Susanne Wegener
Restless Subjects in Rigid Systems

American Studies | Volume 7

Susanne Wegener (Dr. phil.) works on a postdoc project on genre and theory construction in literary criticism. Her research interests are American Studies, Narrative Theory, Critical Theory, Political Philosophy, Theory of Science, and History of Ideas.

SUSANNE WEGENER
Restless Subjects in Rigid Systems
Risk and Speculation in Millennial Fictions
of the North American Pacific Rim

[transcript]

Bibliographic information published by the Deutsche Nationalbibliothek
The Deutsche Nationalbibliothek lists this publication in the Deutsche Nationalbibliografie; detailed bibliographic data are available in the Internet at http://dnb.d-nb.de

© 2014 transcript Verlag, Bielefeld

All rights reserved. No part of this book may be reprinted or reproduced or utilized in any form or by any electronic, mechanical, or other means, now known or hereafter invented, including photocopying and recording, or in any information storage or retrieval system, without permission in writing from the publisher.

Cover layout: Kordula Röckenhaus, Bielefeld
Cover illustration: Christiane Deppe
Printed by Majuskel Medienproduktion GmbH, Wetzlar
ISBN 978-3-8376-2416-8

Content

1   **Introduction: Dealing in Futures** | 7
    1.1 Speculative Fiction | 144
    1.2 Pacific Rim Utopianism | 322
    1.3 Risk Theory | 477
    1.4 The Risk of Close Reading | 60

2   **Are You Paranoid *Enough*? Kathryn Bigelow's *Strange Days* and the Politics of Risk and Speculation** | 699
    2.1 Risk Inside the "Fickle Machine" | 699
    2.2 Establishing Risk | 801
    2.3 State of Speculation | 90
    2.4 The Lure and Trap of Lady Credit | 106
    2.5 Becoming Mace | 1188
    2.6 The Risk Not Taken | 129

3   **Live on the Edge I Say: Edgework, Risk, and Literary Form in Karen Tei Yamashita's *Tropic of Orange*** | 133
    3.1 Edgework – A Subtle Task | 13333
    3.2 Exploding the Grid? Aesthetic Control and the Space-Logic of Synchronicity | 149
    3.3 Confidence Man I: Bobby Ngu and the Confidence Game of Globalized Capitalism | 163
    3.4 Confidence Man II: A Medial Conquista | 1800
    3.5 Now You See Her /Now You Don't: Emi, or the Erotics of Presence | 188
    3.6 Edgework, Unintimidated | 199

4 **Monstrous Politics: Epistemological Empowerment, Natural Science, and New Territories of Empire in Larissa Lai's** *Salt Fish Girl* | 203
 4.1 "The Identity of the Body Has Not Yet Been Confirmed:" Excessive Textuality and Discursive Control in Larissa Lai's Writings | 203
 4.2 Offering Odors – Epistemological Empowerment and Natural Science | 223223
  4.2.1 Useful Poetics | 2233
  4.2.2 The Gaze of Natural Science | 232
  4.2.3 Expanding the Gaze | 240
 4.3 New Territories of Empire | 253
 4.4 Until the Next Time | 2733

5 **Towards a Poetics of Risk and Speculation** | 278
 5.1 United in a State of Fantasy | 282
 5.2 Paratexts | 28890
 5.3 Contexts | 2913

6 **Works Cited** | 297

1 Introduction: Dealing in Futures

In December 2001, shortly after the terrorist attacks on the World Trade Center, Don DeLillo began his by now famous article "In the Ruins of the Future," by summing up a narrative of globalization that he perceived to be related to the attacks:

> In the past decade the surge of capital markets has dominated discourse and shaped global consciousness. Multinational corporations have come to seem more vital and influential than governments. The dramatic climb of the Dow and the speed of the internet summoned us all to live permanently in the future, in the utopian glow of cyber-capital, because there is no memory there and this is where markets are uncontrolled and investment potential has no limit.[1]

DeLillo's opening paragraph can be read as a performative, if sceptical rendition of the world narrative of globalization, a rendition of a utopian narrative of borderless capital markets and a technology-driven political economy that projects disembodied value into a "white-hot future"[2]. While DeLillo was careful to avoid a trifle explanation for the catastrophic events of 9/11 – "there is no logic in apocalypse"[3] – and asserted that it was not the global economy that was the terrorists' primary target, he intuited that, with the attacks, a global contest of narratives and counter-narratives and their implicit temporal trajectories had gained new thrust: while the world narrative of globalization is dealing in futures, "the terrorists of September 11," DeLillo wrote, "want to bring back the past."[4] Against the grain of this constructivist view of history and politics as a

---

1 "In the Ruins of the Future," *The Guardian* (22 Dec. 2001): Web. 5 Jan. 2012. <www.guardian.co.uk/books/2001/dec/22/fiction.dondelillo/print> 1-7, 1.
2 Ibid.
3 Ibid., 2.
4 Ibid., 1.

contest of narratives, the prominent position of DeLillo's own rendition of the narrative of globalization at the beginning of his article insinuates that he considers globalization a meta-process that can explain contemporary changes in economies, states, and societies. He thus views, like many others across the political spectrum, the idea of a globalizing world as a fact that has economic, cultural, political, and social effects on any given society.

Contrary to such a notion of globalization, Wendy Larner, scholar in human geography and sociology, focuses on the discursive framing of the concept and posits that "globalization is a powerful imaginative geography that legitimizes its own production."[5] Larner notes that the 'war on terror' in the wake of 9/11 did not mark the end of transnational flows of capital, goods, services, and people, but became incorporated into an imaginary of globalization that has no problem including national legislative measures and security techniques to contain particular commodities, forms of information, and, above all, population groups that are construed as risky. Strikingly, this imaginary allows the co-presence of economic openness and social closure; it conjoins these seemingly incommensurable aspects of globalization in the imperative to monitor and to select forms of mobility in terms of profit and risk management, terms that both 'deal in futures.' Quoting Nikolas Rose, Larner convincingly argues that the imaginary of globalization and the notion of global flows, networks, and mobilities might best be conceptualized as "'irreal spaces',"[6] produced by different practices and contexts that (and this is Larner's own inference) constitute "'irreal' subjects"[7] whose mobility is naturalized and either facilitated or thwarted.

Nikolas Rose[8] derives his concept of "irreal spaces" from Nelson Goodman and his theory on *Ways of Worldmaking*. A radical constructivist, Goodman denies the existence of one real world; for him there are only different versions constructed of different symbols and symbol systems.[9] Focusing on the different

---

5 "Spatial Imaginaries: Economic Globalization and the War on Terror," *Risk and the War on Terror*, eds. Louise Amoore and Marieke de Goede (Abingdon and New York: Routledge, 2008) 41-56, 49.
6 Nikolas Rose qtd. in Larner, "Spatial Imaginaries," 49.
7 Ibid., 53.
8 See *Powers of Freedom: Reframing Political Thought* (Cambridge, UK: Cambridge UP, 1999) 32. It is worth noting that Rose, while taking the term from Goodman, dismisses Goodman's relativism as "too psychological." Arguing that Goodman conceives of a world version as a picture, Rose makes a point of emphasizing that for him, in contrast, thought constructs reality through practices of inscription, calculation, and action.
9 See *Ways of Worldmaking* (Indianapolis: Hackett, 1978) 3-4.

ways of world making in science and art, Goodman plausibly argues that "we cannot test a version by comparing it with a world undescribed, undepicted, unperceived."[10] The conflicting worlds and spaces fashioned by competing symbolizations are thus not 'irreal' in the sense that they are not consistent or have no validity; however, they can be assessed only as versions that, as Goodman puts it, "mak[e] the world they fit."[11]

It is within this constructivist sense of symbolic world-making and the idea of narratives vying for dominance in a popular imaginary that the present study endeavors to juxtapose the irreal spaces fabricated by symbolic world-making in the service of a political rationality[12] with the irreal spaces and symbolic world-making of film and literature. More precisely, the study sets out to show that the literary and cinematic artifacts of its corpus offer counter-narratives to normative hegemonic discourses and practices that emerged in last the quarter of the twentieth century and have gained impact in the first decade of the twenty-first; it aims to show, above all, that these artifacts and their extrapolating narratives are epistemologically privileged by their openly and boldly fictional aesthetics. The study focuses on three North American fictional texts that were published within a decade around 2000 and belong to the genre of speculative fiction. These texts speculate on the future of political-economic subjectivity at the North American Pacific Rim and thus deal in futures just like the political-economic discourses they tackle.

At the center of the study are close readings of a U.S.-American film by Kathryn Bigelow (*Strange Days*, 1995), a U.S.-American novel by Karen Tei Yamashita (*Tropic of Orange*, 1997), and a Canadian novel by Larissa Lai (*Salt Fish Girl*, 2002).The readings aim to analyze how these fictional texts and their aesthetic strategies comment on the world-making of factual discourses of globalization, economic liberalization, and risk management. Particularly relevant to the texts, albeit not to all three texts in equal measure, is a hegemonic political-economic Pacific Rim discourse that, conditioned by the neoliberalization of governance in both the U.S. and Canada, has emerged in the closing decades of the twentieth century. This discourse has developed its own specific

---

10 Ibid., 4.
11 Ibid., 138.
12 Following Foucault, Wendy Brown defines as a political rationality "a specific form of normative political reason, organizing the political sphere, governance practices, and citizenship. A political rationality governs the sayable, the intelligible, and the truth criteria of these domains." "American Nightmare: Neoliberalism, Neoconservatism, and De-Democratization," *Political Theory* 34.6 (2006): 690-714, 693.

variety of transnational economic utopianism, and has, in the process, construed the 'irreal space' of the Pacific Rim. Challenged by the rise of Asian markets and increasingly successful Asian versions of capitalism, U.S.-American and Canadian economists in the 1980s and 1990s predicted the coming of a golden 'Pacific Century' that, under the aegis of North American nations and imperatives of global free trade, would supersede the expiring 'American Century' in terms of economic growth and vitality. Couched in the neoliberal rhetoric of transnational convergence and the 'free trade zone,' these economic speculations tie in with century-old hegemonic Euro-American constructions of the Pacific region. Like these historical constructions, the utopianist American Pacific Rim discourse strategically conjures homogenizing images of the region, while suppressing contradictions and rifts, such as the uneven regulation of money flows and migration, and the ongoing social and economic injustice along the lines of race and gender in multicultural North American societies. Embedded in the broader imaginary of globalization, and drawing on representational strategies that conceal the racializing and gendering politics on which it capitalizes, this speculative discourse produces an irreal space in order to secure symbolic hegemony and solicit more speculation.

Contesting the utopianism of this discourse, the narratives of the three fictional texts under scrutiny project different millennial visions of a hyper-capitalist, near-future North American Pacific west. All of them bleak dystopias, their perceptive criticism addresses the pervasive economization of the state, the social, and the subject, as well as the re-configurations of race, class, and gender within a new political rationality formed by an alliance of neoliberalism and neoconservatism. While each of the texts tackles different aspects of this new political rationality, they have in common that in their diegetic worlds the impact of an economic free market ideology outweighs other categories of subject formation.

The texts thus seem to position themselves in a theoretical controversy that emerged concurrent with their production. This controversy between scholars and activists of the political Left about the relevance of categories of difference to questions of governance and social justice might best be illustrated by a short digression to a verbal exchange between Judith Butler and Nancy Fraser. Lamenting what she perceives as a new factionalism in the social and political criticism of the Left in her article "Merely Cultural" (1997)[13], Butler defies the notion of a clear-cut distinction between the material/the economic on the one hand, and identity politics and emancipatory social movements on the other.

---

13 "Merely Cultural," *Social Text* 52/53 (1997): 265-277.

Butler criticizes, more precisely, that this distinction implicitly posits the economic as central to the definition of political subjectivity while devaluing identity politics and the struggles of new social movements as belonging to an irrelevant realm of the "merely cultural."[14] Invoking insights of socialist feminists that, already in the 1970s, "sought to establish the sphere of sexual reproduction as part of the material conditions of life, a proper and constitutive feature of political economy,"[15] Butler asks, "why would a movement concerned to criticize and transform the ways in which sexuality is socially regulated not be understood as central to the functioning of political economy?"[16]

Butler's criticism is specifically targeted at a distinction between injustices of recognition and injustices of redistribution that Nancy Fraser has articulated and analyzed in her book *Justice Interruptus: Critical Reflections on the Postsocialist Condition* (1996). As Butler has it, Fraser's distinction "locates certain oppressions as part of political economy and relegates others [specifically hetero-normativity and the misrecognition of lesbians and gays, S.W.] to the exclusively cultural sphere".[17] In her response to Butler's criticism, Fraser rejects the accusation that implicitly identifies her (Fraser's) position with "neo-conservative Marxisms,"[18] and contends that Butler's arguments are not persuasive as they do not afford "an adequately differentiated and historically situated view of modern capitalist society."[19] While asserting that injustices of misrecognition are as serious as distributive injustices, and while disavowing the view of economy and culture as separate spheres, Fraser advocates for the analysis of contemporary capitalist society

an approach that reveals the hidden connections between them. The point, in other words, is to use the distinction against the grain, making visible and subject to critique, both the cultural subtexts of apparently economic processes and the economic subtexts of apparently cultural processes. Such a 'perspectival dualism' is only possible, of course, once we have the economic/cultural distinction.[20]

---

14 Ibid., 265.
15 Ibid., 272.
16 Ibid., 271, italics in the original.
17 Ibid., 269-270.
18 Ibid., 68.
19 Nancy Fraser, "Heterosexism, Misrecognition, and Capitalism: A Response to Judith Butler," *New Left Review* a.228 (1998): 140-150, 143.
20 Ibid., 148.

Fraser's 'perspectival dualism' appears particularly called for in face of the shift to market rationality in governance that has become fully visible only in the first decade of the twenty-first century when the economic/cultural distinction has all but crumbled away. The emphasis in Bigelow, Lai and Yamashita's speculative fictions on the economic as central to the definition of subjectivity on a hyper-capitalist, near-future North American Pacific coast testifies to the authors' clairvoyant perception of a political climate that, as the controversy between Butler and Fraser shows, already in the 1990s began to render precarious familiar categories of critical political thinking.

This is not to argue that Bigelow, Yamashita and Lai can be identified with either Butler's or Fraser's position in the factionalism that, according to Butler, divides the struggles of the Left. It is important to note that the fictional authors' emphasis on the economic implies no underestimation of race and gender as 'merely cultural,' but aptly reflects a political culture that "figures citizens exhaustively as rational economic actors in every sphere of life."[21] Racism, sexism, as well as racialized and feminized labor figure prominently in the texts of all three authors, yet all three texts show these practices of social oppression and regulation to be integrated in and subordinate to the universalizing framework of the market and *homo oeconomicus*[22]. As the study hopes to show, the merit of their extrapolating, fictional representations of a near-future culture that is thoroughly economized lies exactly in making visible and subject to

---

21 Wendy Brown "American Nightmare," 694.
22 In *The Birth of Biopolitics*, Michel Foucault sums up Gary Becker's understanding of individual economic behavior as "[...] any conduct which responds systematically to modifications in the variables of the environment."(269) For Foucault, this "most radical of the American neoliberals"(269) and his conclusion that "any conduct which 'accepts reality' must be susceptible to economic analysis"(269) reflects the classical economic definition of homo oeconomicus as the subject of radical self-interest and rational economic choice. Exposing the pretentiousness of the emphasis on individual self-determination in this universalizing definition, Foucault writes: "From the point of view of a theory of government, homo oeconomicus is the person who must be let alone. With regard to homo eoconomicus, one must laissez-faire, he is the subject or object of laissez-faire. And now in Becker's definition, homo eoconomicus,[...] the person who accepts reality or who responds systematically to modifications in the variables of the environment, appears precisely as someone manageable, someone who responds systematically to systematic modifications artificially introduced to the environment. Homo eoconomicus is someone who is eminently governable." *The Birth of Biopolitics: Lectures at the Collège de France 1978-1979* (New York: Picador, 2010) 270.

critique the precariousness of the economic/cultural distinction that would allow the critical 'perspectival dualism' that Nancy Fraser advocates for an analysis of contemporary capitalist society.

The fictional texts that are at the center of this study thus depict a cultural state marked by a porousness of boundaries, which is generally associated with ideas of liberalization; they make visible, however, that this porousness of boundaries has not per se a liberatory or emancipatory effect. The title of the study "Restless Subjects in Rigid Systems" aims to capture this discrepancy.[23] The subjects of Bigelow, Lai, and Yamashita's speculative fictions are restless subjects in rigid systems, both in a literal and in a figurative sense. As a reference to the texts' protagonists the term 'restless subjects' signifies a subjectivity driven by hopes and speculations that are often prompted by deceptive representations. Many of them migrants or descendants of migrants, these subjects' respective restless pursuit of happiness is often thwarted by the unexpected rigidity of systems of regulation, whose hidden practices and techniques of governance reduce them to economic actors. On a more abstract, if related level, the term 'restless subjects' refers to the unabated relevance of the subjects of race, class, and gender in the texts' hyper-capitalist diegetic political systems, whose multiculturalism incorporates difference without abandoning racism, sexism, and inequality. Finally, the title also applies to the authors and the regulation of authorship in their respective fields of production. The authors' respective position in these fields and these fields' politics of authorship and representation will be addressed in paratextual readings at the beginning of each analytical chapter.

Before these paratexts and the aesthetic strategies and effects of the fictional texts are explored by way of close readings, a survey of the concepts and discourses that are central to the analyses will be given in the following. The starting point for this theoretical survey is a discussion of speculative fiction whose position inside or outside the genre of science fiction is highly contested. A second subchapter introduces the discourse of the Pacific Rim as an instance of economic utopianism and neoliberal speculation, and its reception by cultural critics. A third part presents different theories of risk with a particular focus on more recent conceptualizations of the term by Governmentality Studies and Critical Securitization Studies. And a final section defends 'close reading' as a

---

23 The word "system" is used here in the sense of the *OED* definition I.1 a, as "a set or assemblage of things connected, associated, or interdependent, so as to form a complex unity," *OED Online* (March 2012) Web, 20 Mar. 2012 <http://www.oed.com/view/Entry/196665?redirectedFrom=system#eid>. Its use does not imply a reference to systems theory.

practice that is, once again, becoming subject to debate in contemporary literary studies.

1.1 SPECULATIVE FICTION

Coined in the mid-twentieth century as an umbrella term[24] covering the fantastic from 'hard science fiction' to magic realism, the genre of speculative fiction has, in the past decade, gained a more specific significance of its own, marked by attempts at its redefinition as an extrapolation of contemporary life and society, rather than the fantastic creation of strange, extra-terrestrial worlds associated with science fiction in general. Underlying the struggle for generic redefinition is the decidedly bad reputation of science fiction as a formulaic, aesthetically unsophisticated, low-brow genre and its unrefined readers[25], to whose escapist desires science fiction allegedly provides mere 'fodder.' A statement by Kurt Vonnegut, Jr., author of critically acclaimed novels such as *Slaughterhouse Five* (1969), drastically captures the pervasive critical contempt for the genre: "I've been a sorehead occupant of a file drawer labelled 'science fiction' ever since [my first novel], and I would like out, particularly since so many critics mistake the drawer for a urinal."[26]

Just as Vonnegut had wanted 'out' at a point in time when science fiction was widely considered pulp, critically acknowledged, canonical writer Margaret Atwood, more than a decade later, bent over backwards not to be placed 'in' in the first place. Questioned in an interview, as to whether her novel *The Handmaid's Tale* (1985) could be considered science fiction, Atwood distanced

---

24 The term was first used in 1953 by science fiction writer Robert Anson Heinlein who suggested that "the term 'speculative fiction' may be defined negatively as being fiction about things that have not happened." Qtd. in def.3, *OED Online* (March 2012) Web. 5 Mar.2012.This is, of course, an ironic 'definition;' its staged naivety points, however, to degrees of fictionality as the issue that might be more crucial to a definition of speculative fiction than, for instance, the degree of scientific verisimilitude that is central to many theories of science fiction.

25 Science fiction readers are widely referred to in terms of fandom and addiction rather than literacy. See for example David Hartwell, "The Golden Age of Science Fiction is Twelve," *Speculations on Speculation: Theories of Science Fiction,* eds James Gunn and Matthew Candelaria (Lanham, et al.: Scarecrow, 2005) 269-288.

26 Qtd. as an epigraph to Darko Suvin, *Metamorphoses of Science Fiction: On the Poetics and History of a Literary Genre* (New Haven and London: Yale UP, 1979).

herself from a genre that she described as "filled with Martians and space travel to other planets, and things like that." Rather, she claimed, *"The Handmaid's Tale is speculative fiction in the genre of Brave New World and Nineteen Eighty-Four. Nineteen Eighty-Four was written not as science fiction, but as an extrapolation of life in 1948. So, too, The Handmaid's Tale is a slight twist on the society we have now."*[27] Only a couple of years later, in 2005, Atwood's open contempt had made way for a mild irony and a more differentiated generic model that, strikingly, inverts categorical relations. In a review of Ursula Le Guin's work, Atwood writes:

"Science fiction" is the box in which her work is usually placed, but it's an awkward box: it bulges with discards from elsewhere. Into it have been crammed all those stories that don't fit comfortably into the family room of the socially realistic novel or the more formal parlor of historical fiction, or other compartmentalized genres: westerns, gothics, horrors, gothic romances, and the novels of war, crime, and spies. Its subdivisions include science fiction proper (gizmo-riddled and theory-based space travel, time travel, or cybertravel to other worlds, with aliens frequent); science-fiction fantasy (dragons are common; the gizmos are less plausible, and may include wands); and speculative fiction (human society and its possible future forms, which are either much better than what we have now, or much worse). However, the membranes separating these subdivisions are permeable, and osmotic flow from one to another is the norm.[28]

Obviously Atwood is, at this point, more uncomfortable with both the cultural status of science fiction as a reservoir of "discards from elsewhere" and the generic compartmentalization that excludes science fiction and its subdivisions from the realm of established 'serious' genres, than with the genre itself. Overall, her comment appears more accepting of science fiction (if still slightly derogatory of its more fantastic varieties), and the placement of speculative fiction within it, than her previous statement. It hardly provides, however, more touchstones of generic orientation with regard to speculative fiction, whether considered as a genre on its own or as a subgenre of science fiction. To learn that speculative fiction deals with "human society and its possible future forms" is

---

27 "Interview with Margaret Atwood on her Novel *The Handmaid's Tale*," *Reader's Companion to* The Handmaid's Tale *by Margaret Atwood*," (Doubleday, 1998) Web, 5 Mar. 2012. <http://www.randomhouse.com/resources/bookgroup/handmaidstale_bgc.html#interview>.

28 Margaret Atwood, "The Queen of Quinkdom," *The New York Review of Books* 49.14 (26 Sept. 2002): Web, 5 Mar. 2012 <http://www.nybooks.com/articles/archives/2002/sep/26/the-queen-of-quinkdom/>.

less helpful than the reference to the *Handmaid's Tale* as a "slight twist on the society we have now." While the former definition is so general that it applies to most science fiction 'proper' as well, the latter implies a difference in the degree of non-mimetic representation, a gradual difference on a scale of fictionality as a marker distinguishing speculative from science fiction 'proper,' a differentiation that will be discussed in more detail below.

Atwood's (half-hearted) change of attitude towards science fiction can be read as reflecting a slowly developing critical reassessment of the genre, and points to the fact that the history of science fiction as a genre worthy of academic attention is a fairly short one. This history can be traced back to efforts to dismantle the rigid division between high and low culture and the canon revisions of the 1970s. But even then, the genre was still considered aesthetically so deficient that Darko Suvin, in his preface to *Metamorphoses of Science Fiction* (1979), felt the need to justify the relevance of his book-length study. While admitting that "90 or 95 percent of SF production is strictly perishable stuff," Suvin argues that science fiction is not only one of the largest genres, but "the most interesting and cognitively the most significant one" in what he calls "Paraliterature," or "the noncanonic, repressed twin of Literature," and "even this 90 or 95 percent is highly significant from a sociological point of view."[29] In keeping with this sociological argument (reflecting the *zeitgeist* and political climate of the era) and his broader Marxist convictions, Suvin emphasizes the educational value of science fiction[30], whose "potential cognitive tendency" he considers to be "allied to the rise of subversive social classes and their development of more sophisticated productive forces and cognitions."[31]

Leaving aside for the moment the Marxist utopianism underlying this contention, it is important to note that Suvin's still influential study not only delineates the history of the genre in great detail, but also provides a theory of its poetics, a theory, the most frequently quoted concept of which is probably 'cognitive estrangement.' Drawing on sources as diverse as the Russian Formalists, Bertolt Brecht, and Galileo, Suvin defines science fiction as "a literary genre whose necessary and sufficient conditions are the presence and interaction of estrangement and cognition, and whose main formal device is an imaginative framework alternative to the author's empirical environment."[32] According to Suvin, the experience of estrangement in science fiction is enabled by settings, plots, and characters that are "radically or at least significantly

---

29 *Metamorphoses of Science Fiction*, vii.
30 See ibid., 36.
31 Ibid., ix.
32 Ibid., 7-8, italics in the original.

different from empirical times, places, and characters of 'mimetic' or 'naturalist' fiction," and "simultaneously perceived as not impossible within the cognitive norms of the author's epoch."[33] Suvin's demand for the co-presence of estrangement achieved by a (in most cases techno-scientific) 'novum' and cognition as a guarantee of credibility (often termed 'verisimilitude' in science fiction studies) excludes both realistic fiction and the fantasy tale, a genre which, as Suvin puts it, is "committed to the interposition of anti-cognitive laws into the empirical environment."[34] Suvin goes so far as dismissing "the commercial lumping of it [fantasy, S.W.] into the same category as SF"[35] as a "grave disservice and rampantly socio-pathological phenomenon."

Far removed from such a pathologizing judgment on violations of rigid generic law (a rigor of judgment that may be ascribed to the fundamental rigor marking the founding of discourses, since Suvin's study can, without doubt, be credited with establishing the laws of the genre in the first place), more recent studies of science fiction are less concerned with normative generic demarcation, although taxonomy still looms large in the field. A particularly interesting study, Fredric Jameson's *Archaeologies of the Future*,[36] was published in 2005, the same year, strikingly, in which Atwood's comment on Le Guin's work had asserted the permeability of the membranes separating subdivisions of science fiction and the "osmotic flow"[37] between them. In focusing on theories of political utopia and on utopia as a socio-economic sub-set of science fiction in the first part of *Archaeologies*, Jameson also addresses what he calls "The Great Schism"[38] between science fiction and fantasy.

While, as this chapter title indicates, Jameson does not share Atwood's assumption of permeable membranes and osmotic flow between subgenres of science fiction, his interest is in the structural characteristics of fantasy (and thus epistemologically motivated), and his investigation is descriptive and analytical rather than normative. Stating that fantasy has, in the past decade, conquered a bigger segment of the book market than science fiction in the narrow sense of Suvin's definition (and insinuating with this statement that the vexed relationship between the two might, at least in part, be grounded in economic rivalry), Jameson delineates the structural particularities of fantasy without

---

33 Ibid., viii, italics in the original.
34 Ibid., 8.
35 *Metamorphoses of Science Fiction*, 9.
36 *Archaeologies of the Future: The Desire called Utopia and Other Science Fictions* (London and New York: Verso, 2005).
37 "The Queen of Quinkdom."
38 *Archaeologies of the Future*, 57.

lapsing into the denigrating rigor of Suvin's attitude. For him, fantasy is defined by its "organization around the ethical binary of good and evil, and the fundamental role it assigns to magic."[39] Its historicism often draws on medieval, and sometimes Christian, material, and, while sharing with science fiction a "visceral sense of the chemical deficiencies of our present, for which both offer imaginary compensation,"[40] it is "technically reactionary" and "breathes a purer and more conventional medieval atmosphere."[41] According to Jameson, modern fantasy borrows from medieval struggles between the nobility and the peasantry; its variations on the battle of good and evil often combine incompatible cultural registers such as the feudal *chanson de geste* and the fairy tale that catered to the hopes and desires of medieval peasants.[42]

The most conclusive aspect in Jameson's discussion of the generic schism between fantasy and science fiction is, however, the omnipresence of the motif of magic in the former. Jameson understands the recourse to magic as a regression to the pre-rational, pre-technological era, a regression starkly contrasting the commitment to scientific reason that grants verisimilitude, according to Suvin, and thus allows for "cognitive estrangement" (the co-presence and interaction of estrangement and cognition) in science fiction. For both Jameson and Suvin the true utopia of science fiction lies in its potential of politicizing the masses, whereas the principle of cognition commits the genre to deploying "the certainties and speculations of a rational and secular scientific age."[43] While for Suvin, fantasy's nostalgia for pre-rational, yet otherwise ahistorical magic results in a form of non-cognitive estrangement, and thus merely caters to its audiences' escapist desires, Jameson contends that "history and historical change inscribe themselves in even the most ahistorical forms," and argues that "fantasy can also have critical and even demystificatory power."[44]

The most consequent form of fantasy never simply deploys magic in the service of other narrative ends, but proposes a meditation on magic as such – on its capacities and its

---

39 Ibid., 58
40 Ibid., 59.
41 Ibid., 60.
42 See *Archaeologies of the Future*, 60.
43 Ibid., 63.
44 Ibid., 67.

existential properties, on a kind of figural mapping of the active and productive subjectivity in its non-alienated state.[45]

Jameson identifies the "mode-of-production aesthetic"[46] of fantasy as pre-capitalist, and magic as its expression of disenchantment with "the 'Entzauberte Welt' of capitalism and modern times;"[47] yet he concedes that the "most consequent form of fantasy" uses magic as the demystifying instrument of a cultural critique that is anything but ahistorical. Two aspects in his assessment are striking and point to the reasons for and, simultaneously, beyond the problems of generic definition: first, in speaking of a "form of fantasy,"[48] and in emphasizing that the texts he considers most distinctive are difficult to classify,[49] Jameson foregrounds a decidedly postmodern quality in texts that blend various aesthetic and generic registers, and whose deployment of magic does not signal generic affiliation, but serves as a self-reflexive meditation on magic; he thus implicitly relates the distinctive quality of the texts to an aesthetic paradigm shift whose prominent features are a programmatic challenging of the law of genre[50] and an equally programmatic, representational self-referentiality.

In describing the effect and the purpose of the use of magic as "a kind of figural mapping of the active and productive subjectivity in its non-alienated state"[51] – and this leads to the second, more complex aspect – Jameson points to the literary device of figurative language as a means of addressing a state of alienation that marks contemporary subjectivity. While, for Jameson, alienation is a consequence of the capitalist mode of production, Hans Ulrich Gumbrecht describes an epistemological alienation that might both at once explain the growing popularity of fantastic elements in contemporary literature, and help to identify more precisely the self-reflexive, meta-representational quality in a literary meditation on magic.

In his study *Production of Presence*,[52] Gumbrecht suggests a typology that juxtaposes what he calls "presence culture," exemplified by medieval culture,

---

45 Ibid., 66.
46 Ibid., 59.
47 Ibid., 71.
48 Ibid., 66.
49 See ibid., 68.
50 See for example Jacques Derrida, "The Law of Genre," *Critical Inquiry* 7.1 On Narrative (1980): 55-81.
51 *Archaeologies of the Future*, 66.
52 *Production of Presence: What Meaning Cannot Convey* (Stanford: Stanford UP, 2004).

with "meaning culture," exemplified by early modern culture. For Gumbrecht, "'subjectivity' or 'the subject' occupies the place of the dominant human self-reference in a meaning culture whereas in a presence culture, humans consider their bodies to be part of a cosmology (or part of a divine creation)."[53] While legitimate knowledge is, in a 'meaning culture,' produced, according to Gumbrecht, by the world-interpretation of a subject, knowledge can, in a 'presence culture,' only be revealed by "events of self-unconcealment of the world," a revelation for which the body is the central medium. This implies, for Gumbrecht, that different conceptions of signs underlie the respective cultural forms. Contrasting the 'meaning-culture's' privileging of meaning over the material signifier, in which meaning is encoded, the definition of the sign is in a 'presence culture' close to the Aristotelian sign concept where a sign is a coupling between a substance (something that requires space) and a form (something that makes it possible for the substance to be perceived). This sign concept avoids the neat distinction between the purely spiritual and the purely material for the two sides of what is brought together in the sign. Consequently, there is no side in this sign-concept that will vanish once a meaning is secured.[54]

The alienation of subjectivity and the nostalgia Jameson refers to might thus not only be the alienation by the capitalist mode of production and the nostalgia for the pre-rational ethics of a medieval battle of good and evil. The figurative language of fantasy – and specifically the use of magic – might as well express an alienation that comes with the prevalence of disembodied meaning, and cater to an ensuing desire for presence and an epistemology of embodied experience. The use of magic, defined by Gumbrecht as "the practice of making things that are absent present and things that are present absent,"[55] is thus not only an aesthetic device and, as has been shown above, even less a generic marker; it addresses both an epistemological crisis of modernity and the fundamental epistemological dilemma inherent to literature per se: how to make things that are necessarily absent from a text present by the use of signs.

The highly self-reflexive, meta-representational literary recourse to magic is encoded in a form of figurative language invoking a sign concept that, similar to the one by Aristoteles as quoted in Gumbrecht, conjoins the spiritual and the material. Given the emphasis on substance in the Aristotelian sign concept, the closest approximation to this concept possible in a literary text seems to be the trope of allegory. Significantly, Jameson describes the use of magic in fantastic narratives as a "figural mapping," yet claims, at a previous point in his chapter,

---

53 Ibid., 80.
54 Ibid., 81-82.
55 *Production of Presence*, 82.

that the "allegorical dimension" is "lacking in modern fantasy."[56] This raises the question of what the allegorical dimension signifies for Jameson. It is obviously not the collapsing of the literal and the figural, their 'magical' coexistence in the trope of allegory against the grain of their differing rhetorical status, but rather a specific referentiality and temporality of allegory, a historicizing dimension that the ahistorical genre of fantasy, according to Suvin and Jameson, fails to represent. This suggests that Jameson's understanding of allegory follows that of Paul de Man who discards a definition of allegory as a "sign that points to something that differs from its literal meaning" for its "lack in discriminatory precision," because "this important structural aspect may well be a description of figural language in general."[57] The "figural mapping" that Jameson ascribes to distinctive works of fantasy thus not necessarily refers to allegory, although, as the subsequent paragraph will try to show, allegory would seem the suitable trope to mediate not only magic in fantasy, but the epistemological particularities of the very utopian form that is at the center of Jameson's study.

Strikingly, Jameson makes no further use of de Man's concept of allegory, neither in the chapter on "The Great Schism" nor elsewhere in his book. This is all the more surprising, since allegory, identified by Jameson as "an extreme structure of language itself,"[58] could not only provide an aesthetic framework of analysis across generic subdivisions in the field; as Paul de Man's theorization of allegory shows, it could also tie in with Jameson's understanding of the utopian form as conditioned by a dialectic interplay between identity and difference. In his essay "The Rhetoric of Temporality," de Man analyzes a discourse in European Romanticism on the representational potential of symbol/metaphor and allegory, and ultimately locates the difference between the two in different temporalities:

In the world of allegory, time is the originary constitutive [...] The meaning constituted by the allegorical sign [...] can consist only in the repetition [...] of a previous sign with which it can never coincide [...] since it is of the essence of this previous sign to be pure anteriority.[...] Whereas the symbol postulates the possibility of an identity or identification, allegory designates primarily a distance in relation to its own origin, and

---

56 *Archaeologies of the Future*, 63.
57 "The Rhetoric of Temporality," *Blindness and Insight: Essays in the Rhetoric of Contemporary Criticism* (Abingdon: Routledge, 2005) 187-228, 209.
58 Ibid.

renouncing the nostalgia and the desire to coincide, it establishes its language in the void of this temporal difference.[59]

Significantly, de Man describes as the defining characteristic of allegory a form of intertextuality, a double movement by which allegory draws on and, at the same time, distances itself from a previous signification. If one follows de Man's definition, allegory seems to be the trope ideally suited to capture the historical dimension and the structural ambiguities that Jameson identifies as characteristic of the utopian form:

Utopian form is itself a representational meditation on radical difference, radical otherness, and on the systemic nature of the social totality, to the point where one cannot imagine any fundamental change in our social existence which has not first thrown off Utopian visions like so many sparks from a comet. The fundamental dynamic of any Utopian politics (or of any political Utopianism) will therefore always lie in the dialectic of Identity and Difference, to the degree to which such a politics aims at imagining, and sometimes even at realizing, a system radically different from this one.[60]

Allegory suits the utopian form not only because it rests upon the temporal anteriority of the signification to which it refers, and thus historicizes both the previous sign and its relation to it, but also because it disambiguizes, since it is, according to de Man, "a sign that refers to one specific meaning and thus exhausts its suggestive potentialities once it has been deciphered."[61] What was widely considered a deficiency and even "non-art"[62] in the discourse of European Romanticism, acquires, in the context of utopian representation, the

---

59 "The Rhetoric of Temporality," 207.
60 Jameson, *Archaeologies of the Future*, 4.
61 De Man, "The Rhetoric of Temporality," 188.
62 Ibid. De Man quotes from Hans-Georg Gadamer's treatise on philosophical hermeneutics, *Truth and Method* (1960) where Gadamer, like de Man, traces the history of allegory over the last two centuries and subsumes the aesthetic verdict prevalent among European Romanticists as follows: "Symbol and allegory are opposed as art to non-art." It is worth noting that both Gadamer and de Man argue for a contemporary rehabilitation of the aesthetics, the meaning, and the potential of allegory, regardless of the fundamental differences between hermeneutics and deconstruction in general and the differences in their respective treatment of allegory in practice and theory in particular. See also Steven Mailloux "Hermeneutics, Deconstruction, Allegory," *The Cambridge Companion to Allegory*, eds. Rita Copeland and Peter T. Struck (Cambridge, et al.: Cambridge UP, 2010), 254-265.

status of an epistemological privilege. Moreover, inscribed in the language of allegory is always the mode of production of its origin, a feature privileging allegory to address the problem that, according to Jameson, troubles utopia as a form, and science fiction in general: "[...] our imaginations are hostages to our own mode of production (and perhaps to whatever remnants of past ones it has preserved)."[63]

Yet although his interest is not only in the social and historical conditions of the utopian construct, but also in "the representational relations between them – such as closure, narrative and exclusion or inversion"[64], and is thus not only a political but also an aesthetic interest in science fictional texts, Jameson nowhere acknowledges the importance of allegory to the utopian form or science fiction in general. While his study provides a wealth of philosophical – and specifically Marxist – theorizations of utopia, interesting structural analyses of utopian (and dystopian) representations in science fiction, as well as some insights into the reasons for the generic struggles in the field of science fiction studies, its interest in aesthetic particularities or generic definition is subordinate to its focus on the political and social implications of utopian texts. Even the chapter on the "The Great Schism" between fantasy and science fiction ultimately concedes that the most distinctive texts cannot be easily classified. This seems to suggest that the relevance of generic classification to contemporary criticism of science fiction is waning, and that, in fact, Margaret Atwood's notion of permeable membranes separating subdivisions of science fiction might be reflecting a general tendency.

One of the most provocative, recent contributions to science fiction studies, Seo-Young Chu's *Do Metaphors Dream of Literal Sleep*, offers a radical "science fictional theory of representation"[65] that, at first glance, appears to conveniently affirm Atwood's assessment. More precisely, what Chu calls a science fictional theory of representation not only programmatically questions generic subdivisions within science fiction, but endeavors to overturn the basic epistemological conventions upon which the generic division between science fiction and 'realistic' genres such as realism or naturalism rests. For Chu, science fiction is a mimetic discourse distinct from realism only by a higher degree of elusiveness, characterizing what she calls its "referent" or "object of representation." Contesting the "pervasive characterization [...] of science fiction as a genre that operates beyond mimesis,"[66] and drawing on Suvin's

---

63 *Archaeologies of the Future*, xiii.

64 Ibid.

65 *Do Metaphors Dream of Literal Sleep: A Science Fictional Theory of Representation* (Cambridge, MA, and London: Harvard UP, 2010).

66 Ibid., 3.

definition of cognitive estrangement as achieved by way of "an imaginative framework alternative to the author's empirical environment,"[67] the author outlines the project of her study as follows:

> Transposing this paradigm [that science fiction is generally perceived as a non-mimetic discourse, S.W.] – discovering how it works from the other side – yields a strikingly viable paradigm for reconceptualizing mimesis, science fiction, and the relationship between them. *Do Metaphors Dream* is an argument for such a reconceptualization. Science fiction, I hope to demonstrate, operates fully within the realm of mimesis. The objects of science fictional representations, while impossible to represent in a straightforward manner, are absolutely real. My reconceptualization of science fiction can be understood, more specifically as Suvin's definition turned inside out. Instead of conceptualizing science fiction as a nonmimetic discourse that achieves the effect of cognitive estrangement through "an imaginative framework," I conceptualize science fiction as a mimetic discourse whose objects of representation are nonimaginary yet cognitively estranging.[68]

Chu thus not only sets out to offer a theory of science fictional representation, but, in a sweeping gesture, announces to 'reconceptualize' mimesis in the process. The conceptual foundation for this ambitious project is, however, flawed by an irritating theoretical confusion and lack of terminological precision, as Chu's introductory chapter proves. To begin with, in the above passage, Chu 'transposes' Suvin's idea of cognitive estrangement from its original conceptualization as an *effect* of science fictional representation to science fiction's *objects* of representation: cognitive estrangement is for her not a receptive effect achieved through the dialectic interplay of estranging and cognitively familiar, empirical elements in the diegetic world of a narrative, but inherent to what she calls a text's cognitively estranging, yet 'real' referent. Underlying this 'transposition' is an understanding of a fictional text not as a free play of multiple signifiers, but as a monolithic sign and its unambiguous relation to one determinate referent. This referent, a given science fictional text's (one) object of representation, is, for Chu, in itself cognitively estranging, because its abstract quality challenges representation. Chu elaborates on this assumption by juxtaposing examples of what she considers cognitively estranging science fictional 'referents' with the 'flat' objects of representation that she ascribes to realism. For her, science fictional representation encompasses objects that resist "straightforward representation"[69] such as

---

67 *Metamorphoses of Science Fiction*, 8.
68 Chu, *Do Metaphors Dream of Literal Sleep*, 3, italics in the original.
69 Ibid., 7 and 8.

the sublime (e.g., outer space), virtual entities (cyberspace), realities imperceptible to the human brain (the fourth dimension), phenomena whose historical contexts have not yet been fully realized (robot rights), and events so overwhelming that they escape immediate experience (shell shock). Although impossible to access empirically – cyberspace cannot be weighed on a scale; a traumatic experience cannot be quantified in units of time – these referents can, have, and do become available for representation in SF. Accordingly, SF is distinguished by its capacity to perform the massively complex representational and epistemological work necessary to render cognitively estranging referents available both for representation and for understanding. Realism by contrast, is distinguished by the alacrity with which it can imitate certain kinds of objects, objects such as almonds and nickels, objects themselves distinguished by the alacrity with which they offer themselves up to flat description.[70]

This passage affirms that Chu's understanding of a fictional text is surprisingly unencumbered by theoretical knowledge. It demonstrates that the presuppositions upon which her science fictional theory of representation rests lack any concept whatsoever of fictionality; it painfully reveals that these presuppositions are devoid of a comprehensive concept of realism as a genre in general and of mimesis in realism in particular; and it testifies to her confounding of the concept of theme or subject matter (that is per se an abstract idea) with abstract phenomena that Chu designates as objects of representation; on top of that, Chu considers the capacity to represent such abstract phenomena to be unique to science fiction. In conjunction with the deluded conceptualization of a fictional text as a monolithic sign and its single extra-diegetic referent, this confusion of abstract subject matter with an abstract and, for Chu, therefore 'cognitively estranging object of representation' leads to multiple fallacies. In the first instance, the author, after positing that "all representation is to some degree science fictional because all reality is to some degree cognitively estranging"[71], draws from this stipulative definition and her elaborations in the above passage the conclusion that realism

is actually a 'weak' or low intensity variety of science fiction, one that requires relatively little energy to accomplish its representational task as its referents (e.g. softballs) are readily susceptible to representation. Conversely, what most people call 'science fiction' is actually a high-intensity variety of realism, one that requires astronomical levels of energy to accomplish its representational task insofar as its referents (e.g., cyberspace) elaborately defy straightforward representation. In this book 'realism' designates low-intensity

---

70 *Do Metaphors Dream of Literal Sleep*, 7.
71 Ibid.

mimesis, while science fiction designates high-intensity mimesis. Realism and science fiction, then, exist on a continuum [...] where every object of representation has its place – from shoelaces, dimes, and oak leaves to cyberspace, trauma, black holes, and financial derivatives.[72]

Chu's diction in this passage is telling in many ways. Her description of the representational strategies of a given fictional text as a "task," requiring varying amounts of "energy," again, betrays a striking avoidance of the analytical categories and tools available to literary criticism. The list of 'objects of representation' at the end of the paragraph, again, implicitly suggests that realistic fiction (or what Chu calls "low-intensity mimesis") is incapable of representing abstract ideas such as "trauma, black holes, and financial derivatives." This latter part of the list is in itself conclusive as it, again, confounds the abstraction of subject matter with the abstraction of disembodied empirical phenomena (such as trauma). Most conclusive in this positing of a theorem is, however, the normative vigor marking Chu's attempts to upturn the generic hierarchies that assign minor literary value to science fiction. It is, above all, the tension between her disparaging 'definition' of realism on the one hand, and the ostentatiously unbiased notion of a continuum, expressed in her use of the neutral "high/low-intensity"-modifier, on the other that allows this interpretation.

Built upon the idea of varying degrees of mimesis, Chu's construction of a neutral continuum, by which devaluing positionings of literary texts could be circumvented, reveals that what lies at the bottom of her attempt to reconceptualize mimesis is an anachronistic understanding of the concept. The author obviously ignores that the idea of mimesis (which has been a contentious issue since Plato and Aristotle) has become more complicated with the emergence of critical interrogations of the concept of reality and the relation between art and reality in the twentieth century. For Chu, mimesis clearly means *imitatio*, and her project is motivated by the desire to promote the value of science fictional representations as forms of *imitatio* that are privileged by their capability of depicting abstract subject matter. Ultimately, Chu seems to consider the adjective 'non-mimetic' a devaluing stain, from the traces of which the genre of science fiction has to be purged.

As a consequence of her positing of a neutral mimesis-continuum, on which any given text can be placed according to its "high-" or "low-intensity" mimetic quality, Chu feels free to abandon all generic distinctions. Her theorem not only allows the unproblematic inclusion into science fiction of subgenres such as

---

72 Ibid.

surrealism, utopianism, gothic/horror, slipstream, fantasy, and magic realism,[73] but also the arbitrary designation as science fiction of such unlikely text types as travel writing or Korean American memoir.[74] The degree of Chu's vigor to undo the generic divisions that imply the ascription of minor literary value to science fiction, her eagerness to establish a science fictional theory of representation and science fictional representation as mimetic, equals, however, the degree of theoretical neglect and terminological imprecision impeding her project. This becomes particularly obvious when Chu, after her all-encompassing designation of every given text to some degree as science fictional, dismisses allegory as "What Science Fiction is *Not*"[75], at the end of her methodological introduction. Again, her diction is conclusive in its imprecision:

A narrative in the allegorical mode need not be about something. The purpose of allegory is not to refer to a specific object but to incite the reader's mind to exegesis. Meanwhile, the purpose of science fiction is not to instigate exegetical activity in the reader's mind but to represent a cognitively estranging referent.[76]

Without so much as problematizing her understanding of allegory and its function either as a rhetorical trope, a genre, or a structural element in narrative and/or critical discourse, the author uses the term in this antithetical definition as a negative foil to highlight science fiction's capacity of representing "a cognitively estranging referent." How exactly exegetical activity can be instigated by allegory, if understood as a non-referential text, remains as obscure as the problem how a science fictional text and its representation of a cognitively estranging referent can be recognized and deciphered as such without exegetical activity. This 'definition' contradicts both Paul de Man's contention that allegory is "a sign that refers to one specific meaning"[77] and Chu's own that science fiction is a lyrical form of mimesis[78] marked by its extensive use of figurative language, a contention that she broadly elaborates on. It once more reflects the author's theoretically unencumbered understanding of literary fiction, genre, rhetoric, and, ultimately, fictionality, as well as the decidedly ahistorical and apolitical quality of her science fictional theory of representation. In keeping with the field's inclination towards taxonomy, Chu lists an impressive number of

---

73   See *Do Metaphors Dream of Literal Sleep*, 9.
74   See ibid., 69.
75   Ibid.,76, italics in the original.
76   Do *Metaphors Dream of Literal Sleep*, 76, italics in the original.
77   "The Rhetoric of Temporality," 188.
78   See ibid., 10 -63.

fictional texts as examples to substantiate her claims; yet this abundance cannot make up for or undo the theoretical deficiency that flaws these claims in the first place.

Given the terminological and conceptual imprecision in Seo-Young Chu's theory of science fictional representation, her subsequent abandoning of all generic distinctions does not provide solid ground for any definition of speculative fiction as either a genre on its own or a subgenre of science fiction. As the above exemplary discussion of three studies by critics of science fiction demonstrates, the problem of generic definition has encumbered the field from its beginning and will likely not go away anytime soon. The present study takes advantage of this lack of precise generic definition and resorts to the *OED* definitions of the terms 'speculation' and 'speculative' whose wide range of denotations and connotations permits their application to philosophical/literary and economic registers alike.[79] The study considers the fictional texts of its corpus speculative fiction, because their extrapolations from the society in which they originated are speculative and fictional, while the political-economic discourses and practices regulating this society are speculative and factual. This is not to argue that the factual discourses are more 'truthful' than the fictional discourses of the literary texts. Rather, the privileged status assigned to factual discourses in contemporary Western societies authorizes their powerful and effective construction of both meaning and a social reality that together assign an inferior, marginal status to literary fiction and culture in general. In locating the distinction between factual and fictional discourses in the workings of cultural and political institutions and practices, the present study follows a pragmatic approach to fictionality that is generally associated with the work of John R. Searle.[80] In the spirit of this pragmatic approach, recent theories of fictionality[81]

---

79 *OED* definitions of "speculation" range from the neutral "contemplation, consideration, or profound study of some subject" (def.5a), or an "attempt to ascertain or anticipate something by probable reasoning" (def.5c), to the "disparaging use, usually with adjs.,as bare, mere, pure, etc.; also simply= conjecture, surmise" (def.6c). The definition that most aptly captures the conjectural quality marking both the fictional and the factual discourses relevant to the present study is "as opposed to practice, fact, action, etc" (def. 6b). "speculation, n." *OED Online* (March 2012) Web, 20 Mar. 2012. <http://www.oed.com/view/Entry/186113?redirectedFrom=speculation>.

80 See for example *The Construction of Social Reality* (New York: Simon and Schuster, 1995), and "The Logical Status of Fictional Discourse," *New Literary History* 6 (1974-75): 319-332. In this latter article Searle maintains: "There is no textual property, syntactic or semantic, that will identify a text as a work of fiction" (325), a claim that Dorrit Cohn contests in "Signposts of Fictionality: A Narratological

suggest an understanding of fiction as a complex cultural practice that is regulated by speech act conventions rather than a distinction along the lines of true or false, mimetic or non-mimetic representation.

While, according to speech act conventions prevalent in Western societies, factual discourses are expected to be truthful in that they renounce fictionalizing strategies, fiction is considered a "make-believe"[82]game resting upon an implicit contract or pact between the author of a fictional text and its readership. Alerted by paratextual and textual "signposts of fictionality,"[83] and tacitly acknowledging the specific status of the fictional text, as well as generic particularities (such as the prevalence of unfamiliar or fantastic elements in genres like science fiction), readers of fiction agree to subscribe to the extraordinary "make-believe" contract of fictional narrative. Since in contemporary Western cultures the practice of fiction treats the fictional text as a textual signification that is not committed to an extratextual referent, the notion of mimetic or non-mimetic representation becomes subordinate to coherence and logical consistence within the diegetic world created by fictional narrative. This liberation from extra-textual referentiality does not imply that fictional narrative cannot provide insights or 'truth' beyond its textual boundaries. On the contrary, freed from extra-textual referentiality, a fictional narrative can assume the function of a thought experiment, by which the validity of non-fictional discourses and practices that form the political, social, and cultural reality of a given society can be critically reflected, tested, and challenged. Fictional narrative can thus comment on factual discourses' power of meaning making and subject formation, and it can spotlight contradictions and fictionalizing strategies in these so called discourses of truth.

To consider fiction a practice that is conditioned by speech act conventions and regulated by a given culture's institutions and discourses of truth implies that the notion of degrees or scales of fictionality (which seems to be the assumption underlying both Seo-Young Chu's model of a continuum of mimesis and Margaret Atwood's perception that speculative fiction offers "a slight twist on the society we have now") loses traction. It also implies that, instead, generic conventions and paratextual discourses gain pertinence, since they determine and

---

Perspective," *The Distinction of Fiction* (Baltimore and London: Johns Hopkins UP, 1999), 109-131.

81 See for example Frank Zipfel, *Fiktion, Fiktivität, Fiktionalität: Analysen zur Fiktion in der Literatur und zum Fiktionsbegriff in der Literaturwissenschaft* (Berlin: Erich Schmidt, 2001), esp. 279-299.

82 Umberto Eco qtd. in Zipfel, *Fiktion, Fiktivität, Fiktionalität*, 283.

83 Dorrit Cohn,"Signposts of Fictionality," 109.

navigate the reception of a fictional text. Significantly, the three texts at the center of the present study are hybrid mixes that play with the conventions of genre and elude easy generic classification. Their authorial paratexts even further complicate a convenient placement in terms of genre. It is important to note that the study's classification of the texts as 'speculative fiction' against the grain of their hybridity and complicating paratexts is based on their critical fictional negotiation of factual discourses, whose fictionalizing, speculative strategies they reveal, rather than on a random occurrence of fantastic elements in their diegetic worlds.

Although these fantastic diegetic elements – the elements that would be cognitively estranging nova in Darko Suvin's terms – present various defamiliarizing, imaginary divergences from the empirical framework of contemporary North American societies, they have in common that they highlight and comment on disembodiment as a specific epistemological condition characterizing and enabling the regime of globalized capitalism and its underlying ideology of borderless, global free trade. In Kathryn Bigelow's *Strange Days*, the fantastic element is a technical device that allows the recording and commodification of sensual input from the human brain; in Karen Tei Yamashita's *Tropic of Orange*, the fantastic encompasses such diverse instances as the magical warping of geography and an ambiguous cyborg figure whose representation oscillates between corporeality and digital coding; and in Larissa Lai's *Salt Fish Girl*, a mutated clone transcends her artificially manufactured, genetic code. In terms of temporality, the texts differ significantly: *Strange Days* projects a fictitious Los Angeles on the eve of the new millennium that is only five years ahead of the time of the film's production; the diegetic world of *Tropic of Orange* is set in a fictitious Los Angeles that is contemporaneous with the novel's production and can be regarded alternate history,[84] and *Salt Fish Girl* combines an alternate history

---

84 Gary K. Wolfe designates as 'alternate history' a "narrative premise claimed equally by science fiction and fantasy," and refers to Darko Suvin's definition of the term as "that form in SF in which an alternate locus (in space,time, etc.) that shares the material and causal verisimilitude of the writer's world is used to articulate different possible solutions of societal problems, those problems being of sufficient importance to require an alteration in the overall history of the narrated world." "Coming to Terms," *Speculations on Speculation: Theories of Science Fiction*, eds. James Gunn and Matthew Candelaria (Lanham, et al.: Scarecrow, 2005) 13-22, 14. However, the idea of "different possible solutions of societal problems" in Suvin's definition insinuates an idealistic, utopian thrust that does not apply to *Tropic of Orange*'s rather

strand ,set in China, with a futurist strand, set in a near future British Columbia, where a corporation-governed city has replaced Vancouver.

Regardless of these differences in temporality, all three texts address risks the construction of which is enabled by a technology-driven disembodiment of experience. Conditioned by the encoding of information in signs that no longer have a referent this disembodiment of experience reflects the digitalized, semiotic immateriality that has become a hallmark of globalized capitalism. Beyond this critique, fantastic elements have in all three texts an allegoric, meta-representational and often self-referential function; rather than stereotypical ingredients of a generic formula, they are the medium of a reflection on the cultural practice of fiction, its production and reception, and its culturally coded devaluation vis-à-vis discourses whose authority in the symbolic order is based on their claim to immaculate factuality. This function of epistemological self-reflection, in conjunction with the texts' subtle criticism of an epistemological condition that enables a very specific political-economic rationality, motivates the use of fantastic elements in the texts' narratives among other literary devices. Given the enduring devaluation of fantasy and science fiction, this recourse to the fantastic is a risky endeavor, signaling an author's audacious challenging of the institutions, practices, and conventions that regulate the ascription of artistic value in contemporary Western societies.

Invariably set in a hyper-capitalist Pacific Rim, the critical dystopias projected by Bigelow, Yamashita, and Lai's fictional narratives refer to and position themselves against factual discourses and their utopian construction of irreal spaces and irreal subjects, a speculative, utopian construction whose future-oriented thrust is necessarily fictional and ties in with a general hyper-fictionality characterizing the global economy in the twenty-first century. This hyper-fictionality entails that the space of possibility that global capitalism is persistently carving out for itself is increasingly becoming a space of pure representation; in this space, all agents and operations are part of an endless chain of interacting, mutually referential signifiers, and leave only volatile traces. As fictional speculations on the formation of subjectivity in the North American Pacific Rim, the texts not only address a historically and locally specific manifestation of free market ideology, but tackle the social and political changes in North American societies that came with the growing currency of the ideal of a borderless world market; in other words, the texts highlight how an almost universal subscription to this ideal fosters the

---

dystopian, and at best ironically motivated imaginary divergence from the social reality of an empirical L.A. in the 1990s.

tireless undoing [of] all the social gains made since the inception of the socialist and communist movements, [the] repealing [of] all the welfare measures, the safety net, the right to unionization, industrial, and ecological regulatory laws, [while] offering to privatize pensions and indeed to dismantle whatever stands in the way of the free market all over the world.[85]

Bigelow, Yamashita, and Lai's texts were produced and published within a decade around 2000, and thus at a point in time that, together with the topographical and temporal setting at a millennial North American Pacific Rim and the subtle negotiation of a thorough neoliberalization of governance in their diegetic worlds, suggests their close relation to the emergence of the North American Pacific Rim discourse that in the last decades of the 'American Century' euphorically announced the coming of a golden 'Pacific Century.' The fictional texts seem to respond to and contest a discourse, whose authority and power of meaning-making rests upon the cultural convention that designates the political and the economic as the realm of the factual. The subsequent delineation of this factual discourse and its critical reception hopes to demonstrate, however, that the political-economic utopianism expressed in the imaginary of a borderless Pacific region resorts to fictionalizing strategies that result in the "construction of an optical image from which existence itself [...] has been removed by a sleight of hand, a masterful feat of ideological prestidigitation."[86] Such a homogenizing optical image is, as Fredric Jameson argues, characteristic of early versions of the utopian form and essential to the form's requirement for narrative closure.

1.2 Pacific Rim Utopianism

The utopianist Pacific Rim discourse emerged in the mid-1980s at the North American Pacific coast during a time of economic crisis and political-economic restructuring that affected North-America on both sides of the 49th parallel. In Canada, economic crisis was induced by oil shocks, economic slowdown and a federal deficit, whose growth was, in part, due to generous expenditure by the Canadian welfare state during the 1970s.[87] In the U.S., under the Reagan

---

85 Jameson, *Archaeologies of the Future*, 4.
86 Ibid., 193.
87 See David Ley, *Millionnaire Migrants:Trans-Pacific Life Lines* (Malden, et al., Wiley-Blackwell, 2010) 51.

administration, a huge military buildup sanctioned by the Strategic Defense Initiative[88] caused an enormous expansion of the federal budget deficit. Although the U.S. economy in general saw a favorable development during the Reagan administration and the reasons for restrictions on social welfare were, in the U.S., part of 'Reagonomics' and thus more openly programmatic than those in Canada, the outcome was the same in both North American nations: there was a "new emphasis on markets and in particular to finding new markets,"[89] which was accompanied by radical cutbacks on social programs, contracting out, massive privatization, and the general "re-direction of state power towards an entrepreneurial ethos."[90] This re-direction towards an entrepreneurial ethos and the modeling of the state as a business enterprise is characteristic of the rationality of neoliberalism which, "sustained by a rising neoconservative culture,"[91] increasingly gained ground from the mid-1980s to the mid-1990s in both Canada and the U.S.

For the social reality in both states, the 'freedom' epitomized in neoliberal rhetoric by the promised reduction of state power has proven treacherous, as it translated into substantial tax-cuts for the upper and middle-class, and into benefit cuts and the individual 'freedom' to take care of their own needs for the poor, whose expectations concerning public services have been pervasively disciplined.[92] The need to find new markets on a global scale has, in the legislatures of both states, motivated the removal of national restrictions to the free movement of capital ("such as tariffs, punitive taxation arrangements, planning and environmental controls, or other locational impediments"[93]) and to the mobility of a wealthy class of entrepreneurial migrants (exemplary representatives of *homo oeconomicus*, the ideal-typical actor of the neoliberal state), while "national barriers to the free movement of labour have if anything been strengthened, with more comprehensive and meticulous protection of borders."[94]

The speculative fiction of the Pacific Rim was created during this time of neoliberal restructuring and intensified competition for new markets on a global scale. Incited by the soaring economies of East Asian countries (David Ley emphasizes that, while the burgeoning economies of Japan and the Four Tigers –

---

88 See "Reagan, Ronald Wilson," Thomas L. Purvis, *A Dictionary of American History* (Malden, et al.: Blackwell, 2002).
89 Ley, *Millionnaire Migrants*, 51.
90 Ibid., 53.
91 Ibid., 52.
92 See ibid., 52.
93 David Harvey, *A Brief History of Neoliberalism* (Oxford: Oxford UP, 2005) 66.
94 Ley, *Millionnaire Migrants*, 64.

Hong Kong, Singapore, South Korea, and Taiwan – were praised as economic models, China was, at the time, still considered a target market for North-American export rather than a model) the business sections of North-American mainstream media, in the 1980s, increasingly covered East Asian economic success, and "the Pacific Rim dramatically entered public consciousness."[95] It is important to note, however, that, in contrast to comparable "Atlantic networks which include also military, social and cultural relationships,"[96] "the Pacific Rim as a putative region was shaped in the North-American imagination as a business opportunity and little else."[97]

Joining the praise in the mainstream media, a striking number of motivational guides by North American economists, published from the mid-1980s to the early 1990s, euphorically celebrated Asian economic success, and, conjoining in their rhetoric tropes like 'miracle' and 'dynamism' with ideas of transnational convergence and free trade, greatly contributed to the shaping of the irreal space of the Pacific Rim: books like *The Third Wave* (Alvin Toffler, 1980), *The Chinese Connection* (Michael Goldberg, 1985), *The Pacific Century* (Staffan B. Linder, 1986), *Pacific Destiny* (Robert Elegant, 1990), and *Megatrends 2000* (John Naisbitt, 1990) were highly influential to the general "talking up"[98] of the Pacific Rim, and coined a futurologist lingo that Bruce Cumings has termed "rimspeak."[99] According to Cumings, rimspeak reflects a tendency to gloss over political and cultural differences (such as the 'red scare' of communism) that had seemed insurmountable before the 1970s. Cumings argues that with the emergence of rimspeak and its product 'Pacific Rim,' a thoroughly strategic revaluation of these differences took place: "'Pacific Rim' invoked a newborn 'community' that anyone, socialist or not, could join…as long as they were capitalist. Rimspeakers of course continued to look with curiosity if not disdain upon anyone who did not privilege the market."[100]

Cumings's assessment reflects a widespread rejection by cultural critics of any positivist notion of the Pacific region. Published in *What Is In a Rim*,[101] an

---

95 Ibid,. 41.
96 Ley, *Millionnaire Migrants*, 41.
97 Ibid., 65.
98 Ibid., 46
99 "Rimspeak: Or, The Discourse of the Pacific Rim," *What Is In A Rim: Critical Perspectives on the Pacific Region Idea*, ed. Arif Dirlik (Lanham: Rowman and Littlefield, 1998) 53-72.
100 Ibid., 56.
101 *What Is In A Rim: Critical Perspectives on the Pacific Region Idea*, ed. Arif Dirlik (Lanham: Rowman and Littlefield, 1998).

interdisciplinary volume edited by Arif Dirlik and dedicated to the historicization and deconstruction of the Asia Pacific myth, Cumings's article analyzes rimspeak practitioners' speculative construction of the Pacific Rim as a future capitalist paradise, a borderless, utopian marketplace. Like Cumings, other contributors to *What Is In a Rim* show the Pacific Rim as a construct depending on textuality, the latest narrative version of a historical "earth inscription"[102] whose older mythical narratives were centered around the term 'discovery,' while concealing their ideological agenda and economic interest in the region, as well as their orientalist marginalization and suppression of Asian others. As Arif Dirlik argues, differing perspectives on the Pacific region are contingent upon situated-ness and location within a network of historical relationships; particularly the Euro-American Pacific region idea has, according to Dirlik, always been "a competing set of ideational constructs that project upon a certain location on the globe the imperatives of interest, power, or vision of these historically produced relationships."[103]

While Consuelo Leon traces the beginnings of a Pacific image in American minds back to information about Asia which reached Europe in the thirteenth century and was communicated to Americans through British culture,[104] Arif Dirlik aligns the beginning of an Asia Pacific idea with the global expansion of Europe in the sixteenth and seventeenth century.[105] Both Dirlik and Leon point to the crucial role of commerce as an incentive for the historical 'discoveries' in the Pacific area and the importance of traveler accounts, which were, according to Leon, immensely popular in European countries over several centuries. These early traveler accounts are interesting in the context of the late-twentieth century

---

102 Arif Dirlik, "The Asia-Pacific Idea," *What Is In A Rim: Critical Perspectives on the Pacific Region Idea*, ed. Arif Dirlik (Lanham: Rowman and Littlefield, 1998) 15-36, 19.

103 Dirlik, "The Asia-Pacific Idea," 15-16.

104 Consuelo Leon, "Foundations of the American Image of the Pacific," *boundary 2* 21.1 (1994): 17-29, 18. As an early example Leon mentions Marco Polo's account of his *Voyage to the Orient* (1271). This idea of a mediation of the Pacific image by British culture may also account for the susceptibility to the Pacific Rim imaginary of economists and political leaders in Canada.

105 "The Asia Pacific Idea," 16. See also Dennis O. Flynn and Arturo Giraldez, "The Pacific Rim's Past Deserves a Future," *Studies in the Economic History of the Pacific Rim*, eds. Sally Miller, et al. (London: Routledge, 1998) 1-18. According to Flynn and Giraldez, the birth of European trading in the Pacific area – initiated by Spain and labeled 'Manila Galleon Trade'– can be exactly dated, since it coincided with the founding of the city of Manila in 1571.

Pacific Rim imaginary, because they reflect an inseparability of travel and trade, and, beneath a documentary demeanor, apply decidedly literary, aestheticizing strategies to create images of a Pacific cornucopia, a Pacific paradise inhabited by friendly savages waiting for civilization through European travelers and traders. Their attraction to European readers was based upon a predictable generic structure[106] that allowed a kind of discursive time travel to a stage of primitivism that Europeans had only recently left behind.

At once affirming Europe as their civilized place of enunciation and composing the Pacific area as an empty *terra incognita*, inhabited merely by promiscuous cannibals, fifteenth and sixteenth century traveler accounts laid the foundation for a hegemonic Euro-American strategy of appropriation by representation that was, on both continents, complemented by increasing mapmaking activity. In 1783, the publication of James Cook's *Journal of Captain Cook's Last Voyage to the Pacific Ocean in the Quest of a North-West Passage* ushered in a whole century of Euro-American trade and colonization, an era that historians would later term the 'Age of Cook.'[107] In the Age of Cook, immediately after the American Revolutionary War, the newly independent United States of America started to create a maritime American empire with a China a trade of its own, and intensified the Pacific whaling that played an

---

106 In his reading of Montaigne's essay "Of Cannibals: The Savage 'I'," Michel de Certeau describes the formulaic structure of sixteenth-century traveler accounts as consisting of three basic elements: a framing meta-discourse of the outbound journey to a strange, different place, "starting out in search of the other with the impossible task of saying the truth," followed by an 'ethnological' description of the savage society as seen by a true witness who idealizes the savage community as a beautiful organic body, transforming even cannibalism and polygamy into forms of beauty, and finally the homecoming of the traveler-narrator whose transformed perspective is "augmented with the authority to speak in the name of the other and command belief." "Montaigne's 'Of Cannibals: The Savage 'I'," *Heterologies: Discourse on the Other* (London: U of Minnesota P, 1997) 67-79, 69. Tracing a pattern in eighteenth-century Pacific travel writing, Michelle Burnham argues that "accounts of Pacific travel are characterized [...] by modes of narrativizing risk that reflect a new eighteenth-century conception of numbers and time, and that work to conceal the violence and loss that often characterized these voyages." "Trade, Time, and Risk in Pacific Travel Writing," *Early American Literature* 46.3 (2011): 425-447, 431.

107 See Leon, "Foundations," 18. Michelle Burnham mentions that George Vancouver who explored the northwest coast and particularly British Columbia in the 1790s was a member of Cook's third expedition. See "Trade, Time, and Risk," 433.

important part in the New England economy,[108] long before the idea of a continental empire 'from sea to shining sea' was fully realized. Even Euro-American struggles over territorial claims on the American continent[109] were at least in part motivated by the quest and the international competition for direct access to and control over the Pacific coast.[110] The imperative to write the map of the new American nation in a quest for political cohesion was thus inextricably linked to the quest for economic growth and new markets, an interplay of nation-building and economically motivated imperialism that had characterized the capitalist market society from its beginning in the Early Modern era.[111]

Since U.S.-American nation-building hinged upon an idea of progress that included both the need to sever ties to the European mother country and an imperative for territorial expansion and economic growth, the American pursuit of hegemony over the North-West coast was doubly motivated and fuelled by cartography and literature produced by travelers, traders, and whalers. Consuelo Leon stresses the intense interest in mapmaking and in the exploration of the North-West coast of the Early Republic political elite, and particularly of Thomas Jefferson, "whose vast geographical knowledge was augmented by political pragmatism, [and who] fostered a metamorphosis of the American perception of the Pacific from a rich, but vague notion to one that demanded concrete governmental policies that protected American interests." [112]

By 1820, cartography and literature, commerce and international rivalry about and around the Pacific had shaped the idea of an enormous wealth in the region, as well as the imperative of U.S.-American control over it. As Consuelo

---

108 See Dirlik, "The Asia Pacific Idea," 19.
109 See Paul Giles, "The Deterritorialization of American Literature," *Shades of the Planet: American Literature as World Literature*, eds. Wai Chee Dimmock and Lawrence Buell (Princeton: Princeton UP, 2007) 39-61. While Leon reads smaller conflicts like the Nootka Sound controversy (1789) as instances of historical Euro-American rivalries that are indicative of "the real value placed on the Northwest coast and trans-Pacific commerce" ("Foundations,"26), Giles points to similar reasons underlying the British-American War of 1812 and the Mexican War (1846). Giles emphasizes the importance of geography and maps to American education at the time; he stresses that the reciting of place names functioned as the imaginative appropriation of an unsettled continent. (See esp. 42).
110 See Leon, "Foundations," 26.
111 See Christine So, *Economic Citizens: A Narrative of Asian American Visibility* (Philadelphia: Temple UP, 2008) 16.
112 Leon, "Foundations," 26.

Leon writes, "The United States, as a new nation, understood that, regardless of its relationship to Europe, the Pacific Ocean would be the more decisive element in defining its future." The futurist ring in Leon's diction reflects the utopian fantasy involved in these early American ideas of the Pacific, a utopianist tone that foreshadows the utopianist rhetoric and narrative construction of the late-twentieth-century Pacific Rim ideology. In the formation of this ideology, California and its rapid development played a crucial role. Shortly before the formal incorporation of California into the nation in 1850, the discoveries of gold in 1846 and the ensuing gold rush had "kicked off an unparalleled movement of persons, animals and equipment,"[113] transforming the southern part of the North American Pacific coast region from a thinly settled frontier, controlled by Roman Catholic missions, into a new state, bustling with 250,000 people. Subsuming the impact and implications of the gold disvoveries, Edward W. Soja writes:

Out of practically nowhere, a formidable capitalist presence emerged along the Pacific Ocean rim of the New World, beginning a Californian tilt to the global space economy of capitalism that would continue for the next century and a half. California gold significantly fuelled the recovery and expansion of industrial capitalism after the age of revolution, helped prime the pump for the territorial consolidation and rapid urban industrialization of the United States, and deposited in the San Francisco bay region one of the late nineteenth century's most dynamic centres of accumulation. But the process, once begun, did not end there.[114]

With California having ended its frontier status and having turned into a "dynamic centre of accumulation," the Pacific region had become the new "frontier of capitalist development."[115] What comes to the fore in this perpetual movement of the frontier to ever new territories is the inextricable relationship between the ideology of Manifest Destiny and the market character of the frontier. Emphasizing the centrality of the market to the frontier as a moving concept, Richard White describes the frontier as the middle ground of exchange

---

113 Karen Clay, "Mexican California: Trade, Institutions and Law," *Studies in the Economic History of the Pacific Rim*, eds. Sally M. Miller, et al. (London: Routledge, 1998) 197-209, 191.

114 *Postmodern Geographies: The Reassertion of Space in Critical Social Theory* (London: Verso, 1989) 191.

115 Dirlik,"There is More in the Rim Than Meets the Eye," *What Is In A Rim: Critical Perspectives on the Pacific Region Idea*, ed. Arif Dirlik (Lanham: Rowman and Littlefield, 1998), 352-369, 352.

between different peoples "who engaged in trade [...] and had to arrive at a mutual understanding of what constituted a market, so much so that the exchange relationship could sometimes be indistinguishable from the way of life that surrounded it."[116] This perception of the frontier as a market ties in with a late-nineteenth-century discourse on speculation as a driving force, propelling U.S.-American history from the Columbian expedition to the gradual 'civilizing' settlement and processing of the 'waste spaces' of the continent.[117] According to this discourse, the proverbial 'vastness' of yet unclaimed territories prompted the merging of geographic and economic imagination with the claim to exceptionalism, as a 1889 comment by economic historian George Gibson exemplifies: "The 'magnificent distances' in our country, and its boundless resources, opened a *vista* to the speculator which is not likely to occur again in the history of mankind."[118] This discourse cast immigration as motivated by the speculative projection of future value, and, implicitly, the U.S.-American nation as a nation of speculators.

The official closing of the U.S.-American frontier in the 1890s did not stop the American imagination from projecting speculative vistas in search of "boundless resources"[119] and "the cult of Manifest Destiny never halted at the Pacific shores of California, Oregon, and Washington,"[120] as Arthur P. Dudden asserts. With the Pacific as the new frontier of capitalist development, American speculative vistas were now officially extended to the Pacific region, and the long-standing Euro-American claim to control over its homogenizing symbolic construction became key to frontier negotiations. That the need for symbolic hegemony had gained specific pertinence became evident by the late nineteenth century: not only had the "pacific shores of California, Oregon, and Washington"[121] become target destinations for migrant laborers from Asia and the South, but the American market had become the projection screen for speculative vistas and the target destination for Asian capitalist endeavors.

---

116 Qtd. in William Cronon, George Miles, and Jay Gitlin, *Under the Open Sky: Rethinking America's Western Past* (New York: Norton, 1992), 13.

117 See Urs Stäheli, *Spektakuläre Spekulation: Das Populäre der Ökonomie* (Frankfurt/ Main: Suhrkamp, 2007), 173.

118 George R. Gibson qtd in Stäheli, *Spektakuläre Spekulation*, 182, italics by Urs Stäheli.

119 Ibid.

120 "The American Pacific: How the West Was Also Won," *Studies in the Economic History of the Pacific Rim*, eds. Sally M. Miller, et al. (London: Routledge, 1998) 94-103, 94.

121 Ibid.

Pointing out that early Pacific trade was stimulated by the Chinese economy (a fact that the Euro-American Pacific imaginary tends to ignore), Arif Dirlik particularly emphasizes the role of Japan:

> The Asian contribution to the region's formation, while no less real, was not as readily evident until the late nineteenth century, because up until that point it took the form of resistance to EuroAmerican activity rather than active participation in the region's structuring. Japan's emergence as an economic and political power in the late nineteenth century which paralleled the ascendancy of the United States among EuroAmerican powers, was to bring to the fore a contradiction between the region's form and its content that had been there from the beginning.[122]

Dirlik exposes the Euro-American Pacific idea as a homogenizing discourse that suppresses differences and contradictions. Accordingly, as the example of Japan shows, Asian economic activity was initially denied, and eventually greeted and read as an affirmation of the Euro-American brand of capitalism. Despite Japan's attempt at carving out an Asian space within the Euro-American construct, its attitude – from its beginning until its development into a global player in the world market – has been marked by an eagerness to assimilate to the standards of the Euro-American capitalist order. Instead of introducing an alternative Asian structure to the region, Japan signaled that "it was willing to play according to the rules of the game (including colonialism)." [123]

The competition between Japan and the U.S. has thus been a competition for dominance within the same capitalist system. Even the impulse to secure optimal trade conditions by establishing a Pacific Ocean free trade zone originated in Japan in the 1960s – and was, at that point, met by opposition from the United States, whose attitude did not change before the late 1970s. Further steps towards convergence failed because of the "diversity of Pacific societies and the mutual suspicions that are the legacies of a past of imperialism and colonialism."[124] Instead of shaping an all-encompassing Pacific trade zone, sub-regional groupings have therefore, in the last decades of the twentieth century, implemented smaller zones. In the era of a deterritorialized and globalized

---

122 "The Asia Pacific Idea," 26-27.
123 Ibid., 29.
124 Arif Dirlik, "Introduction: Pacific Contradictions," *What Is In A Rim: Critical Perspectives on the Pacific Region Idea*, ed. Arif Dirlik (Lanham: Rowman and Littlefield, 1998) 3-13, 9.

capitalism, smaller unions like APEC and ASEAN, but also NAFTA,[125] exemplify the contradictory implications of the concept of the free trade zone; they show that this zone can be controlled by trans-national corporations, as it allows capital flows to remain unimpeded by state regulations, while national immigration laws control and navigate the movement of migrant laborers according to the need of capitalist boom-and bust-cycles.[126]

Since the 1960s, economically successful Asian countries like Japan, the Four Tigers, and (more recently and most prominently) China, have not only challenged U.S. economic hegemony by reversing the trajectory of economic activity in the Pacific region, a trajectory that is now targeted at a North American market. They have also created their own Asian brand of capitalism, a successful, competitive product named "communitarian capitalism" whose dynamism threatens to supersede and eclipse the managerial capitalism of the Euro-American school. In terms of economy, these Asian countries have long since outperformed the Third-World-status assigned to them by the Euro-American Pacific region construct. In terms of symbolic dominance and interpretational sovereignty, however, North America struggles to remain in control of a homogenizing discourse.

Like Arif Dirlik and Bruce Cumings, historian Alexander Woodside considers the striking new lingo in the 1980s- and 1990s-publications by U.S. economic 'futurologists' as indicative of a North American struggle for symbolic hegemony over "a common utopianized marketplace:"[127] "The language of the Asia-Pacific myth, with its invocation of 'Third Wave' civilizations and its focus upon the 'basic commonalities' of economic prosperity, rhetorically reconciles the tensely coexisting multiple rival capitalisms and usefully blurs potential

---

125 ASEAN is the Association of Southeast Asian Nation, founded in 1967; APEC signifies the Asia Pacific Economic Cooperation, established in 1989; NAFTA stands for the North-American Free Trade Agreement, implemented in 1992. The founding of these latter economic trade blocs is widely read as an attempt to cope with the competitive challenge posed by the European Union.
126 See Masao Miyoshi, "Turn to the Planet: Literature, Diversity, and Totality," *Comparative Literature* 53.4 (2001): 283-287,esp. 290. See also Masao Miyoshi, "A Borderless World: From Colonialism to Transnationalism, and the Decline of the Nationstate," *Critical Inquiry* 19.4 (1993): 726-751; and Masao Miyoshi "Sites of Resistance in the Global Economy," *boundary 2* 22.1 (1995): 61-84.
127 Alexander Woodside, "The Asia-Pacific Idea as a Mobilization Myth," *What Is In A Rim: Critical Perspectives on the Pacific Region Idea*, ed. Arif Dirlik (Lanham: Rowman and Littlefield, 1998) 37-53.

battle lines among them."[128] Giving an example of what he calls "Pacific Rim prophetic culture" and its decidedly utopian ring, Woodside quotes from John Naisbitt's *Megatrends 2000* (1990):

On the threshold of the new millennium, long the symbol of humanity's golden age, we possess the tools and the capacity to build utopia here and now.[...] The Pacific Rim has rewritten the history of economic development, jumping right over the industrial period and into the information economy where the important resources do come not from the ground but from the people.[129]

The self-assured tone in this euphoric prophecy of the coming of a golden 'Pacific Century' masks a double denial. The striking use of the all-encompassing "we" and "humanity" as well as the conspicuously neutral phrase "the Pacific Rim has rewritten" deny the century-old erasure of the Asian component from the Euro-American Pacific idea. Even more important, the all-embracing vocabulary can hardly gloss over an underlying American anxiety to be excluded from the benefits of the expected golden age. According to Woodside, the American praise of Asian economic dynamism is a pretext for affirming the Western model of export-oriented market economies and for securing the imaginative hegemony over the Pacific discourse. As a prominent feature of the prophetic rimspeak, Woodside particularly highlights

a genteel social Darwinism – the belief in a competitive struggle between civilizations in varying degrees of economic fitness – minus the original Darwinism's tedious fascination with national physique sizes, and with the possibility of peace and prosperity for all through convergence benignly substituted for the older, more brutal outcome of the wholesale elimination of unfit civilizations.[130]

Obviously, the new social Darwinism owes its 'benign' quality to the same weakened position of its discursive founders that also fuels their interest in convergence. It ties in with a reversed orientalism, another characteristic feature of rimspeak, described by Woodside as equally 'benign' and as equally targeted at the creation of an economic Pacific union that could edge out global competitors like the European Community. This new, 'benign' orientalism spreads a reductive image of Asian societies as enjoying the "almost mystical

---

128 Ibid., 49.
129 Qtd. in Woodside, "The Asia-Pacific Idea as a Mobilization Myth," 37.
130 Woodside, "The Asia-Pacific Idea as a Mobilization Myth," 39-40.

consensus" of an "Asian ethos"[131] that is construed as having fostered Asian economic success.

The truly new, and particularly utopianist feature of Pacific Rim prophetic culture, besides these new versions of old stereotypes yielded by a long-standing discursive tradition that ties up power, ideology and representation, is the one that Woodside calls Saint Simonianism. It is named after the early-nineteenth-century French philosopher Henri de Saint Simon who foresaw a golden age in a "future industrial civilization, ruled by an elite of scientists and engineers, undergoing repeated progressive transformations in which supposedly more primitive political struggles disappeared or were marginalized."[132] Saint Simonianism thus designates the utopianism of a prophetic culture, whose idea of an ideal future rests upon an unquestioning belief in the benefits of technological innovations, such as genetic engineering and electronic information flows. While conjuring the illusion of a unified, high-tech Pacific community, the euphemizing, utopianist rhetoric of this culture conceals the lack of a common ethos on which a truly utopian community would have to be based. This lack of "even the rudiments of a moral 'common will' that might cross ethnic barriers"[133] allows the unimpeded organization of a plural society like a factory or a corporation, which is centered around and organized for the sole purpose of production and commerce. In the utopian imaginary of an economic Pacific Rim community, the non-interventionist policy of the neoliberal free market ideology serves as the sole common denominator. Epitomized by the free trade zone (and pursued on a global scale by the World Trade Organization) this ideology creates what Woodside calls a "mobilization myth" in the Pacific region. According to Woodside, this myth conceals the uneven regulation of mobility that is inherent to the concept of the free trade zone; it promotes flows of money, information and commodities, while triggering flows of people and mobilizing "the poor of the region for economic production without representing or encouraging their political and social claims."[134] As a result, "the incompletely defeudalized lives"[135] of subaltern social groups in the Pacific

---

131 Ibid., 40.
132 Ibid., 39.
133 Ibid., 46
134 Woodside, "The Asia-Pacific Idea as a Mobilization Myth," 48. See also page 47, where Woodside, pointing to strategies of various Pacific states to suppress subaltern resistance and labor representation, laconically sums up the problem of non-representation in the region: "It is not fashionable in the Pacific Rim these days to use the strength of labor unions as touchstones of progress."
135 Ibid., 47.

region (whose repressed consumption rates Woodside identifies as the real reason for Asian economic success) are, in the twenty-first century, comparable to those of workers in nineteenth-century Britain.[136]

At this point, the economic utopian fiction created by rimspeak practitioners becomes visible as the very "construction of an optical image from which existence itself [...] has been removed by a sleight of hand, a masterful feat of ideological prestidigitation"[137] that Fredric Jameson describes as characteristic of early versions of the utopian form. As Jameson writes, the narrative closure of this form is motivated by "the unanimity on the need to exclude political discussion and the development of any form of local difference" and "a systemic perspective for which it is obvious that whatever threatens the system as such must be excluded."[138] However, while no less fictional than literary utopias by, say, Edward Bellamy or H.G. Wells, the utopia of the Pacific Rim has the status of a factual discourse, and, accordingly, its lack of a common moral ground and its failure to represent the economic, social and cultural inequality of migrating subaltern groups has dire political consequences: not only are subaltern populations of Asian countries mobilized according to the needs of capital, but the illusion of social mobility motivating their migration is cultivated, whereas the enduring inequality between ethnic majorities and minorities and the racializing practices of governance within multicultural nations like Canada and the U.S. remain concealed by the speculative fiction of a prosperous Pacific community.

While the utopian narrative of a golden 'Pacific Century' provides a form of discursive time travel that projects the idea of a Pacific paradise into the future, it remains invested with the same power of composing and distributing places as the historical traveler accounts that are its epistemological predecessors. This is not immediately obvious, as the utopianist Pacific Rim narrative – different from the center/periphery model of the historical traveler narratives with their clear demarcation of their place of enunciation and the peripheral place they allocated to the colonized other – efficiently hides the co-existence of transnational economic liberalization and restructuring with national practices of social regulation and internal colonization. This co-existence is especially effective in the metropolises of the North American Pacific coast, where it results in a paradox "peripherelization of the core."[139] Los Angeles, in particular, is a point

---

136 See ibid.
137 *Archaeologies of the Future*, 193.
138 Ibid., 205.
139 Edward W. Soja,. *Postmodern Geographies: The Reassertion of Space in Critical Social Theory* (London: Verso, 1989) 215.

in case, as Edward W. Soja shows. Pointing to the impressive rate of Hispanic and Asian immigration to Los Angeles since the 1960s ("including several Pacific island populations"[140]), and emphasizing the centrality of the immigrant population to an economic productivity whose conditions are reminiscent of "Third World Export Processing Zones,"[141] Soja concludes:

> The centre has thus become the periphery, as the corporate citadel of multinational capital rests with consummate agility upon a broadening base of alien populations. The city that more than any other has been built upon the military defence of American shores has become the beach-head for a peripheral invasion.[142]

Soja's diction captures a sense of impending menace starkly contrasting the utopianist rhetoric of the official rimspeak. The passage reflects a "fortress mentality"[143] that has been widely acknowledged as a hallmark of urban communities in southern California, a paranoid obsession with security triggered only in part by "the uncertainties about identity that global flows invariably produce."[144] Mark Davis convincingly argues that urban paranoia and fortress mentality are, in L.A., a reaction to social insulation and "the destruction of accessible public space"[145] in the wake of the "deregulation of the economy and the recession of non-market entitlements."[146]

The "hardening of the city surface against the poor" that Davis considers a result of the neoliberalization of governance in L.A., is strikingly echoed in both David Ley and Katharyne Mitchell's analyses of ethnic conflict and social tensions in Vancouver. Mitchell impressively describes how Vancouver, once "a small city on the edge of the British Empire,"[147] a "provincial backwater,"[148] was

---

140 Ibid., 217.
141 Ibid.
142 Ibid.
143 Mike Davis, *City of Quartz: Excavating the Future in Los Angeles* (London: Verso, 2006) 224. See also Liam Kennedy, *Race and Urban Space in Contemporary American Culture* (Edinburgh: Edinburgh UP, 2000) 6.
144 Arjun Appadurai, *Fear of Small Numbers: An Essay on the Geography of Anger* (Durham: Duke UP, 2006) 7.
145 Davis, *City of Quartz*, 226.
146 Ibid.
147 Katharyne Mitchell, *Crossing the Neoliberal Line: Pacific Rim Migration and the Metropolis* (Philadelphia: Temple UP, 2004) 2.
148 Ibid., 3.

"swept into a process of planetary integration,"[149] and transformed "into a global metropolis, a gateway between East and West."[150] During the closing decades of the twentieth century, in the course of a skyrocketing movement of capital and people (many of them wealthy Chinese immigrants from Hong Kong), property in Vancouver became "the hottest real estate in the world."[151] This economic boom has been widely perceived by Vancouver residents as a Chinese 'invasion' and has triggered conflicts about house styles, landscapes, costs of rental apartments, neighborhood character and zoning amendments.[152] Although these local troubles in Vancouver seem moderate compared to the "class and race warfare"[153] in L.A., there are obvious analogies. Just like Mike Davis sees a relation between "the shift of fiscal resources to corporate-defined priorities" and class and race conflicts in L.A., Katharyne Mitchell and David Ley consider a "market-saturated governance regime"[154] and its promotion of a self-sufficient *homo eoconomicus* as the ideal citizen responsible for the growing social tensions and conflicts in Vancouver.

The striking similarities in the political-economic, cultural and social development of both cities during the last decades of the twentieth century suggest that, despite significant differences in U.S.-American and Canadian history and legislation, the pervasiveness of the neoliberal rationality creates a social reality and a climate of dystopia markedly contrasting the utopian fiction of a golden 'Pacific Century' that it propagates. Situated at the North American Pacific Rim, Los Angeles and Vancouver can be considered 'rim cities' whose close proximity to the new frontier of capitalist development appears to foster and intensify a climate of risk and paranoia. Given the etymological origins of the word 'risk' that the *OED* traces to "the classical Latin verb resecare with the sense 'that which cuts' and hence 'rock, crag, reef' with allusion to the hazards of travel or transport by sea,"[155] the geographical position of both cities at the edge of the North-American continent and their interest in Pacific trade seems to invite a naturalizing perception of danger as risk. Contrary to such a naturalizing notion of risk, the artifacts that are at the center of this study show risk as a construct that is central to the calculations of the neoliberal rationality and its

---

149 Ibid.
150 Ibid.
151 Ibid.
152 See ibid.
153 Davis, City of Quartz, 228-229.
154 Ley, *Millionnaire Migrants*, 7.
155 "risk, n.," *OED Online* (March 2012) Oxford University Press. Web, 20 Mar. 2012. <http://www.oed.com/view/Entry/166306?rskey=5AFGY7&result=1>.

reduction of political subjects to economic actors. In the rim cities of Bigelow, Yamashita, and Lai's fictional speculations on the future of subjectivity at the North American Pacific coast, risk, just like the utopian fiction of a golden Pacific age, is a political strategy to take hold of and 'tame' the future.

1.3 RISK THEORY

At first glance, a definition of 'risk' as a strategy appears counterintuitive. In everyday individual life, risk is generally understood as the probability of a potential danger or unwanted event, an understanding that is reflected in the *OED-* definition of "risk" as the "(exposure to) the possibility of loss, injury, or other adverse or unwelcome circumstance."[156] Accordingly, the avoidance of risk appears to be a natural behavior motivated by self-preservation- or survival-instinct. Ever since Ulrich Beck's analysis of modern society as a "risk society" in 1986,[157] however, a new awareness of risk as a social and political problem has gained currency, and risk – already a focal point of interest and analysis in modern economic theory since the 1950s[158] – has become the object of scientific research in sociology and other social science disciplines. As Jakob Arnoldi shows, "the key insight into risk that sociology has delivered is that risk involves more than simply an objectively given probability."[159]

Arnoldi distinguishes three dominant sociological approaches to risk: Mary Douglas's cultural theory of risk that rests upon a cultural typology and considers risks (their definition and management by a given culture) as dependent upon culturally coded values; Ulrich Beck's notion of modern society as defined by a range of intangible uncertainties, regarding risks as side effects of scientific and technological progress; and a third approach, described by Arnoldi as "inspired by Michel Foucault's notion of governmentality"[160] and represented by a heterogeneous group of scholars from several disciplines, with a focus on risk as a concept that creates social reality and as a technology to govern social problems.[161] What these theories have in common, according to

---

156 Ibid.
157 *Risikogesellschaft* (Frankfurt/Main: Suhrkamp, 1986).
158 See "Risk in economic analysis," "Risk," section 5, *Stanford Encyclopedia of Philosophy* (Fall 2011) Web, 5 Dec. 2011.
159 *Risk: An Introduction* (Cambridge, UK: Polity, 2009) 5.
160 *Risk*, 2.
161 See ibid., 38-66.

Arnoldi, is their assessment that the relevance of risk to contemporary societies has been growing since the 1960s, as well as the notion of the dependence of risk on science and knowledge, and a perception of risk as, "at least to some degree,"[162] "socially constructed."[163]

Yet the assumptions upon which an acknowledgement of the constructed quality of risk is based in each of the three approaches to risk differ considerably, as do the conclusions drawn. For Mary Douglas and her co-author Aaron Wildavsky,[164] the definition of dangers as risks in a given culture is conditioned by community consensus on values and is thus the product of a cultural bias:

This cultural bias is integral to social organization. Risk taking and risk aversion, shared confidence and shared fears, are part of the dialogue on how best to organize social relations. For to organize means to organize some things *in*, and some things *out*. When we say therefore that a kind of society is biased towards stressing the risk of pollution, we are not saying that other kinds of social organization are objective and unbiased but rather that they are biased toward finding different kinds of dangers.[165]

The problem underlying the cultural bias towards risk is, for Douglas and Wildavsky, ultimately the problem of how consensus on values is achieved in a given society, or, to put it differently, the question of whose judgment of value is socially accepted and institutionally enforced. In *Risk and Culture*, Douglas together with political scientist Aaron Wildavsky develops a cultural typology of forms of social organization in which different societal groups seek to ascertain their interests and, accordingly, to establish their respective definitions of dangers as risks. Douglas and Wildavsky also problematize the role of scientific research and the political bias of experts in these processes; yet, while acknowledging "the idea of knowledge as the changing product of social activity,"[166] they renounce "relativist criticism"[167] and insist that "risk is a

---

162 Arnoldi, *Risk*, 66.
163 See ibid,. 65-66.
164 Mary Douglas has also published alone on the subject of risk. See for instance, *Risk Acceptability According to the Social Sciences* (New York: Russell Sage Foundation, 1986), and Risk and Blame (London: Routledge, 1992).
165 Mary Douglas and Aaron Wildavsky, *Risk and Culture: An Essay on the Selection of Technical and Environmental Dangers* (Berkeley and Los Angeles: U of California P, 1982) 8, italics in the original.
166 Ibid., 192.
167 Ibid.

straightforward consequence of the dangers inherent in the physical situation."[168] There is thus a certain tension in Douglas and Wildavsky's cultural theory of risks as constructs, or as depending on culturally shared values that are the basis for the selection of dangers as risks in a given society on the one hand, and their conclusion that risks are 'real' on the other. Their diction throughout *Risk and Culture* signals an understanding of societal organization and structures of hierarchy as conditioned by "dialogue,"[169] "many-sided conversation[s],"[170] "reasonable disagreement,"[171] "open-ended communal enterprise,"[172] and, ultimately, rational choice. This diction indicates the authors' presupposition of a Habermasian understanding of deliberative democracy and an idealistic view of the public sphere of a social-welfare state whose constitutional reality is realized by "a process in which the exercise of social power and political domination is effectively subjected to the mandate of democratic publicity."[173]

Similar tensions can be traced in Ulrich Beck's theory of *World Risk Society* (1999).[174] Beck dismisses Douglas and Wildavsky's *Risk and Culture* as ignoring the recent advent of new and unprecedented dangers that have "the capacity for nuclear and ecological annihilation,"[175] dangers whose scope and uninsurability marks the specific historical situation of what he calls "second modernity."[176] Delineating his distinction between "first modernity" and "second modernity" in his introduction to *World Risk Society*, Beck writes:

The former term I use to describe the modernity based on nation-state societies, where social relations, networks and communities are essentially understood in a territorial sense. The collective patterns of life, progress and controllability, full employment and exploitation of nature that were typical of this first modernity have now been undermined by five interlinked processes: globalization, individualization, gender revolution, underemployment and global risks (as ecological crisis and the crash of global financial markets).[177]

---

168 Ibid., 193.
169 Douglas and Wildavsky, *Risk and Culture*, 8.
170 Ibid., 193.
171 Ibid., 194-195.
172 Ibid., 192.
173 Jürgen Habermas, *The Structural Transformation of the Public Sphere: An Inquiry into a Category of Bourgeois Society* (Cambridge, UK: Polity, 2011) 224.
174 Ulrich Beck, *World Risk Society* (Cambridge, UK: Polity, 1999).
175 Ibid., 23.
176 Ibid., 1.
177 Ibid., 1-2.

According to Beck, the transition between these two stages of modernity is conditioned by "reflexive modernization,"[178] a doubly coded term, coined by Beck to capture both the reflex-like, quasi-automatic, unintentional consequences of conditions that are produced by industrial society (first modernity) without being discursively addressed and reflected upon at the time of their production, and the need for discursive reflection generated by the reality of these consequences in "second modernity" societies. This doubly coded reflexivity of a transformation process from multifarious, dangerous consequences that were unseen and unaddressed by society at the time of their production and therefore challenge a subsequent society to deal with these dangers simultaneously in multi-leveled public discourses is the starting point for Beck's concept of risk society. Confronted with "nuclear, chemical, ecological, and genetic engineering risks" that "(a) can be limited in terms of neither time nor place" and "(b) are not accountable according to the established rules of causality, blame and liability, and (c) cannot be compensated or insured against,"[179] Beck's global risk society is characterized by "the need for reflexive self-definition and redefinition."[180] For Beck, the pressure to deal with dangerous implications of technological progress whose future consequences are of a global scale, unpredictable, and therefore uninsurable on the one hand entails and enables new power struggles:

Risks have become a major force of political mobilization, often replacing references to, for example, inequalities associated with race, class and gender. This highlights the new *power game* of risks and its meta-norms: who is to define the riskiness of a product, a technology, and on what grounds in an age of manufactured uncertainties?[181]

But on the other hand, while emphasizing the existence of a differential between the lack of expert knowledge on the outcome of dangers and the power of decision-making involved in the declaration of dangers as risks, Beck claims that risk society is "tendentially a self-critical society."[182] Even more important, he contends that in "a risk society, which identifies itself as such, critique is democratized."[183] It is worth noting that Beck, at this point, projects his own theory of "reflexive modernization" as having a democratizing effect on critique

---

178   Ibid., 73.
179   Beck, *World Risk Society*, 76-77.
180   Ibid., 78.
181   Ibid., 4, italics in the original.
182   Ibid., 79, italics in the original.
183   Ibid., italics in the original.

in a society, if this society is aware of and acknowledges the processes that he identifies as the reason for an increase of dangers. A risk society "which identifies itself as such" is thus an ideal-typical society that subscribes to Beck's theorization of risks as "second modernity"-consequences of "first modernity"-industrialization while, at the same time, allowing "norms, principles and practices in all society's fields of action to become contradictory – that is, measured by immanent rankings and claims."[184] The idealistic bias in Beck's perspective becomes particularly obvious when he states:

> Risk society is *uncovered* society, in which insurance *decreases* with the scale of the danger – and this in the historic milieu of the 'welfare state', which encompasses all spheres of life, and of the fully comprehensive society. Only the two together – uncovered *and* comprehensively insured society – constitute the politically explosive force of risk society.[185]

Significantly, Beck draws this conclusion after quoting scholars like Niklas Luhmann, Christof Lau, and Jost Halfmann, scholars who foreground the dependence of various risk assessments on decision-makers' respective strategic interest and privileged positionality in a given risk culture. Beck, for instance, quotes Halfmann: "The effective irreconcilability of these various risk assessments turns concrete decisions over acceptable risks into struggles for power."[186] Christof Lau, who elaborates on the role of experts in the power struggles over risks and who argues that these struggles rework existing social divisions and older struggles over justice and distribution, is quoted shortly thereafter:

> Debates over risk definitions and their consequences for society take place essentially at the level of public (or partially public) discourses. They are conducted with the aid of scientific arguments of scientific arguments and information, which serve, so to speak, as scarce resources of the collective actors. The scientifically penetrated public sphere then becomes the symbolic location of conflicts over distribution even if this is disguised by the objectified, scientistic autonomous logic of specialist argument about risk.[...] primary resources in this struggle over risk justice are not immediately strikes, voting figures, political influence, but above all information, scientific findings, assessments, arguments.[187]

---

184 Ibid., 80.
185 Ibid., 85, italics in the original.
186 Qtd. in Beck, *World Risk Society*, 83.
187 Qtd. in Beck, *World Risk Society*, 83.

Beck agrees with Halfmann and with Lau whose position he sums up in an affirmative gesture by differentiating between "those responsible for and those affected by the risks involved."[188] Yet the phrasing of this affirmation already tellingly distorts Lau's assessment that it is the definition of risk and not risk as such that is the object of these contestations. The inconsistency in Beck's argument becomes even more obvious when he delineates Niklas Luhmann's theorization of risk. Significantly, Beck outlines Luhmann's distinction between "those making a decision and those affected by the decision"[189] as the "starting point"[190] of Luhmann's theory. He then quotes passages from Luhmann's study on *Risk*,[191] referring first to a passage in which the author delineates the decision-making involved in individual conduct and the dependence of any distinction between danger and risk on individual knowledge and rational judgment about the probable future consequences of an action or behavior, and, subsequently, to Luhmann's contention that

> the prospect of catastrophe sets a limit to calculation. Under no circumstances whatsoever does one want it – even if it is extremely improbable. But what is the catastrophe threshold beyond which quantitative calculations are no longer convincing? Obviously, this question cannot be answered independently of other variables. It is different for rich and poor, for the independent and the dependent. [...]The really interesting question is what counts as a catastrophe. And that is presumably a question that is answered differently by decision-makers and victims.[192]

Beck comments on this passage by conceding "This may be, but it neglects and underestimates the systemic yardstick of economic insurance rationality,"[193] and it is at this point, after extensive quotation from scholars highlighting the relevance of power and struggle over risk definition, that he emphasizes "the historic milieu of the 'welfare state', which encompasses all spheres of life, and of the fully comprehensive society" as constituting "the politically explosive force of risk society" in the passage quoted above. Beck's insistence on "the systemic yardstick of economic insurance rationality" as an aspect that Luhmann fails to consider ultimately exposes the arbitrariness of his selection of quotes

---

188 Ibid.
189 Ibid., 84.
190 Ibid., 84
191 Niklas Luhmann, *Risk: A Sociological Theory* (New Brunswick and London: Aldine Transaction, 2008).
192 Luhmann qtd. in Beck, *World Risk Society*, 84-85.
193 Beck, *World Risk Society*, 85.

from Luhmann's analysis. Luhmann starts his analysis not, as Beck claims, by merely introducing the distinction between decision-makers and those affected by decisions, but by pointing to the relevance of the specific temporality involved in risk decisions and the dependence of definitions of risk on observation, two factors which, for Luhmann, condition the political brisance of risk:

Within the horizon of the past one at least knows what has happened, even if causal relations remain unclear. Within the horizon of the future precisely this security is lacking – which, from a practical point of view, renders an analysis of causality superfluous. And for precisely this reason a mode of observation attaching importance to causalities exacerbates the discrepancy between the past and the future – especially since the reconciling notion of 'laws of causality' has become questionable.[194]

It is against this background of a mode of observation that attaches importance to causalities which can only be construed by extrapolation that "the gap between decision makers and those affected"[195] who, as Luhmann has it, "constitute an amorphous mass that cannot be given form"[196] becomes visible as a power asymmetry in the struggle over the definition of risk. The fact that those affected by decisions over risks are not a definable group but rather amorphous groupings, comprised of subjects whose allegiance shifts and varies in accordance with concernment, weakens these groupings' opposition to the authority of experts, an opposition that, as Luhmann contends, is increasingly motivated by waning confidence in expert authority. Interestingly, Luhmann points out that a Habermasian understanding that "recognizes only concensus-orientated communication as rational communication"[197] loses traction vis-à-vis these fragmentations and shifting allegiances.[198]

Implicit to Luhmann's definition of risk as depending on the authority of decision-making, the particular relationship between past and future and the causality and extrapolation established by this authority is thus a much more pessimistic view of the effect of risk on societal communication than the idealistic one expressed in Beck's contention that in "a risk society, which identifies itself as such, critique is *democratized*."[199] Beck's perception of the

---

194 Luhmann, *Risk*, 41.
195 Ibid., 111.
196 Ibid., 110.
197 Luhmann, *Risk*, 115.
198 See ibid., 114-118.
199 *World Risk Society*, 79, italics in the original.

democratizing effect of an awareness of uninsurable risk on what he terms 'world risk society' clearly does not account for the asymmetrical power relations marking processes of risk definition and decision making. His objection that Luhmann does not consider the systemic relevance of "the yardstick of economic insurance rationality"[200] raises the question of what this rationality signifies for him, particularly when contextualized with Francois Ewald's theorization of the relationship between risk and economic insurance rationality:

Nothing is a risk in itself; there is no risk in reality. But in the other hand anything can be a risk; it all depends on how one analyzes the danger, considers the event. As Kant might have put it, the category of risk is a category of the understanding; it cannot be given in sensibility or intuition. As a technology of risk insurance is first and foremost a schema of rationality, a way of breaking down, rearranging, ordering certain elements of reality. The expression 'taking risks' used to characterize the spirit of enterprise, derives from the application of this type of calculus to economic and financial affairs.[...] Insurance is not initially a practice of compensation or reparation. It is the practice of a certain type of rationality: one formalized by the calculus of probabilities. This is why one never insures oneself except against risks, and why the latter can include such different things as death, an accident, hailstorms, a disease, a birth, military conscription, bankruptcy and litigation. Today it is hard to imagine all the things which insurers have managed to invent as classes of risk – always, it should be said, with profitable results. The insurer's activity is not just a matter of passively registering the existence of risk and then offering guarantees against them. He 'produces risks', he makes risks appear where each person had hitherto felt obliged to submit resignedly to the blows of fortune. It is characteristic of insurance that it constitutes a certain type of objectivity [...] By objectivizing certain events as risks, insurance can invert their meanings. [...] insurance assigns a new mode of existence to previously dreaded events; it creates value. [...] Insurance is the practice of a type of rationality potentially capable of transforming the life of individuals and that of a population.[201]

Read with Ewald, it becomes obvious that Luhmann's assessment of risk as depending on observation and his inquiry into the constructed quality of catastrophes does not in any way neglect or under-estimate the "systemic yardstick of economic insurance rationality," as Beck criticizes. On the contrary, Ewald's theorization of insurance as a rationality that produces risks spotlights

---

200 Ibid., 85.
201 Francois Ewald, "Insurance and Risk," *The Foucault Effect: Studies in Governmentality*, eds. Graham Burchell, et al. (Chicago: U of Chicago P, 1991) 197-210, 190-201.

contradictions inherent to Beck's theory of a world risk society: although Beck acknowledges "the new *power game* of risks and its meta-norms"[202] in his introduction to *World Risk Society*, his assumption that the plurality and the contradictoriness of "norms, principles and practices in all society's fields of action"[203] leads to democratization in global public forums implicitly downplays the authority assigned to experts and decision-makers, and the subtle, yet powerful effects of their definitions of risk.

Addressing such effects that have become particularly evident in new practices of risk management deployed in the wake of 9/11, scholars in recent Critical Securitization Studies criticize Beck's optimistic view. In a volume dedicated to the theorization of risk as a rationality of government in the 'war on terror,' Claudia Aradau and Rens van Munster, for example, argue that "the representation of catastrophic events" instead of giving way to deliberation in global public forums, as Beck claims, "has brought about exceptional practices beyond and outside the law, imperial reinventions of liberty and democracy and securitization of boundaries of difference."[204] Like Luhmann and Ewald, Aradau and van Munster particularly emphasize the pertinence of precaution and a doctrine of preemption to the rise of risk as a framework of governance:

What is new is not so much the advent of an uncontrollable risk society as the emergence of a "precautionary" element that has given birth to new rationalities of government that the catastrophic prospects of the future be tamed and managed. In conjunction with a neoliberal rationality of risk, the *dispositif* of precautionary risk creates convergent effects of depoliticization and dedemocratization.[205]

While it might be argued that risks have taken on a different quality and status after 9/11 and that the application of new practices of precautionary risk management can be justified by the imperative to deal with new, unprecedented dangers (and the essays in Amoore and de Goede's volume show that this is exactly the argument used to legitimize practices of preemptive risk management) it is important to note that scholars in Governmentality Studies have already criticized Beck's theorization of risk before the 'war on terror.' Mitchell Dean, for example, in his seminal study on Governmentality, traces

---

202 Ibid., 4, italics in the original.
203 Ibid., 80.
204 "Taming the Future: The Dispositif of Risk in the War on Terror," *Risk and the War on Terror*, eds. Louise Amoore and Marieke de Goede (London and New York: Routledge, 2008) 23-40, 24, italics in the original.
205 Ibid.

inconsistencies in Beck's argumentation as early as 1999. For Dean, these inconsistencies are already inscribed in Beck's conceptualization of the transformation from industrial society to post-industrial risk society as "reflexive modernity" and in his assumption that the growing incalculability of once calculable risks is "at the heart of this transformation."[206] Dean argues that Beck's coinage of the term 'reflexive modernity' is motivated by his intention to give a positive account of the present, an account that avoids 'post-isms,' although, according to Dean, risk society "is perhaps more adequately characterized as a post-risk-calculation society."[207] Beck, as Dean has it, identifies risk with insurer's risk and thus with quantitative forms of calculation, without reflecting, as, for instance, Francois Ewald does, that "risk is a form of calculation about reality rather than [...] a naturally occurring entity."[208]

Most important, then, Dean criticizes that Beck "wants to treat risk ontologically."[209] Dean argues that the emergence of multiple, heterogeneous risk rationalities and practices for the government of risk call for a different approach to risk, "a more nominalist position, i.e. one that analyses forms of risk as among the ways in which we are required to know and to act upon ourselves and others today in a range of moral and political programmes and social technologies."[210] It is in this sense of a more nominalist position towards risk that the essays in Amoore and de Goede's collection analyze practices of preemptive risk management in the 'war on terror' as techniques of governance that tie in and intersect with a market-compliant moral behaviorism and the rediscovery of individual responsibility promoted by the rationality of neoliberalism. Drawing on Michel Foucault's notion of the dispositif,[211] Aradau and van Munster, for instance, delineate various historical dispositifs of risk; as its latest manifestation they identify a redirection of the dispositif of insurance from 'spreading risk' (a late-nineteenth century measure developed to mitigate harmful consequences of industrialization by spreading them to the whole

---

206 Mitchell Dean, *Governmentality: Power and Rule in Modern Society*, 2nd ed. (London, et al.: Sage, 2010) 212.
207 Ibid.
208 Ibid., 212-213.
209 Ibid., 211.
210 Ibid.
211 Aradau and van Munster quote Foucault's who defines a dispositif as consisting of "discourses, institutions, architectural forms, regulatory decisions, administrative measures, scientific statements, philosphical, moral, and philanthropic propositions." "Taming the Future," 25.

population) to 'embracing risk' ("a depooling of collective risks towards individual responsibility"[212]):

> The rationality of neoliberalism and the rationality of precaution are not mutually exclusive, but converge in the emphasis on market agents as risk embracing and the simultaneous (if contradictory) need to control the conditions of markets as well as the conditions of the future.[213]

Like Aradau and van Munster, other authors in Amoore and de Goede's volume on risk foreground a continuity in politics of risk, of which the precautionary practices of preemption in the 'war on terror' (such as the surveillance of population groups, the collection of data and border securitization) are only the latest manifestation. In his essay, "Choosing our Wars, Transforming Governance," Jonathan Simon convincingly argues that the "'war on terror' is only the latest effort to redefine the scope of US federal government's power (and especially the executive branch) by invoking the metaphor of war."[214] Identifying the use of the war metaphor by U.S. officials as a mode of achieving popular consent to the shaping of powerful new forms of law, Simon traces its invocation back to the 'war on cancer' in the 1950s and 1960s, to the Johnson Administration's 'war on poverty,' and to the 'war on crime' that was equally declared in the 1960s. Despite the heterogeneous objectives of these declarations of war, they all served to justify exceptional legal measures, exceptional practices outside the law, and a 'zero tolerance' stance that was legitimized by representations of catastrophic consequences.[215]

Similarly, William Walters's essay reads the recent implementation of Homeland Security as closely related to the concept and project of Social Security, and regards the establishing of a "migration-security complex" (officially justified by the discursive construction of migrants as risky subjects) as the latest product of U.S. national politics of risk whose beginning he locates in the "Wetback crisis" of the early 1950s.[216] Like Simon, Walters foregrounds

---

212 Aradau and van Munster,"Taming the Future," 27.
213 Ibid., 29.
214 "Choosing Our Wars, Transforming Governance: Cancer, Crime, Terror," *Risk and the War on Terror*, eds. Louise Amoore and Marieke de Goede (London and New York: Routledge, 2008) 79-96, 79.
215 See Simon, "Choosing Our Wars."
216 "Putting the Migration-Security Complex in its Place," *Risk and the War on Terror*, eds. Louise Amoore and Marieke de Goede (London and New York: Routledge, 2008) 158-177.

the importance of representation and official discourses as speech acts, whose narratives were to legitimate the respective political objectives of a given administration. Accordingly, the problem of 'undocumented migration' that was represented as a risk to social security in the 1950s is now depicted as a form of "risky mobility, a symptom of our broken borders"[217] jeopardizing the security of the American 'home.'

Tying in with Simon and Walters's respective emphasis on the centrality of language and representation to risk as a governance framework, Mark B. Salter's essay on "Risk and Imagination in the War on Terror" highlights the importance of popular risk imaginaries. Salter contends that "the battles over the commanding heights of the popular imagination are just as important as the struggle to control mobile bodies."[218] Accordingly, he considers his analysis of the role of risk imaginaries "a parallel argument"[219] complementing rather than contesting the work of scholars who investigate the biopolitical impetus of securitization practices and market-compliant behaviorism. The question guiding Salter's inquiry is "Why are some mobilizations of fear productive of the consent needed for exceptional measures, while others fail?"[220]

Strikingly, as Salter shows, even decisions of government officials, concerned with questions of risk management, depend, to a large degree, on the persuasiveness of reports presented by experts. Not only are these reports, according to Salter, shaped in the form of narratives that follow literary conventions, but their more or less convincing deployment of rhetorical power and literary devices, such as narrative arcs, ellipses and anachrony, has been held accountable for a failure of the imagination of political decision makers. Using the example of Condoleezza Rice, who claimed before the 9/11 Commission that the risk scenarios presented to her by experts (reports that had depicted Bin Laden and the hijacking of American aircraft as unprecedented dangers) had been lacking in persuasive power, Salter argues that "in her testimony, Rice displaces the failure of analysis into a failure of the imagination, and from there to a failure of narrative. The narrative failed to fire her imagination, which led to a subsequent un-imagining of the threat."[221]

---

217 Ibid., 170.
218 "Risk and Imagination in the War on Terror," *Risk and the War on Terror*, eds. Louise Amoore and Marieke de Goede (London and New York: Routledge, 2008) 233-246, 234.
219 Ibid.
220 Ibid., 235.
221 Ibid., 237.

Salter's reference to the consulting of Hollywood filmmakers by the Pentagon 9/11 Group who were asked to "brainstorm about future terrorist scenarios,"[222] particularly highlights the relevance of fictionality to the risk imaginaries upon which the development of government policies relies, and adds an ironic twist to the power differential between factual and fictional discourses. Pointing to recent TV-series productions that contest the validity of official risk imaginaries, Salter considers these series cultural products that challenge the authority of official risk discourses and practices of risk management. Such cultural products, Salter argues, often resort to humor in their struggle for influence on a popular imaginary that is marked by "a generalized fear,"[223] generated by nightmare scenarios that are disseminated by authorities who seek to justify extensions of governance. "The popular imaginary," Salter concludes, "is akin to a market of ideas in which narratives, identities, and social scripts vie for adherents and credibility."[224] Salter's assessment, like Simon and Walters's emphasis on the manipulative use of representation in risk policy, thus markedly calls into question and challenges a notion of the public sphere as a forum of rational discourse and deliberation.

Underlying these authors' analyses of risk as a framework of governance (a framework that, as Simon and Walters show, has gained pertinence since 9/11, but is by no means a new paradigm) is the assumption that fictionalizing strategies are crucial to the persuasiveness of official representations of dangers as risks; they convincingly expose and foreground a significant entanglement of aesthetic and political practices. As Michael J. Shapiro argues, this entanglement calls for a close examination of both fictional and factual discourses and texts in terms of aesthetics and style:

> To analyze how things in the world take on meanings, it is necessary to analyze the structure of imaginative processes. The imaginative enactments that produce meanings are not simply acts of a pure, disembodied consciousness; they are historically developed practices which reside on the very style in which statements are made, rhetorical and narrative structures that compose even the discourses of the sciences.[225]

In light of Shapiro's argument, a close examination of artifacts such as Kathryn Bigelow's *Strange Days*, Karen Tei Yamashita's *Tropic of Orange*, and Larissa Lai's *Salt Fish Girl* appears particularly productive, since these fictional texts

---

222 Cynthia Weber qtd. in Salter, "Risk and the Imagination in the War on Terror," 235.
223 Ibid., 241.
224 Ibid., 244.
225 Qtd. in Salter, "Risk and the Imagination in the War on Terror," 234.

address factual discourses of risk and speculation in politics and science. Their speculative aesthetics not only correspond with those of political and scientific risk rationalities (for example health and genetic engineering in the futurist strand of Lai's *Salt Fish Girl*), but provide a meta-representational framework to better assess the epistemological conditions of scientific and political discourses. Given the entanglement of aesthetic and political practices in both the speculative, utopianist discourse of the Pacific Rim and the official dystopian speculations on risk in contemporary North American societies, the distinct aesthetics of risk in these fictional narratives seem to advocate a poetics of risk and speculation as a framework of comparison. Such a poetics of risk and speculation could turn the spotlight on the unequal regulation and political efficacy of factual and fictional narratives that equally 'deal in futures' and equally resort to the mode and register of fictionality; it would allow to call into question the devaluation and marginalization of cultural artifacts vis-à-vis factual discourses and the factual discourses' privileged position in a "market of ideas in which narratives, identities, and social scripts vie for adherents and credibility."[226]

Different from the recent TV-series that, according to Mark B. Salter, resort to humor and comic relief in order to counter an imaginary of fear and pervasive risk generated by official narratives, the fictional speculations of Kathryn Bigelow, Karen Tei Yamashita and Larissa Lai pick up and exaggerate this climate of fear in dystopian millennial visions. These visions' aesthetics of risk might raise the question of their potential, if unintended compliance with the respective factual discourses they address: if, as Salter et al. argue, official risk scenarios serve to mobilize a generalized fear that is productive of the public consent needed for exceptional political measures, the classification of the dystopian fictions of this study's corpus as critical counter-narratives becomes complicated and calls for a close examination of the texts' respective representation of risk. A narrow focus on literary devices, imagery and narrative structures is required to identify the exact objects of the texts' critique. Known as close reading, this hermeneutic practice has itself once more become a methodological bone of contention among scholars in literary studies and bears its own hazards.

---

226 Ibid., 244.

1.4 THE RISK OF CLOSE READING

In his essay "Conjectures on World Literature," published in 2000, Franco Moretti argues that "because literature around us is now unmistakably a planetary system," comparative literary analysis requires a new method, if it is to fulfill its responsibility in the face of "hundreds of languages and literatures."[227] At the beginning of the new millennium, in the context of what might be called a narrative of literary globalization, Moretti advocates "distant reading" as a method that would do justice to the abundance of literatures that he considers impossible to cope with otherwise. Distant reading, Moretti explains, would have to draw on "a patchwork of other people's research, *without a single direct textual reading*."[228] This new method would not only be, as Moretti contends, "still ambitious," but "actually even more so than before (world literature!); but the ambition is now directly proportional *to the distance from the text*: the more ambitious the project, the greater must the distance be."[229] While 'distant reading' would allow an understanding of the "world literary system of inter-related literatures"[230] (a system that he considers "simultaneously *one*, and *unequal*"[231] like the world system of international capitalism), 'close reading' "in all of its incarnations from the New Criticism to deconstruction" is, for Moretti, "a theological exercise" whose "very solemn treatment of very few texts taken very seriously"[232] testifies to the narrow-minded, exclusive elitism that provides the ground for canon formations: "you invest so much in individual texts *only* if you think that very few of them really matter."[233]

In Moretti's argument, close reading obviously serves as the outdated, reactionary foil to highlight the boldness, the progressivity and the originality of a theoretical positioning. Ironically, it is a closer look at Moretti's language that reveals that "Conjectures on World Literature" is designed as a manifesto whose timely publication and rhetoric are targeted, above all, at securing for its author the authority and the public attention associated with the founding of discourses and avant-garde provocation. The essay's title, seemingly tentative at first glance and therefore apparently in strange tension with the simplicity of the catchy, apodictic phrasing marking the text throughout, upon closer scrutiny turns out to

---

227 "Conjectures on World Literature," *New Left Review* 1 (2000): 54-68, 54.
228 Ibid., 57, italics in the original.
229 Ibid., italics in the original.
230 Ibid., 56.
231 Ibid., italics in the original.
232 Ibid., 57.
233 Ibid.,italics in the original.

be carefully chosen. It is conspicuously reminiscent of Edward Young's "Conjectures on Original Composition" (1759), one of the founding texts of European Romanticism and the Romanticist cult of the individual author as the locus of genius and originality.

Thus contextualized, "Conjectures on World Literature" becomes visible as a text riddled with contradictions that exceed the level of rhetoric. While the manifesto-style of its rhetoric ties in with the claim to originality subtly inscribed in its title, the essay's claim to newness and egalitarian progressivity rests upon the promotion of a "second hand"[234] literary history. Drawing on methods of sociological formalism and other social-scientific disciplines, the distant reading that, according to Moretti, must be the order of the day for literary critics in the time of globalization would synthecize the research of others in an attempt to discern and delineate broader global patterns of systemic interrelation. Giving an example of such a pattern, Moretti quotes Fredric Jameson's finding that the modern Japanese novel is marked by a tension between the form of the Western novel and "the raw material of Japanese social experience."[235] After pointing to similar results in different studies on the modern novel in various local and historical contexts, he triumphantly concludes: "Four continents, two hundred years, over twenty independent critical studies, and they all agreed: when a culture starts moving towards the modern novel, it's always a compromise between foreign form and local materials."[236]

If this is an example of distant reading and the synthesis that Moretti has in mind, when he speaks of literary criticism as a project that has to become more ambitious, many questions arise. On what evidence, for instance, is the finding of a universal pattern based, if not on the close analysis that traces the tension between form and content in the first place. In other words, how can the discrepancy or tension between an "imported" hegemonic form and social experience in its marginalized target culture be assessed, if not by close reading of individual texts? Ultimately, the ambitious project of distant reading and synthesis not only has to draw on methods of social sciences, but on the findings of literary researchers who are still willing to engage in the "theological exercise" of close reading; such researchers would then, if one takes seriously Moretti's idea of synthesis in 'second hand' comparative literary studies, be assigned the status of petty commodity producers, providing the raw material for the ambitious, globally minded scholar in comparative literature who can hardly conceal his contempt for their work. Even more important, given the

---

234 "Conjectures on World Literature," 57.
235 Jameson qtd, in "Conjectures on World Literature," 58.
236 Ibid., 60.

contemporary "peripherelization of the core"[237] and the neo-colonializing practices of governance effective in multicultural nations of the 'center,' how could distant reading help to assess the artifacts produced by marginalized minorities amid this very center?

While Moretti's call for interdisciplinarity and collaboration is convincing, particularly against the background of the abundance of literary texts written in multiple languages (an abundance of global literary production that cannot be adequately addressed by the cognitive competence of any one single philology, an abundance that requires interdisciplinary scholarship including methods and findings of social science disciplines), his invective against close reading is not. Heather K. Love, in an essay tracing the American controversy about close reading as the traditional method of "depth hermeneutics,"[238] arrives at a similar conclusion. For her, Moretti's promotion of distant reading as a method is exemplary (and the most polemical instance) of a distancing from texts and practices of close reading in what she calls "new sociologies of literature:"[239]

> Distant reading refuses the richness of the singular literary text in favor of the production of knowledge on an enlarged scale. By sacrificing richness – and turning it into data – he is able to handle greater quantities of material, and to observe literature as a vast geographical and historical system. Moretti is clear about what is to be gained through a refusal of the messy intimacies of traditional forms of humanistic inquiry: scientific authority, generality, knowledge, legitimacy.[240]

In emphasizing an anticipated gain of symbolic capital, Love points to an important aspect in recent controversies about method in the humanities. Delineating the institutional history of close reading, she specifically foregrounds its importance to a literary pedagogy of textual exploration that has always been closely related to moral education in literary studies. Love draws on the work of Ian Hunter to problematize the history of a "pastoral instruction"[241] by which the reading of literature became the privileged locus of moral education; she is also critically aware of "the importance of the privileged messenger or interpreter in maintaining a humanist hermeneutics in literary

---

237 Soja, *Postmodern Geographies*, 215.
238 "Close but not Deep: Literary Ethics and the Descriptive Turn," *New Literary History* 41.2 (2010): 371-391, 388.
239 Ibid., 273.
240 Ibid., 274.
241 Ibid., 372.

studies."²⁴² She nevertheless points to the continuity of practices of close reading in the academy whose object of attention has become "the world of text and discursivity"²⁴³ since the 1960s (thus leaving behind the kneejerk association of close reading with New Criticism), and foregrounds its ongoing centrality to a humanist ethics in the study of literature:

Close Reading is at the heart of literary studies, a key credential in hiring and promotion, and the foundation of literary pedagogy; it is primarily through this practice that humanist values survive in the field.[...] Despite intellectual and social changes, the richness of texts continues to serve as a carrier for an allegedly superannuated humanism.²⁴⁴

It seems, however, as if this humanist ethical concern has been widely replaced by other interests. Love lists a number of scholars who have shifted their attention from close examination of individual texts to the sociological study of books and other media, a shift of attention to the conditions of the production, reception, distribution and legal regulation of media.²⁴⁵ Other scholars like John Guillory, James English, Barbara Herrnstein Smith, Pascale Casanova, and Mark McGurl have addressed the role of cultural capital and questions of value in canon formation, academic institutions and the world literary system.²⁴⁶ It is important to note that Love acknowledges the significance of these new developments in the field and does not dismiss their relevance:

This break with the hegemony of close reading presents an opportunity for an interrogation of the relation between literary studies and other disciplines. If, as English argues, literary studies over the past several decades has remained "'all too literary' if viewed from the normative vantage of history, or sociology, or economics, or geography, or philosophy," possibilities for renewed interdisciplinary exchange emerge once this fundamental disciplinary protocol is suspended.²⁴⁷

The work of literary scholars after the 'cultural turn' in literary studies in the last three decades of the twentieth century certainly shows that a lot has been gained by interdisciplinarity. Yet recently, it seems, the desire for interdisciplinary

---

242 Ibid., 373.
243 Hortense J. Spillers qtd. in Love, "Close but not Deep," 373.
244 Ibid.
245 Ibid. Love mentions Leah Price, Roger Chartier, Robert Darnton, Peter Stallybrass, Alan Liu, and Matt Kirschenbaum.
246 See ibid.
247 Ibid., 174.

exchange in literary studies derives from a tacit anxiety to lose ground in a scientific landscape that privileges the exactly measurable and countable. As the apodictic language and triumphant tone in Moretti's essay suggest, the new turn to empirical scientific methods appears to be motivated to a great extent by a need to gain scientific authority, legitimacy and symbolic capital. An example not mentioned by Heather Love is the recent emergence of neo-naturalist approaches in literary and cultural studies. According to Frank Kelleter, two scientific disciplines in particular have gained traction in early twenty-first-century literary studies: "cognitive sciences (encompassing both neurological and linguistic research) and evolutionary theory (especially in its anthropological and psychological variants)."[248] By taking a closer look at neo-naturalist studies, their presuppositions and results, Kelleter shows that the neo-naturalist attempt to establish literary studies as a science based on the systematic analysis of empirical data (a science whose object is not the literary text but the biological processing of literary texts in the human brain) places no importance on the historical and cultural particularity of individual texts. As a consequence, Kelleter argues, the insights provided by neo-naturalist analyses of literary texts as "species literature"[249] are as exact, systematic, measurable, and scientific as they are trivial. "There is a reason," Kelleter writes,

for the neo-naturalist reluctance to study literary texts in their particularity. The reason is a widespread misconception about the way particularity and universality relate in affairs of human history and human culture. This misconception in turn springs from a confusion of human artifacts and natural objects, from a fundamental zoomorphism, probably motivated by the neo-naturalist desire for systematic certainty.[250]

Kelleter says in no uncertain terms that, for him, the current neo-naturalist approaches to literature do not provide an appropriate method for the analysis of cultural artifacts, because they do not "address the most distinct features of their objects of study."[251] Moreover, he considers these approaches not only

---

248 Frank Kelleter, "A Tale of Two Natures: Worried Reflections on the Study of Literature and Culture in an Age of Neuroscience and Neo-Darwinism," *Journal of Literary Theory* 1.1 New Developments in Literary Theory and Related Dsiciplines (2007): Web, 5 Mar. 2011 <http://www.jltonline.de/index.php/articles/article/view/65/258> 153-189, 155.
249 "A Tale of Two Natures," 162.
250 Ibid., 164.
251 Ibid., 168.

"*unwissenschaftlich*"[252] as they are "categorically unsuited for the object," but their disavowal of hermeneutics threatens "to close down research on entire areas of knowledge concerning literature and culture."[253] Kelleter is also unambiguous about the task of literary and cultural studies:

> As long as we still want to know how a specific culture, at a specific point in its historical development, imagined itself, how it struggled with these and other imaginations, how meaning was made where none was probable, we do well not to look simply at (or "into") our own brains, but to make use of them by reading foreign texts.[254]

And, quoting Edward Said, Kelleter leaves no doubt that by 'reading' he means a return to the close reading of primary texts, "a detailed, patient scrutiny of and a lifelong attentiveness to the words and rhetorics by which language is used by human beings who exist in time."[255]

What seems to be underlying the controversies about method in the humanities and the desire for a truly new turn – besides the wish for scientific authority and legitimacy – is a sense of methodological crisis and a skeptical stance towards both practices of close reading and theory in the wake of deconstruction and poststructuralism. The essays of Love and Kelleter delineate new approaches that turn to empirical scientific and social-scientific methods in order to establish universally applicable concepts, abstract formal patterns, and a 'bigger picture' of systemic interrelation; this bigger, universal picture is based upon a distancing from singular texts. Against the grain of this tendency – and at risk of being considered "all too literary"- the present study offers close readings of three individual, fictional texts that emerged in a distinctive historical moment at a specific cultural and geographical site. Both the themes and the aesthetics of risk and speculation that are common to these fictional texts correspond with the aestheticizing, speculative quality of factual discourses and with political-economic practices of risk management, prevalent at a point in time when narratives of globalization more than ever call for re- definitions of the relation between particularity and universality.

As this introduction to concepts and theories relevant to the subsequent analyses endeavored to show, this approach implies no renunciation of interdisciplinarity, or a return to a "theological exercise"[256] in the service of

---

252 Ibid., italics in the original.
253 Ibid.
254 Ibid.
255 Said qtd. in Kelleter, "A Tale of Two Natures," 156.
256 Morretti, "Conjectures on World Literature," 57.

canon formation. On the contrary, the study focuses on fictional texts that are regulated by very specific institutional inscriptions in their respective fields of production and cannot be considered canonical: *Strange Days* failed epically at the box office and has caused a severe career slump for its director Kathryn Bigelow; *Tropic of Orange* has made it into many academic syllabi both in the U.S. and Europe, yet its intricate aesthetics chafe against restrictions, regulating Asian American politics of representation; *Salt Fish Girl* has not met aesthetic recognition outside the discourses of Postcolonial and Ethnicity Studies. The study resorts to the "depth hermeneutics"[257] of close reading in order to identify aesthetic strategies of the texts that have not been addressed so far; it sets out to illuminate the risks they take and tackle, and their exact relation to political and scientific discourses of truth and political-economic practices of subject formation at the Pacific Rim as the new frontier of capitalist development. The study hopes to show that, at this particular historical moment, concepts of risk and speculation might provide an epistemological framework of cultural comparison, and that hope lies in the political empowerment of the alternative epistemologies of cultural artifacts, which, as Fredric Jameson observes, have been relegated to a "frivolous, trivialized space."[258]

---

257 Love, "Close but not Deep," 388.
258 *Archaeologies of the Future*, xv.

2 Are You Paranoid *Enough*? Kathryn Bigelow's *Strange Days* and the Politics of Risk and Speculation

2.1 RISK INSIDE THE "FICKLE MACHINE"

When *Strange Days* was released in 1995 its director Kathryn Bigelow and production firm Twentieth Century Fox had to face a box office disaster nobody could have predicted. The film grossed less than eight million dollars, despite a number of constituents that, at the time of its making, must have appeared particularly promising, as Romi Stepovitch observes: "With a headlining actor in Ralph Fiennes, a blockbuster writer/producer (James Cameron), a large budget from a major Hollywood studio, and with Bigelow being a known action director herself, 20th Century Fox should have had a success on its hands."[1]

Made in retrospect, this assessment implicitly presents *Strange Days*' failure to attract an audience large enough to grant its makers some economic and symbolic profit as the result of an unsuccessful calculation of the probability of future events; the result, that is, of insufficient risk management. Both the use of the past subjunctive and the formulaic nature of the list of constituents supposedly granting success in Hollywood imply the notions of "*known probabilities*" and "statistical *expectation value*"[2] that are essential to the

---

1 Romy Stepovich, "Strange Days: A Case History of Production and Distribution Practices in Hollywood," *The Cinema of Kathryn Bigelow: Hollywood Transgressor*, eds. Deborah Jermyn and Sean Redmond (London/New York: Wallflower, 2003) 144-158, 144.
2 "Risk," *Stanford Encyclopedia of Philosophy* (Fall 2011): Web, 02 Febr. 2012, <http//:plato.stanford.edu/entries/risk> 2, italics in the original.

concepts of risk and speculation. They cast Hollywood as a "fickle machine,"[3] "a unique complex system"[4] comparable to the world economy and filmmakers as speculators who have to project correctly the potential interactions of the industry's many components, in order to make their work profitable, and prevent loss in terms of both economic and cultural capital.

While it is evident that "risks have a central role in economic activities" and that, "in capitalist market economies, taking economic risks is an essential part of the role of the entrepreneur,"[5] the concepts of risk and speculation become more complex when applied to cultural enterprises. As Pierre Bourdieu has shown in his seminal essay "The Market of Symbolic Goods,"[6] it was the autonomization of an artistic field in the seventeenth and eighteenth century by the emergence of an art market after an age of artistic dependence on patronage that endowed works of art with the "two-faced reality"[7] of being commodities *and* symbolic objects. The liberty that came with the development of an impersonal art market formed the artistic profession as a distinguishable category, and subjected 'distinguished' artists to the laws of supply and demand, while, paradoxically, compelling them to demonstrate economic disinterestedness as the hallmark of 'pure' art. As a result, artists not only had to bear the risk that came with a "form of demand which necessarily lags behind the supply of the commodity (in this case, the work of art),"[8] but were caught in the double bind of having to acquire economic *and* symbolic capital, and thus subject to two antagonistic economic logics of the market for symbolic goods.[9]

By distinguishing a "field of large-scale-productions"[10] "with a *short production cycle*, aiming to minimize risks by an advance adjustment to

---

3 Deborah Jermyn, and Sean Redmond, "Introduction: Hollywood Transgressor: The Cinema of Kathryn Bigelow," *The Cinema of Kathryn Bigelow: Hollywood Transgressor*, eds. Deborah Jermyn and Sean Redmond (London/New York: Wallflower Press, 2003) 1-20, 9.

4 "Risk," *Stanford Encyclopedia of Philosophy* (Fall 2011): Web, 02 Febr. 2012 <http//:plato.stanford.edu/entries/risk> 4.

5 Ibid., 10.

6 Pierre Bourdieu, "The Market of Symbolic Goods," *The Field of Cultural Production: Essays on Art and Literature* (Columbia UP, 1984) 1- 34.

7 Bourdieu, "The Market of Symbolic Goods," 3.

8 Ibid.,4.

9 Pierre Bourdieu, *The Rules of Art: Genesis and Structure of the Literary Field* (Cambridge, UK/Malden, MA: Polity, 2010) 141 -173, 142, emphases in the original.

10 Bourdieu, "The Market of Symbolic Goods," 17.

predictable demand,"[11] from the "field of restricted production"[12] with a *"long production cycle* [...] having no market in the present, [and being] entirely turned towards the future,"[13] Bourdieu basically ascribes the lowest predictability, and thus the highest amount of uncertainty and risk, to the latter. Accordingly, it is the cultural productions of the avant-garde that bear the highest degree of risk until their being ahead of their time[14] is fully acknowledged and valued in the form of cultural and economic capital – or not. It is an educated audience – described by Bourdieu as an audience of "producers"[15] as aesthetically refined and trained as the artists themselves – an audience of producers that can determine and ascribe both forms of value and, in return, derive not immediate pleasure, but the pleasure of social distinction from their 'disinterested,' 'purely aesthetic' consumption of 'high' art. At this point, the field of cultural production becomes recognizable as a futures market in which the values at stake are tied to social hierarchy, and risk affects not only the individual producer and her agent(s) of circulation, but the struggle for dominance of a class of producers over a class of consumers, and thus the political-economic structure of a given society.

Against this background that suggests a clear-cut opposition between the two economic logics of the two distinct fields comprising the market for symbolic goods, *Strange Days*, as a Hollywood film, hardly appears prone to risk. Obviously, the Hollywood film industry does not belong to the autonomous

---

11 Bourdieu, *The Rules of Art*, 142.
12 Bourdieu, "The Market of Symbolic Goods," 17.
13 Bourdieu, *The Rules of Art*, 142-143.
14 See Bourdieu, "The Market of Symbolic Goods," 11. According to Bourdieu the "works produced by the field of restricted production" [...] are 'pure' because they demand of the receiver a specifically aesthetic disposition in accordance with the principles of their production. They are 'abstract' because they call for a multiplicity of specific approaches [...].They are 'esoteric' for all the above reasons and because their complex structure continually implies tacit reference to the entire history of previous structures, and is accessible only to those who possess practical or theoretical mastery of a refined code, of successive codes, and of the codes of these codes." Although not mentioned explicitly, 'innovation' and its recognition in relation to existent codes, rightfully belongs to this catalogue of features central to communication in the art market, especially with regard to the avant-garde. See also Niklas Luhmann's definition of art as an autopoietic system."Die Evolution des Kunstsystems," *Schriften zur Kunst und Literatur* (Frankfurt/ Main: Suhrkamp, 2008) 258-275.
15 Bourdieu, "The Market of Symbolic Goods," 17.

"field of restricted production,"[16] marked by a long production cycle and a fetishization of pure aesthetics. On the contrary, as part of the large-scale production system of popular culture, Hollywood appears to aim at reducing risk by relying on short production cycles and a well-tried technical and aesthetic repertoire targeted at an average public. It is this kind of risk management – an openly economic 'interestedness' and a strategy that might be called, with Bourdieu, Hollywood's "quest for investment profitability" – that marks Hollywood productions as "middle-brow art [*l'art moyen*],"[17] a category that, by definition, contrasts the economic disinterestedness of art for art's sake.

Yet, as Bourdieu emphasizes, the two modes of production of symbolic goods rarely occur in unadulterated form, but coexist, and not only share a preference for "a professionalized technical virtuosity,"[18] but also, significantly, a political conservatism that is based on "a covenant with the dominant sections of the bourgeoisie."[19] With their formulaic aesthetic and characteristic recourse to simpler forms of 'high' art themes and devices, middle-brow productions more openly display this political conservatism that is ensconced in 'high' art's discourse of aesthetic purity. In exchange for their political compliance, they become culturally legitimized and are granted participation in the signification processes that shape and perpetuate the symbolic order of a given society – if at the price of an inferior position within that order.

As the example of *Strange Days* shows, however, the entanglement of the two fields of cultural production can be so complex, their interplay so subtle that any categorization becomes moot, and risk (the probability of a future loss of economic, cultural and symbolic capital) grows with structural contingency. In the fickle middle-brow machine that is Hollywood, this contingency, to a large degree, derives from the number of determinations inscribed in the position of the cultural producer, as *Strange Days*' director Kathryn Bigelow exemplifies: her artistic and theoretical education (she was trained as a painter at the San Francisco Art Institute, was an intern at the prestigious Whitney Museum, and enrolled in the master of fine arts program at Columbia University[20]), her

---

16 Bourdieu, "The Market of Symbolic Goods," 17.
17 Ibid.
18 Ibid., 20.
19 Ibid., 20 -21. Bourdieu refers here to a tacit agreement between the artist and the dominant political class which grants the artist's and the intellectual's monopoly on symbolic power in exchange for the social and political indifference of her/his work.
20 See Deborah Jermyn and Sean Redmond, "Introduction," *The Cinema of Kathryn Bigelow: Hollywood Transgressor* (London/New York: Wallflower Press, 2003) 1-19,

independent 'countercinema' debut films, her technical expertise and brilliance as well as her fashioning of a slightly enigmatic, yet highly visible public persona comprise the framework for a biographical narrative that has been told and retold time and again by various observers of the field, regardless of their association with either the academy or the mass-media.

This narrative casts Bigelow as a highly sophisticated *auteur* who, at one point in her intellectual life, made the momentous decision to privilege the democratic sweep of 'accessible' popular culture productions, epitomized by Hollywood, over the elitist distinction lent by high art[21] – and had to bear the consequences of the risk she took with that decision. Paradoxically, risk, in this narrative, functions as an indicator of a progressive political agenda that has no place in the realm of high art, while at the same time serving as a signpost of an economic disinterestedness that, associated with that very realm, contrasts Hollywood's open quest for investment profitability. At this point, the over-determined contingency of risk becomes visible as a marker of the discourse of auteurism that signified a romanticizing self-description (featuring a 'rebellious' political commitment supposedly challenging the middle-brow conservatism of the big Hollywood studios), and the political struggles as well as the marketing of the New Hollywood Cinema in the 1960s and 1970s.[22]

The knee-jerk identification of that discourse with a readiness for taking a political and aesthetic risk – the risk that is associated with a decision for radical, sophisticated aesthetics and a critical political perceptiveness in a politically and aesthetically conservative environment – is thus complicated by the political flexibility and economic adaptability of the Hollywood middle-brow machine. While Hollywood's deployment of an author's name as a branding and marketing strategy immediately highlights the structural double bind it imposes on the cultural producer, this contingency is taken to an extreme in the case of Kathryn Bigelow and the contradictory politics of gender and genre inherent to her authorship. A brief discussion of this authorship will therefore serve as a point of departure for a close reading of *Strange Days*, Bigelow's programmatically speculative film on the contingent politics of risk and speculation that rule the world in the twenty-first century far beyond the fickle machine in which it originated.

---

6 -7. See also Christina Lane, "From *The Loveless* to *Point Break*: Kathryn Bigelow's Trajectory in Action," *Cinema Journal* 37.4 (1998): 59-81, 62.

21 See Jermyn and Redmond, "Introduction," 6 -7.

22 See Derek Nystrom, "Hard Hats and Movie Brats: Auteurism and the Class Politics of the New Hollywood," *Cinema Journal* 43.3 (2004): 18 – 41.

After the failure of *Strange Days* in the mid-1990s and a significant career slump that followed in its wake, nobody could have assumed that Kathryn Bigelow would ever become a member of that coterie of middle-brow artists who become consecrated and defined [23] by receiving one of Hollywood's prestigious Academy Awards.[24] When she received the Academy Award for Best Director in 2009 for *The Hurt Locker*, a film about men in the Iraq war, it was her gender that seemed to be of central importance not only to many observers and commentators in the mass media, but also to the decision of the jury – represented at the award ceremony by Barbra Streisand who was to eulogize and present Bigelow with the illustrious statuette.

Remarkably, as an overture to the announcement of the winner and the actual handing over of the prize, Streisand, after a sensational pause, said: "Well, the time has come,"[25] thus dramatically foregrounding the fact that Bigelow would be the first woman to be awarded the Oscar for Best Director. While this form of staging might belong to the ritualized dramaturgy of anticipation that is an integral part of the ceremony, Streisand's foregrounding of Bigelow's gender does seem significant. It puts into perspective the symbolic capital gained by this Oscar in the "global economy of cultural prestige"[26] as it highlights the 'academy's' decision as guided by a duplicitous political correctness rather than artistic criteria, and thus diminishes that very prestige and the artistic distinction supposedly bestowed by the prize at the very moment of its awarding.

Rather than just illustrating a peculiarity of the cultural awards industry, the Oscar episode tellingly illuminates Kathryn Bigelow's multiply determined position as a producer in the field of popular culture. It ties in with the predominant, yet reductive narrative of Bigelow's strong female authorship in the "all-boys club"[27] that is Hollywood, a narrative that emphasizes more than

---

23 See James F. English, *The Economy of Prestige: Prizes, Awards, and the Circulation of Cultural Value* (Cambridge, MA and London, UK: Harvard UP, 2005) 21.

24 This official name of the film prizes that are better known and popular as the "Oscars" is obviously targeted at investing the awards with the consecrating and legitimizing authority of an educational institution generally associated with the field of restricted artistic production.

25 Barbra Streisand at the 82nd edition of the Academy Awards ceremony, *Kathryn Bigelow Winning the Oscar® for Directing* (10 Mar 2010) Web, 20 Mar 2011 <http://www.youtube.com/watch?v=e-DPBOTlSWk>.

26 English, *The Economy of Prestige*, 247.

27 Matthew Oshinski, "The Hurt Locker Movie Review – Kathryn Bigelow Has a Blast in Iraq," (25 June 2009) Web, 5 Feb 2011. <http://www.nj.com/entertainment/tv/index.ssf/2009/06/the_hurt_locker_movie_review_k.html>.

anything else the gender/genre dichotomy in Bigelow's work and confines Bigelow's artistic persona by redundantly navigating public attention towards that dichotomy. According to that narrative, Bigelow's position is defined by the fact that she is "the sole woman director regularly working in the traditionally male-dominated action movie arena," and her "proficiency" with the action genre, a proficiency that is often perceived as exceeding that of "her male counterparts."[28]

However, the simplistic, oxymoronic casting of Bigelow's artistic persona as "Hollywood's Macho Woman"[29] is complicated by a closer look at the contradictory reception of the representation of gender in Bigelow's most successful movies *Near Dark* (1987), *Blue Steel* (1990), and *Point Break* (1991). All of them hybrid generic blends, these movies have been celebrated by critics in feminist and queer studies as calling into question, subverting and rewriting the signs and codes of Hollywood's gendered generic conventions. Often described as technically brilliant, visually innovative and, above all, "testosterone-pumped,"[30] they have been read as negotiating the social construction and performativity of gender roles, and inscribing hard-bodied heroines into a genre that, according to Yvonne Tasker, is an "almost exclusively male space, in which issues to do with sexuality and gendered identity can be worked out over the male body."[31] And yet, as Christina Lane remarks, Bigelow's work "has been criticized for lacking any new insight into gender politics,"[32] and *Blue Steel*, her movie about a female rookie police officer, might even "be said to enact a conventional scenario which punishes the female character's transgressive desire to become a powerful figure."[33]

---

28 Mark Salisbury qtd. in Yvonne Tasker, *Spectacular Bodies: Gender, Genre, and the Action Cinema* (New York: Routledge, 1993) 176 -177.

29 Salisbury qtd. in Tasker Spectacular Bodies 176-177.

30 Matthew Oshinski, "The Hurt Locker Movie Review – Kathryn Bigelow Has a Blast in Iraq." Film critic Matthew Oshinski's diction echoes the wording used by a striking number of his colleagues. It is quoted this point as a more recent example of a persistent and prevalent perception of Bigelow's action pictures.

31 Yvonne Tasker, Spectacular Bodies: Gender, Genre, and the Action Cinema (New York: Routledge, 1993) 17.

32 Lane, "From *The Loveless* to *Point Break*," 60.

33 Tasker, *Spectacular Bodies*, 160. This critique strikingly echoes the one targeted at James Cameron's muscular heroines who are accused of embodying "an easily consumed feminism" that basically affirms existing power relations, a reference that gains significance in the context of Christina Lane's discussion of *Strange Days* as a "doubly-authored text." "The Strange Days of Kathryn Bigelow and David Cameron,"

Contradictory comments like these abound in the reception of Bigelow's action movies and point to a general instability ingrained in their characters. Read with Bourdieu, this instability, like the masterful play with generic conventions, can be attributed to a conflict between that general compulsion of middle-brow culture "to define itself in relation to legitimate culture" by tapping into techniques and themes borrowed from "the 'bourgeois' art from a generation or so earlier,"[34] and the author's quest for distinction. Consequently, the shaping of an enigmatic, contingent instability of her characters thwarts any unambiguous categorization of her action movies as either progressive avant-garde or conservative middle-brow productions, and, at the same time, strikingly mirrors and contributes to Bigelow's shaping of her own contradictory public persona and her position in the field as an 'auteur.' Only against the background of these circular and contingent politics of auteurism in the cultural field of large scale productions is it understandable that Bigelow has rejected the label of 'feminist' woman director, and has even denied "the centrality of her gender to the style and radical politics of her films and to her position within Hollywood cinema,"[35] although the contingent and transgressive politics of her work have obviously been of special interest to queer and feminist film studies.

In accordance with Bigelow's own, extra-textual self-fashioning in numerous interviews, film critics and scholars in film studies almost univocally represent her as an 'auteur,' who has succeeded in preserving her own distinct 'hand writing,' 'uncompromised' by her career trajectory from independent 'countercinema' to mainstream Hollywood. This reflects, as Christina Lane observes, a

[...] general tendency on the part of film scholars [...] to assume that low-budget countercinema films represent a 'purer', less adulterated vision of the director while mainstream films produced on a larger budget are shaped by so many industrial and ideological factors that authorship becomes moot."[36]

The Cinema of Kathryn Bigelow: Hollywood Transgressor, eds. Deborah Jermyn and Sean Redmond (London/New York: Wallflower Press, 2003) 178 -197, 188,186.

34 Bourdieu, "The Market of Symbolic Goods," 21 -22.

35 Deborah Jermyn, and Sean Redmond, "Introduction: Hollywood Transgressor: The Cinema of Kathryn Bigelow," *The Cinema of Kathryn Bigelow: Hollywood Transgressor*, eds. Deborah Jermyn and Sean Redmond (London/New York: Wallflower, 2003) 1-20, 4.

36 Christina Lane "From *The Loveless* to *Point Break*" 60.

It also reveals a rather uncritical, if unintended, collaboration of the academy with the contingent politics of auteurism in the cultural field of large scale productions. Considering that these politics are compromised by definition, perpetuating the romantic narrative of the uncompromised auteur and applying it to any producer in the field of middle-brow art becomes visible as a contradiction in terms and a demand to hold an impossible position.

The reasons why the concept has nonetheless been attractive to and successful with Hollywood producers and critics since the 1970s are numerous and have been widely discussed. Accordingly, auteurism has been identified as a branding and marketing instrument of the powerful American studio system, as an attempt at catering to an increasingly educated class of consumers[37] (the class described by Bourdieu as aesthetically refined producers who consume the art of other producers in the field of restricted production), and as a class political tool in "the struggle over the organization of film production."[38] From the perspective of the middle-brow producer, auteurism certainly is a strategy to come to terms with the demystification and the "decline of the intellectual artisan in favor of the salaried worker," who is no longer in sole control of his product, but part of "large, collective production units."[39]

It is Kathryn Bigelow's seemingly effortless membership in the avant-garde-art scene and her deconstructionist theoretical education prior to her film-making that connect her even more closely to the European origins of auteurism, and thus add to her specific version of the phenomenon an extra portion of the attraction and the glamour that is generally associated with 'high' theory and French intellectualism in the U.S. It makes sense, then, that Deborah Jermyn and Sean Redmond, editors of a collection of essays focusing entirely on Bigelow's work, rank her among European auteur directors, and appreciate her work for displaying the same innovative, subversive, and often self-reflexive use of film language that marks European auteur films:

One can look at Bigelow's films in the same way; her political play with genre and gender is self-conscious, and the signs of her authorship are a knowing presence in her film-work,

---

37 See David A. Cook, "Auteur Cinema and the 'Film Generation' in 1970s Hollywood," *The New American Cinema*, ed. Jon Lewis (Durham, N.C.: Duke UP, 1998) 11-37, 35; see also Timothy Corrigan, "Auteurs and the New Hollywood," *The New American Cinema*, ed. Jon Lewis (Durham, N.C.: Duke UP, 1998) 38 -63, 40.
38 Derek Nystrom, "Hard Hats and Movie Brats," 18.
39 Bourdieu, "The Market of Symbolic Goods," 23.

so that in much the same way that a Bresson or a Fellini film bears the corporeal traces of their authorship, a Bigelow film will bear the mark of her authorship throughout.[40]

However, Jermyn and Redmond rightfully problematize the patriarchal coding of the Romanticist concept of authorship that is at the origin[41] of the conception of auteurism, and auteurism as a discourse that has primarily canonized male directors as well as Bigelow's extra-textual self-fashioning of an androgynous author persona that appears to collaborate with this discourse. They point out that a similar contradictory tension characterizes the visual artistry of what they call "Bigelow's cinema of transgression," which, on the one hand, "subverts the codes and conventions of dominant film form, in part through employing a range of art-cinema devices [...], and on the other [...] accepts (and pays homage to) these codes and conventions by reveling in their exploration and execution."[42] Characterizations like this one reflect how Bigelow's multiple position-takings further complicate middle-brow art's already complex interplay between the logics of different modes of production. A difficulty of classifying Bigelow's work and politics begins to show, and a paradigm of tension and contradiction that is rooted in a complex interrelation between discourses of authorship, gender and genre becomes visible as the hallmark of her auteurism.

This complex relationship between authorship, gender, and genre also underlies *Strange Days* (1995), the one Kathryn Bigelow film that turned out to be a disastrous failure both in terms of box office results and critical assessment, but is, nevertheless, retrospectively considered one of the artistically most sophisticated films of the 1990s. While the time-lag in these contradictory assessments without question affirms Pierre Bourdieu's observation that

[b]ecause the very logic of the field condemns them to risk their cultural salvation in even the least of their position-takings and to watch, uncertainly, for the ever ambiguous signs of an ever-suspended election, intellectuals and artists may experience a failure as a sign of election, or over-rapid or too brilliant a success as a threat of damnation[,][43]

---

40 Jermyn and Redmond, "Introduction: Hollywood Transgressor," 3.
41 On the origins and the history of the Romanticist concept of authorship as the locus of genius and originality see for example Martha Woodmansee, *The Author, Art, and the Market: Rereading the History of Aesthetics* (New York: Columbia UP, 1994). On the programmatic exclusion of women from that concept see especially chapter 5, "Engendering Art," 103-109.
42 Jermyn and Redmond, "Introduction: Hollywood Transgressor," 3.
43 Bourdieu, "The Market of Symbolic Goods," 28.

even the mere attribution of risk and position-taking is ambiguous in the case of *Strange Days*. Certainly, *Strange Days* bears the signature of Bigelow's authorship, with its fusion of the generic codes of the science fiction film, the film noir,[44] and the action film, its innovative and self-reflexive camera work, and its subversive negotiation of race and gender, a fact that the vanity title card in the closing credits, reading "A Film by Kathryn Bigelow," clearly accounts for. Strictly speaking, however, *Strange Days* is "doubly-authored,"[45] since both James Cameron and Kathryn Bigelow are known to have contributed their respective authorial style, a fact that, according to Christina Lane, "results in the film's ever-shifting meanings."[46] Although Lane, in her discussion of this dual authorship, eventually answers the question of who authored *Strange Days* in Bigelow's favor, the film's multiple logics appear to exceed the contradictions inherent to most Bigelow films.[47] Its "status as a problematic and inconsistent text"[48] certainly calls for a re-reading and new assessment of Bigelow's politics and authorship.

To begin with, a contemporary reading of these multiple logics has to consider the particular chronological conditions involved: by locating *Strange Days'* action in Los Angeles during the last two days of the year 1999, Bigelow chose a near-future scenario that was only a few years ahead of the film's production and release; yet, from the present study's point of view, this scenario lies in the past. In the context of a study targeted at tracing a relation between speculative, fictional texts and a political-economic rationality (the rationality of risk and speculation in the age of free market capitalism), this specific

---

44 In his monograph on film genre and genre theory, Rick Altman traces the "adjective-to noun-trajectory" of the term 'noir' that initially, in the 1940s, denoted a mood and tone rather than the genre which it has gradually come to designate. As Strange Days displays both the mood and tone and other features that are considered standard markers of the genre, it will be used as a generic term in the present chapter. See Rick Altman, *Film/Genre* (London: BFI, 1999) 60-61.

45 Lane, "The Strange Days of Kathryn Bigelow and David Cameron," 186.

46 Ibid., 187.

47 See Lane, "From *The Loveless* to *Point Break*," 61. Challenging "the traditional presuppositions of classical film studies [...] that Hollywood films contain a univocal and unidirectional logic," Christina Lane at this point expresses a fundamental demand to perceive films as "multivocal and contradictory." Responding to Rick Altman's general call for "a 'tension-based,' dialogical approach to mainstream film," Lane suggests that various contradictory positions in Bigelow's films "invite varied reading formations."

48 Lane, "The Strange Days of Kathryn Bigelow and James Cameron," 196.

circumstance appears to be favorable. It allows for a retrospective analysis of the trajectory of those futurist discourses of the dominant symbolic order that have shaped and informed a collective imaginary before the turn of the century and have outlived the time of their fulfillment.

Accordingly, *Strange Days* will be read as an instance of speculative fiction that envisions a chaotically violent and dangerous near-future public sphere in which market concerns and risk management determine the organization of the state, the social, and the subject. The study will thus start from the hypothesis that the film reveals a political and economic subtext that complicates its reception as a mere deconstruction of oppressive race and gender stereotypes, and requires a reading beyond the concerns and paradigms of ethnic and gender studies. The representation of black and white, male and female protagonists in *Strange Days* certainly chafes against the constraints of socially constructed categories of the dominant symbolic order, to say the least. Yet these protagonists are, above all, shown as economic and political subjects that respond to and are transformed by a regime of free-market capitalism and a neo-conservative politics of risk and paranoia. As Bigelow's millenarian vision of a complex and fundamental shift in political subjectivity has rarely been addressed, it is the goal of the present chapter to explore this depiction of political-economic subjectivity in *Strange Days*, and to interrelate it with overlapping discourses of race and gender.

Since *Strange Days* simultaneously depicts, draws on and caters to millenarian anxiety, its paranoid logic appears to co-opt and even contribute to the cultural climate of a society governed by neo-liberalism and neo-conservatism. It thus adds a new aspect to the question of Bigelow's engagement in conflicting progressive and reactionary agendas. It remains to be seen, if and how the political-economic discourse in *Strange Days* further complicates a classification of Kathryn Bigelow's position within Hollywood as it questions the romantic narrative and cultural iconization of Bigelow as a "Hollywood Transgressor,"[49] even beyond the notoriously tense dichotomies of gender and genre, art-house and mainstream cinema, middle-brow and high art.

2.2 ESTABLISHING RISK

Set during the last two days of the century, *Strange Days* presents its audience with a bleak vision of a near future Los Angeles, every image of which radiates

---

49 Jermyn and Redmond, "Introduction: The Cinema: of Kathryn Bigelow," 1.

the presence of risk and incalculable, impending danger. Certainly, a dystopian depiction of a fictitious L.A. at the end of the twentieth century could legitimately be deplored as part and parcel of the stock inventory of a conventionalized postmodern imaginary[50]. Narration in *Strange Days*, however, withholds the usual establishing shot and other expository devices that invite an immediate and unambiguous identification of its setting. Instead, Bigelow uses the first ten minutes of her film to create a highly contingent atmosphere of risk and uncertainty; she elaborately complements and complicates a conventional narrative conversion of her film's diegetic space into a place that conforms to the patterns of "LA disaster fiction"[51] by disrupting it with second order 'narrations' that are marked by a distinct visual style. In fact, the film even begins with one of these narrations, thus self-consciously foregrounding the role of visual representation and competing optic regimes[52] in the production of an overwhelmingly violent and dangerous urban space.[53]

After, literally, setting the film's diegetic time as beginning at 1:06:28 AM on 30 Dec 1999 with a two second shot of a yellow LED embedded in an otherwise completely black screen, the next shot, significantly, shows a tight

---

50 See Mike Davis, *Ecology of Fear: Los Angeles and the Imagination of Disaster* (New York: Vintage, 1999), 275 – 422. Commenting on the impressive and still growing number of fictional dystopias set in L.A., Davis calls Los Angeles "the city we love to destroy" (278), and speaks of the "gleeful expendability of Los Angeles in the popular imagination"(278). See also Mike Davis, *City of Quartz: Excavating the Future in Los Angeles,* (London/New York: Verso, 2006) and Liam Kennedy, "Introduction: Urban Space and Representation," *Race and Urban Space in Contemporary American Culture* (Edinburgh: Edinburgh UP, 2000), 8-16.

51 Davis, *Ecology of Fear*, 279.

52 See Steven Shaviro,"'Straight from the Cerebral Cortex:' Vision and Affect in Strange Days," *The Cinema of Kathryn Bigelow: Hollywood Transgressor,* eds. Deborah Jermyn and Sean Redmond (London/New York: Wallflower Press, 2003) 159-177, 170.

53 While focusing on race as an "eruptive force in the symbolic order of the city," Liam Kennedy emphasizes the general centrality of "vision and visuality," "scopophilic and voyeuristic desires," as well as "visibility and unvisibility" to the production of urban space. "Introduction: Urban Space and Representation," 10. See also Stefan L. Brandt, "The City as Liminal Space: Urban Visuality and Aesthetic Experience in Postmodern U.S. Literature and Cinema," *Amerikastudien/American Studies* 54.4 (2009): 553-581. Brandt links theories of a post-metropolitan discourse to the visual aesthetics of films like Ridley Scott's *Blade Runner* and Alex Proyas's *Dark City*. He suggests the concept of "Postmetropolitan Visuality as a Reading Pattern" (573).

close-up of an eye[54] that blinks once and then closes. During this opening sequence we hear a short dialogue between two male voices, one asking "You ready?" and the other one replying "Yeah, boot it." What follows comes as a shock: almost without transition – there are only fractions of seconds displaying a whirl of illegible, distorted images subsequent to the almost static images of the opening sequence – we are taken on the wild visual ride of an uncut point-of-view shot that lasts almost four minutes. Immersed into a vortex of shaky and partly blurred images, we not only witness the armed robbery of a Chinese restaurant from the perspective of a member of the robber band, but immediately experience the breathlessness and the adrenaline rush of the raid as well as the disappointment at the sight of the almost empty cash register, the panic when armed police arrive at the crime scene, and, finally, the horror of being chased to death. The crude and immediate quality of the shot is enhanced by an equally raw soundtrack, accompanying the action, and giving an unnervingly intrusive account of the breathless clamor and excited yelling of the raiders, the pleading wails of the victims and the invectives barked by the police.

The shot dramatically climaxes when the panting raiders are being chased to the rooftop of the high-rise building where their panic sensibly peaks as the searchlight of a police helicopter pans over and glaringly illuminates the nocturnal scene. Finally, the raider whose point of view we have obviously been sharing tries to jump over to the next building in sheer desperation and crashes into a street canyon. With this the shot ends as abruptly as it began, and, after another, extremely short transition with tumbling, flickering fragments of images and a static noise, we are presented with a scene whose warmer, more saturated colors, balanced soundtrack and conventional shot/reverse shot editing markedly contrast the paler and apparently uncut audio-visual helter-skelter we have witnessed fractions of seconds before. So completely different in acoustic texture and visual style is this ensuing scene that we feel immediate relief at being no

---

54 See Stefan Brandt, "The City as Liminal Space." Brandt reads the eye as a "symbol of urban visuality" (575) and as an "icon of seeing and reading"(573). He plausibly concludes that "the eye-metaphor makes us realize the relationality and subjectivity of the urban gaze." (573-574). Bigelow's use of this icon and metaphor at the very beginning of *Strange Days* quite programmatically evokes connotations of "postmetropolitan visuality" (ibid.). It most certainly has to be read as the first in a number of references to *Blade Runner*. Above all. however, the numerous allusions to visual perception – for instance Lenny Nero's nickname 'Lens,' or Iris, the name of the prostitute whose SQUID-clip recording helps to uncover the LAPD's murder of Jeriko One – will in the present study be read in the context of theories of risk and speculation where they signify the dependence of both concepts on observation.

longer subject to immersion into a contingent, risky ride that turns into an angst ridden nightmare. At this point, we *sense* that we are experiencing the effect of a juxtaposition of different narrative spaces produced by different regimes of representation before we can even begin to *infer* the quality of their diegetic relationship.

Set in a spacious, dimly lit garage, the ensuing scene introduces *Strange Days'* main protagonist, Lenny Nero (Ralph Fiennes) who is shown ripping a hairnet-like contraption off his head while uttering a series of agonized grunts. Only gradually, with the unfolding of a conversation between Lenny and his counterpart Tick (Richard Edson) in this scene, can the spectator infer that she has been seeing what Lenny has been seeing, that the eye of the opening sequence has been Lenny's. And only in retrospect and with the help of textual clues given in the dialogue between the two men can the viewer construe the diegetic meaning of the unsettling POV-shot as the live recording of an unidentified man's last minutes, an anonymous "playback clip" that is about to be traded and marketed as a product.

What is being staged in this scene is thus an epistemological commentary on the signifying function and the power of narration: It becomes obvious that the unframed immersion into an anonymous point of view requires a narrative framework, the introduction of a perceiving subjectivity and positionality in order to 'make sense' and to convert unstable space into a coherent place. As Stephen Heath observes: "What is crucial is the conversion of seen into scene, the holding of signifier on signified: the frame, composed, centered, narrated, is the point of that conversion."[55] Although Bigelow literally establishes a frame by having the shot of the eye in the brief opening sequence precede the long and shaky POV-shot, and introducing Lenny Nero as the owner of the eye immediately thereafter, this narrative frame, at this point, is not only still precarious, but, more important, implies an unnerving gap between signifier and signified. It raises questions as to the legitimacy of the appropriation of the "seen" and the power of meaning-making implicit to its conversion into "scene", and, at plot level, introduces Lenny and Tick – whose name boldly suggests this interpretation – as speculating agents of a parasitic exploitation of somebody else's risk.

Significantly, it is the price for the anonymous disc recording Tick wants to sell to Lenny that is being negotiated in the angry exchange between the two men in the half-lit garage. Lenny, agitated about the fatal ending of the recording, emphatically insists that he will have to cut this ending because of his ethical principles that forbid the dealing of "snuff clips," thereby rendering the

---

55 Stephen Heath, *Questions of Cinema* (London: Macmillan, 1981) 37.

disc worthless to a clientele who appreciate and pay for uncensored merchandise. Notably, Bigelow directs the audience's attention to the conflict between economic interest and ethics at this point in the frame narrative, even before a reliable distinction is fully developed between this particular narrative and the images delivered by a fictitious technology enabling the unmediated consumption of the experiences of others. By picking up the discourse on economic speculation and the contingencies of risk, underlying the second order narrative of the raid, she prioritizes and entrenches it as a key motive that links the seemingly incompatible narrative spaces of both diegetic levels against the grain of their pointedly different aesthetics.

The dialogue, establishing the relationship between Lenny and Tick as a seedy underworld business connection between a drug dealer and his supplier, simultaneously insinuates the pretentiousness of Lenny's claim to have "ethics." This insinuation turns into certainty when Tick, taking this claim for what it is – a speculative attempt at cutting prices –, confronts Lenny with his own, frequently uttered business philosophy: "One man's mundane and desperate existence is another man's technicolor." The cynicism captured in this motto certainly casts doubt on Lenny Nero's moral integrity and introduces him as a prototypical speculator and *homo oeconomicus* at a very early stage in the narrative, a characterization further explored in a later part of this chapter. The utterance also contributes to a self-reflexive discourse on the fragile epistemological boundary between fact and fiction and the role of media within that discourse, an aspect that is addressed throughout the film. Above all, however, in the context of the exposition of diegetic space, it works as a hinge between different narrative levels and their distinct strategies of establishing a fictitious L.A. as an extremely risky, public sphere.

It makes sense that after this risky, public sphere has already been presented from the 'authentic' perspective of "one man's mundane and desperate existence," it is its highly stylized "technicolor" representation that immediately follows the dialogue scene after Lenny has closed his deal with Tick. Yet, for the spectator this connection is not immediately obvious. Again, the scene change happens with an abrupt transition, this time instantly after Lenny has asked Tick: "What else you got?" The question renders the narrative status of the subsequent footage unclear, especially as the next shot presents a street scene, sharply contrasting the garage scene and very similar to the raid and chase of the playback clip, as it, too, shows a band of raiders on the run from the police. For a few seconds, the viewer is uncertain as to whether this is the beginning of yet another playback clip, offered to Lenny by Tick. The effect is a feeling of ambiguity that serves as the ideal emotional framework for the reception of the brilliantly dramatized series of shots that is about to follow.

Adding to this affective ambiguity is the panning camera movement that not only persecutes the fleeing raiders, but, although delivering sharper, more stable images, even seems to mimic the movement of the POV-shot of the playback clip. Not until the camera movement comes to a halt, showing the front of Lenny Nero's gold-colored Mercedes as it emerges from a cloud of smoke and slowly approaches, does the narrative status of the scene become clear. With this symbolically charged image that openly, if not ironically, flaunts its own histrionics, however, all ambiguity surrounding the narrative mode and status of the sequence ends. At this point, the staging of Lenny Nero as someone between netherworldly demon and *deus ex machina* clearly signals that the series of shots subsequent to the garage scene belongs to the frame narrative of a film that indulges in its own masterful use of dramatic composition and 'technicolor' spectacularity.

Using conventional, yet technically ingenious shot/ reverse shot montage, the sequence presents a nightly urban street scene that is reminiscent of a war zone. It shows burning cars and smoke filled streets immersed in gloomy low-key-lighting, bands of armed raiders looting convenience stores, or engaging in one-on-one-assaults – among them, notably, three drag-queens ambushing Santa Claus, – people getting arrested by or running from heavily armed riot police, tanks set up as road blockade, and wary, notably Asian store owners, armed with machine guns, trying to protect their property.

Except for similar subject matter – in particular, the shot of a police helicopter whose search-lights restlessly pan a high-rise facade strikingly parallels the final scene of the POV-sequence – these images have little in common with the shaky, blurred images of the playback clip. Highly stylized, most of them swish-pans and tracking shots, many taken from a high, slanted camera angle, the images of this sequence are clearly designed to convey the drama and the oppressive, intensely heated atmosphere of an explosion-risk area. Moreover, the feelings of tension and paranoia these shots inevitably and reliably evoke are pointedly heightened as they are intercut with eye-level shots of Lenny Nero sitting in his car and gliding through this war scene, obviously unaffected and strangely unfazed.

Like the long POV-sequence of the playback clip, this nightmare scenario of mayhem and unbridled violence comes with a soundtrack that enhances its dramatic effect. The quickly alternating images of street life, Lenny's car, and Lenny in his car are the visual clues suggesting that the quick succession of stylistically diverse pieces of music that accompany the images originate from

Lenny's car radio as he randomly switches stations. Thus diegetically motivated, the interplay between music and images appears coincidental, the soundtrack a random genre mix of alternative rock, non-descript instrumental music, and, finally, a choir singing a solemn Gregorian chant. In addition, these musical pieces are intercut with pieces of a dialogue between a talk radio host discussing the coming of the new millennium with various callers on the phone.

Alternating with the musical pieces, this verbal exchange is placed over some of the dramatic images of the sequence as a voice-over that further directs the audience's reception of the scene, and initially offers a form of disambiguation. It is with the help of the clues given in this radio phone-in that all uncertainty concerning the time and place of the action is dispelled. To be precise, it is the host of the show who confirms an assumption that the avid moviegoer and *connoisseur* of 'Los Angeles disaster fiction' must at this point already have deduced: this is L.A., the 'city of the future' and relentlessly immoral, capitalist metropolis that always has been and eternally will be on the brink of apocalyptic doom, in the night of 30 December 1999, the night before the last day of the century.

Yet ambiguity and uncertainty, the dominant affective reactions clearly marking the reception of *Strange Days'* beginning, are not completely dispelled, as the arsenal of apocalyptic L.A. stereotypes staged in the sequence is simultaneously ironized and charged with iridescent economic and religious connotations. Contrary to what the narration has the spectator believe, it is precisely *not* a coincidence that the sequence's first images of fleeing looters are accompanied by the aggressive beats and vocals of Skunk Anansie's "Selling Jesus." To be sure, the theme of 'losing one's religion,'[56] and replacing it with materialist greed, conveyed by the interplay between song and shot, implies a programmatic cultural critique. Its introduction can be read as the overture to a critical discourse that is informed by Walter Benjamin's notion of capitalism as a "pure religious cult"[57]. At this point of the film, however, as this very theme is picked up acoustically in a solemn choral hymn and visually, with bold sarcasm, by another shot showing the assault on Santa Claus, its critical impact collapses in an ironic exaggeration of apocalyptic clichés.

---

56 I am aware that the phrase "to lose one's religion" is idiomatic and basically means "to lose one's temper". However, its rich blend of connotations (mingling ideas of moral support through religious beliefs with ideas of emotional turmoil and loss of control) perfectly captures the subtext of the images and music under scrutiny.

57 Walter Benjamin, "Capitalism as Religion," *The Frankfurt School on Religion: Key Writings by the Major Thinkers*, ed. Eduardo Mendieta (New York: Routledge, 2005) 259-262, 259.

Appropriately, this elaborately tuned and highly ambiguous, apocalyptic audio-visual symphony ends abruptly on a religious drumbeat. After two male callers of the radio show have voiced their expectations of the future in the new millennium – the first one decidedly pessimistic, calling into question the propriety of a millennial celebration in face of social and economic disaster ("What the hell *are* we celebrating? The economy sucks, gas is three bucks a gallon, kids are shooting each other at recess, I mean, the whole thing sucks"), the second one, Dwayne, articulating in black vernacular his hope for a social and political sea change ("2 K, comin up tomorrow night, out with the old, in with the new… you know, for the man, the end of the old is good news, I mean we're gonna take it 'n make it new, make it our own, history is gonna start right here, you know what I'm saying) – the third caller, a woman named Lorrie, points out the alarming prevalence of 'war-talk' in the media, and, with reference to the Bible, urgently warns that "there won't be another thousand years." She thus articulates a premonition of the impending apocalypse that the talk radio host ridicules with relish:

Talk radio host: "Now, just so the rest of us know how much time is left: when is

the rapture supposed to hit exactly? Is it midnight New Year's Eve?"

Lorrie: "That's right."

Talk radio host: "Aha. Is that midnight L.A. time, or Eastern Standard Time, or

what? I mean, what time-zone is God in anyway?"

Lorrie (tearful): "I pray for you all."

Here, the American jeremiad – and thus the American genre that traditionally bewails society's moral corruption – meets its cynical deconstruction. With this rhetorical climax of religious drama, the 'technicolor' sequence that has lasted three minutes ends, and, before its iridescent blend of sarcasm and pathos can fully unfold, another abrupt transition indicates yet another narrative shift to the 'authentic' perspective of yet another man's (or woman's) "mundane and desperate existence," captured in another one of Lenny's playback clips. The spectator is left with feelings of ambiguity and uncertainty prompted by an audio-visual puzzle that constantly oscillates between gestures of authenticity and mocking references to representational stereotypes.

While withholding the certainty that an establishing shot or any other unambiguous expository device would provide, the brilliantly orchestrated alternation of the different aesthetic modes of two different narrative levels at the beginning of *Strange Days* succeeds in conveying an intensely unsettling climate of risk and contingency within the first ten minutes of the film. Equally contributing to this atmosphere, besides the bleak imagery projecting a violent, catastrophic future, is a narration that subjects its audience to an unnerving experience of depersonalized affect,[58] mockingly refuses a reliable subjective perspective, and deliberately heightens ambiguity through misleading cues. Undeniably, Kathryn Bigelow has composed a distinct aesthetics of risk, an aesthetics that owes as much to her sophisticated use of state-of-the-art cinematic technology[59] as it draws on the visual language of the historical images documenting the beating of Rodney King by the LAPD in 1991 and the violence and the chaos of the 1992 L.A. riots that followed in its wake.[60]

---

58 See Shaviro, "'Straight from the Cerebral Cortex'," 164-166.

59 Especially the effort and technological refinement that went into the visual style of the POV-sequences in *Strange Days* is remarkable and certainly exceeds the nostalgic concept of "technicolor" representation. Bigelow states that, in order to achieve the effect of an unbroken sequence, "a tremendous amount of coverage" had to be produced. She also reports on the impossibility of finding a camera that had the capacity of mimicking the movement of an eye. Accordingly, a special camera had to be built that was light enough "to give it the flexibility of an eye," and the POV-shots had to be filmed with a helmet-camera. See Gavin Smith, "'Momentum and Design': Interview with Kathryn Bigelow," *Hollywood Transgressor: The Cinema of Kathryn Bigelow*, eds. Deborah Jermyn and Sean Redmond (London/New York: Wallflower, 2003) 20-31, 22-23.

60 See Shaviro, "'Straight from the Cerebral Cortex'," 160. On the political significance of the transgressive LAPD action and the raw aesthetics of its video recording see Donald E. Pease, The New American Exceptionalism (Minneapolis/London: U of Minnesota P, 2009), esp. 43- 67. After emphasizing the centrality of representational strategies to the fostering of U.S. citizens' identification with successive state fantasies in the course of the twentieth century, Pease argues that the Rodney King documentary threw a wrench into the gears of such representational strategies:
"When the film from the handheld camera that documented the LAPD's beating of Rodney King was broadcast across television screens in 1991, this image could not be integrated within the state fantasy of the New World Order that the Gulf War was designed to inaugurate. Rather than settling into the image repertoire of the newly forged state fantasy, this documentary instead spontaneously recovered the memories – of slaves beaten by their masters, of migrant laborers forced into transfer centers, of Indians slaughtered by the thousands, of Vietnamese families dragged from their huts and shot and burned, of Iraqis forcibly separated from their homeland – that haunted the present with its record of injustice from the historical past at the very moment

Against the background of these widely disseminated images of race and class warfare, *Strange Days*' 1995 fictional projection of L.A. at the end of the twentieth century can certainly be considered a "disciplined extrapolation[s] to explore the possibilities of the near future."[61] It is definitely an instance of speculative fiction that foregoes "invasions from outer space or technological Frankensteins."[62] Instead, its speculation on a risky and contingent near future L.A. city life impressively stages and extrapolates from developments that Mike Davis has described as characteristic of "post-liberal Los Angeles."[63] Read against the foil of Davis's political diagnosis, the oppressive images of the robber's last view before he crashes into the street canyon in the opening POV-sequence appear as a brilliant dramatization of "the programmed hardening of the urban surface in the wake of the social polarizations of the Reagan era."[64]

Simultaneously, the 'technicolor' street scene perfectly – and only with negligible exaggeration – captures the warfare, the policing, the militarization, and the fortress mentality that, according to Davis, came along with the economic, social and cultural stratification of that era.[65] However, *Strange Days*' elaborate exposition of a city governed by catastrophic contingency already suggests that there are more fundamentally political notions of risk and speculation underlying both the film's aesthetics and its subject matter.

---

when the New World Order was systematically expunging that record from official historical narratives." (38)

In picking up the visual grammar of the Rodney King documentary in the playback sequences of her fiction film, Bigelow thus invokes historical images that, according to Pease, "opened up an empty space in between the dismantling of one state fantasy and the emergence of another" (43), and "brought about a change in U.S. citizens' identificatory relationship to the state's fantasy work." (67)

61 Mike Davis, *Ecology of Fear*, 362.
62 Ibid. Davis, at this point, refers to the novels of William Gibson and Octavia Butler and their strategy "to project existing trends along their current downward-sloping trajectories."
63 Davis, *City of Quartz*, 223.
64 Ibid.
65 See ibid.

2.3 STATE OF SPECULATION

Pointing beyond the historically, politically, and geographically narrow focus of "post-liberal L.A.,"[66] these notions of risk and speculation on the one hand correspond to a much older and distinctly American discourse, and, on the other, presciently project a pervasive, transnational political rationality that fully unfolds only in the twenty-first century, and is only recently being addressed by the fairly new fields of Governmentality and Critical Securitization Studies.[67]

In his study of the history of economic speculation and *homo oeconomicus* as a speculator,[68] sociologist Urs Stäheli traces a late-nineteenth/early-twentieth-century American discourse that identifies speculation as deeply ingrained in the founding and the political self-definition of the American nation. According to economic historians and social psychologists of that time, it was speculation that propelled U.S.-American history from the Columbian expedition to the gradual 'civilizing' settlement and processing of the continent's 'waste spaces'. The proverbial 'vastness' prompted the merging of geographic and economic imagination with the claim to exceptionalism, as economic historian George Gibson's 1889 comment exemplifies: "The 'magnificent distances' in our country, and its boundless resources, opened a *vista* to the speculator which is not likely to occur again in the history of mankind."[69]

Accordingly, the immigrants attracted by these unique vistas were cast as sharing the very orientation towards the future and the love for risk that characterizes the speculator. Indeed, the qualities associated with the spirit of speculation clearly resonate in the proverbial rugged individualism and the self-reliance of the American pioneer. John M. Findlay, in his monograph on the history of gambling in America, even compares pioneers and frontiersmen to bettors and gamblers with whom they share "high expectations," as well as a proclivity for "grasp[ing] the chance to get something for nothing" and "cherish[ing] risks in order to get ahead."[70] It is, then, high hopes and the love for risk (and, as Urs Stäheli emphasizes, a highly individualized form of risk best

---

66 Ibid.

67 A comprehensive sociological characterization of neoliberalism as a transnational political project was published even more recently in 2009. See Loïc Wacquant, *Punishing the Poor: The Neoliberal Government of Social Insecurity* (Durham: Duke UP, 2009).

68 Urs Stäheli, *Spektakuläre Spekulation: Das Populäre in der Ökonomie* (Frankfurt/Main: Suhrkamp, 2007).

69 George R. Gibson qtd. in Stäheli, *Spektakuläre Spekulation*, 182, Stäheli's italics.

70 John M. Findlay qtd. in Stäheli, *Spektakuläre Spekulation*, 184.

captured in the slogan 'use your chance') that define the identities of both the speculator and the immigrant.[71]

Significantly, the discourse on the identification of the American nation with the spirit of speculation peaked with the closure of that empty space of possibility that had triggered speculative fantasies in the first place. By way of explanation, Urs Stäheli points to the discursive pressure to perpetuate the idea of speculation that had been cast as the origin and the source of the American national identity. This pressure heightened considerably when the closing of the frontier and the gradual 'filling up' of the sites that had been attractive because of their emptiness and possibility seemed to put an end to speculation and thus seemed to threaten that very identity. The speculative lure of the empty and waste spaces of "a new world waiting to be made"[72] that had so starkly contrasted the backdrop of an overcrowded, "small, already partially exhausted and rigorously partitioned Europe"[73] had thus, paradoxically, pushed ahead its own destruction. Consequently, with an increasing population and with the gradual closing of the frontier, both the American idea of speculation and the characterization of the risk-loving, Emersonian individualism of the American pioneer as diametrically opposed to decadent European masses saw a crisis and required a redefinition.[74]

Without the empty spaces that had invited and catered to the speculator's love for risk, and with the presence of a growing number of other speculating immigrants from Europe, the clear-cut opposition between the ruggedly individual American speculator and the decadent European mass began to crumble. Increasingly, during the nineteenth century, cities populated by crowds began to replace the empty spaces in the American imagination, thus calling for and gradually inducing changes in the prevalent perceptions of the 'masses.' Yet, as Stäheli shows, despite a general acceptance of the prevalent modern concept of 'the public' as based on a distinction between 'the masses' and the democratic idea of 'the people,' this very distinction remained unstable in the American context.

Accordingly, representations of crowds and masses could, in the American political discourse of the nineteenth century, both signify an amorphous mob considered "wholly unfit for any political structure"[75] and a danger to the American polity, because it displayed 'contagious' European vices such as

---

71 See Stäheli, *Spektakuläre Spekulation*, 184.
72 Ralph Hale Mottram qtd. in Stäheli, 182.
73 Ibid.
74 See Stäheli, *Spektakuläre Spekulation*, 183 -190.
75 Joel T. Headley qtd. in Stäheli, *Spektakuläre Spekulation*, 177.

Socialism, atheism and alcoholism; or it could, as Walt Whitman's political texts show, embody the desire for an all-inclusive American mass-democracy whose political subject would ideally combine the mass and the individual.[76] Whether rejected as dangerously suggestible mobs, or celebrated as embodiments of a radically inclusive, democratic pluralism, crowds represented the individual's loss of personality and were often captured in conventional tropes "as oceans, streams, seas, swarms and masses that press, jam, crush, flock, mob, throng, and pack their way into being."[77]

This animalistic, depersonalized irrationality in the depiction of the nineteenth-century crowd points to a paradox not only inherent to a definition of the USA as a nation of speculation, but also to the nation's democratic ideals. If, as Mary Esteve observes in her study of nineteenth-century crowd representations, "critical or reflective judgment, the constitutive disposition of a political and aesthetic reasoning being within a liberal polity, is supplanted by universal physiological affection,"[78] and if the representation of crowds as depersonalized affective entities served to justify what Stäheli calls the functional inclusion/exclusion management of the public sphere,[79] fundamental questions arise: How can the crowd that is defined by "universal physiological affection" provide, at the same time, as Stäheli claims, the new democratic space of possibility for the speculating projections of the immigrant? How can a purely affective entity devoid of individuality and reason, perform the calculation of probabilities that is the basis of political and economic speculation? Can the other of the reasonable subject take a risk?

Although projecting a public sphere a hundred years after the era of crowds described by Stäheli, Esteve and others,[80] *Strange Days* picks up both the topos of speculation and the doubly coded topos of the teeming multitude that epitomizes the promise of inclusive democracy while, at the same time, embodying a danger to its social and political order. The film indulges in the same spectacle of the motley crowd comprised of radically self-interested individuals that Stäheli associates with the speculating street mobs of Wall Street around 1900, only locating it at the North American Pacific Coast in the twenty-first century, which means locating it exactly at the new "frontier of capitalist

---

76 See Stäheli, *Spektakuläre Spekulation*, 174-179.
77 Mary Esteve, *The Aesthetics and Politics of the Crowd in American Literature* (Cambridge, UK: Cambridge UP, 2003) 6.
78 Ibid., 27.
79 See Stäheli, *Spektakuläre Spekulation*, 179.
80 See also David A. Zimmermann, *Panic! Markets, Crises, Crowds in American Fiction* (Chapel Hill, University of North Carolina Press, 2006).

development"[81] that offered new, decidedly economic spaces of possibility after the closing of the frontier as a moving concept.

In the new political order of *Strange Days'* L.A., individuals comprising crowds still "grasp the chance to get something for nothing" and "cherish risks in order to get ahead"[82], but Bigelow leaves no doubt that their action is not motivated by "high expectations." What is at stake for the desperate, criminal *lumpenproletariat* that is introduced within the first minutes of the film, besides economic profit or loss that would grant them the subsistence that an only nominally existing welfare system obviously denies them, is punishment by the penal system of a de-democratized state governed by sheer market rationality and police authority.

Bigelow thus projects a political culture that centers on the primacy of the market. Generally subsumed under the tag of neoliberalism, this market rationality neither merely prioritizes free trade and entrepreneurial concerns nor just casts the priority of these concerns as "occurring by dint of nature."[83] Rather, it depicts the priority of the market as "*achieved and normative, as promulgated through law and through social and economic policy.*"[84] What is more, according to Wendy Brown, "the state itself must construct and construe itself in market terms, as well as develop policies and promulgate a political culture that figures citizens exhaustively as rational economic actors in every sphere of life."[85] What *Strange Days'* street scenes show, then, is the idea of the speculative mob adapted to a political culture in which, as Michel Foucault writes,

the subject is considered only as *homo oeconomicus*, which does not mean that the whole subject is considered as *homo oeconomicus*. In other words, considering the subject as *homo oeconomicus* does not imply an anthropological identification of any behavior whatsoever with economic behavior. It simply means that economic behavior is the grid of intelligibility one will adopt on the behavior of the new individual.[86]

---

81 Arif Dirlik,"There's More in the Rim than Meets the Eye," *What Is In a Rim*, ed. Arif Dirlik (Lanham: Rowman and Littlefield, 1998) 352 -369, 352.
82 John M. Findlay qtd. in Stäheli, *Spektakuläre Spekulation*, 184.
83 Wendy Brown,"American Nightmare: Neoliberalism, Neoconservatism, and De-Democratization," *Political Theory* 34.6 (Dec. 2006): 690 -714, 694.
84 Ibid., italics in the original.
85 Ibid.
86 Michel Foucault, *The Birth of Biopolitics: Lectures at the College de France`1978 - 1979* (New York: Palgrave MacMillan, 2008) 252.

It becomes evident, at this point, that the destitute and completely de-politicized individuals roaming the streets of Bigelow's dystopian L.A. in scattered bands are produced as amoral, radically self-interested subjects by the gaze of a penal system that defines criminals not on the basis of moral concepts, but treats them "as anyone whomsoever who invests in an action, expects a profit from it, and who accepts the risk of a loss."[87] The gaze of this penal system scans the crowded streets not for the criminal, but for "the supply of crime" on "the market of crime."[88] Bigelow stages the omnipresence of that gaze by using the searchlights of the police helicopters as a leitmotif, with their restless panning movements occurring not only on, but connecting both narrative levels of the film, and immersing almost every scene in a vaguely flickering light.

Far more than the symbol of a ubiquitous urban surveillance, or instances of intertextual reference to films like Ridley Scott's *Blade Runner* or Fritz Lang's *Metropolis* in which they serve this function, these searchlights represent in *Strange Days* the subjectivizing gaze of neoliberal culture and its penal enforcement. If, as Foucault states, neoliberal penal policy "has renounced the objective of the complete suppression and exhaustive nullification of crime,"[89] the 'vista' the searchlights enable is a thoroughly speculative one. It allows for the penal system's cost-benefit-analysis of the supply of crime in relation to the amount of expenditure in terms of law enforcement required to penalize it. What appears to be the erratic behavior of a paramilitary police force intent on controlling, containing and directing the movements of the marauding bands, rather than attempting to stop and arrest them all in the street scene at the beginning of *Strange Days*, thus becomes recognizable as the result of a profoundly economic calculation based on questions such as "How many offences should be permitted?" and "[…] how many offenders should go unpunished?"[90].

---

87 Ibid. 253.
88 Foucault, *The Birth of Biopolitics*, 255.
89 Ibid.,256.
90 Gary Becker qtd. in Foucault, *The Birth of Biopolitics*, 256. 90 *Strange Days*' 1995 discourse on the nexus of economic restructuring, the retrenchment of welfare measures, and crime management in a thoroughly neoliberal culture thus discerningly anticipates a characterization of the "neoliberal Leviathan" (xviii) and "its distinctively paternalistic visage" (xx-xxi) as would be delivered by Loic Wacquant, more than a decade later: "The state," Wacquant writes in the prologue of his study, "stridently reasserts its responsibility, potency, and efficiency in the narrow register of crime management at the very moment when it proclaims and organizes its own impotence on the economic front, thereby revitalizing the twin historical-cum-

It is thus neither the Rule of Law, nor exclusively the force of law that defines the state, the social, and the subject in Bigelow's film, but a neoliberal political culture whose speculative economic rationality produces its subjects by responding solely to its population's economic behavior. Government is in this culture precisely *not* defined by despotism or merely restricted to the coercive force of the police state as which it is publically denounced by Jeriko One (Glenn Plummer), a charismatic African American rap star and political leader of a black civil rights movement intent on uncovering the racism and the lack of democratic values in the governance of the film's diegetic L.A. Significantly, as Mark Berrettini observes, Jeriko One's "prominent introduction as a character coincides with the announcement of his death" in the framework of an "amalgamated televisual format of music video and newscast."[91] This sensational televisual commodification of the news of the murder of Jeriko One, however, points to an increasing indistinguishability of the economic and the political, rather than just emphasizing "the hybridity of Jeriko's work and his public persona," or "the ways his work straddles the supposedly discrete spheres of entertainment and politics,"[92] as Berrettini claims.

More important, the televisual assemblage of the Jeriko One murder report with the news coverage of the LAPD street-operation that immediately precedes it relates both events to the concept of insurance and thus points to the central role of risk in the political culture of Bigelow's diegetic L.A. It is the female news-anchor's voice-over accompanying the news report's images of police in riot gear who struggle to regulate the overwhelmingly criminal L.A. street life that gives some decisive clues on that role:

New Year's Eve, 1999. It's being called the party of the century, but it may be the biggest party ever. No one has ever seen preparations like this, but preparations require care and insurance, and the LAPD is one insurance company that doesn't want accidents.

A teaching play on televisual editing, the conjunction of televised images and voice-over comment reinterprets as 'party preparations' the bleakness, the violence, the desperation and the chaos that *Strange Days*' viewers have been introduced and subjected to in the expository sequences of the film.[93] What is

---

scholarly myths of the efficient police and the free market." *Punishing the Poor: The Neoliberal Government of Social Insecurity* (Durham: Duke UP, 2009) xviii.
91 Mark Berrettini, "Can 'We All' Get Along? Social Difference, the Future, and *Strange Days*," *Camera Obscura 50* 17.2 (2002):155 -189, 156.
92 Mark Berrettini, "Can 'We All' Get Along," 156-157.
93 See ibid., 156.

more, it delivers a revised version of that specifically American blend of speculative imagination and exceptionalism that had offered, in the late nineteenth century, a "vista to the speculator that is not likely to occur again in the history of mankind,"[94] according to George R. Gibson's aforementioned 1889 comment on the "boundless resources" of the country.

Strikingly, read against this background, Kathryn Bigelow's representation of a finely tuned mass-media representation of political crowd management a century later suggests that it is now the state whose speculations on a contingent future are targeted at and justified by the 'vista' of the doubly coded masses: Under the pretext of a mass-celebration that is supposed to keep up the appearance of an enduring validity of liberal democratic ideals, the "magnificent distances"[95] of a century ago are replaced by images of unruly masses cast as wayward 'party guests' who have to be taken 'care' of, and whose notorious, yet incalculable irrationality requires precautionary measures – "preparations" and "insurance" – from the LAPD. Bigelow's representation of a near-future L.A. thus not only conjoins the idea of the American nation as a nation of speculation with the rationalities of neoliberalism but, at this point, explicitly evokes, adds, and relates to these concepts the vocabulary that epitomizes the ideal of the welfare state with its pastoral care of the population and its emphasis on security – an ideal that Michel Foucault, drawing on Plato's dialogue *The Statesman*, has famously termed the "shepherd-flock game."[96]

Rooted in early Christianity when it signified the relationship between God, the pastor and the Christian community (the pastorate), the secularized shepherd-flock metaphor represents the idea that the state should care for the welfare of its citizens. Foucault's analysis shows, however, that despite its connotations of Christian charity and philanthropy, both the early Christian and the modern secular version of pastoral power are forms of subjection and use technologies for "the constitution of subjectivity" that can be understood as a "prelude to governmentality."[97] Particularly, the demand for the pastor to have intimate knowledge of all individuals comprising his 'flock' in order to judge and analyze

---

94 George R.Gibson qtd. in Stäheli, *Spektakuläre Spekulation*, 182.
95 George R.Gibson qtd. in Stäheli, *Spektakuläre Spekulation*, 182.
96 See Michel Foucault, *Security, Territory, Population* (London: Palgrave, 2007) 169 - 173. See also Mitchell Dean, *Governmentality: Power and Rule in Modern Societies* (Los Angeles et. al.: Sage, 2010 [1999]) 92, and Colin Gordon," Governmental Rationality: An Introduction," *The Foucault Effect: Studies in Governmentality* Eds. Graham Burchell, Colin Gordon, and Peter Miller (Chicago: University of Chicago Press, 1991, 1 -51, 8.
97 Foucault, *Security, Territory, Population*, 184-185.

their worthiness of salvation, reprimand their faults and coerce them to work on their self-improvement – combining the imperative of 'care for others' with that of 'care for the self' – is continuous with the rule of an 'ethically responsible' sovereignty and the political technologies of the twentieth-century welfare state, as Mitchell Dean observes in his seminal work on governmentality.[98] In both versions of pastoral power, according to Dean, "subjection and subjectivity […] encounter each other. However, there is one point on which contemporary pastoral power differs from its early Christian version: the individual is now 'normalized' in relation to a scientific knowledge of populations."[99]

In *Strange Days*' projection of a near-future L.A., the state's attempt at gaining "scientific knowledge" of its population is not restricted to the ubiquitous monitoring of this population's movements and activities, or the application of 'psy'-disciplines to access and govern the individuals' inner existence.[100] In order to illustrate how the market rationality governing the film's diegetic political culture is supplemented by the exercise of pastoral power, Bigelow makes a point of letting the audience in on the diegetic back-story of the fictitious playback technology called SQUID, around which action in *Strange Days* centers: By way of a seemingly casual aside uttered by protagonist Max Peltier (Tom Sizemore) she lets the film's audience know that SQUID (short for Super Conducting Interference Device) was developed by military intelligence as an instrument of surveillance before its escapist possibilities were discovered and commodified on the black market of *Strange Days*' diegetic L.A. The fictional state's invention of a technology enabling the recording and the consumption of an individual's live experience quite literally represents a dreadful vision of an all-encompassing 'scientific' knowledge of the population, a vision that can certainly be read as a critical comment on a Reaganite 'military machine.'[101]

At a more fundamentally political level, it vividly accounts for the pastoral power's ambition to gain total insight into the lives of the individuals comprising its 'flock.' The conspicuously objectifying disrespect for individual borders and privacy implicit to this technology, however, also insinuates that pastoral power is not primarily interested in the individuals' well-being, but in the normalizing formation of bio-political subjects. Given its appropriation and commodification

---

98 See Dean, *Governmentality*, 92.
99 Ibid.
100 See Dean, *Governmentality*, 92.
101 Both the SQUID-device's speaking acronym and its octopus-like attachment to the human body highlight that this knowledge is obtained through a 'sucking' intrusiveness.

by black market dealers and customers, the SQUID-technology can be read as representing both a success and a failure of bio-political governance in a political culture dominated by market rationality. That it can even assume the function of a revolutionary *machine de guerre* as described by Gilles Deleuze and Felix Guattari in *A Thousand Plateaus*, a subversive and tactical war machine whose transformational potential is directed against a static state apparatus will be shown in a later part of this chapter. As a metaphor for the state's pursuit of an all-encompassing knowledge of its population it can at least be said to point to and to reveal the true colors of contemporary pastoral care.

A less science-fictional illustration of the diegetic state's exercise of pastoral power is implied in the news-anchor's sarcastic comment that reinterprets the LAPD as "one insurance company that doesn't want accidents." By having the word "insurance" mentioned twice in the news-anchor's voice-over, Bigelow draws attention to a concept that Francois Ewald has described as a calculative rationality centering on the definition of risks and the estimation of the probability of future events, a rationality that has been constitutive to the emergence of the modern welfare state. According to Ewald, technologies of insurance became a method of governing the increasing number of social problems that came with the rise of industrial capitalism in the late nineteenth century. Instead of dealing with work accidents, illnesses or unemployment as individual hazards and matters of individual responsibility, the possibility of such incidents was defined as insurable risk requiring solidarity and a collectively borne compensation granted by social insurance. Pointing to the political impact of this historical shift from a societal concept based on the individual responsibility of an abstract, legal subject to one based on social insurance and risks that are collectively borne and shared among the individuals of a group, Ewald writes:

Beginning at the end of the nineteenth century, risk designated the collective mode of being of human beings in society: it had become social. Similarly, evil was no longer the opposite of good, but resided in the relation between goods; risk was no longer inscribed in the relation between humanity and a simultaneously benevolent and hostile nature, but in the relation between human beings, in their common quest for good. Thus insurance could no longer be optional, a fruit of the private virtue of foresight. It became mandatory, a moral and social obligation – two types of obligation that would henceforth be seen as one. Insurance could then become a state-function sanctioned by law: the punishable offence was now to neglect to insure oneself. The age of the security societies was dawning. A new order was born, with its own way of conceptualizing the relations between the whole and the part, the individual and society, good and evil.[102]

With the state as "the greatest social insurer,"[103] the purpose of the socialization of risk was certainly not to tackle capitalist inequality or overturn the structures of society.[104] On the contrary, social insurance was a political technology designed to mitigate and to compensate for the negative effects of exploitation, oppression and poverty, while leaving its structural origins unaffected. It is important to note, however, that risk insurance by enforcing solidarity as a moral and social obligation did establish social rights and social citizenship. It did so not in the sense of the liberties of citizens as individuals, but by contractually binding individual members of a collectivity to "accept responsibility for each other's burden."[105] Although the distribution of risk according to an insurance calculus required the monitoring and registration of intimate details – scientific knowledge – of all individuals comprising a collectivity and reflected existing social inequalities in the varying proportional shares it ascribed, it was a political technology that at least alleviated the social problems of a society defined by the capitalist mode of production.[106]

In the neoliberal culture of *Strange Days*' fictional L.A., the principle of social insurance has deteriorated to a cynical joke. The newscast's composition of televised images and voice-over comment unmistakably conveys that what is enforced by the LAPD is neither the socialization of risk nor the moral and social obligation to mutual responsibility of the individuals comprising the 'party' crowd. On the contrary, the interplay between bleak images of self-interested brutality and the text that sarcastically designates police in riot gear as an "insurance company" whose "preparations require care and insurance" turns the spotlight on cuts in social services, social rights drawbacks, societal disintegration and lack of solidarity. Significantly, the police force represent not the state or its law, but a privatized "company," offering not the contractual spreading of risk over a collectivity of insurance holders, but precautionary

---

102 Francois Ewald, "Two Infinities of Risk," *The Politics of Everyday Fear*, ed. Brian Massumi (Minneapolis /London: U of Minnesota P, 1993) 227.
103 Claudia Aradau and Rens van Munster, "Taming the Future: The Dispositif of Risk in the War on Terror," *Risk and the War on Terror*, eds. Louise Amoore and Marieke de Goede (London/New York: Routledge, 2008) 23-40, 27.
104 See Aradau, and van Munster,"Taming the Future," 27, and Dean, *Governmentality*, 215.
105 Dean, *Governmentality*, 215.
106 See ibid.

crowd management to a government which is organized like a firm of which they are but a branch. It is the irrational, unpredictable crowd that poses a risk to a government whose priority is not the social welfare of its citizens, but the provision and the preservation of free enterprise and free market conditions; and it is the task of the police to handle the risk that might induce a crisis of governance.

Here, the concept of risk that, according to Niklas Luhmann, is by definition a "calculation in terms of time,"[107] distinguished from 'danger' by its dependence on observation and decision making, begins to show as a polyvalent calculative rationality that can be invested with and tied to different political programs and goals.[108] It is important to recall, at this point, that the perception and definition of risk by recent Governmentality and Critical Securitization Studies as a dispositif or a rationality to govern social problems differs decisively from Ulrich Beck's diagnosis of a new global "prominence of risk" uniting "new transnational politics with the question of cosmopolitan democracy" in a "world risk society."[109] Scholars like Francois Ewald, Mitchell Dean, Claudia Aradau, Rens van Munster, Jonathan Simon, Marieke de Goede and others have called into question the ontological claim implicit to Beck's conceptualization of a world "of dangers and risks" that he casts as the result of a failure of "second modernity" (his term for postmodernity) to come to terms with the unforeseen consequences of processes of functional differentiation initiated during "first modernity."[110] Following Michel Foucault's lectures on bio-politics and governmentality, these scholars foreground instead "the virtue of adopting a more nominalist position, i.e. one that analyses forms of risk as among the ways in which we are required to know and to act upon ourselves today in a range of moral and political programmes and social technologies."[111]

Read in light of this conceptualization of risk as a polyvalent, calculative political rationality or a historically defined dispositif, the distinct aesthetics of risk described above as well as the representation of crowds and their management in *Strange Days* can be recognized as complementary elements of an intricate representational strategy, designed to spotlight risk as a new

---

107 See Niklas Luhmann, *The Concept of Risk: A Sociological Theory* (New Brunswick/ London: Aldine Transaction, 2002) 11.
108 See Dean, *Governmentality*, 220.
109 Ulrich Beck, *World Risk Society* (Cambridge/ Malden: Polity Press, 2009), 4.
110 Ibid., 3-4.
111 Dean, *Governmentality*, 211. See also Mitchell Dean, "Questions of Method," *The Politics of Constructionism* Eds. R. Williams and I. Velody (London: Sage, 1998) 182-199.

paradigm of organizing economic and political discourse, and risk management as an instrument of governance. Clearly, Bigelow's emphasis on and ironic contextualization of the term "insurance" alludes to the varying manifestations and functions of different historical risk rationalities. While invoking the logic of social insurance, according to which the concept of risk was instrumental to the moral ideals of the welfare state at the end of the nineteenth and for most of the twentieth century, the sarcasm in this emphasis, at the same time, points to the change in the way risk is being instrumentalized at the end of twentieth century. In presenting this change by way of a diegetically motivated, and cunningly edited televisual interplay of text and images, Bigelow's film foregrounds the role of media representation in risk management and thus anticipates a non-ontological understanding of risk as a political rationality that Claudia Aradau and Rens van Munster identify at the center of US American post 9/11 security politics, more than a decade later:

Importantly, the identification of risk is not the same as recognizing the uncertainty of future events. On the contrary, the identification and management of risk is a way of organizing reality, taming the future, disciplining chance and rationalizing individual conduct (Hacking 1990). Identifying the future as bearing catastrophic risks is therefore linked with visions of order and ways to constitute and reproduce it.[112]

It testifies for the astute political perceptiveness of Bigelow's 1995 speculation on governmental risk management in a near-future L.A. that observation and representation have a crucial role in the complex set of political practices and techniques her film depicts. Rendering undistinguishable political from economic speculation, risk in this political culture on the one hand caters to a bio-political framework within which the political decision makers are clearly distinguished from those who, affected by the decisions made, "constitute an amorphous mass that cannot be given form."[113] Within this framework, the bodies comprising the crowd, whether selectively regulated, disciplined and distributed by police power as in the first street scenes of Bigelow's film, or condensed and constantly monitored as in the spectacular mass scenes at the "Retinal Fetish Club" or the New Year's Eve Party at the end of the movie, are subjected by the bio-politics of pastoral power to the decision making of a sovereign state authority that distinguishes risk from danger.

---

112 Aradau and van Munster,"Taming the Future," 25-26.
113 Niklas Luhmann, *The Concept of Risk*, 110.

Cast as "wholly unfit for any political structure,"[114] like the amorphous mob in the late nineteenth century, the 'animalistic' crowd in *Strange Days'* near- future L.A. presents the limits of scientific knowledge and cannot be captured in terms of known probabilities; it poses a risk to the social order that is comparable to natural disasters and is thus uninsurable. On the other hand, "insurance *is* the art of making the seemingly incalculable subject to calculation."[115] Ultimately, then, the 'art' of insurance in *Strange Days* is depleted of its socializing meaning and evoked as an instrument of subjection, while the concept of uninsurable, catastrophic risk serves in this bio-political framework to justify precautionary measures of a sovereign power that suspends the law in a permanent state of exception.[116] Like the ubiquitous and permanent war talk[117] inducing talk radio caller Lorrie's premonition of an impending apocalypse, the representation of the teeming multitude as posing a risk of catastrophic proportions feeds a collective imaginary germane to governmental practices and techniques in the neoliberal culture that Bigelow unerringly projects.

While showing that there is not much left of the ethical imperative of 'care for others' in *Strange Days'* neoliberal L.A., Bigelow, on the other hand, poignantly stages how, within that very culture, rationalities of risk are being individualized and integrated into the subjectivizing governmental techniques of 'care for the self.' With many of its protagonists responding to the diegetic city's pervasive and oppressive climate of risk with a feeling of constant and excessive anxiety,

---

114 Headley qtd. in Stäheli, *Spektakuläre Spekulationen*, 177.

115 Aradau and van Munster,"Taming the Future," 28, italics in the original.

116 See Giorgio Agamben, *State of Exception* (Chicago/London: U of Chicago P, 2005). See also Richard V. Ericson,"The State of Preemption: Managing Terrorism Risk through Counter Law," *Risk and the War on Terror* Ed. Louise Amoore and Marieke de Goede (London and New York: Routledge, 2008) 57 -76.

117 See Agamben, *State of Exception*, 21. Significantly, Agamben emphasizes that, in the American context, "because the sovereign power of the president is essentially grounded in the emergency linked to a state of war, the metaphor of war, over the course of the twentieth century becomes an integral part of the presidential political vocabulary whenever decisions considered to be of vital importance are being imposed." (21) Donald E. Pease even argues that "with the inauguration of the National Security State in 1950, the United States officially entered into a permanent state of war with the Soviet Union" thus "taking up the site of exception" and installing "a permanent alternative to the normative order that it called the National Security State." *The New American Exceptionalism*, 24.

this city is created as a space of paranoia,[118] and paranoia made visible as a concept that is central to a new city-citizenship. Bigelow unmistakably foregrounds and underlines the programmatic political meaning of paranoia by having it explicitly addressed and accentuated at various points in the plot.

In the first instance, it is musical producer Philo Gant (Michael Wincott) who when accused of being paranoid after too much 'wire-tripping,' as the consumption of SQUID clips is termed, defends himself: "Paranoia is just reality on a finer scale." Notably, this idea is picked up and commented on in a later scene by protagonist Max Peltier (Tom Sizemore), shortly before he is exposed as the film's monstrous villain in disguise who will eventually kill Philo after literally frying his brain on a wire-trip overdose. Although addressing Lenny Nero who is devastated after the vexing 'experience' of a perfidiously orchestrated, sadistic 'snuff' clip that will turn out to be another one of Max's vicious schemes, it is Max, of all people, who in effect seems to counter Philo's previous remark with the pithy phrase: "The issue's not whether you're paranoid [...] the issue is whether you're paranoid *enough*."

Strikingly, the two statements implicitly prefigure the two opposing conceptualizations of risk informing the contemporary theoretical discourse on risk as sketched above. While Philo Gant's definition of paranoia as "reality on a finer scale" reflects the realism inherent to an ontological notion of risk, Max Peltier's phrasing implies a relational, constructivist understanding of both risk and paranoia. At plot level, these different understandings of risk and paranoia reflect the asymmetry of power underlying the two men's relationship. With his undercover persona as a bodyguard in Philo's service suggesting the contrary, it is Max whose power over representation in the form of SQUID clips generates and manipulates the experience of a depersonalized risk and an intensely individualized paranoia, finally leading to Philo's gruesome death, a twist in the plot that ultimately affirms Max's constructivist notions of risk and paranoia.

However, despite these fundamental differences, both statements seem to presuppose a definition of paranoia as a required and adequate epistemological adaptation of political subjects to the hazards of an environment that is construed as risky. In concert with its elaborate aesthetics of risk, the film's discourse on paranoia casts an excessive anxiety, bordering on the pathological, as a normalizing coping strategy. Moreover, the subtext of speculation in Max's

---

118 I draw here on Jacques Donzelot's phrase: "In order to make fear reign a space of fear must be created," qtd. in Brian Massumi, "Everywhere You Want to Be: Introduction to Fear," *The Politics of Everyday Fear* (Minneapolis/ London: U of Minnesota P, 1993) 3-37, 23. See also Mike Davis's reference to L.A.'s "paranoid spatiality." *City of Quartz*, 239.

wording when he claims "the issue is whether you're paranoid *enough*" suggests an understanding of paranoia as a rationally calculating self-technology against the grain of its decidedly irrational connotations, a 'practice of the self' within the paradigm of neoliberal 'prudentialism.' Paranoia in *Strange Days'* near-future L.A. thus caters to a privatized logic of risk management complementing the speculating, 'pastoral' bio-politics of the state which construe the entire population as a "locus of risk."[119] It is represented as one of the self-governing practices in a neoliberal society "in which subjects are required to prudently calculate and thereby minimize the risk that could befall them." [120]

Drawing on the work of Pat O'Malley, Mitchell Dean points out that the 'practices of the self' exercised by the prudential subject ideally conjoin responsible, rational, moral and calculating behavior in order to cope with health and crime risks.[121] As a self-technology applied by the good citizen who compliantly functions as a self-governing subject, prudentialism, at the same time, however, caters to the socially virtuous conduct benefitting the social body of the ideal city modeled on the Greek *polis*: The imperative of being independent from the state and bearing one's own risk (if with the help of hired professionals and experts) is, after all, closely linked to the moral obligation not to burden the civic community.[122] Significantly, this moral obligation of the political subject to prudently apply a rationally calculating self-technology and thus minimize individualized risks ties in with the trajectories of the pastoral power that it thereby exonerates from the imperative of 'the care for others.' It is at this point that risk becomes visible as a rationality working at more than one governmental level in *Strange Days'* diegetic political culture. Obviously, as the film's aesthetics impressively underline, the political practices related to risk rationality have generated in the film's fictional L.A. one of those societies that, according to Michel Foucault, "are really demonic since they happen to combine those two games – the city-citizen game and the shepherd-flock game – in what we call modern states."[123]

Rather than producing uncontrollable panic, a "universal physiological affection,"[124] as in the culture of Victorian modernity, the representations of

---

119 See Dean, *Governmentality*, 157.
120 Aradau and van Munster, "Taming the Future," 27.
121 See Dean, *Governmentality*, 221.
122 Ibid., 105.
123 Michel Foucault, "Politics and Reason," *Politics, Philosophy, Culture: Interviews and Other Writings, 1977 -1984*, ed. Lawrence D. Kritzman (New York: Routledge, 1988) 57 -85, 71.
124 Esteve, *The Aesthetics and Politics of the Crowd in American Literature*, 27.

teeming multitudes and the bleak atmosphere of ubiquitous risk in *Strange Days'* near-future L.A. are shown as creating the ideal political climate for the radically individualized anxiety and affective alertness that it casts as a prudently calculating governmental self-practice. This practice responds to the disintegration of a society that is not bound by social contract to mutual responsibility, a society in which "humanity itself [...] has become a dangerous class."[125] While speculative decision making within a rationality of risk defines the bio-political relationship between the pastoral state and the population it produces as an amorphous, dangerous mass, the pastoral power neither provides a common moral ground nor effective protection against the consequences of this ethic void at the level of citizenship. The citizen is thus required to individually embrace and prudently manage the risks that are no longer collectively borne by way of social insurance.

It is evident, then, that in *Strange Days*, Kathryn Bigelow sketches a political culture beyond the scope of "post-liberal L.A." Resonating in the film's complex discourse on risk and speculation are the historical U.S.-American investments in these concepts as well as the risk-related governmental technologies that, since the last decades of the twentieth century, increasingly define the politics, not only of the U.S. but of capitalist Western 'states of speculation' in general. Moreover, with its subtle discourse on paranoia, *Strange Days* can even be said to sagely prefigure the notion of "a precautionary logic that normalizes suspicion"[126] as it has emerged in post-9/11 U.S. The oxymoronic absurdity of the imperative to be "paranoid *enough*" highlights the interminably calculating effort prudentialism requires and the enormous affective strain it imposes on the neoliberal subject within a culture of normalized suspicion. With its subtext of speculation the demand to be "paranoid *enough*" also expressly underlines Bigelow's representation of most of her film's protagonists as radically self-interested individuals who comply with the rationality of the market even at the level of affectivity. The economy of affective compliance captured in this phrase thus boldly affirms Foucault's conceptualization of *"homo oeconomicus* as the surface of contact between the individual and the power exercised on him,"[127] and points to a transcendent economization of political subjectivity beyond the universalist and normative economic fiction of 'rational economic man.'

---

125 Giorgio Agamben, "No to Bio-Political Tattooing," *Le Monde* (10 Jan. 2004): Web, 4 May 2011 <http://www.ratical.org/ratville/CAH/totalControl.html>.

126 Richard V. Ericson quoted in Louise Amoore and Marieke de Goede, "Introduction: Governing by Risk in the War on Terror," *Risk and the War on Terror* Ed. Louise Amoore and Marieke de Goede (London and New York: Routledge, 2008) 5-19, 16.

127 Foucault, *The Birth of Biopolitics*, 252-253.

2.4 THE LURE AND TRAP OF LADY CREDIT

While the film's discourse on paranoia already suggests a surprising affective susceptibility and adaptation to the logic of the market, its discourse on love seems even more conclusive and reveals significant differences among the protagonists' political-economic subjectivities. At first glance, it seems as if *Strange Days* affirms the conventional notion of an irreconcilability of love and market concerns, as much of its narrative dynamic derives from the protagonists' romantic relationships that seem to complicate their compliance with the rules of the market. Upon close scrutiny, however, the film's discourse on love and sexuality proves an insightful and eye-opening allegory on different versions of *homo oeconomicus* and the nature of speculation. Lenny Nero's relationships both with his ex-girlfriend Faith (Juliette Lewis) and his black female buddy Mace (Angela Bassett) in particular are revealing and corroborate the notion of *Strange Days'* critical investment in the politics of speculation.

Shortly after Lenny Nero has been introduced as the calculating merchant of SQUID-recorded second-hand risks in the expository scenes of *Strange Days*, the spectator learns that Lenny has lost Faith, the woman with whom he is still madly in love even though she has left him for musical producer Philo Gant. Notably, Faith is introduced by way of a SQUID clip that Lenny nostalgically indulges in before the viewer is informed, in a later scene, that her relationship with Lenny belongs to the past. The scene in which Lenny revels in his SQUID-recorded happy days with Faith is remarkable in many ways. It starts when Lenny returns to his apartment to rest after a night of negotiations with Tick and other suppliers of SQUID-clips, just seconds too late to pick up the receiver and take a call from Iris (Brigitte Bako), a prostitute who is on the run from the police and desperately trying to reach him. Leaving behind the mayhem of the streets and shutting out the interminable police sirens and helicopter noises, Lenny closes the door of his apartment, sits down, and rummages through a box of SQUID-clips. Eventually, he picks a clip with the caption "Faith" and a pair of eyes sketched on its label, pours himself a drink, dons the SQUID-headset and pushes the 'Start' button.

After the usual split-second transition of illegible blur we are immersed into a sunny beach scene sharply contrasting the gloomy, half-lit scene of its reception. The POV-shot whose instability we have learned to identify as characteristic of the SQUID recordings shows a young woman on roller skates, scantily dressed in over knee-stockings, black panties and a crop top. Skating backwards she dances before the 'recording' eyes of the person wearing the SQUID-device, who, as we soon infer, is Lenny. With gyrating hip-movements and appealing laughter she appears to try to seduce the viewer into following her, moving back and forth, offering both her hands to support him as he laughingly staggers along. From the woman's encouraging pep-talk – "You're doing good, Sweety" significantly echoed by Lenny's lovestruck reply "You're looking good, Baby" – and the camera movement panning between her seductive body and her protegé's roller skates, we can conclude that Lenny is reliving a romantic skating-lesson at the beach on a sunny California afternoon. The SQUID-sequence stops when Lenny stumbles and falls and Faith approaches him to help him up, intermittently beaming at him, laughing and apologizing somewhat exaggeratedly: "Oh, I'm sorry, Lenny! Lenny, are you alright?"

Different from the first SQUID-clip at the very beginning of *Strange Days*, the Faith-clip is not shown as the long, uncut POV-shot that the viewer has, at this point, come to expect. Instead, this SQUID sequence is intercut with extreme close-ups of Lenny's face unmistakably displaying feelings of enraptured pleasure and even a pointedly innocent, childlike bliss. The quick change between the distinctly different types of light defining the two quickly alternating narrative levels underlines both the bleak atmosphere of Lenny's apartment that is eerily illuminated by the shine of flickering red and blue neon signs filtering through a glass brick wall from the world outside and the strikingly bright, happy-go-lucky appeal of the clip. It is no accident that this SQUID sequence is one of only two scenes set in bright daylight in the whole film, which further emphasizes its importance The effect of sunshiny brightness is enhanced and reflected by the almost gleaming whiteness of Faith's beautiful, seductively moving body, while Lenny's face, as he's reliving the happy moment, appears dark and soft with desire.

It is this desire and its production that the scene artfully, yet clearly stages and foregrounds. When Lenny is shown pushing the 'Fast Forward' button of his deck and the SQUID sequence continues, the spectator begins to understand that it is this second part of the clip, a sex scene after the skating lesson, that is the actual destination of Lenny's nostalgic time travel. Sharing Lenny's gaze, we follow Faith to her apartment at the beach, watch her dancing into the bathroom, undressing and splashing water onto her body sweaty from skating in the sun, while a non-diegetic soundtrack of rhythmic reggae-music plays along. It is at this point with the music and the setting of the sunny beach apartment conjuring a carefree holiday atmosphere that the impression of witnessing a pointedly artificial stage act rather than a 'natural' scene between lovers sharpens. We begin to realize – and retrospectively reassess – the staged artificiality of Faith's behavior in the skating scene before this equally artificial performance of erotic seduction. This initially vague feeling heightens and is explicitly confirmed when Faith, who has been posing and flirting with Lenny's recording senses all along, asks Lenny "Are you gonna watch or are you gonna do?" and Lenny replies "Watch and see."

Strikingly, the opposition between "looking," "watching" and "seeing" on the one hand, and "doing," on the other, that the previous exchange between Lenny and Faith during the skating lesson has already introduced is picked up here and accentuated in a way that leaves no doubt as to its centrality. What Lenny re-lives in this scene becomes evident here as the production of a simulacrum of erotic love, a celebration of scopophilic fetishization that climaxes in Faith's confession during sex: "I love your eyes, Lenny, I love the way they see." Yet it is clearly not Lenny who sees what is obvious in the scene, but the audience who share his gaze without sharing his obsession: Evidently, Faith, contrary to Lenny, is not carried away by sexual arousal and sensual bliss, and if she is feeling pleasure at all, it is Lenny's susceptibility to her seductive performance that induces it.

As an elaborate commentary on the objectifying, male coded cinematic gaze, the scene evokes the theoretical discourse on the cultural construction of the female body by a cinematic voyeurism and fetishism considered as inevitably encoded in the very institution of the cinema. Read in light of this discourse, which, originating in the nineteen-seventies, "denies the neutrality of the cinematic apparatus itself,"[128] the fictitious SQUID technology in general and the Faith-clip scene in particular form a dense meta-cinematic text that interrogates the construction of sexual difference by "phallocentric mechanisms"[129] even beyond the visual 'terrorism' of the camera.[130] If, as Mary Ann Doane writes, "vision, which had formerly quite clearly 'belonged' to the individual subject is expropriated by the machine,"[131] the technology that enables the disc-recording of not only visual, but all sensory input directly from the human cerebral cortex must clearly entail an even more radical "restructuration of subjectivity and perception."[132]

The impulses recorded by SQUID not only provide seemingly unlimited possibilities for the consumption of the risky experience of others – advertised

---

128 Mary Ann Doane, *Femmes Fatale: Feminism, Film Theory, Psychoanalysis* (London / New York: Routledge, 1991) 165.
129 Ibid., 195.
130 See ibid., 165.
131 Ibid., 193.
132 Ibid., 190.

by Lenny at one point as "a piece of somebody's life"[133]– they also imply a radical alienation in the 'recording' subjectivity from its perceptions and experiences: The eye of the 'I' that knowingly *is* the camera, the ear of the 'I' that knowingly *records* a soundtrack, and the touch of the 'I' that knowingly *produces* a tradable sensual experience transform the living organism into an assemblage of prosthetic devices, and, ultimately, signify the subject's absence from his or her own life. While this alienation seems to affect anybody who consents to functioning as a living recorder in *Strange Days*, the film clearly conveys that it is mostly men who, wearing the device, record and sell pieces of other people's lives for economic profit, and it is women who are objectified and whose lives are being sold, sometimes without them even noticing it. Evidently, the black-marketing of the SQUID technology mirrors and even reinforces the dominant economic and gendered hierarchies of the symbolic order regulating *Strange Days'* diegetic society.

It is no surprise, then, and in keeping with the concern of feminist avant-garde-cinema with the deconstruction and interrogation of the phallocentric

---

133 Significantly, this formulaic praise is an advertisement not only within the diegetic world of *Strange Days*, but also in the official Twentieth Century Fox trailer version that has been "approved for all Audiences by the Motion Picture Association of America"(see "*Strange Days* Teaser," 20th Century Fox (22 Apr. 2008) Web, 15 Febr. 2011. *<http://www.youtube.com/watch?v=s0zaqWQiXG8&feature=related>*. While using diegetic clips and images of a film may be a production firm's usual strategy and part of any cinematic advertising campaign, it is noteworthy that in this version of a trailer for *Strange Days*, it is not the original diegetic situation in which we see SQUID-disc dealer Lenny Nero who wants to sell his "forbidden fruit." In this trailer version the counterparts whom Lenny addresses in the original diegetic scenes have been eliminated, so that only the shots showing Lenny Nero's intensely seductive sales promotion remain. Thus decontextualized, these fragmented shots – all extreme close-ups of Ralph Fiennes's face – directly address the audience whose attention and desire they are supposed to solicit. Putting the audience in the position of potential SQUID addicts, the editing not only mimics the now-you-see-it-now-you-don't-aesthetics of TV-ads, but identifies Hollywood with the same concept of a seductive and immoral wish-fulfilling machine as the wire-tripping enabled by SQUID. As a paratextual seduction, this trailer navigates audience expectations and reception attitudes towards *Strange Days* as a dangerous, illicit product, and pointedly charges the consumption of a movie with connotations of a grittily glamorous incrimination. Moreover, while pretentiously flaunting critical self-reflexivity, it simultaneously adds to and capitalizes on Bigelow's image as "Hollywood Transgressor."

cinematic production of sexual difference that *Strange Days* casts men as the main clientele of SQUID-clip consumption and thus addresses the male gaze as constitutive of a dominant masculine subjectivity. Notably, the film's female protagonists either categorically reject the concept (like Lenny's African American friend Mace), or, in two instances, are forced by men to wear the recording headset in the framework of intricate exploitation schemes, within which their experience of debasement, rape, horror, and – in the instance of Iris – even death is multiplied as they are simultaneously "wired" to the SQUID device of their violent, masculine tormentor. What Iris and, at the end of the film, Faith are forced to go through in the framework of this elaborately vicious arrangement is their own suffering *and* the lust it induces in the male perpetrator by way of a SQUID circuit that superimposes the affective 'reality' of both positions.

Compared to these exploitation schemes, the Faith-recording and its re-living by Lenny appear harmless. With the retreat to his den and his own romantic memories signifying within the plot a regressive and recreational intermission, both Lenny's 'production' and consumption of the clip seem to involve neither risk nor exploitation. Obviously recorded with mutual consent, the clip clearly displays Faith's exaggerated and conspicuous posing as a provocative compliance with Lenny's male voyeurism that she appears to enjoy and that further inspires her performance. There is no discernable discomfort in her posing for Lenny, and she needs no male authority to give her stage directions.[134] On the contrary, in the first part of the clip, the playful skating lesson, Faith mockingly plays the encouraging mother guiding her 'baby's' insecure first steps, and, however unconvincing her performance of the good and soothing mother may appear to the extra-diegetic audience, the childlike happiness on Lenny's face confirms the enticing effect it has on him. Similarly, the significant change in Faith's performance after the fast-forward induced ellipsis, when the seduction turns unambiguously sexual, is reflected in the almost ecstatic arousal on Lenny' face and the involuntarily groping movements of his hands as he re-lives the moment, although, obvious to extra-diegetic spectators of the scene, a form of deception is going on.

What Bigelow clearly evokes in the scene is the figure of the *femme fatale*, that stereotypical, enigmatic 'deadly woman' "who destroys the hero, and ultimately herself with her monstrous desires,"[135] a female figure that has always occupied a central place in cinematic representation, particularly in the film noir.

---

134 See Doane, *Femme Fatales*, 166 -167.
135 Yvonne Tasker, Spec*tacular Bodies: Gender, Genre, and the Action Cinema* (London and New York: Routledge, 1993) 150.

Faith's assuming of "a 'mask of feminity' in order to become photographable (filmable) as though femininity were synonymous with the pose,"[136] as well as her "overrepresented,"[137] gleaming white body certainly convey the secret and the threat represented by the *femme fatale* in the film noir. If, at first glance, the skating lesson-part of the clip seems incompatible with this role of the *femme fatale* that signifies, after all, "the antithesis of the maternal,"[138] it can be argued that it is exactly Faith's unconvincing parody of the maternal that calculatedly enhances and underlines her dubious *femme fatale* identity, while her seductive body language pointedly betrays the artificiality of her masking performance. With its foregrounding of a female performativity that cannot be anything but duplicitous, the Faith-clip scene thus fits in with *Strange Days'* bleak film noir aesthetics in general, and with Lenny Nero's equally film noir inspired, melancholic ex-cop-turned-drug-dealer existence and nostalgia[139] in particular.

Even more important, Faith's identification with the *femme fatale* stereotype ties in with the salience of the theme of 'seeing' in the clip. Read against the background of the relevance of the *femme fatale* stereotype to a cinematic discourse on vision and truth, the visual instability marking the SQUID clips appears as an epistemological equivalent to the destabilizing threat of deception that the *femme fatale* poses according to her connotations. The stagger and sway of the Faith-clip images signal an already weakened perceiving male subjectivity whose looking and watching will not necessarily amount to seeing the truth, an epistemological gap poignantly underlined by Lenny's explicit desire to "watch and see." Significantly, this desire is articulated in front of a mirror, where Lenny is watching himself standing behind Faith and tenderly drying her with a towel. It is the only instance in the Faith-clip, where the spectator actually sees Lenny – notably at a moment in which Lenny's admiring gaze at Faith is reflected by the mirror in a deluding image of shared identity and togetherness. Doubly misleading, the image reflected by the mirror not only confirms Lenny's fantasy of Faith and himself as lovers, but, by assuming the function of a stable reverse shot, complementing the shaky SQUID-recorded POV-images, purports the illusion of Lenny as a coherent subjectivity whose identity is stabilized and corroborated in and by the act of voyeuristic fetishization.[140]

---

136 Doane, *Femmes Fatales*, 166-167.
137 Ibid., 2.
138 Ibid.
139 See Paul Schrader, "Notes on the Film Noir," The Film Genre Reader II, ed. Barry Keith Grant (Austin: U of Texas P, 1995), 213-226.
140 See Doane, *Femmes Fatales*, 165.

Besides being a comment on the "lure and trap"[141] of both cinematic vision and the *femme fatale*, the deceptively coherent image of the mirror shot enhances the effect of SQUID-related instability and epitomizes the climax of a discourse on confidence and belief that is essential to the film's speculation on a near future political-economic subjectivity. A closer look at the contextual situated-ness of the Faith-clip in the plot suggests that its narrative function is neither limited to an invocation of a conventionalized generic stereotype nor restricted to an illustration of that precarious male perspective associated with the crisis of masculinity characterizing the Reagan era.[142] Rather, read in light of *Strange Days'* economic discourse, the use of the *femme fatale* stereotype and its conjunction with the gendered discourse on vision in the scene of the Faith-clip become visible as a boldly allegoric negotiation of a crisis of confidence inherent to a gendered concept of speculation originating in a late-nineteenth century discourse and the classical economic fiction of 'rational economic man.'

Preceded by Lenny's exposition as a cunningly speculating dealer and commissioner of custom made SQUID clips, and followed by a scene showing Lenny's engagement with a customer in a highly speculative sales pitch, his retreat to his apartment and his regression to a nostalgic re-living of the Faith-clip represent a disruption in an otherwise coherent narrative. With its melancholy atmosphere and display of affective vulnerability, the scene clearly belies the narrative of the parasitic speculator as the cool agent of rational choice who calculatingly exploits and capitalizes on the risks of others. It thus calls into question the idealized economic fiction of the male, yet neutralized *homo oeconomicus* who has rid himself of any particular features that might be in the way of a cool and unaffected assessment of the market.[143]

Although Lenny is not a speculator at the stock market and does not deal in shares, his actions are certainly guided by the logic of "the something for nothing"[144] that has been identified as the central feature of the speculator by late-nineteenth and early-twentieth century critics of the money market business. Like the stock market speculator, he lives and capitalizes on the products of others, while returning only a minimum of a fair equivalent. And like the stock

---

141 Ibid. 196. Doane contends that "much of the work of the contemporary independent cinema is [...] predicated upon a slippage – a movement from the idea that vision is threatened to the notion that vision itself is threatening. It is the image itself which is a lure and trap."

142 See Susan Jeffords, *Hard Bodies: Hollywood Masculinity in the Reagan Era* (New Brunswick: Rutgers UP, 1994).

143 See Stäheli, *Spektakuläre Spekulationen*, 266.

144 Findlay qtd. in Stäheli, *Spektakuläre Spekulationen*, 184.

market speculator, Lenny is compelled to keenly observe the market in order to foresee and cater to the contingent, and often unarticulated desires of his customers.

Notably, Lenny presents only the latter part of these complex professional challenges in the scene of the sales talk following the Faith-clip scene, when he solicits his customer's trust with the words: "You can trust me, 'cause I'm your priest, I'm your shrink, I'm your main connection to the switchboard of the soul, I'm your magic man, I'm the Santa Claus of the subconscious." Casting himself as the economically disinterested provider of a wish-fulfilling machine and the risky "forbidden fruit" whose danger-less consumption it enables, and foregrounding a spiritual, intuitive, and empathetic quality of his service, Lenny's advertisement-line is multiply coded. It betrays a keen and accurate assessment of the psychological needs of the self-governing subject in *Strange Days'* diegetic society that neither provides social cohesion nor an ethical common ground for the individual who has to manage his or her own highly individualized risk with the hired support of experts like 'shrinks.' This subtle subtext is even carried further with the words 'priest' and 'Santa Claus' boldly pointing to the idea of pastoral care and – especially when contextualized with the Santa Claus mugging episode at the beginning of the film – its commercialization and depletion of Christian values. Moreover, with their strikingly parallel construction, the five sub-clauses of the statement pointedly suggest and promise the 'magic' fulfillment of a plethora of affective desires while withholding anything that could point to the rational calculation behind such a phrasing.

Most important, however, Lenny's advertising self-description explicitly picks up the discourse on trust and confidence that is at the center of the Faith-clip scene. While tying in with the general cultural climate of normalized suspicion in *Strange Days'* diegetic L.A., the crisis of confidence negotiated in the elaborate Faith-clip scene displays a more specifically economic meaning when contextualized with the gendered scripts of speculation described by Urs Stäheli. Stäheli traces what he calls the drama of a rationally calculating *homo oeconomicus* who is confronted with a ubiquitous logic of female coded, irrational masses in a late-nineteenth century classical economic discourse. In order to be successful, the ideal-typical speculator and economic man cast by the authors of this discourse is compelled to coolly observe the masses and their 'hysterical' economic behavior, while bracing himself against seduction by their wayward and irrational movements. Moreover, although universally and unambiguously cast as male, the classical economic speculator needs to discipline and neutralize himself with the help of procedures of self-mastery aimed at securing his practice of cool deliberation which he needs in order keep intact his distinction from the irrational masses.[145]

What emerges from the framework of this gendered and eroticized discourse on the psychology of money market dynamics is a surprisingly detailed, tangible and clear-cut image of the ideal-typical speculator. A coolly calculating, self-denying and somewhat disembodied male subject, the speculator oscillates between constant market observation and a marked auto-centrism that makes him susceptible to depression, euphoria or melancholia. It is this psycho-pathological disposition, reflected in a host of psycho-pathological vocabulary used in late- nineteenth-/early-twentieth-century descriptions of the speculator that, according to Urs Stäheli, suggests that the neutralized universality of this ideal-typical figure is a *desideratum* whose programmatic articulation already implies its limits, if not its failure. Not only is the speculator predestined to become a paralyzed melancholic, according to the subtext of these programmatic descriptions, but, as the simultaneous emergence of female metaphors and allegories of speculation suggests, he must also remain a man with heterosexual desires.

It is easy, against this background, to recognize features of the speculator in Lenny Nero. His detached acquisition, shrewd commissioning, and cunning marketing strategies certainly rely on a keen and cool observation of the mass-market from which he stays at a safe distance. When asked about his outlandish "Armani" designer clothes, he replies, "It's the only thing that's between me and the jungle." Yet this distinction is precarious as it relies on signs and labels that, like counterfeited banknotes and those withdrawn from economic circulation, have lost their referentiality. *Strange Days'* dramaturgy leaves no doubt that Lenny's "Armani" clothes cannot protect him as they cover a body too weak to defend itself in the jungle of the film's diegetic market place. In a similar way, Lenny's fake gold Rolex watch emblematically signifies a loss of the referentiality of signs in the de-materialized hyper-fictional economic era of the

---

145 See Stäheli, *Spektakuläre Spekulation*, 266. Stäheli particularly focuses on the figure of the "contrarian" speculator, whose observation of and distinction from the irrational masses is even more explicitly constitutive to his subjectivity, since his risk and profit depend on his ability to make anti-cyclic decisions. The difference between this very particular figure and the more general descriptions of the ideal-typical speculator that mark the new economic heyday of the stockmarket is only gradual. Within the scope of the present study, it is more important and noteworthy – and Stäheli explicitly points to this nexus – how exercises in self-mastery anticipate the self-technologies and the prudentialism that characterize the neoliberal subject a century later, 232.

late twentieth century. With its imitation gold almost explicitly evoking the loss of the gold-standard as the reliable measurement of value of a century ago, Lenny's watch and his belief in its mystical powers of economic persuasion appear like fossils in a highly de-referentialized, post- gold-standard economic environment.

It is no accident, then, that, in the close-up shots showing Lenny's preparation for the consumption of the Faith-clip, his watch is pointedly exposed as he gets ready to start the clip. In two shots the camera appears to dwell on the watch and thus connects the nostalgia for a world of referentiality and long-gone values to the private nostalgia Lenny indulges in. More important, the pointed exhibition of the fake Rolex invokes the theme of trust and confidence that the Faith-clip programmatically negotiates and sets the tone for the duplicitous performance of Faith, whose name already indicates a figurative potential exceeding the conventionalized film noir enigma of the *femme fatale*.

If Lenny Nero can be read as the speculator whose detached and rational observation of the masses and their desires is germane to his success, and whose retreat to his apartment exemplifies one of those self-mastering measures of regression and introspection that the speculator needs after excessive contact with the masses, the ensuing Faith-clip reveals an allegoric quality whose consistent correlation with the gendered late-nineteenth/early-twentieth- century scripts of speculation, described by Stäheli et al., is surprising. Contextualized with these scripts, *Strange Days'* representation of Faith becomes visible as one of those highly sexualized and feminized metaphors of speculation that the economic semantics dominant in reflections on the newly emerging money market business have juxtaposed in opposition to the male speculator. Tellingly named "Cyn(thia) Speculation" or "Lady Credit," and attributed with an abundance of beauty, charm and intelligence, speculation is cast by these semantics as a seductive, vamp-like prostitute who, after soliciting trust, calculatingly deceives and manipulates her suitors into venturing dangerous investments. With its connotations of a treacherous surface hiding a cunning internal wickedness, the semantics used to describe "Cyn Speculation" and "Lady Credit" obviously tap the same imagery of a dangerous beauty and sinful (as phonetically conveyed by the abbreviation 'Cyn') female sexuality as the *femme fatale* stereotype discussed above.

With Faith's scanty and glittery costumes exposing and highlighting the almost dazzling white surface of her body throughout the film, *Strange Days'* visual discourse foregrounds a superficiality in Faith's charms that corresponds to the allegoric casting of the body of speculation as a "mere empty shell."[146] This staging of Faith's body as a hollow and superficial 'retinal fetish' is subtly, yet unmistakably augmented by the seemingly casual depiction of her habit of washing by splashing water onto her sweaty body – a habit that, introduced in the Faith-clip, becomes recognizable as such when Lenny meets her backstage after her performance at the "Retinal Fetish Club." Conjoining connotations of a seductive and enticing bodily presence and a sinful uncleanliness, this visualizing of a smeary superficiality is, significantly, contextualized in both instances with a display of Faith's merciless and unsympathetic cruelty towards Lenny, a cruelty that exposes the excessive contingency of her charms.

Tying in with this visual staging of the promise and the lure of her body as the vessel of a bountiful, if contingent potential, is Faith's rock singer identity. Her equally melodramatic and stereotypical back-story of the desperate, yet talented young drug addict hoping to 'make it' as a rock-star in L.A. adds some late-twentieth-century local color to the late-nineteenth-century imagery of a seductive Lady Credit. Still catering to the semantic construction of credit as a "flighty young maiden,"[147] this representation of Faith as an up-and-coming rock-star motivates her strategic change of lovers within a pattern of artistic patronage: Having left Lenny Nero for musical producer Philo Gant, and ending up with the cunning Max Peltier at the end of the film, Faith's series of lovers within *Strange Days*' narrow diegetic time frame indicates that what Faith demands from her lovers is faith itself, i.e. the recognition of and the belief in her potential. Lenny Nero, Philo Gant, and Max Peltier become visible, at this point, as different and, above all, differently successful models of the speculating *homo oeconomicus* whose rational choice and cool deliberation supposedly enable a reliable assessment of the future prosperity of his investments.

Quite in accordance with the late-nineteenth-century semantics of speculation, Faith's seduction – her soliciting of the confidence and the investment of a succession of male speculators – is a precarious game. It requires a speculator who is susceptible to her charms – the charms of speculation – yet one who has to discipline, control and master himself in order to resist delusion by the equally female coded market. With the Faith-clip showing how the male subject of speculation is constituted in the act of the voyeuristic fetishization of a

---

146 Robert Smitley qtd. in Stäheli, *Spektakuläre Spekulationen*, 268. Stäheli quotes from Smitley's 1933 monograph *Popular Financial Delusions,* a guidebook whose purpose of defending the stock market against popular prejudice appears to be inconsistent and adversely affected by Smitley's recourse to the sexualized allegory of 'Cyn Speculation.' See Stäheli, 269.

147 See Stäheli, *Spektakuläre Spekulation*, 271.

hyper-feminine and seductive "Lady Credit," the scene of its reception clearly stages this subject as weakened and paralyzed by melancholia. Although Lenny Nero has been left by Lady Credit who, in keeping with her flighty connotations, has bestowed favors on another, more promising speculator, his continuing affective infatuation with her attractions enduringly impairs his capacity of *seeing*, and thus the capacity that is crucial to a successful observation of the market. Having become a sentimental melancholic after Faith has left him, and still blinded by the radiant surface of her body, Lenny is unable to see the deception in the performance of a Lady Credit whose excessive contingency multiplies in a de-referentialized economy of fiat money and post-gold-standard economics. Clearly, Lenny Nero is no longer a 'man of rational choice' and his materialist fetishization of the signs and symbols of an outdated economic value system signals that he is neither well adapted to the ubiquitous and thoroughly dematerialized market economics that define *Strange Days'* diegetic society.

Conjoining the discourse on cinematic vision, the film noir and the *femme fatale* in a boldly gendered allegory of the male coded speculator's seduction by a female coded epitome of speculation, the Faith-clip scene elaborately illuminates Lenny's 'loss of Faith' as a fundamental crisis of confidence. Read in light of the film's economic discourse, this crisis of confidence designates the failure of a political-economic subjectivity that has become obsolete. It unmistakably shows the classical economic model of 'rational economic man' as weakened and ill-equipped for a political culture whose ubiquitous market rationality does not allow for a recreational retreat from the market.

Interestingly, Bigelow further comments on the scope of destabilization in Lenny's subjectivity immediately after the Faith-clip scene and subtly insinuates its relation to a complex discourse on race and gender. When Lenny is shown as he is awakened by the alarm-mode of the TV-set, it is the above mentioned news report on the murder of Jeriko One that is on. Its images are intercut with images of Lenny slowly getting up and dressed for business. While the diegetic report on the murder of the black rap singer aestheticizes and commodifies the one political subject of the film engaging in critical public discourse, the spectator sees Lenny's soft white body in his underpants languidly moving to the fridge, opening the deep-freeze compartment and taking out a red, white and blue popsicle. With Lenny dreamily, yet intensely sucking the red upper part of the oblong, phallic popsicle throughout the rest of the scene, Bigelow makes a point of flaunting Lenny's provocative disinterest in the murder report. Besides its connotations of political indifference and childish regression, the sexual subtext of this pointedly lascivious consumption of a popsicle suggests a no longer unambiguously heterosexual orientation in a man, whose gender will be presented as precarious from that point on throughout the film. The scene thus further contributes to a deconstruction of the economic fiction of a universally masculine, rational economic subject whose intense psychological interaction with the market is imagined to be propelled by universally heterosexual drives.

Even more important, the intricate interplay between the news footage on Jeriko One and the erotic undercurrent in Lenny's indulgence in the popsicle subtly suggests a relation between the passive compliance of a political subject reduced to mere libidinal consumption of U.S.-American goods and the subtle racism of a U.S.-American multiculturalism that fetishizes and commodifies the fixed positions of minoritized identity.[148] Doubly silenced by the execution-style murder and the news report, Jeriko One and his political intervention are to be consumed like a popsicle by a political subject that is in turn silenced by its reduction to a compliant economic function. In contextualizing this silencing of Lenny Nero with the violent, execution-style silencing of Jeriko One and his outspoken critical stance Bigelow sets the stage for the introduction of Mace.

2.5 BECOMING MACE

Pointedly contrasting Faith's seductive and treacherous *femme fatale* character, Lenny Nero's African American friend Lornette "Mace" Mason (Angela Bassett) is cast as the epitome of a moral strength and reliability that is reflected in her striking physical power. Easily recognizable as one of the doublings familiar from earlier Bigelow films "in which monstrous characters or creatures echo and parody the heroes and heroines with which we are called to identify,"[149] Mace, however, does not merely invite identification by embodying a moral rectitude that further highlights Faith's immorality. A closer reading reveals that her character, although not at the center of the plot, is intricately designed as a model of the self-governing, moral-political subject that is central to the film's diegetic political culture.

---

148 See Brian Carr, "*Strange Days* and the Subject of Mobility," *Camera Obscura 50* 17.2 (2002): 191-217. Discussing a potential reading of the experiences enabled by SQUID in the sense of Kaja Silverman's "emphasis on identification as a journey, abduction, and transformation of the normative subject," Brian Carr critically interrogates a contemporary tendency to theorize "mobility, estrangement, or crossing" as "essentially progressive" that is "logically similar" to "commodified versions of contemporary multiculturalism." (208-209).

149 Tasker, *Spectacular Bodies*, 156.

It is noteworthy and emphatic of this centrality to *Strange Days'* political subtext that Mace is the only protagonist throughout the film that Bigelow endows with a history by way of a genuine flashback.[150] Motivated by a sentimental moment between Mace, who loves Lenny, and Lenny, who considers Mace a female buddy, the flashback in which Mace remembers their first encounter is conclusive, even though it lasts only thirty seconds. As one of the film's few sequences that are set in broad daylight, it shows an utterly distraught, younger Mace, who, desperately running towards her home, watches helplessly as her husband gets arrested by an LAPD officer in front of the house. After stopping briefly and furiously slapping her handcuffed husband, Mace continues to run into the house anxiously yelling her young son's name. Eventually, she finds the approximately six-year-old Xander in his room together with Lenny Nero, who, wearing an LAPD uniform, is reading to Xander from a children's book. The flashback ends with the image of the child sweetly and composedly introducing his newly found friend, the empathetic LAPD cop Lenny Nero, to his relieved mother.

While the somewhat sentimental drama presented by this short flashback sequence fails to deliver a satisfying explanation for Mace's indulgent and unwavering romantic love for Lenny, and thus contributes to a crisis in credibility in particular affecting the reception of *Strange Days'* oft-criticized ending, it is immensely conclusive with regard to the political subjectivity it depicts. Instead of just delivering the background to a romanticized interracial love story, the flashback supplies images of a younger Mace, whose short pink waitress uniform and straightened bobbed hair, together with the uncontrollable emotional turmoil openly displayed by her body language conjure a constructed, assimilated feminity sharply contrasting the equally constructed African Americanized masculinity of Mace's action heroine role in the film's diegetic present. Contextualized with Mace's tough and strong body and stance throughout the rest of the film, the flashback can be read as representing the 'before'-part of a classic makeover story which – while skipping the actual

---

150   See Christina Lane, "The Strange Days of Kathryn Bigelow and James Cameron," *The Cinema of Kathryn Bigelow: Hollywood Transgressor* Eds. Deborah Jermyn and Sean Redmond (London/ New York: Wallflower Press, 2003) 178 -197, 192. Lane interprets the "subjective camerawork" of the flashback as identifying Mace's "visual field with authenticity and authority." (193) Different from authors like Paul Gormley who reads Bigelow's emphasis on Mace's affinity to 'the real' as an alignment (and thus an epistemological privileging) of African American culture with 'authenticity,' Lane focuses on Bigelow's and screen writer Jay Cocks's elaboration of Mace's character as a more differentiated political comment.

makeover process – highlights the spectacular 'after'-images as the result of an enormous investment of time, labor and self- discipline.

With the help of the flashback sequence, Bigelow implies the story of a 'toughening up,' a hardening of both muscles and attitude, and thus, without actually telling that story, adds a political dimension to the stereotype of the action film heroine that Mace embodies and simultaneously exceeds. Sleek and neutralized from top to toe, sporting tight cornrows and an austere black and white driver's uniform, Mace is introduced to *Strange Days'* audience as Lenny's friend who comes to the rescue whenever Lenny is in need of help. As a bodyguard and driver employed, significantly, with a private security firm, Mace has to combine physical strength with social constraint; she is trained in close combat and keeps her cool in the most critical and dangerous situations, quite contrary to Lenny, who badly needs her physical and moral support. Read in light of the flashback sequence, this depiction implies that fundamental changes must have happened in the time preceding the film's diegetic present.

As in the Faith-clip sequence, where Lenny Nero's 'decline' to a female coded passivity is cast very subtly as a speculation-induced crisis of confidence and the paralyzed melancholia of an ill-adapted, outdated model of economic man, the film equally subtly insinuates a political paradigm change at the bottom of Mace's transformation. Both her job and her hard-bodied muscularity can be read as symptoms of and responses to a generalized hardening and 'toughening up' of the social in a neoliberal political culture that prioritizes market concerns, favors individualized market solutions to – and thus the de-politicization of – social and political problems, and in which risk functions as a rationality of governance on both the level of the state and the individual. Not only must security in this culture be hired from private entrepreneurs, who capitalize on a generalized climate of paranoia, but the individual is compelled to prudently apply an entrepreneurial self-management that requires interminable, self-improving efforts exempting neither soul, nor mind or body.

Mace's outward austerity and stern facial expression, while being part of her new identity as a professional bodyguard and driver of wealthy, risk-avoiding clients, clearly convey the strain of a constant managerial care of the self, a care made necessary by a retreat of the state from the care for others. Bigelow emphasizes how this retreat imposes a burden especially on the most marginalized of political subjects in late-twentieth-century U.S.-American political culture with the help of an interesting chiastic movement that suggests an exchange of an institutionalized paternal for an individualized maternal form of care: while the flashback scene shows Mace as a pointedly feminine, 'hysterical' black mother and then-cop Lenny Nero as the epitome of white male authority blending features of the pastoral and the paternal, the Mace- Lenny figuration at the beginning of *Strange Days*' suggests a significant role reversal: Mace is not only introduced as a toughened African American 'hard body,' but, more specifically, as a toughened, single African American mother who both faces and is bent on fighting the risk of a social decline that preemptive calculation – another characteristic of risk rationality in neoliberal culture – statistically associates with her demographic group.[151] Lenny Nero, the dominant culture's white, male, heterosexual measure of all things, on the other hand, has lost all authority together with his ability for rational deliberation, and appears passive and weakened.

The subversive political subtext that this back-story of a role reversal seems to convey gets complicated, however, on a closer reading of the striking moral attitude that Bigelow attributes to Mace's character throughout the film. To begin with, it is noteworthy how restrained the seemingly spectacular bodily strength corresponding to this strict moral attitude appears upon close scrutiny. Reading Bigelow's casting of a black woman as the muscular sidekick of her film's weakened white hero with Yvonne Tasker, *Strange Days*' construction of gender and sexuality through racial discourse becomes visible as tamed by generic convention. Tasker, in her seminal work on gender and the action cinema, names three conventionalized strategies of the action movie genre which "castrate" threatening images of a black, masculine, muscular body that the hegemonic white culture has constructed as hyper-sexualized and inherently violent: first, the "casting of black and Asian women as sidekicks to the white hero" with the "already castrated" woman confirming the "white hero's difference and strength;" second, the comic image that "undermines notions of masculine power," and third, a narrative leading the white hero into "situations in which he is subjected to torture and suffering."[152]

It becomes evident, at this point, that Bigelow's negotiation of all three of these conventions produces Mace's body as inherently compromised and castrated by gender and race; in addition it is ironically fractured by Lenny's weakness and the comedy of the role reversal between Mace and Lenny. Accordingly, the action scenes in which Mace rescues Lenny appear to revel in her keen alertness and the precision of her martial arts techniques rather than a display of the muscularity of her body that is fully visible only in the final scene,

---

151 See Robert Castel, "From Dangerousness to Risk," *The Foucault Effect: Studies in Governmentality*, eds. Graham Burchell, et al. (Chicago: Chicago UP, 1991).

152 Yvonne Tasker, *Spectacular Bodies: Gender, Genre and the Action Cinema* (London / New York: Routledge, 1993) 40-41.

in which Mace is wearing a short and slinky black dress, notably, with a 'phallic' handgun strapped to her inner thigh.

With her body strikingly contained by her high-necked driver's suit in most of the scenes, Mace's physical strength is thus staged as a product of hard work, self-discipline and, above all, an unfaltering moral rectitude rather than an untamable 'hyper-sexual' muscularity. Contrary to the decidedly racialized and gendered connotations of black, masculine, physical strength, Mace is presented as neutralized rather than masculinized, and, given the similarity of her austere black and white driver's suit to a priestly robe, is even associated with notions of purity and sacrality in many scenes. If, as Yvonne Tasker writes, the body of the action heroine is "almost the last certain territory of the action narrative" and "the sole narrative space that is safe," the religious undertones in Bigelow's depiction of Mace's body certainly castrate that body even further by endowing it with connotations of a subtle moral-political conversion narrative and casting its mission as a war against a moral cesspool.

In keeping with the visual clues, the discourse on Mace's affinity to morals rather than muscles is picked up by her text that further points to the specific quality of Mace's stern morality. Significantly, the first shot of Mace in *Strange Days* is an extreme close-up of her mouth as she answers Lenny's emergency phone call. With the camera capturing even the slightest twitch of a muscle in Mace's lips, Bigelow subtly highlights and enforces notions of restraint and self-control resonating in the question that is Mace's reaction to Lenny's call, before he can even begin to tell her his reason for calling: "So, Lenny what happened to your car *this* time?" Magnified by the close-up and enhanced by the matt red color of her lipstick, the image of Mace's twitching lips introduces her character as struggling for control over a paradox blend of emotions. Subtly relating connotations of a repressed erotic tension to the forced calm and patience habitually mustered by mothers of notoriously wayward children, Bigelow artfully establishes the emotional asymmetry associated with unrequited love, while simultaneously accentuating how that asymmetry is counteracted and inverted by Mace's attitude of moral superiority. Even more important, by insinuating at this very early point in the narrative that Lenny Nero's sloppy morals serve not merely as the contrasting backdrop to Mace's moral rigor, but are the target and center of her moral mission, Bigelow intricately links her film's discourse on love to its discourse on a very special political agenda.

The reprimanding, yet indulgent tone set by this first shot of Mace and the subsequent sequence, in which Mace is further introduced as a reliable and law-abiding citizen, marks the ironic banter of Lenny's and Mace's dialogues throughout the film. In these dialogues, Bigelow pointedly and without exception plays off Lenny's lack of values against Mace's value conservatism. While it might be easy, given the comedy of this figuration, to overlook the moral message, a closer look reveals this message to be surprisingly political. It is a call to order when Mace reminds Lenny that the predicaments he constantly finds himself in result from his disrespect of a moral code of conduct. It is a critique of his primitive version of economic self-interest, when she rejects his offer to pay her for driving him to the "Retinal Fetish Club" by reminding him: "This may be a hard concept for you, but friends don't have to pay their friends."[153] And it is an attack against Lenny's careless self-neglect and evident lack of prudentialism when Mace, furious because Lenny made her "lose it in front of a client," accuses him:

Your ass is always broke, you go from one score to the next, and you're getting strung out ... It's *your* brain, so you do whatever it is you wanna do with it, but not on my watch. I got a child, I got rent, and I got an ex-husband doin' hard time who doesn't send me a dime of support. I'm just tryin' to hold on.

It is the tough stance on Lenny's SQUID abuse in this emotional sally that helps to identify more precisely Mace's ideological position. While underlining the discipline that her precarious economic situation requires, her responsibility as a single mother, and her selfless love for Lenny, Mace's critique is targeted at a lifestyle in which neither discipline, nor responsibility or altruistic love have a place. Already at this point, Bigelow leaves no doubt that the values promoted and represented by Mace are, strikingly, the family values generally associated with the conservatism of an American Right, and that her concern basically expresses a general "angst about the declining or crumbling status of morality within the west"[154] that Wendy Brown locates at the core of contemporary American neo-conservatism.

---

153 Notably, the "hard concept" that Mace refers to goes back to the Old Testament. With reference to the Fifth Book of Moses which forbids the charging of interest when money is being lent among brothers, but explicitly allows it when the exchange involves 'only' strangers, Dirk Baecker points to the necessity that came with the emergence of a market economy to develop a universal ethical code that licensed the charging of interest from someone to whom one is closely related by brotherly love. See "Volkszählung," *Kapitalismus als Religion*, ed.. Dirk Baecker (Berlin: Kulturverlag Kadmos, 2009) 265 -282, 267. In the case of Mace, this reference to a concept rooted in the Old Testament further illuminates her moral-religious affiliation.

154 Brown, "Neoliberalism, Neoconservatism, and De-Democratization," 697.

Mace's stern rejection of the SQUID technology that Bigelow foregrounds throughout *Strange Days'* narrative particularly illustrates this notion of a neoconservative trait in Mace's political subjectivity, a trait that seems incompatible, at first glance, with the neoliberal subtext suggested by the flashback scene. While it is true that Mace, as Paul Gormley states, "knows the difference between 'playback' and real life and 'real-time,'"[155] and is thus cast in stark contrast to Lenny, whose nostalgic use of SQUID might be read as an indication of the dominant white culture's propensity for an "empty simulation of life,"[156] the film certainly does not associate her critical stance on SQUID with the "construction of black American culture as cool and hip" or "the hipness that black culture signifies."[157] On the contrary, resonating in Mace's categorical rejection of SQUID is a decidedly 'uncool' indignation and a rigid, conservative attitude strikingly echoing the concept of 'zero tolerance' that originated in a 1960s U.S. American environmental discourse, and that has served as a policy in increasingly conservative contexts ever since. Tracing the 'zero tolerance'-concept as a defining attitude in a succession of U.S. American domestic and international 'wars' (against cancer, against crime, and against terror), as well as its political shift from left to right, Jonathan Simon concludes:

The Bush [sen., S.W.] Presidency highlighted the potential for zero tolerance from the highest level. This example has been followed by the application of the concept farther and farther from its original entry point of toxic chemicals and drugs. Its promoters are not shy in taking exactly the view that our framework suggests, i.e. that zero tolerance is not so much a policy as a mentality of governance.[158]

Read against this background, Mace's rigorous 'zero tolerance-,' "just-say-no-stance"[159] on SQUID becomes visible as the symptom of a moral behaviorism

---

155 Paul Gormley, "Trashing Whiteness: *Pulp Fiction, Se7en, Strange Days* and Articulating Affect," *Angelaki: Journal of the Theoretical Humanities* 6.1 (2011): 155-171, 167.
156 Ibid.
157 Ibid.
158 Jonathan Simon, "Choosing our Wars, Transforming Governance: Cancer. Crime, and Terror," *Risk and the War on Terror*, eds. Louise Amoore and Marieke de Goede (London / New York: Routledge, 2008) 79 -96, 88.
159 The "just-say-no"-formula was coined by First Lady Nancy Reagan. It restates the Reagan administration's zero-tolerance policy against drugs and crime as a rule for individual behavior. See Simon, "Choosing our Wars," 87.

that, while targeted at fighting "dealers who put poison in our society,"[160] compliantly responds to the "strong, state-led and legislated moral-political vision" that is the hallmark of neo-conservatism, according to Wendy Brown. Delineating the basic features of neo-conservative ideology, Brown writes:

The open affirmation of moralized state power in the domestic and international sphere is what sets off neoconservatism from an older conservatism, what makes it *neo*. [...] Unlike its predecessor, it is animated by an overtly avowed power drive, by angst about the declining or crumbling status of morality, and by a concomitant moralization of a certain imaginary of the west and its values. Thus while many neoconservatives decry the 'social engineering' they attribute to socialism and liberal democratic egalitarian projects such as affirmative action, integration, and poverty reduction, neoconservatism no more rejects state-led behaviorism than neoliberalism does. Rather, it identifies the state, including law, with the task of setting the moral-religious compass for society, and indeed for the world.[161]

As Mace's family values and zero-tolerance-stance on SQUID reflect a neo-conservative model of the state's moral-religious authority translated into the moral behavior of its political subject, they seem to contradict and call into question Mace's compliance with the immoral market rationality of neoliberalism suggested by the makeover story and her self-governing prudentialism. In fact, as Wendy Brown emphasizes, neo-conservatism is rooted, at least in part, in resistance to "capitalism's erosion of meaning and morality," and thus seems to clash with neoliberalism's prioritizing of the market and entrepreneurial calculation. Brown convincingly argues, however, that the de-politicization, the de-democratization, and the erosion of moral values that come with the *oikodizee*[162] of the market and the reductive interpellation of the neoliberal subject as an actor of rational economic choice produce a void that, in turn, fosters the subject's susceptibility to the moral authority of neo-conservatism:

---

160 George H.W. Bush qtd. in Simon, "Choosing our Wars," 88.
161 Brown, "Neoliberalism, Neoconservatism, and De-Democratization," 697.
162 Drawing on Gottfried Wilhelm Leibniz's eighteenth-century concept of *theodizee*, Joseph Vogl coins the term *oikodizee* to describe how economic science drew on theology to construe a complex system of legitimation to uphold the idea of a self-regulating market in times of economic crisis. *Das Gespenst des Kapitals* (Berlin: Diaphanes, 2011)

As neoliberalism produces the citizen on the model of the entrepreneur and consumer, it simultaneously makes citizens available to extensive governance and heavy administrative authority. We have already seen that neoliberals themselves have a keen appreciation of the production of certain kinds of subjects and behaviors through market incentives and deterrents. But apart from express governance aims, there's the basic critical and theoretical insight that the choosing subject and the governed subject are far from opposites; individual rational action on one side and state or religious authority on the other, while operating in different semiotic registers, are quite compatible.[163]

It is thus the "state-led behaviorism" of a new political subject produced at the intersection of neoliberal and neo-conservative rationalities that Bigelow's action heroine character represents. While Mace's uncritical and de-politicized stance throughout the first two thirds of *Strange Days* corroborates Brown's notion of a de-democratizing effect of both rationalities on the political subject, Bigelow, however, projects the possibility of a political sea change, a transformation generated in, through and by that political subject, despite and against its internalized moral-political script in the scene in which Mace, finally and against her principles, consents to experiencing a SQUID-clip.

The scene is set on New Year's Eve at the house of Mace's brother in an African American neighborhood, where Mace brings Lenny who feels no longer safe in his own apartment. Bigelow uses the connotations of the risk implicit to the transgression of a white guy entering a black 'hood' to highlight the degree of Lenny's paranoia. By having Mace explain to her friends and relatives "He's with me," she underlines, at the same time, the cultural hermeticism of the African American milieu that Paul Gormley describes as being depicted as 'hip,' 'authentic,' and strongly defined by familial ties throughout the film.[164] Importantly, however, the atmosphere of cheerful familial togetherness and 'hipness' is restricted to this scene and conveyed mainly by racializing stereotypes, such as black rap music and the black extras' exaggerated swagger, back-slapping, and casual style of dress. Particularly Mace's outfit, consisting of black combat pants, a sleeveless belly top, and a broad-shouldered leather jacket with an eye-catching animal print appliqué strikingly contrasts her usual austere driver's uniform.

Thus exposed by music and style the scene stages nothing less than a political awakening. After reluctantly giving in to Lenny Nero, who insists on her watching the clip that Iris has slipped him, Mace experiences with her first SQUID-clip the execution of Jeriko One by LAPD officer Steckler. Physically

---

163 Ibid., 705.
164 Gormley, "Trashing Whiteness," 166 -169.

jolted and emotionally shocked by both the initiation to the medium she has rejected as "porno for wire-heads" only shortly before and the political content conveyed by the clip, Mace is in tears when she reopens her eyes, choking and unable to speak for a few seconds. When she finally speaks – and Bigelow underlines the importance of that moment as a moment of evangelical conversion by Mace's pointed silence and a close-up of her face with its painful expression and tilted posture boldly evoking a Christian *mater dolorosa* iconography – she replies: "I could see the world opening up and swallowing us all." Here the religious theme of millennial apocalypse – explicitly introduced at the beginning of the film with talk radio caller Lorrie's jeremiad on the impending millennial doom and a subtext throughout the film – is picked up and reinterpreted as the signal to yet another moral-political conversion of the de-politicized, political subject that, as the narration subtly and elaborately suggests, has been moulded at the intersection of neoliberal and neo-conservative governance.

It is noteworthy that Bigelow, at this point, not only connects the religious connotations of apocalypse with the religious undertones in her representation of the repressed, 'castrated' sexuality of Mace's body, but foregrounds the biblical meaning of apocalypse as revelation and connects it to the film's discourse on risk as well as its self-reflexive discourse on seeing. Only with the political subject taking the risk of deviation from the script of state-led behaviorism can the revelatory subtext of apocalyptic doom work its mind-altering effect and the political truth be revealed. Bigelow visualizes the degree of risk involved in Mace's decision to watch the clip by having Mace's body language pointedly stage her reluctance to give in to the powers of the medium she has rejected as seductive and poisonous, and the force of will she has to muster in order to overcome this reluctance. At the same time, she unmistakably conveys that this resistance has to be read in the context of political delusion by having Lenny, in preparation of Mace's first playback experience, advise her: "You gotta keep your eyes closed, or otherwise you'll see double." It is one of the scene's political messages that revelation can only be had after the dominant symbolic order's prescribed framework of representation has been blinded out and supplanted by the 'risky' experience of that, which is demonized by that order as poison to society.

And it is in this scene that the SQUID-technology functions as the subversive war machine that Gilles Deleuze and Felix Guattari have described in *A Thousand Plateaus* as being opposed to the "state apparatus, which divests the war machine of its power of metamorphosis."[165] Alienated from its original function as a technology in the service of pastoral power, SQUID, in this scene, induces a process of 'becoming' that promises to undo the rigor of the moral-political scripts of a state-led behaviorism at the busy intersection of neoliberalism and neo-conservatism. Mace's however reluctant succumbing to the danger implied by the forbidden SQUID experience not only makes her 'see,' but triggers, along with the political awakening, a whole-sale transformation that might be captured in Deleuze and Guattari's terms as 'becoming woman' and 'becoming minority.' By encoding connotations of an African Americanized 'savage' belligerenc in Mace's costume in this scene, Bigelow boldly suggests that Mace herself becomes a politicized, revolutionary war machine, a hard-hitting *mace* in the war against the racism and the corruption of the dominant symbolic order.

Yet it is no smooth transformation from the rigid, castrated hard body produced by a fusion of neoliberal and neo-conservative rationalities to the "anthropomorphic assemblage"[166] of a politically empowered, liberating, phallic woman that Bigelow presents in *Strange Days* finale. With both models of political subjectivity encoded in the stereotypes of Christian iconography, images of Mace's body are not only "overdetermined with multiple image histories"[167] of African American racialization and oppression in the U.S., but are, at the same time, defined – and thus limited – by the privileging of mind over matter and the oppression of sexuality implicit to a conservative Christian value system. Even as a war machine Mace remains castrated; she is becoming a 'phallic mother' rather than 'becoming woman.' Only with the phallic support of the hand-gun strapped to her inner thigh can she "transgress the male space of a men's restroom […] to take the destiny of the tape and its possible cultural effects into her own hands."[168] Likewise, only with the authority and by the intervention of white male authority – Deputy Director Palmer Strickland (Josef Sommer) – can the SQUID-clip of the murder of Jeriko One be revealed to the public. Evidently, the hardened black female body in *Strange Days* cannot become a revolutionary mace as it remains tamed and confined by the

---

165 Gilles Deleuze and Felix Guattari, *A Thousand Plateaus: Capitalism and Schizophrenia* (Minneapolis, University of Minnesota Press, 1991) 513.
166 Ibid.
167 Lane, "The Strange Days of Kathryn Bigelow and James Cameron," 195.
168 Ibid.

"boundary-maintaining images"[169] of religious iconography and psychoanalytic tropes.

2.6 THE RISK NOT TAKEN

It is thus the persistence of a conservative and conventionalized imagery in *Strange Days'* visual discourse that renders inconsistent the film's otherwise surprisingly accurate critique and politically perceptive speculation on a subtle, yet fundamental political paradigm-shift. Affecting not only the credibility of its much criticized ending, the inconsistency of using conventionalized religious imagery is at least in part affirmative of the symbolic order that the film so meticulously criticizes. This recourse to well-tried, conservative images has evidently prevented the film from becoming one of the symbolic war-machines that Bigelow invokes with the scene of Mace's SQUID-experience. Quoting Bigelow's own comment on *Strange Days* as a film that is "at war with itself," Barry Keith Grant argues that "the film's ideological contradictions speak quite eloquently of the tensions inherent in the situation of a woman making action movies about the traditionally male genre of action movies."[170] This defense reiterates, however, the stereotypical casting of Bigelow as "Hollywood's Macho Woman"[171] and the reductive reception of *Strange Days* as a film that renegotiates the vexed nexus between gender and genre in Hollywood. It does not account for the film's complex comment on the U.S. as a state of speculation, its subtle depiction of the formation of political subjectivity in L.A. at the end of the American century, or its perceptive critique of risk as a technology of governance. Barry Keith Grant's defense of *Strange Days* against Robin Wood's critical assessment of the film as "a tease and a cheat"[172] reflects and builds upon the 'cult of personality' that is a widely acknowledged hallmark

---

169 Donna Haraway qtd. in Marcia Ian, *Remembering the Phallic Mother: Psychoanalysis, Modernism, and the Fetish.* (Ithaka, NY: Cornell UP, 1996) x. Quoting from Haraway's *Simians, Cyborgs, and Women: The Reinvention of Nature,* Ian identifies "the so-called 'phallic mother' as the very archetype of 'boundary-maintaining images' in British, European, and American literary modernism."

170 "Man's Favorite Sport?: The Action Films of Kathryn Bigelow," *Auteurs and Authorship: A Film Reader,* ed. Barry Keith Grant (Malden et al.: Blackwell, 2008) 280-291, 289.

171 Salisbury qtd. Tasker *Spectacular Bodies* 176-177.

172 Robin Wood qtd. in Grant "Man's Favorite Sport?" 289.

of the American transformation of the original French *politique des auteurs* into auteur theory.

As Edward Buscombe argues, "the development of '*la politique des auteurs*' into a cult of personality gathers strength with the emergence of Andrew Sarris, for it is Sarris who pushes to extremes arguments which in *Cahiers* were often only implicit."[173] Significantly, Andrew Sarris's translation of *la politiques des auteurs* into auteur theory reveals a programmatically apolitical quality when read with Sarris's positing of auteur theory rules: not only are cinematic aesthetics considered the sole product of an auteur personality, according to Sarris, but auteur personalities have to "be wrenched from their historical environments."[174] This ahistorical understanding of auteur aesthetics ties in seamlessly with the conservatism and open quest for investment profitability marking the Hollywood middlebrow-machine as a field of large-scale-productions. Obviously, this field requires from its producers a strong authorial signature while curtailing the political potential of their aesthetics.

It is worth noting how Bigelow's own assessment of *Strange Days* as a "film at war with itself"[175] mirrors the conceptualization of art in early Romantic art theory. The obfuscation of her own authorship and authorial responsibility captured in this phrasing casts her film as a product assuming a life of its own, an existence independent from the aesthetic decisions of an original author. The phrase thus strikingly reflects the Romantic notion of the ingenious author who merely gives birth to original creations, a Romantic idea of authorship exemplified by the following quote from Coleridge's work on Shakespeare: "An Original may be said to be of *vegetable* nature; it rises spontaneously from the vital root of genius; it grows, it is not made."[176] Considering *Strange Days* a *vegetable* rising from the "vital root" of Bigelow's genius, however, spotlights contradictions in American auteur theory, "its Romantic conception of the director as the 'only begetter' of a film,"[177] and its demand for personal signature, rather than exculpating the film's inconsistent aesthetics.

There is no point in denying that *Strange Days*' ending compromises its otherwise complex and perceptive political critique; what is more, it does so in a way that cannot be read as a performative compliance targeted at revealing the restrictions inscribed in the political-economic workings of the fickle Hollywood

---

173 "Ideas of Authorship," *Auteurs and Authorship: A Film Reader*, ed. Barry Keith Grant (Malden, et al.: Blackwell, 2008) 76-92, 79, italics in the original.
174 Qtd. in Buscombe, "Ideas of Authorship," 79.
175 Qtd. in Grant, "Man's Favorite Sport," 289.
176 T.S. Coleridge qtd. in Buscombe, "Ideas of Authorship" 78, Buscombe's italics.
177 Buscombe "Ideas of Authorship" 78.

middlebrow-machine. Twenty minutes long, this ending, with its conventional imagery, signals an irritating, risk-avoiding compliance of "Hollywood transgressor"[178] Kathryn Bigelow with what might be called Hollywood's zero-tolerance, political conservatism. The inconsistency in Bigelow's aesthetics of risk has to be read as an aesthetic risk not taken that, ultimately, translates into a political risk not taken: *Strange Days'* elaborate aesthetics of risk are epistemologically inconsistent as they are eventually disarmed by an imagery that fails to render unidentifiable and unrecognizable traditional structures and conventions of representation.[179] Obviously, this aesthetic deficiency not only entailed economic failure, but, while not completely erasing the film's political critique, has lastingly impaired its power of political intervention.

---

178 Jermyn and Redmond "Introduction: Hollywood Transgressor," 1.
179 See Deleuze and Guattari *A Thousand Plateaus*, 513.

3 Live on the Edge I Say: Edgework, Risk, and Literary Form in Karen Tei Yamashita's *Tropic of Orange*

3.1 EDGEWORK – A SUBTLE TASK

"Live on the edge I say. Live to the max. It's like riding the crest of a wave, staying current with it, right there on top, top of the news, before it breaks." (22) With these words, Emi, a Japanese American news producer for a local L.A. TV-station, and certainly the coolest and sassiest of the protagonists in Karen Tei Yamashita's *Tropic of Orange* (1997),[1] is introduced and characterized as a risk loving, fast living, postmodern young woman in the first of the novel's seven chapters that are focalized on her perspective. Addressed at Gabriel, her Chicano lover, whom she meets for lunch in a stylish L.A.-restaurant "cushioned in pastels and glass bricks and remakes of David Hockney" and populated by "an assortment of Hollywood types – screenwriters, producers, wannabees" (23), Emi's advice sarcastically imitates and exaggerates the elliptic catchphrases of media-talk and its love for novelty.

Beneath the parody, however, the pithy phrasing of the 'live-on-the-edge' motto reveals another, more important layer of meaning, particularly when contextualized with a previous remark placed a few lines above, where Yamashita has Emi describe her relationship with Gabriel: "It's really just a test. Rigorous, but hey, some fail. Like *Human Feats* on cable. Like paddling across the Pacific in a canoe. Crossing the Sahara on bikes. Climbing Mount Whitney."(21-22) In both instances, Emi not only recommends risk experiences as a way to professional and personal satisfaction and growth, but uses high-risk sports activities as metaphors to illustrate the audacity, the skills, and the

---

1 Karen Tei Yamashita, *Tropic of Orange* (Minneapolis: Coffee House Press, 1997). All further references to the novel will be given in parentheses in the text.

presence she expects her nostalgic boyfriend to develop. With these metaphors, Emi unmistakably evokes a concept that sociologist Stephen Lyng has termed "edgework,"[2] and, using the allegories of surfing and "paddling across the Pacific" as a pun, playfully casts L.A. and the Pacific Rim as "the mystical space at the edge, where one's individual skills, power of concentration, capacities for control, and will to survive are the most critical determinants of one's continued existence."[3]

Originally developed to theorize the growing popularity of high-risk sports activities such as sky diving and mountain climbing[4], the edgework concept's connotations of "determination, stamina, and cool decision making"[5] as well as its emphasis on personal skills and control in narratives of individual empowerment soon suggested its application to other areas of voluntary risk taking. In a recent, revised version of the theory, Lyng describes as 'edgework' all activities in which the experience "of controlling the seemingly uncontrollable"[6] is considered to compensate for the encumbering experiences of hyper-consumption, alienation, and reified social structures in post-industrial capitalist societies. According to this broad definition, the edgework concept includes —besides extreme sports activities — a wider range of risk management practices such as stock market investments, police and military work, business entrepreneurship, managerial science, and coaching, but also socially deviant behavior such as criminal delinquency or drug experiences.[7] What characterizes all edgework across this spectrum, is, as Lyng states in his recent, most abstract definition, "an encounter with a particular edge or boundary condition," which

---

2   Stephen Lyng, "Edgework, Risk, and Uncertainty," *Social Theories of Risk and Uncertainty: An Introduction*, ed. Jens O. Zinn (Malden: Blackwell, 2008) 106-137.
3   Lyng, "Edgework, Risk, and Uncertainty," 124.
4   See Stephen Lyng, "Edgework: A Social Psychological Analysis of Voluntary Risk Taking," *American Journal of Sociology* 95.4 (1990): 851-886.
5   Jakob Arnoldi, *Risk: An Introduction* (Malden: Polity, 2009) 141.
6   Lyng, "Edgework, Risk, and Uncertainty," 124.
7   See also Tom Baker and Jonathan Simon, "Embracing Risk," *Embracing Risk: The Changing Culture of Insurance and Responsibility*, eds. Tom Baker and Jonathan Simon (Chicago: U of Chicago P, 2002) 1-25. Baker and Simon locate the growing popularity of edgework within a "larger cultural trend of embracing risk" (6) that, since the 1980s, gradually displaces the strategy of 'spreading risk' that industrializing societies had pursued since the late nineteenth century in order to mitigate the negative side effects of industrialization.

consists of the line separating form and formlessness, order and disorder, expressed more concretely in terms of the distinction between life and death, sanity and insanity, consciousness and unconsciousness, or other consequential limits. In confronting either the life and death challenges of Himalayan mountain climbing or the psychic dangers of hallucinogenic drug use, making sure that one does not 'cross the line' into formlessness and annihilation is a critical goal of the enterprise. However, the real significance of the 'edge' in these activities is reflected in how edgeworkers of all stripes ultimately seek to get as close to this critical line as possible without actually crossing it.[8]

Against the background of this abstract definition, Emi's ironic recommendation of a life on the edge becomes visible as a programmatic motto, a motto that points to the centrality of edgework as a pivotal idea contolling *Tropic of Orange* on several levels. Accordingly, the present chapter aims to trace edgework as an aesthetic principle organizing the novel's form, and as a paradigm of political-economic governance negotiated at its level of content. That the edgework concept also defines Yamashita's authorial position in the field of Asian American literature will be shown in the following brief discussion of Asian American literature preceding the analysis of the novel.

Like *Tropic of Orange* all novels by Japanese American writer and professor of literature Karen Tei Yamashita have been perceived as outstanding in many ways. While deeply and continuously concerned with struggles of immigrant citizenship and its involvement in constructions of the nation state, they have all been praised for establishing trans-Pacific and inter-American perspectives on multiculturalism and processes of globalization, for their creative amalgamation of postmodern cyberpunk with magic realism, and, not least, for their respective elaborate narrative structure and form. Yet Yamashita's work has not met easy acceptance in the field of Asian American literature.

What seems to complicate her position in the field is, strikingly, the fact that Yamashita's novels are based upon a profound knowledge of French 'high' theory. In particular Yamashita's masterful use of narrative form that stages transgressive concepts such as fluid hybridity and heteroglossia clearly displays a reverence for and a familiarity with poststructuralist modes of discourse that have been critically received within Asian American studies. This theoretical knowledge, a knowledge and theoretical proficiency that would be considered educational capital and an asset in other fields of cultural production, has, in the late 1990s, begun to be frowned upon by some Asian American scholars as calling into question Asian American authors' ideological integrity.

---

8   Lyng, "Edgework, Risk, and Uncertainty," 111.

It is no coincidence that *Tropic of Orange*, Yamashita's L.A. novel, whose aesthetics particularly draw on poststructuralist imagery to represent the hazards and contingencies of geopolitical and identitarian mobility was written and published during this time of epistemological crisis. It indicates, rather, that Yamashita's creative prose with its elaborate narrative aesthetics not only addresses, but also performs the risk-taking that is inherent to any violation of boundaries. Similar to Kathryn Bigelow, whose position as an avant-garde filmmaker and critical negotiation of risk as a political rationality have been shown to be complicated by her entanglement with conservative politics of risk effective inside the 'fickle' Hollywood machine, Yamashita's educated avant-garde aesthetics appears to garner for the author a complicated and hazardous position in the field of Asian American literature.

Illustrating her own judgment of that field as highly contingent and uncertain, and, implicitly, the even higher degree of contingency inherent to a decentered position on the field's 'edge,' Yamashita has voiced the perception that "[…] for the Asian American or the Asian-Anglo-omniphone writer […] the blank page is a kind of mine field, a field of pitfalls."[9] Strikingly, the drastic metaphor of the mine field in this comment echoes and visualizes the principle of territorial and conceptual border violation that is at the center of Yamashita's work. It casts the space of Asian American articulation as a "riskscape,"[10] and Asian American writing as an endeavor that cannot be anything but transgressive. More specifically, the metaphor of the mine field signals an awareness of the 'subterraneous,' invisible hazards inherent to the complex "dialectic of articulation and power" within which "Asia/America is produced."[11] It illustrates that the Asian American author's compulsion to tackle and/or circumnavigate these hazards relies on vigilance, sensibility, and skillful control. With this emphasis on skillful, individual control, Yamashita represents Asian American fictional writing *per se* as a practice of extreme, voluntary risk taking, a risk embracing practice whose connotations of decentered positionality and the will to individual empowerment strikingly mirror Stephen Lyng's

---

9   Karen Tei Yamashita, "Traveling Voices," *Café Creole: Circle K* (June 2000): Web, 12 Jul. 2011. <http://www.cafecreole.net/travelogue/karen/circleK2.html#june2000>.

10 In her reading of Don DeLillo's *White Noise*, Ursula Heise attributes the term to geographer Susan Cutter. "Die Zeitlichkeit des Risikos im amerikanischen Roman der Postmoderne," *Zeit und Roman: Zeiterfahrung im historischen Wandel und ästhetischer Paradigmenwechsel vom sechzehnten Jahrhundert bis zur Postmoderne*, ed. Martin Middecke (Würzburg: Königshausen und Neumann, 2002) 373-394, 385.

11 David Palumbo-Liu, *Asian/American: Historical Crossings of a Racial Frontier* (Stanford: Stanford UP, 1999) 388.

conceptualization of 'edgework.' Reading the aesthetic sophistication of Yamashita's narratives as a very specific form of edgework, and analyzing its reception in terms of risk will, in the following, serve to trace and sketch some of the ideological snares and rifts that mark the field of Asian American literature as a 'mine field.'

Rone Shavers's review[12] of Yamashita's recent *I-Hotel* (2009), for instance, not only captures Yamashita's position in terms of risk, but, in the process, subtly conveys a wealth of information on the risks associated with Asian immigration to the U.S. and the subtleties of its discursive regulation. More specifically, in concluding his praise of the National-Book-Award-nominated novel that compiles an "encyclopedic"[13] history of Asian American activism organized around San Francisco's International Hotel, Shavers associates risk with Yamashita's technical brilliance and her decision to present the political agenda of her novel in a complex narrative structure:

> *I Hotel* will almost certainly serve as a model that future Asian-American authors will follow, especially since what differentiates this book from countless others is the attention Yamashita gives to narrative form, and the risks she takes with it. This is a very careful, cleverly constructed novel—to say that Yamashita defies conventional storytelling is an understatement.[14]

While Shavers's projection of Yamashita's potential avant-garde position within the field of Asian American literature casts the distinctive narrative form of her novel as a risky investment in a prospective gain of symbolic capital, it conveys the nature of the stakes involved only by way of its rhetoric. Instead of defining the specific risk taken by the Asian American author who breaks from or reformulates literary traditions – the risk inherent to any avant-garde defiance of "conventional storytelling,"– the assemblage of the terms "model," "future" and "differentiation" from "countless others"[15] in Shavers's concluding remark implicitly imparts some of the multiple meanings risk has assumed in the context of Asian American political discourse, and subtly relates them to the subfield of Asian American literature.

---

12 Rone Shavers, "Review of *I Hotel* by Karen Tei Yamashita," *The Quarterly Conversation* 23 (7 Mar. 2011): Web, 5 Nov. 2011<http://quarterlyconversation.com/i-hotel-by-karen-tei-yamashita>.
13 Ibid.
14 Ibid.
15 Shavers, "Review."

Unmistakably, if perhaps inadvertently, this seemingly casual collection of keywords evokes and reiterates the 'yellow peril' anxieties of an excessive Asian mass – "countless others" – that has been cast as a risk to the nation by a dominant cultural narrative since the beginning of Asian immigration to the U.S. Resonating in this projection of "future Asian-American authors" and their "countless" books is the idea of a dangerous Asian economic excess, an idea whose persistence can be traced in recent examples of economic Pacific Rim utopianism. In this discourse, a celebratory rhetoric only thinly veils a perception of the contemporary rise of Asian capitalism as a danger to U.S. American economic hegemony.[16]

Shavers's speculation on "future Asian-American authors" and their "countless" books not only implicitly suggests that the century-old, yet persistent nativist fears associated with Asian immigration to the U.S. have come true, but, equally important, links them to a notion of stiff competition defining the field of Asian American literature. In doing so, it subtly relates both the racist anxieties that have been instrumental to the construction of the nation[17] and the transnational economic imaginary of a pretentious Pacific Rim utopianism to the cultural myth of the model minority that continues to essentialize an alleged Asian American adaptivity to U.S. national values, such as ambition and competitiveness. In suggesting that Yamashita's novel will serve as a "model that future Asian-Americans will follow," Shavers's comment, at the same time, insinuates a lack of originality in Asian American literary productions that ties in with an equally stereotyping perception of Asian economic success as based solely on violations of western intellectual property rights in the realms of industrial and post-industrial production.

By identifying as the distinctive feature of *I-Hotel* "the attention Yamashita gives to narrative form"[18] Shavers's concluding remark not only celebrates her

---

16 See the section on Pacific Rim utopianism in the introductory chapter and Arif Dirlik, "The Asia Pacific Idea: Reality and Representation in the Invention of a Regional Structure," *What Is In A Rim: Critical Perspectives on the Pacific Region Idea,* ed Arif Dirlik (Lanham e.a.: Rowman and Littlefield, 1998) 15-36; Alexander Woodside, "The Asia-Pacific Idea as a Mobilization Myth," *What Is In A Rim: Critical Perspectives on the Pacific Region Idea,* ed Arif Dirlik (Lanham e.a.: Rowman and Littlefield, 1998) 37-52; Bruce Cumings, "Rimspeak, or, The Discourse of the 'Pacific Rim'," *What Is In A Rim: Critical Perspectives on the Pacific Region Idea,* ed Arif Dirlik (Lanham e.a.: Rowman and Littlefield, 1998) 53-72.

17 See David Leiwei Li, *Imagining the Nation: Asian American Literature and Cultural Consent* (Stanford: Stanford UP, 1999), esp. 2-15.

18 Shavers "Review."

novel as setting new standards in the field of Asian American literature, but implicitly ascribes a conventionality and a lack of "careful," clever narrative construction, i.e. a lack of formal complexity, to Asian American literary texts of the past and the present. Rather than doing justice to the field it purports to describe, this boldly generalizing, sweeping gesture betrays the existence of a racialized literary market and its conditioning of a separate, yet formally deficient, ethnic canon, defined by "exhortation to common experience and Asian American peoplehood,"[19] rather than refined aesthetics. Encoded in Shavers's recognition of Yamashita's narrative style as a distinctive, contingent asset in a contested subfield of literary production is thus a conventionalized receptive attitude that has been collaborative with the discursive formation and regulation of Asian American citizenship in an era of "Asian abjection,"[20] and constitutive to struggles for Asian American entry into U.S. American literary culture.

It is the interpretative filter of this conventional receptive attitude, the decision to prioritize the perception of political representation over the recognition of aesthetic representation that has put at risk Asian American authors and, by extension, the field of Asian American literature.[21] The denial of aesthetic criticism – a "loss of form in current criticism, especially the very

---

19 Li, *Imagining the Nation*, 34.
20 Ibid. Drawing on Etienne Balibar's notion of the "historical reciprocity of nationalism and racism" (4) and Julia Kristeva's description of the abject (6-7), Li identifies a persistent American orientalism as a core constituent of the construction of the U.S. nation and the formation and definition of American citizenship. He delineates transformations of this orientalism in relation to changes in political culture and modes of production in a global economy from the mid-nineteenth to the end of the twentieth century and, in sketching a genealogy of U.S. national politics on Asian immigration, distinguishes a period of "Oriental alienation" from a subsequent period of "Asian abjection." In this ongoing era of "Asian abjection" Asian Americans, although given equal protection under the law, do not experience" full inclusion" because "apparatuses of social and cultural reproduction, mass media and systems of education continue to secure the common sense of Asian Americans as aliens, thus both precluding their sense of national entitlement and inhibiting their American actualization." (6) David Leiwei Li, *Imagining the Nation: Asian American Literature and Cultural Consent* (Stanford: Stanford UP, 1999).
21 See Jinqui Ling, *Narrating Nationalisms: Ideology and Form in Asian American Literature* (New York, et.al.: Oxford UP, 1998), 4.

criticism that purports to link literature and politics"[22] – fails to acknowledge that "the aesthetic experience of form is implicated, through its necessary tie to critical discourse, in the social and political conflicts inherent in the formations of the public sphere."[23] It disregards the fact that "the work's inner form gives shape to a rift it cannot overcome in the heterogeneous incommensurate materials it works on."[24] In doing so, the reductive reading convention that precludes aesthetic judgment deprives writers of 'ethnic' literature of an instrument of persuasion in the "open-ended, contentious *valuing* at stake in literary and political criticism."[25] More precisely, it deprives them of an *equalizing* instrument of persuasion in a public sphere that is cast by the dominant symbolic order as defined by rational judgment,[26] yet is, in fact, conditioned and marked by social and political inequalities and struggles. It is at this point that the double entendre in Shavers's praise begins to show, and Yamashita's investment in elaborate narrative structures becomes visible as political edgework, the embracing of political risk by way of aesthetic control.

Contrary to the connotations of avant-garde innovation that critics ascribe to narrative form in her latest novel, Yamashita's decision to model her novels in complex narrative structures can be traced throughout her work. More important, the perception of narrative composition as a risky endeavor marks not only an – albeit duplicitous – highpoint of recognition and consecration as reflected by Shavers's concluding remark, but also an initial failure to be admitted into the canon. It allows for a more conclusive assessment of the risk taken by an Asian American writer who invests in elaborate narrative, when Yamashita, writing a travelogue in preparation of her second to last book *Circle2Cycles* (2001), during a research trip to Japan, recalls critical reactions to her second novel *Brazil-Maru* (1992):[27]

---

22 John Brenkman, "Extreme Criticism," *What's Left of Theory: New Work on the Politics of Literary Theory*, eds. Judith Butler, et al. (New York: Routledge, 2000) 114-136, 120.

23 Brenkman, "Extreme Criticism," 120.

24 Ibid., 118.

25 Ibid., 120, italics in the original.

26 See Ibid.

27 The fact that an American *sansei* author recounts the critical reception of her novel on a Brazilian *issei* community during a stay in her American *issei* ancestor's country of origin is in itself a dense cultural text whose implications of fluid transnationality and diaspora indicate its political and historical situatedness in a period marked by market multiculturalism and the widespread assumption of the declining significance of the nation state. In addition, the quote's publication/mediation in the borderless

In my own novel, *Brazil-Maru*, I created five separate narrators to tell a story based on the history of Japanese immigration to Brazil. I received the complaint by some American critics that they could not hear the differences in the voices of the narrators even though I, as the writer, knew them to be distinct. Still I could understand their difficulty. All of the narrators, except for the last speaker, are speaking in Japanese. (The final narrator is speaking in Portuguese.) It's a very subtle task: how to make English look Japanese on the page.[28]

Although *Brazil Maru* is set in the eponymous country,[29] the quote points to a fundamental "predicament of Asian American articulation"[30] as David Leiwei Li has termed the complex and shifting relations between Asian racialization in the U.S., Asian American identity politics, and the politics of Asian American aesthetic representation. By expressing a compliant understanding for the "difficulty" experienced by "some American critics" to recognize and decipher the complexity of her narrative technique, and by attributing this difficulty to her own failure to adequately cater to the subtleties of cultural translation, Yamashita's comment, like the prefatory passage preceding the beginning of *Brazil Maru*, implicitly acknowledges the Asian American author's obligation to

---

"nonwaters of cyberspace" (Palumbo-Liu, *Asian/American*, 372) further enhances these connotations of fluid transnational mobility, connotations that according to David Leiwei Li distract from the ongoing racializing abjection of Asian American subjects in the U.S. See Li *Imagining the Nation* 6-7.

28 Yamashita, "Traveling Voices," *Café Creole: Circle K* (June 2000) Web, 12 Jul. 2011.

29 While pointing out that Yamashita has used Brazil as a setting for most of her creative prose, Kandice Chuh expressly underlines the importance of an informative introductory passage that the author has placed at the beginning of *Brazil Maru*. According to Chuh, this passage "frames the novel for U.S. audiences for whom the story of Japanese migration to Brazil may be seen as foreign" and "emphasizes the impact of US exclusionary immigration policies on that migration". Chuh foregrounds the "triangulation" and "interconnectivity" between the U.S., Japan, and Brazil as establishing an East-West- as well as a North-South- nexus in Yamashita's prose-texts that, as Chuh argues, invites their reception in the framework of Asian American hemispheric studies. Regardless of the display of "interconnectivity" and an "imagination unbounded by territorial constraints" (635) in *Brazil Maru*, it is noteworthy that the passage also documents the Asian American writer's need to cater to a U.S. literary market. Kandice Chuh, "Of Hemispheres and Other Spheres: Navigating Karen Tei Yamashita's Literary World," *American Literary History* (2006): 618 – 637.

30 Li, *Imagining the Nation*, 21.

provide a text that is comprehensible according to the conventions of the dominant symbolic order represented by (white) "American critics." It is, moreover, strikingly polite and cautious in relating the critics' inability to hear the differences in the narrators' voices to the cultural producer's "very subtle task" of making "English look Japanese on the page."

With this phrasing, Yamashita identifies herself as the "Pacific Rim subject *par excellence*,"[31] the American subject of Asian descent whose abilities of cultural translation demonstrate the "distinguishable sensibility" that the dominant cultural narrative ascribes to "the true Asian American."[32] At the same time, the phrasing conveys an allusion to a subtle form of resistance, since the essentialist stereotype of Asian American sensibility was in the 1970s strategically appropriated and translated into a self-ascribed cultural ideal and the "measure of being an Asian American"[33] by Frank Chin and his co-editors of *Aiiieeeee!* (1975).[34]. While defying the codification of the stereotype that both discourses – the racist essentialism of the dominant symbolic order and the Asian American strategic "alter-essentialism"[35] represented by Chin – define as male and U.S.-centered, Yamashita's display of a programmatic sensibility can be traced in *Brazil Maru* as well as in her comment on the novel. Her decision to employ multiple narrative voices certainly reflects an awareness of the ideological implications inherent to the question of point of view that Frank Chin and his co-editors have pronounced as the central feature of Asian American literary sensibility.

On the other hand, Yamashita's choice of setting and her polyphonic narrative technique in *Brazil Maru* and throughout her creative work indicate her affiliation with more recent ideological position takings in the field. Contrary to the strategic essentialism of a "nation- and nativity-bound Asian American sensibility"[36] they document an investment in the "postidentitarian" and "postnational"[37] concepts promoted by poststructuralist modes of discourse that

---

31 Palumbo-Liu, Asian/American, 345.
32 Li, Imagining the Nation, 31.
33 Ibid.
34 Frank Chin; Jeffery Paul Chan; Lawson Fusao Inada; Shawn Wong, eds. Aiiieeeee! An Anthology of Asian-American Writers (Garden City, NY: Anchor-Doubleday, 1975). The publication of this important study marks, according to David Leiwei Li, the "ethnic nationalist phase" (122) of Asian American criticism. Imagining the Nation.
36 Ibid., 117.
37 See ibid., 186.

have gained impact in the context of a " turn towards the transnational"[38] in American Studies and in Asian American Studies alike. Beginning in the late 1980s, Asian American scholars like Lisa Lowe, Elaine Kim, Shirley Geok-lin Lim, Amy Ling, and King-Kok Cheung increasingly promoted notions of 'diaspora,' strategic 'positionality,' fluid 'hybridity,' 'multiplicity,' and individualized 'difference' in their attempts to re-conceptualize Asian American subjectivity. While recognizing the necessity of an "ongoing work of transforming hegemony,"[39] these authors have questioned the conceptual efficacy of the received and mutually constitutive paradigms of fixed identity and the nation, and have challenged both "the narrowness of a cultural nationalist identity politics and critical mode"[40] and "the discursive centrality of the US."[41]

This ongoing dismissal of the "the old jargon and schema"[42] in favor of a rhetoric of fluid mobility, transgression and dissolution of boundaries inspired by poststructuralist theory has not met unreserved and general approval in Asian American studies. Since the late 1990s, scholars like David Leiwei Li, David Palumbo-Liu, and Jinqi Ling, although acknowledging the need to overcome the ethnic nationalist approach from a generation earlier, have criticized the new paradigm and interrogated its power of political intervention. They discern in the euphoric promotion of 'difference' and 'diaspora' as concepts liberating from naturalized categories not only the danger of overlooking historical and geopolitical conditions – "the material production of difference"[43] in specific "chronotopes" as Palumbo-Liu has termed the "time/space constructions"[44] that determine the production of any given identity – but also the danger of a depoliticizing atomization of group allegiance. Paradoxically, as David Leiwei Li observes, the conceptualization of a diasporic "self in difference"[45] that was intended to counter the racializing essentialisms of the preceding phase even

---

38 Chuh, "Of Hemispheres and Other Spheres," 618.
39 Lisa Lowe, "Heterogeneity, Hybridity, Multiplicity: Marking Asian American Differences," *Diaspora* 1.1 (1991): 22-44, 39-40.
40 Zhou Xiaojing, "Introduction: Critical Theories and Methodologies in Asian American Studies," *Form and Transformation in Asian American Literature*, eds. Zhou Xiaojing and Samina Najmi (Seattle and London: U of Washington P, 2005) 9.
41 Chuh, "Of Hemispheres and Other Spheres," 619.
42 Elaine H. Kim, *Asian American Literature: An Introduction to the Writings and their Social Context* (Philadelphia: Temple UP, 1982) 14.
43 Ling, *Narrating Nationalisms*, 8.
44 Palumbo-Liu, *Asian/American*, 344.
45 Li, Imagining *the Nation*, 194.

caters to the neo-racist and the neo-conservative politics of an ongoing "conservative revolution"[46] that interprets racial equality exclusively as "a matter of individual rather than group or collective concern."[47] About the resulting 'individualized difference, Li writes:

The historically alienated and abjected Asian American is suddenly believed to be in full possession of the power of meaning-making and self-invention. Identity, rather than being the outcome of normative regulation and contestation, becomes a matter of personal choice like picking up groceries at the supermarket. [...] When difference is finally coded as an idiosyncratic merit or drawback to be either cherished or conquered by the individual its depoliticization via personal choice is complete: Personal biography overrides collective history, the sovereign individual is favored over a critical sense of community, and the past and present forms of historical and social determination are eventually dismissed as extraneous.[48]

Li's comment reflects how closely both the "conservative revolution" and the "difference revolution"[49] are related to the borderless omnipresence of global consumer capitalism and its economic mantra of individual free choice. The sarcastic invocation of the "sovereign individual" – a term that, in this context, could easily be replaced by 'rational economic man' – further enhances this nexus, and points to the conflicting race and class identifications that came with the emergence of a professional Asian American middleclass and, in particular, the professionalization and institutionalization of Asian American intellectuals. Stating a growing distance between this privileged class of institutionalized intellectuals – "subject[s] of speech within the ivory tower,"[50] who can indulge in the luxury of personal choice without too many restrictions – and the muted Asian American 'other' in whose name they claim to speak, Li criticizes the professional class's adoption of poststructuralist ideas and concepts as epistemologically, ethically and politically inconsistent: "Asian American academic critics are turning their alienation and abjection within the nation into its compulsory claims, but the effect of appropriating poststructuralist theory to articulate an anxiety rooted in structural unevenness is not without its irony."[51]

---

46 Ibid., 193.
47 Michael Omi and Howard Winant qtd. in Li, *Imagining the Nation*,193.
48 Li, *Imagining the Nation*, 194.
49 Rey Chow, *The Protestant Ethnic and the Spirit of Capitalism* (New York: Columbia UP, 2002) 134. Subsequently abbreviated to *The Protestant Ethnic*.
50 Li, *Imagining the Nation*, 186.
51 Li, *Imagining the Nation*, 186.

The tone of sarcastic fervor in Li's critique resembles that of other critics, regardless of their affiliation with either a neo-marxist historical materialism or a constructivism influenced by French theory, and is characteristic of this Asian American debate over conflicting theoretical and institutional conceptualizations of resistance and subversion, a debate that has been perceived as a "'crisis' of Asian American cultural studies."[52] According to Rey Chow, this tone expresses an "impassioned sense of discomfort,"[53] and indicates that the stakes are high in a controversy concerned with nothing less than the "politics of writing [...] about ethnic and multicultural identities in our post-civil rights age."[54] In her attempt to analyze the positions involved, Chow's reference to a "distinctive affective dissonance" [55] that divides theoretical from creative writing is as general as it is unsatisfying. More interesting and conclusive, especially in the context of Yamashita's fiction, is the aspect of temporality that Chow deducts from Pheng Cheah's work on hybridity theory:

[F]reedom, as implied in the difference revolution and in hybridity theories, is the futurist, anticipatory mode of speech. Creative writers, on the other hand, tend to go in a different temporal direction because their mode of speech is derived from looking backward even as they are propelled forward in time: When the subject matter involved is of the nature of injustice – such as controversial issues of ethnicity, cultural diversity and racism – these fundamental discursive incommensurabilities in time (and its value production) simply become critical.[56]

Read in context with her analysis of "coercive mimeticism" in autobiographical 'ethnic' prose that is at the center of her book, Chow's diagnosis of different and incommensurable temporal modes of speech as the reason for conflicting positions in the controversy about poststructural theory's (in)adequacy makes perfect sense: With its source in the emotional experience of injustice, the 'ethnic' autobiography's mode of speech is definitely "derived from looking backward,"[57] and clearly distinguishable from the abstract and rational discourse of theoretical writing whose "futurist, anticipatory mode of speech"[58] is defined by its purpose of political intervention. Yet writers of contemporary Asian

---

52 Ling, *Narrating Nationalisms*, 4.
53 Chow, *The Protestant Ethnic*, 135.
54 Ibid.
55 Ibid.
56 Ibid., 136.
57 Ibid.
58 Ibid.

American fiction have found ways to resist the "coercive mimeticism" of the autobiographic genre, with their texts displaying a potential of political intervention that is founded precisely in their subversion of a hegemonic Anglo-American definition of literary genres[59] and their resistance against integration into a racialized literary canon, whose receptive conventions would curtail their literary potential.

As can be derived from the previous discussion of Karen Tei Yamashita's creative work and its reception in terms of risk, her novels are a case in point. While it could be argued that non-linear polyphonic narrative – perceived here in conjunction with the theme of migratory and identitarian mobility as a marker of underlying poststructuralist concepts – is indeed tied to a backward looking perspective in *I-Hotel* and *Brazil Maru*, since the subject matter of both novels is historical, the same cannot be said about *Tropic of Orange* (1997). Published in the middle of the crisis of Asian American studies, and negotiating topics of geopolitical, migratory, and identitarian fluidity in contemporary L.A., Mexico, and the U.S./Mexican border area, *Tropic of Orange* clearly stages postmodern and poststructuralist concepts and, in particular, draws on Deleuzian imagery such as maps, layers and rhizomatic multiplicity. At first glance, it thus appears to make a claim that these concepts' power of political intervention is not restricted to theoretical discourse. The temporality of its mode of speech is, however, not unambiguously identifiable, a fact that Yamashita boldly emphasizes by placing a reader address before the beginning of her novel, a reader address that explicitly activates the very issue of different temporalities:

Gentle reader, what follows may not be about the future, but is perhaps about the recent past; a past that, even as you imagine it, happens. Pundits admit that it's impossible to predict, to chase such absurdities into the future, but c'est L.A. vie. No single imagination is wild or crass or cheesy enough to compete with the collective mindlessness that propels our fascination forward. We were all there; we all saw it on TV, screen and monitor, larger than life.

A classic *captatio benevolentiae*, this appeal to the reader mimics the conventionalized topos of the intrusive narrator of the Victorian novel whose interventions were to grant the educating effect of the narrative. Placed before a contemporary novel whose narration relies on the relativism of an unmediated juxtaposition of different narrative perspectives, the gesture of the reader address can only draw attention to the fact that there is no such thing as narrative

---

59 See Xiaojing, "Introduction: Critical Theories and Methodologies in Asian American Studies," 4.

guidance through the dense textual web resulting from the narrative perspectives' multiple interactions. As a kind of paradox intervention, it thus formally announces and prepares an experience of uncertainty and risk that its content explicitly addresses.

Strikingly, Yamashita illustrates the effect of uncertainty by playing with the arbitrariness of the temporal distinction between past, present and future that is at the center of any definition and representation of risk. This dizzying blurring of the boundaries between temporal categories sets a tone of playful contingency for an appeal to the readers' willing suspension of disbelief, an appeal that is not restricted to the conventional announcement that what is about to follow pushes the limits of what is credible. Rather, Yamashita uses the conventionalized association of such an appeal with the genres of fantasy and science fiction to subtly discredit the futurist mode of speech marking predictions of "pundits" and thus a theoretical 'discourse of truth' and its power of defining risk. Clearly, this is a plea for speculative fiction, intended to highlight the speculative nature of theoretical discourse and expertise.

Even more important, Yamashita uses the epigraph to flaunt her refusal to grant an unambiguous temporal mode of speech and a secure vantage point from which to assess both her novel's genre and the credibility of its plot. It becomes obvious that, applied to *Tropic of Orange*, a novel that is not only no autobiography or memoir but defies any generic categorization, the distinction between different temporal modes of speech as defining the political adequacy of poststructuralist concepts for "writing about ethnic and multicultural identities in our post-civil rights age"[60] loses traction. At the same time, the epigraph's renunciation of a present that is independent from a historical past without any doubt rejects the ahistorical "temporality of immediacy"[61] that critics have associated with the adoption of poststructuralist theory by Asian American literary discourse. Knowing this discourse to be a "mine field"[62] and perhaps even anticipating a critique of her novel as being shaped by "poststructuralist ghost writing,"[63] Yamashita programmatically embraces the epistemology of risk that her epigraph addresses and performs. By destabilizing the boundary between theoretical and fictional discourse and soliciting her readers' trust in the "wild or crass or cheesy" imagination of her novel's speculative fiction, her confident play with contingency signals the author's refusal to be categorized as either a

---

60 Chow, *The Protestant Ethnic*, 135.
61 Ling, *Narrating Nationalisms*, 4.
62 Yamashita, "Traveling Voices."
63 Li, *Imagining the Nation*, 186.

creative writer or a "subject of speech within the ivory tower,"[64] and the claiming of a politically and aesthetically perceptive position outside the dichotomy that marks the crisis of Asian American critical thinking.

Thus keyed to the epistemology of risk, readers encounter a novel that addresses the politics of contemporary capitalism and the hazards created by its border transgressing global excess. Significantly, various forms of speculation drive forth *Tropic of Orange*'s plot, and the novel's cross-generic and fragmented narrative makes almost palpable the climate of risk that dominates its diegetic political culture. While using L.A. and its connotations of a stereotypically dystopian fictionality as a backdrop much like Kathryn Bigelow in *Strange Days*, Yamashita's novel differs from Bigelow's clairvoyant futurist speculation on the governmentality of risk not only by its focus on multiculturalism, transnational migration and immigrant citizenship, but by the indeterminacy of its temporal mode.

It is important to emphasize that *Tropic of Orange* is a novel that does not project its diegetic world into a near future, but offers a speculative account of political and economic events just prior to or concurrent with the time of its writing. Merging elements of noir fiction, cyberpunk, and magic realism, the "radical fictionality"[65] of the novel nevertheless invites its reading as a piece of speculative fiction. An instance of alternate history rather than futurist extrapolation, its imaginative account of a political-economic culture 'on the edge' of late-twentieth-century U.S. America is neither ahistorical nor depoliticizing, despite its conspicuous recourse to poststructuralist concepts of representation. In order to assess more precisely how close the edgework of Yamashita's creative writing brings her to a "critical line without actually crossing it"[66] and the risk she takes with that authorial position, the present chapter aims to analyze closely the nexus between *Tropic of Orange*'s negotiation of risk and the risk of literary form.

---

64 Li, *Imagining the Nation*, 186.
65 Walter Benn Michaels, *The Gold Standard and the Logic of Naturalism* (Berkeley and Los Angeles: U of California P, 1987) 87. Michaels uses the term to describe the genre of the American romance as introduced by Nathaniel Hawthorne.
66 Lyng, "Edgework, Risk, and Uncertainty," 111.

3.2 Exploding the Grid? Aesthetic Control and the Space-Logic of Synchronicity

Tropic of Orange is set in Los Angeles, Mexico, and the U.S./ Mexican border area, but the space of this 'empirical'[67] topography undergoes a fantastic change in the course of the plot; it warps and folds, and thus signals the ending of all certainties granted by historical facts and geopolitical claims to power. Narration in the novel is comprised of 49 episodes told from the perspectives of seven protagonists of different ethnic descent. These protagonists' simultaneous experiencing of seven subsequent weekdays and their relationships among each other multiply to produce a combinatorial explosion, a dense, web-like informational structure that, ultimately, forms a complex narrative space.

Yamashita foregrounds and illustrates the simultaneity of the episodes experienced by the seven focal protagonists by implementing, in addition to a conventional, linear table of contents, a second content page in the form of a grid. This grid, a kind of Cartesian coordinate system, bears the caption "HyperContexts." Its horizontal axis lists the seven days of the week by forming a timeline from Monday to Sunday, while its vertical axis is comprised of the names of the seven focal protagonists with their respective episodical chapters filling the coordinate space. While the grid suggests and visualizes a juxtaposition of synchrone and diachrone temporality, its caption evokes connotations of the unregulated, unlimited, and egalitarian textuality generally associated with the Internet. It thus triggers connotations of a fluid 'spatial' connectivity markedly contrasting the 'flat,' merely diachrone and linear narration suggested by the conventional table of contents that precedes it. Placed before the novel's beginning and even before the epigraph discussed above, the contradictory trope of the linear-geometric grid, whose interstices are determined by the chapters' individual settings and 'filled up' by exuberantly growing relationships among the protagonists –"criss-crossing story-lines featuring the

---

67 It is worth noting that the empirical topography is, in fact, the product of imperialistic 'engineering,' as Alex Hunt shows. In his article on the U.S.-American appropriation of what is now the US-American South West, Hunt traces how this expansion of U.S.-American territory was realized and, at the same time, naturalized by an instance of cartographic "earth-writing" (130) performed by Major William H. Emory of the Army Corps of Topographical Engineers in the aftermath of the Mexican War of 1846-48. See "Mapping the Terrain, Marking the Earth: William Emory and the Writing of the U.S./Mexico Border," *American Literary Geographies: Spatial Practice and Cultural Production 1500-1900*, eds. Martin Brückner and Hsuan L. Hsu (Newark: Rosemont, 2007) 127-146.

diversity of characters" [68] – draws attention to a complex and paradox temporality, and in the process establishes spatiality as *Tropic of Orange's* structural principle.

A timetable rather than a table of contents, HyperContexts visualizes how the time-act of reading when applied to a non-linear narrative produces a spatiality that no reading of linear narrative can achieve. With the oxymoronic image of the HyperContexts grid, Yamashita not only confronts her novel's readers with the confounding spatialization of narrative time that is also a spatialization of narrative form, but attunes them to a challenging reading process. Notably, both the concept of reading as a demanding processual task concerned with the spatialization of form produced by the logic of synchronicity and its representation by the spatio-temporal trope of the grid are not restricted to the level of narrative discourse and structure. Instead, the vertiginous fusion of time and space so prominently exposed by the paratextual HyperContexts grid and the reader address proves to be central to a plot, in which time stops and geographical space warps as the Tropic of Cancer becomes magically attached to a Mexican orange and is dragged northward to L.A. when the orange is carried across the border.

Throughout *Tropic of Orange*, Yamashita boldly presents spatio-temporal processuality as a key concept of the plot – a concept that, at times, even assumes the anthropomorph traits of a protagonist – and her protagonists' extraordinary capacity of reading it (or the lack thereof) as the distinctive feature of their respective subjectivity. The meta-narrative challenge to decipher the spatialization of narrative form in order to produce the spatialization of narrated time posed to readers of the novel by the paratextual grid thus corresponds to the challenge of reading a fantastic spatio-temporal processuality that the protagonists have to face at plot level. Significantly, the most complex and hazardous time-act of 'reading space' in *Tropic of Orange* is performed by Manzanar Murakami, the oldest and most eccentric, but, at the same time, the most emancipated, and, eventually, the most liberating protagonist. And it is in the chapters focalized on Manzanar Murakami that Yamashita picks up the trope of the grid as a concept requiring an extraordinary literacy.

Endowed with a speaking pseudonym encoding some of the complex spatial, historical and cultural entanglements of twentieth-century Japanese American relations,[69] this Japanese American character is an ideal-typical reader of spatio-

---

68 Seo-Young Chu, *Do Metaphors Dream of Literal Sleep: A Science-Fictional Theory of Representation* (Cambridge: Harvard UP, 2010) 98.

69 By having another protagonist mention that he is "the first sansei born in captivity" (108), the text suggests that Manzanar was born in the eponymous detention camp for

temporal formations that are not perceptible to others. Introduced as an artist who has given up the safety of his bourgeois existence as an honorable member of L.A.'s Japanese American community, Manzanar is the composer and conductor of an imaginary urban music that only he can hear. A traumatised freak and a social dropout, he is considered a shameful "blight on their image as the Model Minority" (37) by the Japanese American community, yet has become a "fixture on the freeway overpass" (36) on which he stands perennially, orchestrating symphonies comprised of the eternal roar and buzz of L.A. traffic and the movements of human migration. "To say that Manzanar Murakami was homeless was as absurd as the work he chose to do. No one was more at home in L.A. than this man," (36) writes Yamashita, thus introducing Manzanar, above all, as an 'expert' Angeleno, a competent reader of the city space of which he has become an integral part. Manzanar is an eccentric urban reader, economically impoverished yet equipped with an exceptional sensorium for the vibrancy of L.A., *the* postmodern American city on the Rim that is eternally 'on edge.'

Accordingly, Manzanar's synesthetic urban literacy is exposed in terms of musical edgework in "Traffic Window," the first of the seven episodes focalized on his character:

The Third Movement was excruciatingly beautiful. But that was his rule about third movements. One should hang breathlessly on every note, a great feeling of anguish nearly spilling from one's heart. It was mostly strings, violins accompanied by violas and cellos, exchanging melodies with the plaintive voice of the oboes. When it was really good it brought tears. He let them run down his face and onto the pavement, concentrating mightily on the great work at hand. *One slip of the baton, one false gesture, and he might lose the building intensity, might fail to caress each note with its tender due. In some deep place in his being, he wanted desperately to lose his way through these passages, but he would not give up his control.* He must hear every measure, cue every instrument at its proper moment, until the final note, this was the work of the great conductor and the right of the composer.(33-34, italics added)

Although *Tropic of Orange* eventually presents Manzanar as having already crossed the line that according to the Japanese American community's bourgeois binary logic separates "sanity and insanity,"[70] this expository passage introduces

---

Japanese immigrants during World War II, a biographical detail that allows to perceive him in terms of Giorgio Agamben's "homo sacer." His self-chosen surname seems to refer to Haruki Murakami, a Japanese writer of postmodern, often surreal fiction that is widely received and critically acclaimed in the U.S.

70 Lyng, "Edgework, Risk, and Uncertainty," 111.

"the great work" (33) of his art as a demanding rapprochement of "the line separating form and formlessness,"[71] and thus as a precarious artistic struggle for formal control. The vague connotation of a yet to be named, impending danger implicit to the loss of control over "building intensity" in the passage subtly evokes an idea of chaos lurking beyond the critical line of his edgework. At one level these connotations correspond to the host of clichéd apocalyptic L.A.-scenarios that are ironically invoked throughout *Tropic of Orange*'s narration; at another, meta-textual level they serve to foreshadow the bleak climax of the novel's own building intensity.

Read as a self-reflexive comment, this exposition of the eccentric Japanese American protagonist, who conducts the multiple instruments of an invisible orchestra to play the third movement of an imaginary classical symphony, turns out to be an allegory on the complexity and the difficulty of mastering the narrative voices of a polyphonic postcolonial novel that is deeply invested in the deconstruction of hegemonic dichotomies. With its emphasis on "third movements" (33) and its lyrical metaphoricity, it introduces Manzanar as a skillful and intuitive aesthetic edgeworker who struggles for focus vis-á-vis the political task of 'moving' an audience without losing aesthetic control. Displaying the "shifting identities" and the "particularly productive, postindustrial subjectivity" that the "Asian American has come to symbolize," [72] Manzanar is a "cultural translator," a "Pacific Rim subject *par excellence*,"[73] in short, an Asian American edgeworker whose voluntary embracing of risk parallels that of the Asian American author and intellectual. In addition to the subtext of 'movements' whose multiple coding evokes, besides musical connotations, notions of political activism and art as political intervention, the expository passage thus introduces an understanding of *aisthesis* and authorship that privileges cultural literacy, translation and composition over the Romanticist notions of genius and original creation. Manzanar's ingenuity is exposed as being "disguised" (56) as it finds expression 'merely' in his ability to read and re-compose an abundance of preexisting urban material.

It is this material that is represented in terms of the grid in "Rideshare," the second of the chapters focalized on Manzanar. "Manzanar's grids" (237) are formed and filled by "mapping layers" (56), and thus by numerous strata of those cultural formations that have been shaping L.A. In a particularly conclusive passage of "Rideshare," Yamashita uses the metaphor of the grid not only to depict *the* multicultural metropolis that is generally considered to

---

71 Ibid.
72 Palumbo-Liu, *Asian/American*, 343.
73 Ibid.

3.2 Exploding the Grid? Aesthetic Control and the Space-Logic of Synchronicity | 153

exemplify the development of postmodern urban space *per se* exactly because it neither has nor forms a center of any kind. She applies it, moreover, to expose and to underline the simultaneous presence of synchrone and diachrone patterns in the formation of its spatiality as well as to highlight Manzanar's extraordinary kinesthetic capacity to decipher its spatio-temporal complexity:

There are maps and there are maps and there are maps. The uncanny thing was that he could see all of them at once, filter some, pick them out like transparent windows and place them even delicately and consecutively in a complex grid of pattern, spatial discernment, body politic. Although one might have thought this capacity to see was different from a musical one, it was really one and the same. For each of the maps was a layer of music, a musical instruction, a clef, an instrument, a change of measure, a coda.

But what were these mapping layers? For Manzanar they began with the very geology of the land, the artesian rivers running beneath the surface, connected, diverging, shifting and swelling. There was the complex and normally silent web of faults – cracking like mudflats under a desert sun, like the crevices in aging hands and faces. Yet, below the surface there was the man-made grid of civil utilities: southern California pipelines of natural gas; the unnatural waterways of the Los Angeles Department of Water and Power, and the great dank tunnels of sewage; the cascades of poisonous effluents surging from rain-washed streets into the Santa Monica Bay; electric currents racing voltage into the open watts of millions of hungry energy-efficient appliances; telephone cables, cable TV, fiber optics, computer networks.

On the surface, the complexity of layers should drown an ordinary person, but ordinary persons never bother to notice, never bother to notice the prehistoric grid of plant and fauna and human behavior, nor the historic grid of land usage and property, the great overlays of transport – sidewalks, bicycle paths, roads, freeways, systems of transit both ground and air, a thousand natural and man-made divisions, variations both dynamic and stagnant, patterns and connections by every conceivable definition from the distribution of wealth to race, from patterns of climate to the curious blueprint of the skies. (56-57, italics in the original, underlining added)[74]

With the help of the grid metaphor, Yamashita represents Los Angeles as a city whose three-dimensionality is produced by overlapping layers of geological sediments and the traces of successive historical populations, a city forming both a tangible, ontological and an ideologically hybrid, fictional space. Using the

---

74 Obviously, the passage also echoes and thus refers to the principle of paradox temporality that Mike Davis has captured in the phrase *Excavating the Future in L.A.*, which is the subtitle of his seminal *City of Quartz*.

grid in conjunction with a striking imagery of layers, lines and maps, she introduces, in this passage, the motif of a spatiality whose decidedly haptic quality is almost palpable, a spatiality boldly contrasting the two-dimensionality of discursive representational concepts such as geographical maps and other forms of geopolitical 'earth-writing' as well as their naturalizing function. By italicizing the first sentence of the passage, Yamashita places particular emphasis on the difference between these two-dimensional concepts and the haptic spatiality enabled by the "mapping layers" that Manzanar artfully selects, conducts, and re-composes to form new and, above all, different kinds of maps.

Resonating in this passage is a by now widely acknowledged notion of "the urban not as an one-directed abstraction of time-space, but as a site where multiple spatialities and temporalities collide."[75] Resonating in the rigidity of the grids that have been formed by the colonizing regulation exercised by successive power regimes and the respective infrastructures they have deployed in the form of "sidewalks, bicycle paths, roads, freeways, systems of transit both ground and air" (57) is, however, also already the rhythm of an alternative mapping mobility and the potentiality of the ungovernable movements it might produce. By introducing Manzanar's creative musical reading and re-composition of "mapping layers" as appropriating, spatially filling and threatening the two-dimensionality of "man-made grid[s] of civil utilities"(57), Yamashita conspicuously evokes and refers to a number of seminal theorizations and conceptualizations of urban space ranging from Georg Simmel's analysis of metropolitan life to Virilio's age of the accelerator, Lefebvre's city rhythms, and de Certeau's spatial practices.

Most conspicuously, though, the imagery of grids, maps, lines and layers in this passage of "Rideshare" mirrors the pictorial language that marks the philosophy of Gilles Deleuze and Felix Guattari. In "Ridehare," Yamashita, quite obviously, 'shares a ride' with Deleuze and Guattari in drawing on the French philosophers' metaphors of layers, mapmaking, multiplicity, and, above all, the rhizome. In depicting L.A. not as the epitome of postmodern space *per se*, but as a multi-layered, rhizomatic Pacific Rim city, she casts it as an urban space that is characteristic of the "special case" of the "American rhizome"[76]

---

75 Kirsten Simonsen, "Spatiality, Temporality, and the Construction of the City," *Space Odysseys: Spatiality and Social Relations in the 21st Century*, eds. Jorgen Ole Baerenholdt and Kirsten Simonsen (Burlington: Ashgate, 2004) 43-62, 45.

76 Gilles Deleuze and Felix Guattari, *A Thousand Plateus: Capitalism and Schizophrenia* (Minneapolis: U of Minnesota P,1991) 19. Subsequently abbreviated to *A Thousand Plateus*.

and the rhizomatic American West, as described by Deleuze and Guattari in their introduction to *A Thousand Plateaus*:

[And] directions in America are different: the search for arborescence and the return to the Old World occur in the East. But there is the rhizomatic West with its Indians without ancestry, its ever-receding limit, its shifting and displaced frontiers. There is a whole American "map" in the West, where even the trees form rhizomes. America reversed the directions: it put its Orient in the West, as if it were precisely in America that the world came full circle; its West is the edge of the East.[77]

Read with Deleuze and Guattari, Manzanar becomes visible not just as the ever-changing product of those interminable, rhizomatic processes of discursive formations that generate postmodern subjectivity,[78] but as the particular product of an American, and, even more specifically, an American Pacific Rim version of rhizomatic processuality. Not "an ordinary person" who "should [be] drown[ed]" by the "complexity of layers"(57), Manzanar is the homeless, deracinated other of both East and West, and therefore an expert in the detection of neuralgic lines of flight and desire in the dense mesh of overlapping cultural and political-economic grids and maps. His expertise relies on the hybrid, shifting identity of the nomadic subject that Deleuze and Guattari define as not being restricted by fixed and sedentary boundaries; his edgework draws on an intuitive capacity for reading and re-composing non-discursive cultural formations, and clearly exemplifies what the French philosophers have termed "nomad art."[79]

Temporarily positioned on the freeway-overpass – and thus on a bridge of sorts that allows for a "close vision," "which maybe as much visual or auditory as tactile," and which by that kinesthetic quality produces "haptic space"[80] – Manzanar is able to discern and to conduct multiple, delimiting movements that carve out haptic "smooth spaces composed from within [the] striated space"[81] determined by L.A.'s historic and prehistoric grids. An emblem of the city's

---

77 Ibid.
78 See Alfonso de Toro, "*Jenseits* von Postmoderne und Postkolonialität: Materialien zu einem Modell der Hybridität und des Körpers als transrelationalem, transversalem und transmedialem Wissenschaftskonzept," *Räume der Hybridität. Postkoloniale Konzepte in Theorie und Literatur*, eds. Christof Hamann and Cornelia Sieber (Hildesheim: Olms, 2002) 15-52, 17.
79 Deleuze and Guattari, *A Thousand Plateaus*, 492.
80 Ibid., 493.
81 Ibid., 507.

struggles over parcelised space, the grid of the freeway-system is deciphered by Manzanar who can read between its binary lines and can thus reframe it as "a great root-system, an organic living entity." (37) The freeway system is thereby transformed into a rhizomatic metaphor symbolizing L.A.'s flows of people and their affective states, an affective mobile multiplicity that is most aptly reflected by music as the most abstract sign-system. True to the Deleuzian idea of the rhizome as "an acentered, nonhierarchical, non-signifying system without a General,"[82] Yamashita leaves no doubt that Manzanar's role as a conductor implies no form of guidance or the exercise of signifying authority:

As far as Manzanar was concerned, it was all there. A great theory of maps, musical maps, spread in visible and audible layers – each selected sometimes purposefully, sometimes at whim, to create the great mind of music. To the outside observer, it was a lonely business; it would seem that he was at once orchestra and audience. (57)

The role of the conductor thus consists of selecting and composing various layers; he is a part and an agent of the 'becoming' of a metropolitan rhizome in which the boundary between subject and object becomes irrelevant vis-à-vis circulating, heterogeneous states of being.

Throughout the novel, Manzanar comments on the dramatic collapsing of urban structures as well as the changing patterns of human movement and behavior in terms of the layers and grid-imagery. After the maelstrom of L.A.'s freeway traffic has been caught in a dramatic moment of stasis, and a flow of migrants from the South gushes into the city in which "the percussion of war" (240) is by then prevailing, Manzanar states "Once again the grid was changing." (239) While sensing a growing feeling of helplessness vis-á-vis the enormous intensity of the changing process, he cannot be at ease with his task of composing and conducting the rhizome until he realizes: "There was no need to conduct the music any longer. The entire city had sprouted grassroots conductors of every sort."(254)

The grassroots metaphor, used here to describe the urban paradigm change, strikingly parallels the imagery of grass and weed used by Deleuze and Guattari to illustrate the ethic dimension of their conceptualization of the rhizome.[83] In the case of the novel's grassroots conductors, this ethic dimension consists of a decidedly political subversion and appropriation of L.A.'s dilapidating structures: the homeless develop a dense grassroots network, taking residence in abandoned cars that have turned into immobile shells on the clogged freeway

---

82 Ibid., 21.
83 Deleuze and Guattari, *A Thousand Plateaus*,18-19.

3.2 Exploding the Grid? Aesthetic Control and the Space-Logic of Synchronicity | 157

system – all of them 'nomad artists,' forming new lines of flight and using their chance to re-territorialize the de-territorialized urban layers.[84] The bleak, dystopian atmosphere of chaos that marks *Tropic of Orange's* fictitious Los Angeles at the end of the novel can be read, then, as an instance of that "turning point" at which, according to Deleuze and Guattari, lines of flight cannot only be "obstructed or segmented, but turn into destruction or death."[85]

By negotiating the dense mesh of grassroots relations growing across and suffusing the ruins of the dualistic order in Los Angeles, Yamashita adds a decidedly political dimension to the "mapping layers" of both the city and her novel. She depicts the postcolonial reframing of space and calls into question "the *topos* of territory, native soil, city."[86] But in drawing on Deleuze and Guattari, she also comments on a philosophy whose concern is the "Ruin of Representation,"[87] as the title of Dorothea Olkowski's eponymous study indicates. What this philosophy has to offer "to philosophers and to feminist and minority theorists"[88] precisely because of that concern is, according to Olkowski,

the shift from a psychoanalytic to a semiotic perspective, the pragmatics that allows thinking to arise out of and in terms of actual practices rather than seeking metaphysical grounds, the critique of binarism as hierarchical, the breaking down of massive social and political structures into microentities, the refusal of any single and explanatory paradigm and any single philosopher or philosophy and finally the positive accounts of bodies and desire [...].[89]

In 'sharing a ride' with Deleuze and Guattari, Karen T. Yamashita obviously acknowledges and addresses the political need for the 'ruin' of binarily structured systems of representation at the plot level of her novel, particularly in the episodes that are focalized on Manzanar Murakami. Yet, while Manzanar's

---

84 Their urban net-working and forming of new lines of flight affirms a linkage between the concept of the rhizome and the tactics of minority rights movements that Dorothea Olkowsky points out in her reading of Deleuze. See Dorothea Olkowski, *Gilles Deleuze and the Ruin of Representation* (Berkeley and Los Angeles: U of California P, 1999) 55.

85 Deleuze and Guattari, *A Thousand Plateaus*, 510.

86 Jacques Derrida, *Specters of Marx: The State of the Debt, The Work of Mourning and the New International* (New York and London: Routledge, 1994) 83.

87 Dorothea Olkowski, *Gilles Deleuze and the Ruin of Representation* (Berkeley and Los Angeles: U of California P, 1999).

88 Ibid., 57.

89 Ibid.

non-discursive, pragmatic edgework of conducting and re-composing "an entire civilization of sound" (35) seems to get out of hand as it climaxes in a cacophonic crescendo threatening to explode the two-dimensional urban grids that form "planes of consistency"[90] in *Tropic of Orange*'s fictitious L.A., Yamashita's discursive edgework successfully approaches the line separating order and chaos, form and formlessness, without ever crossing it.

Significantly, the HyperContexts grid exposed at the novel's beginning as a key metaphor of spatio-temporal processuality provides a surprisingly contradictory 'plane of consistency' to the textual strata of the novel, despite the connotations of fluid connectivity encoded in its caption. While this connectivity obviously alludes to Deleuze and Guattari's ideal of a rhizomatic book composed of "plateaus that communicate with one another across micro-fissures, as in a brain,"[91] the linear-geometric metaphor of the grid, at the same time, points beyond "any single and explanatory paradigm"[92] and "any single philosopher or philosophy."[93] More precisely, it is its quality of being a timetable rather than a table of contents that points beyond the ahistorical aesthetics of 'becoming' and the "temporality of immediacy"[94] generally associated with poststructuralist philosophy. A closer look at the historical emergence of the idea of spatialization of narrative form as achieved by the "space-logic of synchronicity"[95] reveals that the HyperContexts grid epitomizes in Yamashita's novel a complex discourse on the nexus between art and historicity.

Notably, spatialization of literary form – although exposed here by a grid preceding a 'postmodern' novel that is concerned with transnational global flows, migratory mobility, and postcolonial processes of hybridization – is by no means a 'postmodern' concept. In fact, literary critic Joseph Frank has described it as characteristic of avant-garde novels of high modernism in his essay "Spatial Form in Modern Literature,"[96] as early as 1945. In analyzing the spatiality of form in Flaubert, Joyce, Proust and Djuna Barnes, Frank identifies as its constituents a "breaking up of temporal sequence"[97] and the fragmentation of the

---

90 Deleuze and Guattari, *A Thousand Plateaus*, 72.
91 Ibid., 22.
92 Olkowski, *Gilles Deleuze and the Ruin of Representation*, 57.
93 Ibid.
94 Ling, *Narrating Nationalisms*, 4.
95 Joseph Frank, "Spatial Form: An Answer to Critics," *The Idea of Spatial Form* (New Brunswick and London: Rutgers UP, 1991) 67-106, 76.
96 Joseph Frank, "Spatial Form in Modern Literature," [1945] *The Idea of Spatial Form* (New Brunswick and London: Rutgers UP, 1991) 4-66.
97 Ibid., 17.

narrative into smaller "units of meaning" in which "the time flow of the narrative is halted; attention is fixed on the interplay of relationships within this immobilized time area."[98] The consequences of this modernist narrative technique that juxtaposes aspects of the past and the present, and fuses them in "one comprehensive view"[99] are fundamental, according to Frank:

By this juxtaposition of past and present [...] history becomes ahistorical. Time is no longer felt as an objective, causal progression with clearly marked-out differences between periods; now it has become a continuum in which distinctions between past and present are wiped out. *And here we have a striking parallel with the plastic arts.* Just as the dimension of depth has vanished from the sphere of visual creation, so the dimension of historical depth has vanished from the content of the major works of modern literature. Past and present are apprehended spatially, locked in a timeless unity that, while it may accentuate surface differences, eliminates any feeling of sequence by the very act of juxtaposition. Ever since the Renaissance, modern man has cultivated both the objective visual imagination (the ability to portray space) and the objective historical imagination (the ability to locate events in chronological time); both have now been abandoned.[100]

It is obvious that the linear-geometric form and the multiple, interrelated coordinates of the grid in *Tropic of Orange* visualize exactly this spatialization of form. At the beginning of her novel, before its fragmented narrative unfolds, Yamashita uses the grid to expose the complexity and the challenge of a reading process that sets the reader the same task of "connecting allusions spatially and gradually becoming aware of the pattern of relationships"[101] that readers of, for instance, James Joyce's *Ulysses* have to tackle.

At content level, she even addresses, in her representation of Manzanar's artistic work as a cultural conductor, the "parallel with the plastic arts,"[102] used by Frank to identify spatialization of form as a modernist cultural paradigm. After introducing Manzanar's occupation as a "skilled surgeon" (56) in his bourgeois past, the narrative continues: "Perhaps the skill had never left his fingers, but the will had. He could as easily have translated his talents to that of a sculptor in clay, wood, or even marble – any sort of inanimate substance, but strangely, it was the abstraction of music that engulfed his being."(56) Strikingly, this short passage contains several unmistakable references to cultural

---

98 Ibid.
99 Frank,"Spatial Form in Modern Literature," 63.
100 Ibid. italics added.
101 Ibid., 21.
102 Ibid., 63.

theories that form the basis of Joseph Frank's theory of a modernist spatialization of literary form: the conspicuous reference to the plastic arts, the term "will" – although evoked here in the negative – and the term "abstraction, all point to the work of Wilhelm Worringer and his adoption of Alois Riegl's idea of *Kunstwollen* or will-to-art. According to Worringer, the high degree of abstraction, achieved by non-naturalistic art styles resorting to linear-geometric patterns rather than striving for mimetic representation, stems not from a lack of artistic refinement, but expresses a will-to-art that is propelled by a cultural climate of disharmony and crisis. In its representation of the Asian American protagonist, whose capacity for and 'will-to' cultural readings and re-composition parallels that of the Asian American author and intellectual, the passage thus aligns *Tropic of Orange* with a cultural theory that is anything but a-historical.

It is with these allusions to Worringer and Riegl that Yamashita adds a highly contradictory layer of meaning to her use of both Deleuzian philosophy and the spatialization of literary form as theorized by Joseph Frank. Notably, Deleuze and Guattari, like Frank, refer to Worringer and Riegl in their description of nomad art. They praise the two art historians for providing "excellent analyses" of the reduction of space to the plane and to the abstract line that both academics identify as characteristic of Egyptian art,[103] while criticizing, on the other hand, Worringer's definition of the abstract line as grounded in recti-linearity and motivated by cultural crisis and anxiety.[104] By suggesting replacing this definition by a reading of the abstract line as a nomadic "affect of smooth spaces"[105] in a desirable and timeless process of becoming, they erase the decidedly historical quality in Worringer.

Significantly, Joseph Frank's reading of Worringer is similarly eclectic. Although celebrating the relevance of Worringer's theorization of the emergence of linear-geometric patterns in art as a response to cultural climates of instability and anxiety, Frank uses Worringer to underline his claim that in modernist texts historical time is transformed into timeless myth. At first glance, the paradox inherent to the parallel that Frank draws between the spatialization of narrative form and the domination of the plane in Worringer's theory of artistic abstraction might occlude the eclecticism in his reading of Worringer, as spatialization appears to contradict the 'flat' linearity of the plane. The relation between both concepts becomes much clearer in Frank's response to criticism of his influential essay, a response in which he argues:" I stated what has become a

---

103 Deleuze and Guattari, *A Thousand Plateaus*, 495.
104 Ibid., 496-497.
105 Ibid., 497.

platitude — and what I can now put in more precise linguistic terminology — that the synchronic relations within the text take precedence over diachronic referentiality."[106]

The spatialization of literary form that Frank had identified as a distinctive feature of modernist novels is thus achieved by a privileging of internal synchronicity over diachronic referentiality. As a non-naturalistic mode of artistic expression, narrative spatiality therefore parallels, as Frank concludes, the "space-shyness"[107] that, according to Worringer, characterizes the modernist abstraction achieved by dominance of the plane in the plastic arts. Whereas this somewhat paradox parallel becomes more comprehensible in Frank's retroactive defense of his theorization of literary spatiality, his conclusion that by this narrative technique "history becomes ahistorical"[108] remains obscure.[109] Being itself historically situated and ideologically biased by Frank's identification with the concepts of the New Criticism,[110] his notion of a mutually exclusive *privileging* of the space-logic of synchronicity over diachrone referentiality is, above all, hardly convincing.

Rather than simply aligning her novel with either a timeless temporality of immediacy or an equally timeless, mythic universality, the subtle web of triangular cross-references to Deleuze, Frank and Worringer in both *Tropic of Orange*'s narrative and the paratextual HyperContexts grid identifies Yamashita's will-to-art as a will to comment on and to contribute to a discourse

---

106 Joseph Frank, "Spatial Form: An Answer to Critics," *The Idea of Spatial Form* (New Brunswick and London: Rutgers UP, 1991) 67-106, 75.
107 Worringer qtd. in Frank, "Spatial Form: An Answer to Critics," 85.
108 Frank, "Spatial Form in Modern Literature," 63.
109 It is noteworthy that Frank, in a 1991 defense of his 1945 article, quotes as "the most profound recent interpretation of the modern literary situation" (95) Octavio Paz's *Children of the Mire* (1974), in which the Mexican poet and critic argues that, "twentieth century poets have set against the linear time of progress and history the instantaneous time of eroticism or the cyclical time of analogy or the hollow time of the ironic consciousness. Image and humor: rejections of the chronological time of critical reason and its deification of the future"(qtd. in 95-96). Frank's claim that the "anti-capitalism," the "impassioned rejection of the modern age," and the "aversion to the world of the bourgeoisie" that Paz identifies as a common denominator of Anglo-American, European and Latin-American avant-gardes result in the abolition of historical imagination as "the ability to locate events in chronological time" (Frank 1945, 63) dismisses the very historical situatedness of these positions.
110 Frank explicitly dedicates his work on literary spatiality to Allen Tate, one of the founders of the New Criticism.

on the severed relation between time and space that marks modernity as a time of cultural crisis and anxiety. If, as Anthony Giddens has pointed out, "the dynamism of modernity derives from the *separation of time and space*"[111] and if, as Giddens continues to argue, the timetable is the "time-space ordering device" allowing for "coordination across time and space,"[112] then the HyperContexts grid doesn't simply signal a will to control the narrative space of a novel, its spatio-temporal organization. More important, its linear-geometrical structure can be read as an abstraction that renders visible the cohesive control exercised by the ordering of time and space implicit to all forms of discursive representation. An avowal rather than a denial of historicity, it neither signals that distinctions between past and present are "wiped out"[113] in the novel, nor that representation is ruined.

The combinatorial explosion of possibilities visualized by the grid is contained, and the grid not exploded as its time/space construction provides chronotopes that, despite their fantastic mobility, reflect a cultural crisis firmly situated in historical time and place: While Yamashita's (and Manzanar's) will-to-art can be described as artistic edgework – the voluntary embrace of political hazards without losing aesthetic control – the political risks negotiated by *Tropic of Orange*'s plot are defined by the border transgressing, transnational capitalism of post-NAFTA America at the end of the twentieth century and the nation's simultaneous construing of a paradox "security/economy nexus."[114]

This setting might be read, with Anthony Giddens, as one of those "'environments of risk'," – and Giddens, like Ulrich Beck, understands risks as consequences of modernity – "that collectively affect large masses of individuals,"[115] and "'security' as a situation in which a specific set of dangers is counteracted or minimized."[116] *Tropic of Orange*'s narrative, however, calls into question such a naturalizing perception of risk. Rather than facing hazardous consequences ontologically 'evolving' from modernity, its protagonists have to tackle risks that are construed and imposed by very specific political decisions. These decisions are, on the one hand, guided by a strategic geo-political

---

111 Anthony Giddens, *The Consequences of Modernity* (Stanford: Stanford UP, 1990) 16.
112 Ibid., 20.
113 Frank,"Spatial Form in Modern Literature," 63.
114 See Mathew Coleman,"U.S. Statecraft and the U.S.-Mexico Border as Security/ Economy Nexus," *Geopolitics*. Vol. II , ed. Klaus Dodds (London et al.: Sage, 2009) 209-235.
115 Giddens, *Modernity*, 35.
116 Ibid. 35-36.

territorialism of the nation-state, and, on the other, by the border transgressing ideology of free trade as represented by the utopianist Asia Pacific imaginary and the NAFTA.

Tropic of Orange addresses and exposes the contradictions inherent in discourses of both the nation and the transnational trade zone where they are glossed over by a homogenizing language of global excess. It stages how the euphemistic official promotion of what amounts to an oxymoronic "gated globalism"[117] is designed to occlude both the interest in control over geo-political and geo-economic space, and the risks it implies for the migrant laborer on whose "speculative vistas"[118] of America it relies. In doing so, *Tropic of Orange* brings its 'postmodern' plot in line with the historical late-nineteenth discourse that identified speculation as being deeply rooted in the founding, the political self-conception, and the geo-political development of the American nation. Affirming the characterization of the American immigrant as a speculator who believes and invests in America's utopian promise, *Tropic of Orange* foregrounds how faith and trust in this promise are prompted by deceptive representations that blind out contingencies and dangers. Particularly two of the novel's protagonists, Bobby Ngu and Arcangel, both of them representatives of a class of migrant labor whose subjectivity is cast as excessively fluid, embrace these dangers with confidence.

3.3 CONFIDENCE MAN I: BOBBY NGU AND THE CONFIDENCE GAME OF GLOBALIZED CAPITALISM

The novel's most obvious negotiation of an economic trans-Pacific imaginary takes place in the seven chapters that are focalized on Bobby Ngu, with the chapter headings blatantly signaling the primacy of money in the prevailing U.S. American value-system: "Benefits" – "Car Payment Due" – "Second Mortgage" – "Life Insurance" – "Visa Card" – "Social Security" – "American Express." These headings, on the one hand, indicate that the immigrant Bobby Ngu has 'made it,' because he has successfully crossed the "new line of hegemony" as Hans Ulrich Gumbrecht has termed "the absolute line of social division between

---

117 Hilary Cunningham, "Transnational Politics at the Edges of Sovereignty: Social Movements, Crossings and the State at the U.S.-Mexico Border." *Global Networks* 1 (4): 369-387, 371.

118 Urs Stäheli, *Spektakuläre Spekulation: Das Populäre in der Ökonomie* (Frankfurt/Main: Suhrkamp, 2007) 173.

those [...] who have a Social Security number and those who don't."[119] On the other, they seem to reduce Bobby to a mere economic factor as they emphasize his absorption into a powerful finance and insurance system, which produces dependency as a form of subjection, and which implies the possibility of ubiquitous surveillance and control. While this subtle form of sovereign governance applies to contemporary first world subjects regardless of nationality, race, and/or ethnicity, the chapters focalized on Bobby foreground, however, "the ways that global capitalism has inexorably and powerfully defined the Asian American subject."[120]

Accordingly, Bobby's history is shown to be economically motivated from scratch, and simultaneously provides various instances of U.S. encroachments across the Pacific. As the narrative gradually reveals, Bobby's real name is Li Kwan Yu, and he is not, as the pseudonym he has cunningly chosen suggests, a Vietnamese but a Chinese immigrant from Singapore. After his father's small Singaporean bicycle plant has been ousted by a globally expanding U.S. venture destroying his family's basis of existence, Bobby follows a piece of advice that resonates with confidence in America as the land of future potential: "Dad says, you wanna future? Better go to America. Better start out something new."(15) Thus incited by confidence in America, Bobby becomes an economic refugee at the age of twelve. A victim of U.S.-capitalist expansionism, he pretends to be a Vietnamese war refugee and manages to emigrate to the U.S under this label. Disguised as a "bonafide Vietnamese" (79), yet guided by 'good faith' in the utopian American promise, Bobby is depicted as an ambiguous 'confidence man,' who tricks his way into the promised land.

By investing Bobby's story with this twist of fraudulent mimicry, Yamashita very skillfully contextualizes the racializing Western construction of 'the Asian' as shrewdly and excessively economic with the duplicitous principles of a hegemonic moral economy, which grants immigration permits as compensation for U.S. military transgressions in Vietnam. Implicitly, this representation of U.S. imperialism, political-economic entanglement and arbitrary immigration policy also negotiates the calculatedly produced, yet deceptive illusion that immigration grants access to the economic abundance of wealthy first world

---

119 Hans Ulrich Gumbrecht, "Epilogue: Untenable Positions," *Streams of Cultural Capital* Eds. David Palumbo-Liu and Hans Ulrich Gumbrecht (Stanford: Stanford UP, 1993) 249-262, 225.

120 Christine So, *Economic Citizens: A Narrative of Asian American Visibility* (Philadelphia: Temple UP, 2007) 32.

nations.[121] Most important, however, it casts serious doubt on the assumption that access and excess stand as signs of social equality.[122]

In keeping with this dense trans-Pacific backstory, Yamashita sketches Bobby's life in the U.S. as an instance of perfect assimilation to American consumerism. Contrary to his Mexican wife Rafaela, a community college student, whose term paper titles clearly signal her heightened political awareness, he is not dissatisfied with this life, although he and his wife "remain at the bottom of the U.S. socioeconomic hierarchy."[123] As the owner of a small service enterprise, Bobby works tirelessly not minding the long hours or the primitive nature of his janitor job. He considers this job a mere means to achieve a better life for himself and his family, and it is in perfect conformity with the all-American notion of consumption as the key to happiness, that his dream of a better life is basically one of affluence, with little or no monetary limitations. "Gotta make money" is the mantra that makes Bobby tick, a mantra, though that not only pushes him to work harder and harder but forces him to replace enjoyment of life and vitality with self-destructing indulgence in liquor and cigarettes. A Kung-Fu fighting, hard-working, law-abiding, and apolitical citizen, Bobby perfectly combines the excessive features ascribed to a stereotypical 'Asianness' (including those attributed to Asian Americans as the well-assimilated model minority) with neoliberal practices of interminable self-improvement – at least until the shock of his wife and son leaving him induces a gradual process of change.[124]

It seems to contradict this total integration into the world of American consumerism and fiat money only at first glance when the narrator dryly sums up Bobby's existence by stating "Bobby's a cash-man" (266) at the end of the novel, just in the chapter entitled "American Express." In fact, it is characteristic of the bold symbolism that Yamashita uses in her depiction of neoliberal politics when Bobby gains access to the spectacular wrestling match between SUPERNAFTA and his Mexican opponent, in the climactic scene at the end of the novel, only by giving up his habit of paying cash and using his American Express card instead.

---

121 See Susanne Wegener, "Lines and Layers, Grids and Maps: das Konzept des Rhizoms als Ausdruck postkolonialer Hybridität in Karen Tei Yamashitas *Tropic of Orange*," *LiLi: Zeitschrift für Literaturwissenschaft und Linguistik 37*.147 (2007): 164-177, 168-169.

122 See So, *Economic Citizens*, 27.

123 Claudia Sadowski-Smith, *Border Fictions: Globalization, Empire, and Writing at the Boundaries of the United States* (Charlottesville and London: U of Virginia P, 2008) 63.

124 See Wegener, "Lines and Layers," 168-169.

While the label "cash-man," once again, caters to the long-standing, racializing Western tradition of casting 'the Asian' as excessively, yet primitively economic, Bobby's acquisition of privileged access by his use of the credit card – "American Express gets him the best"(266) – reflects the equally threatening stereotype that constructs Asians and Asian Americans as embodying an excessive "economic overachievement and adaptability."[125] The scene thus ironically amalgamates the worn-out 'Yellow-Peril' clichés of the first half of the twentieth century with the less obvious anxieties underlying both the cultural construction of Asian Americans as a model minority and the economic Pacific Rim discourse at the end of the century.

Although enthusiastically greeting the twenty-first century as the 'Pacific Century' and embracing Asian 'miracle economies' as models of capitalist success, the North American authors of the utopianist Pacific Rim discourse can hardly conceal their fear in view of "the possibility of Asia's economic expansion (more often characterized as domination) and the specter of billions of Asian buyers, laborers, and sellers,"[126] or gloss over their hegemonic agenda in a climate of stiff economic competition. Using the trope of the Pacific Rim to evoke connotations of physical boundaries, totality, and coherence, their rhetoric of free trade, transnational convergence and border-free economic spaces in the Pacific region aims to disguise the fact that the Pacific has become "a site of contestation between the United States and various East Asian competitors."[127]

In this struggle for hegemony over the region, language plays a crucial role, as Alexander Woodside points out: "The language of the Asia-Pacific myth, with its invocations of 'Third Wave' civilizations and its focus upon the 'basic commonalities' of economic prosperity, rhetorically reconciles the tensely coexisting multiple rival capitalisms and usefully blurs potential battle lines among them."[128] It is important to recall that this rhetorical suppression of differences and tensions invents and constructs the homogenous and borderless space that it pretends to describe. In fact, the "newly invented space of the Asia Pacific"[129] is a product of "rimspeak,"[130] as Bruce Cumings has trenchantly

---

125 So, *Economic Citizens*, 11.
126 Ibid., 8.
127 Arif Dirlik, "Introduction: Pacific Contradictions," *What Is In A Rim: Critical Perspectives on the Pacific Region Idea,* ed Arif Dirlik (Lanham e.a.: Rowman and Littlefield, 1998) 3-13, 5.
128 "The Asia-Pacific Idea as a Mobilization Myth," *What Is In A Rim: Critical Perspectives on the Pacific Region Idea,* ed. Arif Dirlik (Lanham: Rowman and Littlefield, 1998) 37-53, 49.
129 Palumbo-Liu, *Asian/American*, 343.

termed this very specific variety of the language of global excess. In the sense of Baudrillard's "precession of simulacra,"[131] its floating signifiers engender not just a territory but a hyper-real space governed by representation and designed to solicit speculation.

By casting Bobby Ngu as an excessive 'Asian' *homo oeconomicus* who is lured across the Pacific by America's utopian promise of equal opportunity, *Tropic of Orange* addresses this discourse on representation and speculation beyond the racist stereotype of 'the Asian' and the racist politics of exclusion underlying the inclusionary language of global excess. The novel's depiction of a profound "bankerization"[132] of his Asian American existence suggests a correspondence between an increasingly elusive monetary nominalism that dematerializes economic exchange, and a fluid, equally elusive subjectivity whose succession of masquerades replaces identity in an interminable process of abstraction, displacement and deferral. In showing Bobby's reluctant development from a "cash-man," whose reliance on the banknote signifies his confidence in the imaginary of a foundational stability and a protected value granted by the state, to a user of an American Express credit card, *Tropic of Orange* depicts Americanization as adaptation to an economy that is founded on credit and confidence, and the credit card as an entrance ticket to a confidence game that is no longer confined to the nation. Misled by 'good faith' and misleading by his masquerade as a "bonafide Vietnamese," Bobby Ngu eventually becomes an American when he embarks on the electronic frontier of capitalism and its elusive realm of fiat money. Although increasingly disillusioned with the American promise, his use of the plastic card that grants worldwide credit while being backed by nothing than electronic signs suggests that he has become a late-twentieth century version of the confidence man that Herman Melville depicted in his eponymous last novel. Published in 1857, *The Confidence Man: His Masquerade* reflects a historical climax of a distrust of paper money that had haunted the U.S nation from the beginning of American history.

Throughout this history, periods of currency backed by specie – gold or silver – and/or acknowledged by government guarantees alternated with periods

---

130 Rimspeak: Or, The Discourse of the Pacific Rim," *What Is In A Rim: Critical Perspectives on the Pacific Region Idea*, ed. Arif Dirlik (Lanham: Rowman and Littlefield, 1998) 53-72.

131 Jean Baudrillard, *Simulations* (New York: Semiotexte, 1983) 2.

132 Jean Joseph Goux, "Cash, Check, or Charge?" *The New Economic Criticism: Studies at the Intersection of Literature and Economics*, eds. Martha Woodmansee and Mark Osteen (London and New York: Routledge, 1999) 114-128, 122.

in which the circulation of large amounts of paper money printed by hundreds of banks and not backed by specie rattled the very confidence of Americans that fueled American economic growth. Since value in the speculative American economy was created by confidence – "a mysterious sentiment that permitted a country poor in specie but rich in promises to create something from nothing"[133] – and confidence was further shaken by counterfeiters who, capitalizing on the lack of a single issuing authority, channeled false banknotes into the monetary circuit, "the American economy rose and fell on a tide of paper credit that tended to promise more than they could deliver."[134] This volatile interplay of confidence and value resulted in a number of financial crises. It was at the peak of one of these crises, the financial panic of 1857, when debates about the gold standard resurged, since "the money supply became a great confluence of ten thousand different kinds of paper that continually changed hands,"[135] and the approach of the Civil War created growing economic needs, that Melville's novel *The Confidence Man: His Masquerade*[136] was delivered to the bookstores.

Set on a Missisippi steamer, conspicuously named Fidèle, on its journey from St. Louis to New Orleans on April 1st, Melville's narrative introduces the boat as a "ship of fools,"[137] its passengers as a "flock of fools,"[138] and the issue of trust and confidence as its central concern. In Melville's novel, confidence is solicited by a mysterious impostor who, in various pious disguises, persuades his fellow passengers "to donate or lend money; purchase stocks, strange machines, and herbal medicines."[139] Melville leaves no doubt, however, that the confidence man's schemes do not merely reflect the corrupt business practices of the period, as in the course of both the narrative and the journey his confidence games become more complex and the quality of his sales pitches decidedly

---

133 Stephen Mihm, *A Nation of Counterfeiters: Capitalists, Con Men, and the Making of the United States*, (Cambridge, MA: Harvard UP, 2007), 10.
134 Ben Tarnoff, *Moneymakers: The Wicked Lives and Surprising Adventures of Three Notorious Counterfeiters* (London: Pengouin, 2011), 4.
135 Mihm, *A Nation of Counterfeiters*, 3.
136 Herman Melville, *The Confidence Man: His Masquerade* (New York e.a.: Norton, 2006).
137 Melville, *The Confidence Man*, 23.
138 Ibid., 1.
139 Yvonne Elizabeth Pelletier, "False Promises and Real Estate: Land Speculation and Millennial Maps in Herman Melville's Confidence Man," *American Literary Geographies: Spatial Practice and Cultural Production 1500-1900*, eds Martin Brückner and Hsuan L. Hsu (Newark: U of Delaware P, 2007) 191-205, 195.

philosophical.[140] Conjoining a discourse on Christian philanthropy – "Charity never faileth"[141] – with a discourse on faith in signs – next to his stall the ship's barber has placed a gilded sign that reads "NO TRUST" – *The Confidence Man: His Masquerade* is more than "a parable about the market economy."[142] While its religious subtext suggests "that Christianity and the Bible are 'confidence tricks'"[143] as they rely on a deceptive economy of faith, its discourse on signs is a self-reflexive, semiotic meditation on the severed relation between signifier and signified with fundamental implications, as Mark C. Taylor observes in his reading of the barber's gilded "NO TRUST" sign:

> The sign that Melville names a sign is no ordinary sign, for it calls into question the very meaning and significance of signs. Were we to follow the counsel of the sign by refusing to trust, we could not have confidence in any sign. If, however, signs are not to be trusted, then we cannot even have confidence in the sign that reads "NO TRUST." The challenge of the sign creates a double bind. The barber's sign bends back on itself to create a distrust of distrust. The sign, in other words, discredits itself by encouraging an attitude that is precisely the opposite of what it seems to promote. When we distrust distrust, it once again becomes possible to credit signs. [...] It is not insignificant that the sign upon which Melville's questions turn is "gilt." A gilded sign is almost as good as gold: its surface is gold but its substance is a matter of little value. This play of surface and substance inverts the customary relation between signifier and signified to create a simulation whose value is uncertain. Throughout human history, gold is not so much a sign as the transcendental signified that is supposed to ground the meaning and value of other signs. Gold, in other words, is the sign that is constructed to erase its status as a sign.[144]

What is encoded in Melville's gilded sign, besides a comment on the economic crisis marking the period of *The Confidence Man*'s production and publication, is, according to Taylor, a fundamental distrust in the symbolic economies of language, writing and fiction. Like Edgar Allan Poe's "Gold Bug"(1843), Melville's 1857 novel is, above all, a meta-fictional text on the crisis of language and aesthetic representation, and as such strikingly prefigures "the collapse of referents, the dissolution of exchange standards, the dissociation of the sign from what it signifies, the evacuation of all 'presence' or of any 'treasure' regulating

---

140 See ibid.
141 Melville, *The Confidence Man*, 12.
142 Mihm, *A Nation of Counterfeiters*, 4.
143 Pelletier, "False Promises," 195.
144 Mark C. Taylor, "Discrediting God," *Journal of the American Academy of Religion* 62.2 (1994): 603-623, 606-607.

the play of signifiers, the indefinite deferral of meaning, in the pure operations of writing,"[145] whose climax in electronic money would be pinpointed by Jean Joseph Goux more than a century later.

For Goux, the credit card marks the ultimate highpoint of the increasing dissociation of sign and substance that had been inherent already in the first appearance of coins whose inscribed value did not, in many cases, match their metallic purity or weight. [146] Encoded in the credit card are the ultimate abstraction of the monetary sign and the processing of automatic banking operations in the form of electronic signals that are "further and further removed from human labor."[147] However, different from Melville's gilded "NO TRUST" sign and its paradox double bind, the electromagnetic plastic card – while being itself a worthless 'gilded' sign – solicits trust in an excessive promise of worldwide credit that is based on an indefinite deferral of debt. It thus epitomizes the highpoint of an economy of confidence that constantly projects the realization of value into a distant future.

As a late-twentieth-century confidence man Bobby Ngu is both the object of and an operative subject in this economy of confidence that banks on the future in a representational space in which "signs are left to float freely on a sea that has no shores."[148] Characterized by constant oscillation between trust and distrust, hope and disillusionment, the story of his Americanization negotiates the same circular relation between confidence, representation and future value that Melville's *Confidence Man* depicts as grounded in the speculative quality of the American market economy. *Tropic of Orange* picks up the nineteenth-century anxieties about currency and credibility, caused by "more than ten thousand of different kinds of paper that continually changed hands,"[149] by relining Bobby's development from a cash-man to the confident holder and user of a credit card with a complex discourse on paper and value, trust and identity throughout the chapters that are focalized on his perspective.

Beginning with the passport and the dollar notes that his father "saved from the black market"(16) in order to enable Bobby's entry to America, this discourse suggests that representational constructions of both national identity and currency are vulnerable to fraudulent deception. Moreover, it implicitly

---

145 "Cash, Check, or Charge?" 115.
146 Marc Shell, "The Issue of Representation," *The New Economic Criticism: Studies at the Intersection of Literature and Economics*, eds. Martha Woodmansee and Mark Osteen (London and New York: Routledge, 1999) 53-74, 54.
147 Goux, "Cash, Check, or Charge?" 120.
148 Taylor, "Discrediting God," 607.
149 Mihm, *A Nation of Counterfeiters*, 3.

exposes the purely fictional and arbitrary quality of legal tender that is invested with value by mere state power – including the authority to decide who and what crosses the nation's border – when representative papers of identity and currency are traded as commodities in the framework of a shadow economy and thereby assume the "archaic and almost incredible"[150] quality of 'commodity money' that precious metals used to have. Equipped with the supposedly 'golden' passport and with the dollar notes sewn into his pants – and thus 'safely' endowed with the "documentary proof" and the "plain paper"[151] that Melville's novel had already ridiculed as deceptive fictional significations – Bobby manages to shirk all legal restrictions and immigrate to the land of plenty, only to learn that what this land holds in store for him is plenty of primitive work with little or no prospect to better his situation. And even in this primitive work, as Yamashita shows, paper and trust, representation and confidence have a crucial role.

In "Benefits," Bobby's expository chapter, immediately following the passage on the representative papers that enable Bobby's immigration, Yamashita makes a point of letting the reader know that Bobby's janitor job is not restricted to *trabajo de limpieza*, the cleaning work usually done by illegal Hispanics, who are as eager to make money as Bobby is, but includes the sorting of mail in the mailroom of a "big-time newspaper"(16) and the disposal of secret documents in a bomb producing company that "still got defense contracts" (16). While the mail sorting job indicates a certain degree of confidence in the immigrant, who is entrusted with a task that at least requires the ability to read, Yamashita's mention of this detail can also be read as a reference to Melville's short story "Bartleby, the Scrivener," whose eponymous protagonist is a mysterious character, who politely but firmly rejects his task of copying legal documents. The only hint at an explanation for Bartleby's melancholy refusal and alienation is offered at the end of this narrative, when the reader learns that Bartleby's previous job was the sorting through of undeliverable mail in a postal 'Dead Letter Office.' Confined to sorting mail in the mailroom of a "big-time newspaper" (16) Bobby Ngu is as excluded from the circuit of signification and meaning making as a dead letter. And still, although melancholic and alienated like Bartleby, who refuses to write by stubbornly repeating "I would prefer not to,"[152] Bobby equally politely, if taciturnly 'would prefer not to" read the

---

150 Jean Joseph Goux, *Symbolic Economies* (Ithaka, NY: Cornell UP, 1990), 121.
151 Melville, *The Confidence Man*, 21.
152 Giorgio Agamben reads both the formula and the 'rumor' about the Dead Letter Office, mentioned at the end of Melville's narrative as references to a biblical passage in Paulus. Thus contextualized with, "And the Commandment, which was

duplicity encoded in what he proudly perceives as signs of confidence in his reliability as a putatively legal immigrant.

As the following passage from "Life Insurance," Bobby's fourth chapter in *Tropic of Orange*, illustrates, however, the duplicity of the immigration confidence game is inscribed in and suffuses the language of Bobby's narrative discourse. Marked by the floating mode of free indirect speech and an elliptic syntax, this discourse reflects both his fluid subjectivity and his distrust in language as information encoded in signs:

Bobby don't ask no questions. He just comes in twice if they give him the call. [...] maybe it's the place in El Segundo makes bombs. Gotta haul out the shredded paper. Anybody ask any questions, he's got a clearance. After everything, they never figured out he's not Vietnam. *Not no orphan with no connections to nothing.* Orphan refugee can't be communist. Gotta be happy he's alive in America. Saved by the Americans. New country. New life. Working hard to make it. American through and through. Clearance proves it. He can haul out all the shredded documents he can carry. Doing America a favor. Doing his duty. That's it. (158-159, italics added)

While the passage foregrounds Bobby's Americanness as a decidedly apolitical 'pledge of allegiance,' based on gratitude, work ethic, and 'no questions' asked (in this case the turning of a blind eye to classified documents that might impair an idealizing perception of America) the fourfold negation in the phrase "Not no orphan with no connections to nothing"(159) subtly slips in an element of distrust of the state's signifying power as it casts Bobby's subjectivity as a vacancy, a blank position in the dominant symbolic order. Blending the trope of pleonasm with the dysgrammatism that marks Bobby's discourse throughout, the irritating accumulation of negations can only be deciphered in the context of the sentences immediately surrounding it. Strikingly, these sentences are, like the pleonasm they frame, negative constructions describing hegemonic fictions of national identity and security, rather than pinning down Bobby's subjectivity. Framed by "not Vietnam"(a synecdoche signifying a denied political U.S. trauma rather than denoting a citizen of a South-East Asian nation) and "can't be communist" (a phrase summarizing the construction of a risk construed to justify

---

ordained to life, I found to be unto death" both the dead letters and the formula, express a fundamental (and, as Agamben suggests, legitimate) distrust of scripture and/as law. If Bartleby can be read as a messianic redeemer figure (as Deleuze and others gave argued), redemption would, according to Agamben, have to result, ultimately, in the destruction of the Tora. See *Bartleby oder die Kontingenz* (Berlin: Merve, 1998) 69-72.

the United States' self-appointed political and military mission in the Manichaean world order of the Cold War era) Bobby's political subjectivity becomes visible as not definable by fictions of national identity and security, which it eludes in a flurrying play of negative signifiers.

It is the second word in the phrase "Not *no* orphan with no connection to nothing," the dysgrammatical 'no' that can be read as a resistant linguistic residue rejecting the narrow space ascribed to the immigrant subject by the hegemonic symbolic order, amidst and despite the affirmative pledge of allegiance. It is this 'no' that carves out a "clearance" beyond the approval that signals the official authorities' trust that Bobby will not pose a security risk. Gained by a confidence trick, the "clearance" that allows Bobby to haul away documents of a bomb producing company "that still got defense contracts" is itself a confidence trick, since the paper that Bobby disposes of is shredded and thus unreadable. What this clearance 'proves,' then, is not trust in the immigrant laborer, but the duplicitous workings of a subtle economy of confidence designed to form and to keep in place a political subjectivity that has "gotta be happy to be alive in America." (158) With the pleonasm inserted into Bobby's avowal of gratitude and civic duty, the text signals, however, that Bobby evades this reduction to 'bare life.'[153] It indicates that, although Bobby can and will not read the classified documents, he is about to carve out for himself a 'clearance' in a different sense, a free inhabitable space, in which trust in signs is not only possible again but allows a reading of the state's duplicitous confidence game.

In conveying details of the nature of Bobby's janitor job, Yamashita not only subtly links the process of his gradual disillusionment to a discourse on a contemporary version of distrust in paper, but illustrates this discourse as closely related to constructions of national security and risk. In this process of Bobby's disillusionment, the pleonastic negations in the phrase "not no orphan with no connection to nothing" mark a turning point. Like the barber's gilded "NO TRUST" sign in Melville's *Confidence Man*, the phrase expresses a "distrust of distrust,"[154] and captures a double bind in a speculative economy of confidence of which mutual deception is an integral part. If, as Mark C. Taylor claims in his reading of Melville, "when we distrust distrust, it once again becomes possible to credit signs,"[155] and if, as Jean Joseph Goux argues, "money *is* language, information, writing,"[156] the benefits alluded to in Bobby's eponymous

---

153 See Giorgio Agamben, Homo Sacer: Sovereign Power and Bare Life (Stanford: Stanford UP, 1998).
154 Taylor, "Discrediting God," 606.
155 Ibid.
156 "Cash, Check, or Charge," 121, italics in the original.

expository chapter are earned in "Life Insurance," the chapter in which Bobby finally decides to give paper and language the benefit of the doubt.

In a passage placed shortly after the pleonasm of negations that already contains a linguistic seed of resistance, the text subtly insinuates that Bobby's life is 'insured'– a 'clearance' beyond bare life carved out – by his reading of his Mexican wife Rafaela's college papers. The titles of Rafaela's papers indicate that the benefits Bobby draws are not to be stacked in cash, but consist in a growing trust in the language of cultural critique and an ensuing rise of political consciousness:

Maquiladoras & Migrants, Undocumented, Illegal & Alien: Immigrants vs. Immigration. Talks about *globalization of capital. Capitalization of poverty. Internationalization of the labor force. Exploitation and political expediency. Devaluation of currency and foreign economic policy. Economic intervention.* Big words like that. Enough to get back smoking again. Maybe he's been too busy. Maybe. But it's not like he don't understand. Prop 187. Keep illegals out of schools and hospitals. They could pass all the propositions they want people like him and Rafaela weren't gonna just disappear. (161, italics in the original)

Being neither an orphan nor having "no connection to nothing" (158), it is by way of his ties to Rafaela that Bobby gradually overcomes his denial of the state's distrust in and internal exclusion of the immigrant on whose labor it capitalizes. Yet, different from Rafaela, whose writing – for all its political critique – still signals her belief in the U.S. as a deliberative democracy, Bobby remains a confidence man, willing to outplay the state in a confidence game that relies on faith in the elusive, operative signs of monetary economic exchange.

In a confidence plot that is set in the novel's diegetic present, Yamashita plausibly amalgamates Bobby's memories of his own immigration plot and the discourse on paper and confidence with a representation of the workings of a trans-nationalized political economy, transnational family ties, and charity. After receiving a letter that, allegedly written by his father, requests Bobby's help in financing the purchase of immigration papers for a 'cousin' that he cannot remember, Bobby meets with a Chinese contact in L.A.'s Chinatown. Presented with the photograph of a twelve-year-old Chinese girl, a sentimental backstory and an appeal to his sense of family, Bobby decides to help the girl, although he quickly realizes that he is being deceived by a confidence trickster. Shunning the Chinatown "snakehead" (99) and beating down the price of his "Chinese connection"(99) that capitalizes on trafficking undocumented migrants across the U.S. /Mexican border, he uses his money and the experience gained in the confidence plots of his own and his wife's immigration to smuggle the twelve-year-old Chinese girl from Tijuana across the U.S./Mexican border to L.A.

As in all episodes focalized on Bobby Ngu, several details in this narrative of his altruistic support for and protection of a girl that is not at all related to him, can be read as references to Melville's *The Confidence Man*. However, while strikingly reminiscent of key tropes in Melville's novel, the Chinese herbal medicine that Bobby buys in a Chinatown pharmacy before he meets the Chinese con man, the use of the term "snakehead" (99) for this criminal character, and charity as a motif propelling Bobby's readiness to help the orphaned girl cast Bobby as an object rather than a subject of confidence schemes. This chain of referents suggests that not only the "Lucky Golden Dragon" (99), the boat that brings across the Pacific Chinese immigrants hoping for and speculating on a golden American future, but, at the same time, Chinatown, L.A., and all of the U.S. are, like Melville's Fidèle, a "ship of fools"[157] inhabited by "a flock of fools"[158] whose most prominent feature is blind trust in treacherous promises and deceptive representational schemes.

Yet it is just with its representation of Bobby's family ties and the motif of charity that *Tropic of Orange* introduces the symbolism of an alternative economy to contrast the operative signs of the capitalist economy in which "the libidinal, the intersubjective, and the semantic are completely divorced from economic relations."[159] Bobby's barter with the Chinatown snakehead sets the tone for an economic exchange that can be associated with the "primitive" intertribal economy that Jean Joseph Goux, drawing on the work of Géza Róheim and Marcel Mauss, describes as "pre-oedipal" and "embedded in a dual maternal signifying economy."[160]

In this barter economy, social and commercial relationships are inseparable and constituted, in many cases, by tribal rituals such as the exchange of children's umbilical cords. Intertribal commerce thus not only works without mediation by the law of an abstract general equivalent, but rests upon social ties established by the symbolic exchange of bodies and body parts. As Goux observes, "in barter a harmony of desires and a reciprocity of ties implies that the exchange is also a commerce of bodies."[161] On the one hand, Bobby's barter with the human trafficking snakehead seems to indicate that even the commerce of bodies becomes detached from social ties in the paradox context of

---

157 Melville, *The Confidence Man*, 23.
158 Ibid., 1.
159 Goux, *Symbolic Economies*, 125.
160 Ibid. 123.
161 Ibid.

transnational capitalism and U.S. immigration legislation. On the other, however, it prepares a confidence plot that channels into the abstract operational symbolization of a 'bankerized' capitalist society, a "cryptophoric symbolism" laden with inter-subjective affect and a "surplus meaning"[162] of social ties and libidinal value.

Sigificantly, the chapter in which Bobby smuggles the Chinese girl across the U.S./Mexican border bears the title "Visa Card," and it is basically a bankerized shopping transaction that enables the girl's illegal crossing of the highly lit up and heavily policed, fourteen-mile border zone. Having paid the Chinese con man with his Visa card that "drags itself through the slit"(201) in an abstracted and automatized economic exchange of de-semanticized signs deferring "convertibility to the point where it becomes imaginary,"[163] Bobby meets his Chinese "cuz" in Tijuana and slyly uses this imaginary economy and its elusive play of signifiers: after ridding the girl of all visible traces of her Chinese background, he, again, uses the Visa card to fit her out with a conspicuously American attire. Dressed in Levi's, Nike's sneakers, a T-Shirt that reads "Malibu," and with a Barbie doll in her arms the girl enters the U.S. as his daughter without even being asked to show a passport that she does not possess.

Notably, this intriguingly simple narrative affirms with subtle, yet conclusive details Bobby's adherence to the unwritten laws of a primitive, tribal economy that his barter with the snakehead has already foreshadowed. Read in light of the barter economy described by Goux, Roheim and Mauss, the cutting off of the girl's pigtails can be read as a bold metaphor alluding to the ritualized exchange of umbilical cords that establishes both social and commercial ties. It presents the symbolical replacement of a biological relation between two members of a 'tribe' that the text, in addition, labels "two celestials" (204). Referring, at one level, to "Celestial Empire," a traditional name for China, the term "celestials," at another level, further invests the narrative with connotations of the "sacred signs" and the "cryptophoric symbolism" that characterize, according to Goux, "all pre-capitalist societies, whether they are tribal, Asiatic, ancient or feudal in type."[164] What is being cut off with the Chinese girl's pigtails in the process of her visible Americanization is, read against this background, the umbilical cord to a pre-oedipal, maternal signifying economy. In pushing this process and in posing as the girl's father, Bobby initiates "the little celestial" to the oedipal, profane, and operative signifiers of a political economy which mark her body as 'alien' and exploitable. It is, however, his affective and social investment – an

---

162 Ibid., 121.
163 Goux, *Symbolic Economies*, 130.
164 Ibid., 129.

investment clearly exceeding the duplicitous Christian charity ironized in Melville's *Confidence Man* – that smuggles in, together with the little celestial's 'alien' body, the affective 'surplus' of which this economy is utterly devoid.

While this subtle negotiation of contrasting symbolic economies casts him as a *homo oeconomicus* who cannot be reduced to the "rationality of atomistic behavior"[165], Bobby Ngu is, at the same time, represented in the narrative of this confidence plot as the "economically well-educated subject"[166] of a political sovereignty that, according to Foucault, "will cover the totality of the economic process with a gaze [...] in the uniform light of evidence."[167] It is his intimate knowledge of the U.S./Mexican border as a liminal and ambiguous political-economic space, in which flows of capital and goods, and flows of migrant bodies are unevenly regulated, that enables Bobby's delusion of this sovereign gaze and its reliance on "the uniform light of evidence." Based on this knowledge, his confidence trick draws on performativity and the persuasive 'evidence' of a disguise that can be purchased with a Visa card. It is not without irony when Bobby covers the Chinese girl's 'alien' body with garments whose American brand names encode their production in sweatshops by workers, whose disenfranchisement is legally sanctioned and allows for the exploitative creation of surplus value, thereby granting the profit margins of transnational corporations whose capital and goods travel across borders unimpeded by restrictions.

Staging the political duplicity of the tri-national North American Free Trade Agreement (NAFTA), this satiric representation of Bobby's border-violating confidence trick extends *Tropic of Orange*'s critique of the free trade ideology and its disguising schemes. It refers to conditions sanctioned by a treaty whose official implementation in 1992 has legalized an ongoing "de facto absorption of Mexico into the US economy,"[168] and has for decades to come locked up provisions for a lopsided distribution of economic and political power in favor of the U.S. Similar to the utopianist Pacific Rim discourse, a rhetoric of freedom and transnational convergence obscures the downside of the treaty in its official promotion. Behind the smokescreen of neoliberal rhetoric, private, U.S.-based and state-subsidized, 'transnational' corporations (the true beneficiaries of NAFTA) capitalize on the agreement's imposition of a "mixture of liberalization

---

165 Michel Foucault, *The Birth of Biopolitics: Lectures at the Collège de France 1978-1979* (New York: Palgrave Macmillan, 2004), 282.
166 Ibid., 285.
167 Foucault, *The Birth of Biopolitics*, 286.
168 Pamela Maria Smorkaloff, "Shifting Borders, Free Trade, and Frontier Narratives: US, Canada, and Mexico," *American Literary History* 6.1 (1994): 88-102, 88.

and protection, designed to keep the wealth and power firmly in the hands of the masters of the 'new imperial age'."[169] Resorting to less emotive language, the Labor Advisory Committee's critical report on the treaty, published shortly after NAFTA's legal implementation, precisely pinpointed its negative implications in predicting that it would

> have the effect of prohibiting democratically elected bodies at [all] levels of government from enacting measures deemed inconsistent with the provisions of the agreement,[...] including those of the environment, workers' rights, and health and safety, all open to challenge as 'unfair restraint of trade.'[170]

Only a couple of years later, a soaring number of maquiladoras in North Mexico and the desperate reality of their employees have vigorously corroborated the LAC's prediction. With the poor working conditions and mere survival wages granted by NAFTA – and although working on Mexican soil – maquiladora workers must be considered an indirect export of cheap workforce, which, in conjunction with direct labor export in the form of Mexican migration to the U.S., drain Mexico of the resources necessary for its reproduction.[171] NAFTA thus secures the "contraction of part of the Mexican economy, which is compelled to serve as a labor reserve for foreign capital."[172] This process of economic restructuring – sold by NAFTA rhetoric as 'economic liberalization' – was accompanied by a highly racialized anti-immigration discourse urging the escalation of rigid U.S. American immigration control. It has led to the criminalization of immigrants who risk their lives crossing an intensely policed U.S-Mexican border zone in the hope of improving their own and their families' economic situation. With congressional laws construing the subjectivity of migrants as 'criminal aliens' and as risks to national security, health, wealth, and culture,[173] the late-twentieth century militarization of the U.S.-Southwest border

---

169 Noam Chomsky, "Notes on NAFTA: The Masters of Mankind," *Juarez: the Laboratory of Our Future* ed. Charles Bowden (Hong Kong: Everbest, 1998) 13-20, 14.
170 Qtd. in Chomsky, "Notes on NAFTA," 19.
171 See Raul Delgado Wise, and Mariana Ortega Breña, Migration and Imperialism: The Mexican Workforce in the Context of NAFTA," *Latin American Perspectives* 33.2 (2006): 33-35, 35.
172 Ibid.
173 See Mathew Coleman, "U.S. Statecraft and the U.S.-Mexico Border as Security/ Economy Nexus,"*Geo-politics*. Vol. II, ed. Klaus Dodds (London, et al.: Sage, 2009) 209-235, 215. Coleman traces telltale changes in the diction of a succession of immigration laws passed by Congress since 1986. According to his analysis, the

must be regarded a "geopolitical frontier regime"[174] that strangely coexists with the de-territorializing economic transnationalism promoted by the ideology of free trade.

In its complex representation of Bobby Ngu, *Tropic of Orange* conjoins a critique of the utopianist Pacific Rim discourse with a critical comment on the hemispheric "security/economy nexus"[175] that emerged in the wake of NAFTA. It shows that both phenomena are related manifestations of late-twentieth-century, global capitalism, a political-economic regime in which euphemistic representations of a border transgressing global excess gloss over irreducible contradictions between the interests of national sovereignty and economic liberalization. In choosing the chronotope of a post-NAFTA U.S. Southwest, and in depicting Bobby as a twentieth-century Asian American confidence man, Yamashita makes extensive and artful use of the potential of literary discourse to uncover the denial of dangers and tensions inherent to these official representations as a deceptive globalized confidence game. With a subtle web of references to Melville's *Confidence Man*, she relates the speculative economies of this global confidence game to a historical U.S.-national discourse on economic speculation and confidence in representation. In activating the intertextual 'coin' of Melville's little read novel, she re-introduces it into a circuit of competing symbolic economies, and with this cross-reference, adds a historical dimension to her novel's criticism of discursive representation initiated by the HyperContexts grid. In the chapters focalized on Bobby Ngu, this criticism seems to suggest that it is the language of literature and the language of cultural critique – represented by Rafaela's college papers – that are worthy of trust and confidence.

Permeating the narrative of Bobby's Americanization as a confidence man in the age of neoliberal governance, this critical negotiation of representation culminates in the rich and multiply coded text of the confidence plot, by which Bobby 'americanizes' the Chinese girl's alien body. In staging the commerce of

---

1986 Immigration and Reform Control Act (IRCA) was "motivated by congressional fear of demographically driven migration through the U.S.-Mexico 'backdoor' [...] and by purported medical risks, contagion possibilities, so-called cultural enclavism, and fiscal burdens posed by such migration." The category of the "criminal alien," initially denoting "an incarcerated alien subject to deportation" was in subsequent legal texts increasingly generalized "to name a larger perceived problem of immigrant criminality." As an umbrella term it thus rhetorically paved the way to construing immigrant workers as a risk and a threat to the nation..

174 Ibid., 214.
175 Ibid., 213.

alien bodies that are disenfranchised by economic restructuring and construed as a risk to national security this plot is, significantly, a performance. Its theatricality reveals and exploits a decidedly histrionic quality inherent to the disciplinary practices of a seemingly incoherent "gated globalism."[176] The performativity of Bobby's counterfeiting border game not only suggests the formation of national identity by "the citational performance of selves and others," but reflects a notion of the border as a stage and the escalation of border control as an "audience-directed performance."[177] Even more important, by disguising the alien body with the logos of transnational corporations, Bobby's performance affirms a reading of the border as the stage for a grotesque theatrical play of national statecraft *in the service* of global free trade, rather than a mere coincidence of incoherent disciplinary practices.[178]

3.4 CONFIDENCE MAN II: A MEDIAL CONQUISTA

This notion of the performativity of the border as an important tool in the service of free trade is corroborated by the narrative discourse of those chapters in *Tropic of Orange* that focalize on Arcangel. A timeless Pan-American trickster figure, introduced as a poet and a "one man circus act" (47), Arcangel literally embodies the cultural history of the American continent from its 'discovery' in 1492 to the present. Inscribed in his body is, above all, the history of Latin-

---

176 Cunningham, "Transnational Politics," 371.
177 Peter Andreas qtd. in Coleman, "U.S. Statecraft and the U.S.-Mexico Border," 210.
178 While acknowledging Peter Andreas's work on the performative function of border policing and the "expressive role of law enforcement" in the performance of the border, Mathew Coleman calls into question the subordination of "geo-political" immigration policing to "geo-economical" trade interests. Counter to a notion of U.S. statecraft as privileging and enforcing the primacy of its interests in free trade by means of its immigration policy, Coleman advocates a reading of the Southwest border as "a security/economy nexus of relatively incoherent practices buoyed by a range of sometimes countervailing policy identities." (213) Yamashita's depiction of Bobby's border performance clearly affirms, however, the instrumentality of the border region to the goals of the free trade ideology. This becomes particularly obvious in the context of *Tropic of Orange*'s critique of neoliberal capitalism. This critique not only addresses the homogenizing free trade rhetoric of both the Asia Pacific myth and the official NAFTA promotion, but suggests a transcendent omnipresence of the neoliberal rationality.

American suffering inflicted by the colonization, the oppression, and the exploitation of the indigenous population by white colonizers. Ironically flaunting both the virility stereotypically ascribed by the hegemonic symbolic order to Latin-American men and the stigmata acquired by hard physical labor – with a purple stain on his neck marking him as the proverbial redneck – Arcangel's body is presented as an archive of cultural knowledge; his 'tricks' draw on cultural artifacts which he remembers, quotes, enacts, or ridicules, *ad libitum*. A "true performer" equipped with a suitcase full of disguises, he wanders about the southern hemisphere, alternately working alongside the rural population, reciting poetry, or staging circus acts and superhuman feats.

While jocosely amalgamating in his depiction the playful elusiveness of the indigenous trickster with the carnality of a stereotypical, if aging Latin lover, Yamashita leaves no doubt that Arcangel is a decidedly political redeemer figure, the heroic working class leader of a potential Latin American revolution, a "Conquistador of the North" (198). Drawing on an abundance of literary and political inter-texts, she casts him as a political performance artist whose message – albeit most explicitly delivered in traditional, lyrical incantations – is a critique of the neo-colonializing workings of free trade. His mission is to solicit the attention and the confidence of an indigenous audience that is jaded and brainwashed by the consumption of TV-images designed to create and to cater to transnational markets.

Accordingly, Arcangel's journey towards the North is depicted as the spectacular road trip of a Latin American confidence man whose magical tricks have to compete with the sedating and misleading images of capitalism's transnational confidence game as televised on the "tube of plenty."[179] The media critique inherent to his inverted medial 'conquista' becomes particularly explicit in a passage of "To Dream," the chapter in which Arcangel is about to cross the "New World Border" (198). After having dragged to the North a broken bus carrying, alongside a crowd of migrants, the magical orange with the Tropic of Cancer miraculously attached to it, Arcangel attempts to exploit the power of television for the spectacle of a border performance that is about to upturn the neoliberal restructuring of space and time:

Televisa, Univision, Galaxy Latin America and local border stations congregated to eyeball the event. If there were a dozen local and national stations, there were a dozen eyes, translating to a dozen times a dozen times a dozen like the repetitious vision of a common housefly. Arcangel strained for this vision even though live television had no

---

179 Erik Barnouw, *Tube of Plenty: The Evolution of American Television* (New York: Oxford UP, 1975).

way of accommodating actual feats of superhuman strength. The virtually real could not accommodate the magical. Digital memory failed to translate imaginary memory. Meanwhile, the watching population surfed the channels for the real, the live, the familiar. But it could not be recognized on a tube, no matter how big or how highly defined. There were not enough dots in the universe. In other words, to see it, you had to have been there yourself. (197)

In juxtaposing and mingling the lyrical language of magic realism with the sober lingo of information technology, the passage is representative of Yamashita's use of an aesthetics that blends and re-composes the linguistic registers of cultural discourses whose value and validity within the hegemonic symbolic order could not be more disparate. At this point, the edgework of negotiating the value of competing symbolic registers that shapes *Tropic of Orange*'s narrative throughout is dedicated to a very specific media critique: television, the novel's narration suggests, is a cultural practice that is compliant with the disciplinary performance of the border.

It is noteworthy that the TV stations listed in the first sentence of this passage, different from what their Spanish names might suggest, belong to transnational media corporations whose headquarters are situated in the U.S. The products sold by these stations to commercial sponsors are Spanish-language news and entertainment formats targeted mainly at Spanish speaking minorities in the U.S. What is evoked with the listing of these names is thus a highly commercialized entertainment industry that capitalizes on the ideology of free choice and free trade, while being firmly embedded in the rationality of neoliberal governance, which it, in addition, protects and furthers by anaesthetizing its audience of disenfranchised migrant laborers on both sides of the border.[180]

---

180 On the economic rationality dominating television production see Mimi White. White emphasizes the central role of advertising as "an integral part of television program flow" (143). She understands the television viewer as a consumer and a commodity, a "token in the system of exchange between networks, stations, ad agencies, and commercial sponsors" (145). "Ideological Analysis and Television," *Channels of Discourse: Television and Contemporary Criticism*, ed. Robert C. Allen (Chapel Hill and London: U of North Carolina P, 1987), 134-171. John Fiske draws on the work of Antonio Gramsci and Stuart Hall to foreground the ideological role of television. He points to the "necessary correlation between people's social situations and the meanings that they may generate from a television program" (260). For Fiske, television is a hegemonic instrument of the ideological struggle by which "a dominant class wins the willing consent of the subordinate classes to the

This parasitic, ideological relationship is visualized in the passage by the metaphor of the "common housefly" (197). The housefly metaphor invests television's border transgressing penetration with the connotations of an insect whose ubiquitous presence is commonly considered a 'pest,' a transmitter of contagious diseases that will not be stopped by a border. In the phrase "the repetitious vision of the common housefly" (197) the metaphor acquires an allegoric quality, suggesting a synchronized cooptation of any number of commercial TV stations: Like the facets of the housefly's eye, the multiple cameras of these different channels cover the same events, producing – with minor adaptations to the habits of specific viewer segments – a multiplicity of similar images that are broadcast as 'news' to the multiple screens of millions of American households. With the phrase "a dozen eyes, translating to a dozen times a dozen times a dozen" impressively illustrating the dizzying multiplication of images, the similarity of which serves as 'evidence' of a medially construed 'truth,' the passage exposes the TV-stations' power of meaning-making and deception. At the same time, this phrasing evokes the African American tradition of 'playin' the dozens,' a tradition of expressive public signifying contests "that has its origins in the slave trade of New Orleans where deformed slaves [...] were grouped in lots of a 'cheap dozen' for sale to slave owners."[181] The subtext of a signifying competition between different performances of the border as a public spectacle is thus enriched with connotations of racism and African American slavery in the U.S.

In servicing the 'contagious' economic rationality of neoliberal governance, the multiplicity of televised images cannot "accommodate" Arcangel's magical border performance of superhuman strength by which he drags across the border "the great multitude" (211) of cheap 'alien' bodies – and with it the southern hemisphere. Strikingly, in this passage, the antithetic juxtaposition of "the magical" and "the virtually real" ascribes to the former a multiply coded physical presence – represented by Arcangel's magical muscle, the multitude of migrant bodies, and the geophysical body of the hemisphere – a physical

---

system that ensures their subordination. This consent must be constantly won and rewon, for people's material social experience constantly reminds them of the disadvantages of subordination and thus poses a constant threat to to the dominant."(259) "British Cultural Studies and Television," *Channels of Discourse: Television and Contemporary Criticism*, ed. Robert C. Allen (Chapel Hill and London: U of North Carolina P, 1987) 254-289.

181 Mona Lisa Saloy, "African American Oral Traditions in Louisiana," *Louisiana's Living Traditions* (May 1998):Web, 22 Nov. 2011, <http://www.louisianafolklife.org/LT/Articles_Essays/creole_art_african_am_oral.html>.

presence, which is cast as an epistemological privilege: "to see it, you had to have been there yourself" (197). The "virtually real" – represented by mere "dots" transmitted to a "tube, no matter how big or highly defined" – is, in contrast, marked by a vacancy, an absence of the body resulting in representational failure: Although time stops and the 'solid ground' of the geopolitical order warps in this magical process, the televised news report fails to "accommodate" the "real, the live, the familiar" (197), and thus cannot deliver the political truth inherent to this literal re-volution of bio-political disciplinary practices.

Whereas this negotiation of contrasting medial representations and their respective epistemologies convincingly exposes the compliance of electronic abstraction with the bio-political navigation of bodies in the service of free trade, it appears highly contingent when contextualized with the novel's discourse on art. Read against the background of Worringer's theory on art and abstraction evoked by the HyperContexts grid and discussed in the previous subchapter, the comment on representation articulated in the above passage proves ambiguous. While the decidedly figurative quality of magic realism can be considered suspended and, in a way, abstracted by the convention of the fantastic, Yamashita's emphasis on the presence of the body appears to overturn this abstraction: the chapters that are focalized on Arcangel suggest that it is just the physicality and the immediacy of bodily presence that privileges the collective cultural archive of Latin America over the ultimately abstracted and disembodied, virtual representation governing the postmodern public sphere of the North. However, the cultural critique conveyed by the different performances of the border, in which these contrasting patterns of representation culminate, seems to be in tension with the novel's identification with abstract form as encoded in the HyperContexts grid and the character of Manzanar Murakami.

The avowal of abstract form as the appropriate artistic response to and articulation of cultural crisis, as formulated by Worringer's art theory, is thus diametrically opposed to the critique of abstract representation articulated at the novel's level of content. In addition to this paradox relation between form and content, and even more important, the epistemological privilege and the cultural superiority that the representation of the clashing border performances ascribes to the presence of the body raises questions as to the epistemological status of the literary per se. If the inherent incapacity of literature to capture the presence of bodies only by degree differs from the total erasure of bodily presence from "the virtually real" of electronic signification, how, then, can the literary "accommodate" "the real" and "the live"?

This contradictory epistemological subtext is carried to extremes in the climactic scene of the wrestling match of "El Contrato Con América" (256) at the end of *Tropic of Orange* where Yamashita's criticism of the free trade ideology and its speculative, representational confidence game loses all subtlety. The spectacular fight, in which Arcangel, impersonating "El Gran Mojado," challenges "SUPERNAFTA," the embodiment of the North American Free Trade Agreement, is – in keeping with the official broadcasting of NAFTA's 'birth'– a loud and shrill affair staged at L.A.'s Pacific Rim Auditorium and simultaneously broadcast to four giant screens. It is a bold, political allegory when Yamashita has SUPERNAFTA enter the stage as "a masked man in a Titanium suit with a head of raging fire" (256) and pretentiously address the "multicultural rainbow of kids out there" (257). His pithy invitation to "get a piece of the action" (257) and his prophetic promise of a golden economic future propelled by technological progress blatantly mimic the rhetoric of free trade that conceals its agenda of mobilizing and navigating the transnational migration of subaltern social groups and classes according to the varying needs of capitalist boom and bust cycles.[182]

This subaltern aspect of 'global flows' is flashily embodied and represented by El Gran Mojado, the 'great wetback,' aka Arcangel who has already dragged the North-South divide of the hemisphere into L.A., bringing with him tens of thousands of illegal Mexican migrants. As with her depiction of SUPERNAFTA, Yamashita does not skimp on symbolic excess in her representation of his challenger. The trickster's somewhat ridiculous outfit – he is wearing a "ski-mask of camouflage nylon, blue cape with the magic image of Guadalupe in an aura of gold feathers and blood roses, leopard bicycle tights and blue boots" (258) – and his ironic American superhero posture – he "stood, arms crossed and legs spread like a Power Ranger or a Ninja Turtle or Zorro" (258) – satirically display both the officially required process of immigrant Americanization and a self-mockingly Hispanic interpretation of it. In addition, as Mojado appeals to a transnational, pan-American resistance against the policy of NAFTA in his speech, he also ironically and playfully invokes the stereotype of a lascivious Latin-American machismo, thus winning his audience's sympathy and laughter. But while conspicuously contrasting this self-ironic parody of the Northern stereotype of Latin-American masculinity with SUPERNAFTA's humorless,

---

182 See Masao Miyoshi, "A Borderless World: From Colonialism to Transnationalism, and the Decline of the Nationstate," *Critical Inquiry* 19.4 (1993): 726-751; see also Masao Miyoshi, "Sites of Resistance in the Global Economy," *boundary 2* 22.1 (1995): 61-84; and Masao Miyoshi, "Turn to the Planet: Literature, Diversity and Totality," *Comparative Literature* 53.4 (2001): 283-287.

self-important, and pompous performance, Yamashita makes it clear that the migrant diaspora that Mojado leads and represents is not just an urban carnival: what the masses in the audience – and the novel's readers – witness is a dramatic life and death fight, in which the fate of thousands of 'wetbacks' and maquiladora workers is at stake.

Predictably, the pathos in this archaic encounter of good and evil climaxes when SUPERNAFTA – in keeping with his reputation – kills El Gran Mojado with a secret weapon. Yet Yamashita's excessive symbolism does not allow the scene to end with the folk hero's melodramatic death after a "highly stylized match."[183] The author has the chapter end, instead, with the remark that "somewhere the profits from the ticket sales were being divided" (263), thus accomplishing its purpose of exposing the function of a discursive propaganda machine that conceals the sheer economic rationality of its agenda. Against this background, the victory of SUPERNAFTA over El Gran Mojado in the Pacific Rim Auditorium comes as no surprise. Always oscillating between counter-narrative and parody, its excessively allegoric, at times even cheesy, representation conspicuously parallels the representational strategies of the ideology it depicts. It thus seems to justify the cautionary reader address of the epigraph that Yamashita has placed before the beginning of the novel like a disclaimer: "[...] No single imagination is wild or crass or cheesy enough to compete with the collective mindlessness that propels our fascination forward [...]."

According to Molly Wallace, it is just Yamashita's imaginative use of puns and metaphors that highlights "the gap between the cultural and the economic"[184] that non-fictional globalization discourse and its metaphors tend to efface. Wallace argues that in taking the homogenizing metaphors of the official language of global excess literally and unmasking their "conflation of the cultural and the economic," Yamashita taps the full metaphoric potential of the fictional text "to figure the operation of language without committing to a referent."[185] While Wallace clearly recognizes the subtlety of Yamashita's literary edgework in her boldly unsubtle depiction of the wrestling match, she does not elaborate on *Tropic of Orange*'s comment on the pervasiveness of the neoliberal market rationality as a "political culture that figures citizens

---

183 Molly Wallace, "Tropics of Globalization: Reading the New North America," *symplokē* 9. 1-2 (2001): 145-160, 157.
184 Ibid., 150.
185 Ibid., 158.

exhaustively as rational economic actors in every sphere of life,"[186] which is at the bottom of a conflation of the cultural and the economic.

Yamashita creates an imaginary that suggests, however, that neither the spectacle of Arcangel's attempted revolution nor the audience it addresses can evade a political rationality, which imposes the economic as the homogenizing "grid of intelligibility"[187] on the subjects it produces, and thus renders irrelevant any differentiation between the cultural and the economic. Her representation of Bobby Ngu as a confidence man and the 'bankerization' of his life illustrate how this political culture is suffused by an economic rationale, and relies, like literature, on "the operation of language without committing to a referent."[188] Arcangel's chapters add to this discourse on representation and speculation in the electronic age the critique of a medial spectacularity that is equally dematerialized. His pronounced physicality contrasts and challenges a medial culture, in which all forms of bodily presence and resistance become absorbed and transformed into electronic signs and the spectacle of technologically produced virtual images. In the different ways in which both 'confidence men' address and embrace the risks construed by statecraft in the service of economic restructuring, the absence of the body becomes visible as key to the representational confidence game of capitalism in the age of neoliberal governance.

But the dystopian perception of the effects of information technology, underlying the novel's clairvoyant political discourse on representation and confidence, leads to a fundamental epistemological dilemma. While the narrative discourse focalized on Bobby Ngu suggests the trustworthiness of literature in a subtle negotiation of competing symbolic economies, the bold allegory in Yamashita's representation of Arcangel appears to undermine rather than affirm the potential of literature to compete with the treacherous simulacra of presence produced by electronic media. It pointedly exposes writing as a medium whose incapacity of 'truly' representing time and space as well as physical presence only by degree differs from the digital media's time/space compression and erasure of physicality. Neither the timeless immediacy of a Deleuzian 'becoming' that Yamashita has encoded in the uninflected verbal infinitives that serve as headings for Arcangel's chapters nor the literary edgework of a blatantly tasteless, revolutionary spectacle can paper over the epistemological cracks that gape open in all operations of signs that are not committed to a

---

186 Wendy Brown,"American Nightmare: Neoliberalism, Neoconservatism, and De-Democratization," *Political Theory* 34.6 (2006): 690 -714, 694.
187 Michel Foucault, *The Birth of Biopolitics*, 252.
188 Wallace, "Tropics of Globalization," 150.

referent. On the contrary, Yamashita's attempt to conjoin a critique of postmodern digital technology with a somewhat idealizing homage to magic realism in a decidedly referential allegory brings her novel dangerously close to the line separating a deliberately "cheesy" literary imaginary from the "larger than life" projections on "TV, screen, and monitor" that the novel's epigraph programmatically discredits.

3.5 NOW YOU SEE HER / NOW YOU DON'T: EMI, OR THE EROTICS OF PRESENCE

In the chapters that are focalized on Emi, Yamashita's critical representation of information technology further explores the production of presence in the digital age and, in the process, keeps on tapping the potential of allegory. The Japanese American TV-producer, who has already been introduced as the energetic proponent of the live-on-the-edge-motto at the beginning of this chapter, boldly impersonates the 'here-and -now'-immediacy that marks the live broadcasting of the television shows by which she makes a living. Yet Emi's depiction is iridescent, and transcends a simple reflection of the temporal condition and effect of television. As Yamashita conjoins in her representation an allegory of mediality with a satiric discourse on sexuality and genetics, she not only spotlights the centrality of the body to contrasting concepts of time and space but further negotiates the epistemological potential of competing representational practices.

At the beginning of "Weather Report," Emi's expository chapter, named after a TV program segment like all other chapters focalized on her perspective, her witty, colorful superficiality, which is presented as her most distinctive feature, is highlighted by a dialogue with her boyfriend Gabriel, a Chicano newspaper journalist with a proclivity for film noir. Characteristically, this dialogue takes place in a bar at the "very center of the Westside power plays, cushioned in pastels and glass bricks and remakes of David Hockney," (19) and thus in a Hollywood setting whose subdued surfaces and cool, educated middleclass appeal pointedly contrast the heat of the competitive "power play" of the meaning-making machine, in which its customers are involved. Yamashita effectually uses the muted, cool colors of this setting to accentuate the different shades of hot red dominating Emi's flashy appearance. Emi is introduced as stirring a Bloody Mary, sporting "a big ruby ring," "red nail polish" (19), and "reformulating" her lips with the twirling "baton" of a lipstick (24) in the course of her conversation with Gabriel, while bashing her boyfriend's penchant for classic Hollywood movies with the opening line: "The film noir stuff is passé. Don't you get it?" (18) This rant continues after Emi's habit of watching and "scanning the ongoing surrounding scene" (19) is exposed as her compulsion to take in and take hold of any situation "as if she had produced it herself" (18):

Stop being such a film buff. Raymond Chandler. Alfred Hitchcock. Film nostalgia. I don't give a damn if *Chinatown*, *The Player*, or everybody in Hollywood owes these old farts their asses. I'll give you this: at least *they're* in color. Except for *Roger Rabbit*, if I have to spend another evening with you watching another video in black and white, this relationship is over." She laughed, tossing the silky strands of her straight hair over her padded shoulders. She didn't mean it. She never did. (19, italics in the original)

Significantly, Emi's critique of auteurism and film noir cinema in this invective is directed against the technological obsolescence of older film noir classics rather than the modern instances of the genre that she mentions, or their contents. Corresponding to her own colorful appearance in the scene, Emi emphasizes the importance of color as the one criterion that makes a movie acceptable. The superficiality of this 'aesthetic assessment' is further enhanced by her outspoken resentment of the historicizing, backward-looking perspective of a "film nostalgia" that reveres the aesthetic refinement and the influence of 'great' authors like Raymond Chandler and Alfred Hitchcock. In drastically disparaging these authors as "old farts," and in dismissing the historiography and ideational genealogy implicit to the assumption that "everybody in Hollywood owes [them] their asses," Emi foregrounds what is, at another point in her conversation with Gabriel, cast as her dedication to "strictly current affairs" (22). What is inscribed in her rant against anything "passé" – the word is picked up twice and applied to different contexts in the course of the dialogue – is an avowal of the 'liveness' and the presence associated with television broadcasting. At the very beginning of Emi's exposition, Yamashita thus introduces as a leitmotif the opposition of analog and digital media and their respective temporal directions, an opposition that media scholar Paddy Scannell characterizes as follows:

To find and tell the story in the live, phenomenal now of television is to articulate a prospective, forward looking narrative. This in contrast [sic] with written histories that are backward-looking retrospective narratives. […] the present is alive because it is the now-becoming-future of the lives of the living. The liveness of television is not its technological effect, but the condition of its existence in a double sense: its possibility and its manifest, expressed effect.[…] Analog time's immediate now is expressed […] as being in a relationship with its before and after, neither of which exists in digital time. The now of analog time [...] is an immediate present that exists only by virtue of the historic and future present, which are the conditions of its possibility, of its coming-into-being.[189]

The "prospective, forward-looking perspective" that Scannell associates with the "live, phenomenal now of television" is clearly exemplified by the weather report that programmatically provides the title for the expository chapter and that is central to Emi's professional concern within this chapter: Emi finds herself in a predicament caused by the disappearance of a commercial-recording for a tanning lotion; being responsible for the in-time broadcasting of that commercial in the weather report slot, Emi has to break off her lunchtime chitchat with Gabriel. While this detail of the plot illustrates 'presence' as a non-stop availability that television's forward-looking liveness demands from its makers, it also shows this liveness to be dictated by the rationale of a market "in which advertisers demand and buy audiences."[190]

The films that Emi finds acceptable only because they are in color, on the other hand, indeed display the "backward-looking, retrospective narratives" that Scannell ascribes to analog media: Roman Polanski's award winning *Chinatown* (1974) is a modern film noir set in 1937 L.A., featuring Jack Nicholson, who plays a private eye character in the tradition of Chandler, and Faye Dunnaway, who impersonates a 'bad good girl' version of the *femme fatale* stereotype. Robert Altman's noir comedy *The Player* (1992), though not explicitly backward looking, fits the analog pattern in that it satirizes the workings of the Hollywood movie machine and thus implicitly invokes its mythic history. It is worth noting and points to an identification with digital mediality going far beyond the professional identification of a TV producer with her job that the only film that finds Emi's approval in the quoted passage is Robert Zemeckis' *Who Framed Roger Rabbit* (1988), a fantasy-comedy-noir film, starring live actors and digitally animated cartoon characters.

While Emi's pointed exposition as a 'digital girl' could be read as the parody of a postmodern subjectivity – characterized, according to Fredric Jameson, by "a flatness or depthlessness, a new kind of superficiality in the most literal

---

189 Paddy Scannell, "Television and History," *A Companion to Television*, ed. Janet Wasko (Malden, et.al.: Blackwell, 2008) 51-66, 59-60.
190 Eileen R. Meehan, "Watching Television: A Political Economic Approach," *A Companion to Television,* ed. Janet Wasko (Malden et.al.: Blackwell, 2008) 238-255, 241.

sense"[191] – a dense web of signifiers in the quoted passage and throughout the chapter call into question whether Emi *is* indeed a human subject at all. Subtle clues in the text insinuate that she can be read as the paradoxical embodiment of the disembodied information processing of digital media. At first glance, this subtext of Emi's non-human quality seems to be concealed underneath the discourse of seduction, as the passage stages as Emi's signature feature a proclivity for deliberate provocation that blends the insult of her ostentatious superficiality with a decidedly gendered, erotic tease. In correspondence with the flashy red, feminine accessories accentuating Emi's appearance, the gesture of laughingly "tossing the silky stands of her straight hair over her padded shoulder" is quite obviously a flirty invitation for Gabriel to pick up one of the playful fights that mark their relationship throughout her narrative discourse. As this gendered, flirtatious gesture enhances the subliminally erotic image conjured by Emi's lascivious licking of her fingers after she has spiced up and stirred with a celery stick the "hot colors" (19) of her Bloody Mary, it invites an interpretation of Emi as a postmodern *femme fatale* at the very beginning of the chapter.

Significantly, given Emi's Japanese American background, the gesture of tossing "silky strands of straight hair" is doubly coded in a literal sense, as it implicitly evokes connotations of a glossy blackness complementing the red 'hotness' conjured by this chain of rather stereotypically gendered, gestural and color signifiers. The stereotypical and decidedly corporeal sensuality ascribed to Emi is thereby captured in a binary code that contrasts the color red with the non-color black. The binary pattern of this code is picked up by the two sentences immediately following the one describing the hair-tossing gesture: "She didn't mean it. She never did" (19), and, even more conspicuously, a few lines below, where the relationship between Emi and Gabriel is reported as having been "on again/ off again" (19).

These oppositions of red/black, did /didn't, on/off strikingly resemble the 1/0, current-supply/no-supply-code that conditions the electronic differential of digital information processing. The chain of signifiers evoking connotations of a seductive, if stereotypical, femininity is thus complemented by a subtext of electronic signals that captures this very femininity in the form of a digital code. And it is, paradoxically, this digital code that adds philosophical depth to the representation of the seductive attraction of Emi's witty superficiality. Contrasting the meaning-making of the erotic signifiers that charge Emi's

---

191 Qtd. in Doug Kellner, "Critical Perspectives on Television from the Frankfurt School to Postmodernism," *A Companion to Television*, ed. Janet Wasko (Malden et.al.: Blackwell, 2008) 29-47.

exposition with connotations of the *femme fatale* stereotype, the absolute meaninglessness of this code – in conjunction with Emi's preference for colorful surfaces – seems to affirm Jean Baudrillard's claim that "surface and appearance" is "the space of seduction."[192] According to Baudrillard,

[D]istinctive signs, full signs never seduce us. Seduction only comes through empty, illegible, insoluble, arbitrary, fortuitous signs, which glide by lightly, modifying the index of the refraction of space. They are signs without a subject of enunciation, nor an enounced. They are pure signs in that they are neither discursive nor generate any exchange. The protagonists of seduction are neither locator nor interlocutee, they are in a dual and antagonistic situation. As such the signs of seduction do not signify; they are of the order of the ellipse, of the short circuit, of the flash of wit (*le trait d'esprit*).[193]

In the exposition's subtext of seduction, Yamashita conjoins a pointed exhibition of gendered corporeality – highlighted by physical markers and gestures – with the disembodied mediality of signs that "do not signify."[194] Read with Baudrillard, Emi is introduced as being seductive, because she is neither "a subject of enunciation, nor an enounced."[195] The image of the *femme fatale*, 'enounced' by the signal surfaces of shiny red in Emi's appearance and her codified gestures, becomes visible as the 'product' of the adaptability of a pure and vacant mediality: relying on shiny surfaces, this mediality, however, merely reflects its object of communication. It does not produce anything, but seduces with a superficial reflection of anything it takes in. As Baudrillard has it, "seduction is not that which is *opposed* to production. It is that which *seduces* production."[196]

Notably, this relation of seduction and production is spotlighted by Emi's habit of watching and "scanning the ongoing surrounding scene" (19) and her compulsion to take in and "take hold" of any situation "as if she had produced it herself" (18), within the first paragraph of her expository chapter, immediately before her invective challenges Gabriel's penchant for film noir. Rather than just staging the *déformation professionelle* of a TV-producer, the prominent exposition of the habit compelling her to scan and "take hold of" (18) every situation, prepares the stage for a performance of the non-productivity of pure

---

192 Jean Baudrillard, "Seduction, or the Superficial Abyss," *The Ecstacy of Communication,* ed. Sylvere Lotringer, (New York, Semiotexte: 1988) 57-75, 62.
193 Ibid., 59-60.
194 Ibid., 60.
195 Ibid., 59.
196 Ibid., 58, italics in the original.

mediality. While playfully and wittily pushing Gabriel's buttons with her rant against *Chinatown,* Emi's seductive posture, gestures, and coloring strikingly reflect the film's representation of the *femme fatale* character played by Faye Dunnaway. With the 'bad-good-girl'-connotation simultaneously evoking the binarism of the digital code, it becomes obvious that she does not, in fact, produce anything in a way that is comparable to film makers, who produce a movie by using narrative to turn into scene what is supposed to be seen, but instead turns the seen into its shiny reflection.[197]

Against this backdrop, a reading of Emi as the paradoxical embodiment of a disembodied and, in itself, meaningless digital mediality appears conclusive. At first glance, such a reading seems to be substantiated by Emi's name, which encodes an acronym that is widely used in digital tech language, where it can signify 'External Machine Interface,' 'External Memory Interface,' or 'Electromagnetic Interference.' These references clearly support an interpretation of Emi as a mere digital interface, an interpretation that is further corroborated by Emi's depiction as a telecommunication addict who feels most alive when she simultaneously watches four TV screens, when she is 'hooked up' with a computer, a cellular phone, a fax, or even when she is being alerted by her pager. Her sleek car is to her not only what Baudrillard calls "a partner in a general negotiation of lifestyles,"[198] but, more important, a decidedly erotic partner as the quote from "NewsNow," Emi's second chapter, shows: "'I love to shift gears,' she gripped the stick and confessed over the wailing Tango." (61)

It is this subtext of erotic interaction that interferes with and disrupts an unambiguous reading of Emi as a mere interface. Strikingly often, her inclination for provocation that propels and motivates the plot throughout the chapters focalized on her perspective is contextualized with allusions to physical sex and

---

197 Drawing on Jacques Lacan's theorization of the "mirror phase," Jean Baudrillard acknowledges the transition from "a system of objects" and "the critique of objects as based on signs saturated with meaning" (11) to the symbolic 'flatness' of digital mediality as a gradual process that he describes as follows: "All this still exists, and simultaneously is disappearing. The description of this projective imaginary and symbolic universe was still the one of the object as the mirror of the subject. The opposition of the subject was still significant, as was the profound imaginary of the mirror and the scene. The scene of history as well as the scene of the everyday emerge in the shadow of history as it is progressively divested of politics. Today the scene and the mirror have given way to a screen and a network." "The Ecstacy of Communication," *The Ecstacy of Communication,* ed. Sylvere Lotringer (New York, Semiotexte: 1988) 11-27.

198 Baudrillard, "The Ecstasy of Communication," 13.

images of a decidedly sensual ingestion of food. While seduction is doubly coded and can be related to the "superficial abyss"[199] of a meaningless mediality that seduces 'production' and 'takes in' products of meaning-making which it merely reflects, the repeated allusions to physical sex and corporeal ingestion, at the same time, counteract the subtle discourse of a merely medial seduction. They appear to insist on a very carnal physicality, which, in conjunction with the digital subtext, charges the representation of Emi's body with a presence/absence dichotomy strikingly reminiscent of the 'now-you-see-it/ now-you-don't-aesthetics' that TV-commercials apply in order to prompt desire. Given the similarity of this dichotomy to the electronic binarism of the digital code, it is indeed enticing to read Emi as a mere interface, a cyborg, and thus as a post-human techno-body that is the "subject of our prosthetic culture in a complex web of dynamics and technologically mediated social situations."[200] The text, however, offers occasional glimpses of Emi's corporeality, while simultaneously giving clues to its sheer digital mediality in an intricate interplay that mimics the aesthetics' of TV advertising. It thus at once both teases out and problematizes a desire for the apparition of the body as a naturalized unit.

At one point in her expository chapter, Emi's provocative banter even assumes the form of a genetic and genealogical quest. It is in a moment of self-reflection that Emi recalls a conversation with her mother who, commenting on her provocative "big mouth" (21), scolds her "Whatsa matter with you? Your dad and I don't talk like that. Your brother and sister don't talk like that. In fact no J.A. talks like that."(21) With characteristic sarcasm, Emi replies:

"Maybe I'm not Japanese American. Maybe I got switched in the hospital. There were three sets of switched kids in the daytime Donahues last week: *Montel Williams*, *Rikky Lake*, and *Sally Jesse Raphael*.(Ratings were all up. Caress sold a lot of Caress.) But get this, they discovered each other by genetic testing. If three talk shows found three different sets, imagine how many more of us there must be! There's probably a support group out there for people like me. I should check the net."(21, italics in the original)

While using a fantasy frequent among children who, coming of age, express feelings of familial disconnection and alienation in order to assert a still precarious individuality, the passage provides a host of conclusive allusions to constructions of the body as the "unambiguous locus of identity, agency, labour, and hierarchicalized function" that Donna J. Haraway has shown to be "crafted"

---

199 Baudrillard, "Seduction," 57.
200 Rosi Braidotti, *Transpositions: On Nomadic Ethics* (Malden, M.A. and Cambridge, U.K.: Polity, 2006) 37.

by "post eighteenth century life sciences."[201] Whereas her mother's scolding reveals an unquestioning acceptance and perpetuation of the dominant symbolic order's ascriptions of familial and ethnic identity – with the acronym J.A. pointedly exhibiting the essentializing function of hegemonic catachresis – Emi's reply draws attention to scientific, medical, and media practices that are compliant with that hegemonic order in that they construe and reiterate a notion of the organic body as the site of identitarian essence.

With the theme of children who were switched at birth, the quoted passage evokes the practice of labeling newborns with bracelets that spell out their family names. An instance of practices of assistance, medical pedagogy, and "forms of record-keeping allowing the production of new types of statistics"[202] that emerged at the beginning of the nineteenth century, this practice is representative of a clinical gaze that focused on the individual body, a practice that is not hard to read as an initiation to the workings of Althusserian interpellation. Cast as a risk to familial and individual identity, the switching of babies at birth – resulting in their interpellation by an 'improper' name – indeed denotes the failure of a clinical practice of bio-political subject formation that ascribes inheritable racial markers to biological bodies. The fact that this failure is considered a melodramatic sensation worthy of extensive media coverage, the high attendance figures of which document a surprising amount of public interest, shows the 'knowledge' expressed in that practice to be deeply engrained in the social fabric of a political culture that markets itself as liberal and multicultural. It reveals the pervasiveness and the discursive reproduction of a biological positivism and determinism underneath the celebration of diversity – a diversity exemplified in the quoted passage by the talk show hosts. Their names refer to popular American television personalities, whose belonging to various ethnicities – African American, Jewish, and Caucasian – together with their success, seems to provide evidence for the irrelevance of ethnicity to a social hierarchy that is, in fact, based on and perpetuated by racializing discursive practices of interpellation and catachresis.

It should be noted that, although the construct of race and skin color as its physical marker is nowhere in the passage explicitly mentioned, it is subtly slipped in by way of the bracketed phrases interrupting Emi's reply. While the insertion of these phrases mimics the insertion of a commercial break and thereby structures this reply exactly like the TV-shows Emi refers to, it is no

---

201 *Simians, Cyborgs, and Women: The Reinvention of Nature* (New York: Routledge, 1991) 211.
202 Nikolas Rose, *The Politics of Life Itsself* (Princeton and Oxford: Princeton UP, 2007) 10.

coincidence that the label whose products are advertised is Caress, a label that sells skin care products. Inserted in the commercial break of a talk show, whose guests were supposedly switched at birth, the speaking name of this label on the one hand fittingly enhances the affective charge of the topic of the show, and, on the other, subtly directs attention to skin and, implicitly, skin color. In doing so, the commercial break not only dramatically stages but ideologically prepares the finding of persuasive identitarian evidence as inscribed in the genetic code, the 'discovery' of an ontological, physical 'truth' by "genetic testing." Subtly charged with connotations of skin and race by the label Caress, this physical truth is effectually 'disclosed' after the commercial's broadcasting.

Simultaneously, the now-you-see-it/now-you-don't-aesthetics of the commercial reflect, perform, and delineate the paradigm shift from a subjectivizing clinical gaze, focused on the visible tissues and surfaces of the body, to the gaze of experts, whose technological equipment renders visible a molecular level of the body that was concealed before. With Emi's sarcastic conclusion, "imagine how many more of us there must be. There is probably a support group out there for people like us. I should check the net," the passage, in addition, illustrates how the expert knowledge produced by this new scientific gaze postulates a bio-political normativity based on statistical projection and its calling for prudent behavior and self-management on the side of the normalized subject. By affirming, refining, and enhancing a perception of the body as the locus of identity, this molecular scientific gaze enables a form of bio-political governance that ties in with neoliberal governmentality as it increasingly rests on risk predictions made on the basis of molecular evidence and the moral behaviorism that relies on the subject's responsibility for prudent, risk avoiding conduct.[203]

What Yamashita has artfully put in Emi's mouth with her reply in the quoted passage is thus a critique of subject formation by new practices of bio-political governance. Articulated by an elusive protagonist, whose representation constantly oscillates between corporeality and disembodiment, and encoded in that elusive protagonist's seemingly non-reflective rendition of TV-images that are compliant with these practices, this critique, at the same time, stages what it criticizes, as it heightens the reader's desire for disambiguating clues to the protagonist's identity; a desire, paradoxically, for the apparition of her body as the site of identity. With its performative structure suggesting that it merely

---

203 See Robert Castel, "From Dangerousness to Risk," *The Foucault Effect: Studies in Governmentality*, eds. Graham Burchell, Colin Gordon, and Peter Miller (Chicago: U of Chicago P, 1991) 281-298; and Jacques Donzelot, "The Mobilization of Society," *The Foucault Effect: Studies in Governmentality*, eds. Graham Burchell, Colin Gordon, and Peter Miller (Chicago: U of Chicago P, 1991)169-180.

mirrors what Emi has seen in her favorite medium, her reply can be read as the performance of a pure mediality that only reflects its object of communication. Even the deconstruction of an ontological notion of the body as the naturalized site of identity and the biological determinism that have been shown as inscribed in that reply can be read as affirming this interpretation, since Emi's rejection of a place in the duplicitous hegemonic order corresponds with other passages in later chapters, where she, for instance, playfully claims, "I hate being multicultural," and, in her usual provocative manner, exposes the pretentiousness of a multiculturalism that signifies nothing beneath its celebration of diversity.

Yamashita, however, thwarts this reading of Emi as a mere interface, or an "anti-identitarian, postmodern creature of the web"[204] by picking up the discourse on genealogy and genetics with a twist in the plot towards the end of Emi's narrative, when Emi learns that Manzanar Murakami, the 'crazy' conductor of L.A.'s urban music, is her grandfather. Thus endowed with a history and a 'revolutionary' lineage, Emi dies a decidedly physical death after she has been hit by a bullet on the roof of the NewsNow van. Although the interplay of simultaneous clues to physicality and mediality keeps producing contingency and irony until the very end (for instance, when Gabriel receives Emi's email messages after her death – among them a confession that she cheated on him by having digital sex), the genealogical discourse provides Emi with a history that the presence of digital mediality denies.

At this point, it becomes obvious that, in Emi's narrative discourse, Yamashita conjoins the temporality and the production of meaning ascribed to analog narration –"the now of analog time [...] that exists only by virtue of the historic and future present, which are the conditions of its possibility, of its coming-into-being"[205] – with the ahistorical, 'meaningless' presence of digital mediality. It is no coincidence that *The Framing of Rogger Rabbit*, the movie, in which real actors play alongside digitally animated cartoon characters, is introduced as the one instance of film noir that Emi approves. Its aesthetics programmatically provides a model for a hybrid cyberpunk/ noir narrative that not only shows the cyborg as "text, machine, body, and metaphor"[206] but curtails the symbolic polyvalence of the cyborg metaphor by constantly juxtaposing it with clues to biological physicality. In doing so, Yamashita's cyberpunk narrative exceeds a mere discourse on digital mediality and its blatant

---

204 Caroline Rody, "The Transnational Imagination: Karen Tei Yamashita's *Tropic of Orange*," *Asian American Identities Beyond the Hyphen*, eds. Eleanor Ty and Donald C. Goellnicht (Bloomington: Indiana UP, 2004) 130-148, 146.
205 Scannell,"Television and History," 60.
206 Haraway, *Simians, Cyborgs, and Women*," 212.

superficiality. Oscillating between metaphors of disembodiment and references to biological corporeality, this narrative produces a desire for presence that counters and subverts its critical deconstruction of physical positivism and postmodern mediality. What is more, its blending and shifting of linguistic registers and referential modes appears to complicate, much like Arcangel's narrative discourse, the task of distinguishing figural from literal language that Paul de Man considers essential to any reading process:

If to read is to understand writing [...] then it presupposes a possible knowledge of the rhetorical status of what has been written. To understand, primarily means to determine the referential mode of a text and we take for granted that this can be done. We assume that a referential discourse can be understood by whoever is competent to handle the lexicological and grammatical code of a language. Neither are we helpless when confronted with figures of speech. As long as we can distinguish between literal and figural meaning, we can translate the figure back to its proper referent. [...] Even if, as is often said to be the case for poetic language, the figure is polysemous and engenders several meanings, some of which might even be contradictory to each other, the large subdivision between literal and figural still prevails. Any reading always involves a choice between signification and symbolization, and this choice can be made only if one postulates the possibility of distinguishing the literal from the figural. This decision is not arbitrary, since it is based on a variety of textual and contextual factors (grammar, lexicology, tradition, usage, tone, declarative statement, diacritical marks, etc.) But the necessity of making such a decision cannot be avoided or the entire order of discourse would collapse.[207]

Similar to the edgework of a 'cheesy' amalgamation of the language of cultural critique with the lyrical symbolism of magic realism in Yamashita's allegoric representation of Arcangel, her version of cyberpunk activates a choice between signification and symbolization, literal and figural language. At the same time, it thwarts this choice by blending these linguistic registers and refusing any disambiguation of their rhetorical status: only provided with a genetic lineage and a physical death, and thus by an amalgamation of the figural and literal, can the allegory of digital mediality be experienced as the very desire for metaphysical presence that it deconstructs. As Emi's narrative discourse performs and addresses the very epistemological cracks that the cheesiness of Arcangel's medial spectacle makes palpable, both protagonists become visible as

---

[207] Paul de Man, "Allegory," *Allegories of Reading: Figural Language in Rousseau, Nietzsche, Rilke, and Proust* (New Haven and London: Yale UP, 1979) 188-220, 201.

figures of speech in "allegories of reading"[208] that court the collapsing of "the entire order of discourse."[209]

3.6 EDGEWORK, UNINTIMIDATED

But which order of discourse does Yamashita's aesthetic edgework ultimately jeopardize? From the perspective of ethnic and postcolonial studies, Emi's cyberpunk depiction alone could be accused of catering to a stereotypical "Japanimation,"[210] a new techno-Orientalism that, driven by resentment and envy of Asian economic success, casts Japan as "the figure of empty and dehumanized technological power."[211] But while Yamashita certainly invokes this novel version of the racializing 'yellow peril' stereotype, she clearly ridicules and ironizes it. Emi's precarious corporeality – a corporeality that is fully invested with meaning only by a patriarchal lineage – could, on the other hand, provoke the justified objection of feminists like Elizabeth Grosz.[212] Yet it could be argued that the fluid oscillation between corporeality and digital mediality in Yamashita's representation of Emi evokes the "generalized and indeterminate in-betweenness, a transgressive movement in itself"[213] that Grosz associates with an "escape from the systems of binary polarization of unities that privilege men at the expense of women."[214]

Ultimately, there seems to be much more at stake in *Tropic of Orange* than a risky position within the field of Asian American literature at the highpoint of its ideological crisis. Legitimized by the lack of conventions for speculative fiction that allows for the ambiguous rhetorical status of a boldly fictional narrative, the novel articulates a desire for presence that exceeds and cannot be folded back to

---

208 De Man "Allegory" 188.
209 Ibid., 201.
210 Toshiya Ueno, "Japanimation: Techno-Orientalism, Media Tribes, and Rave Culture," *Aliens R Us: The Other in Science Fiction Cinema,* eds. Ziauddin Sardar and Sean Cubitt (Sterling: Pluto, 2002) 94-110.
211 David Morley and Kevin Robbins. "Techno-Orientalism: Japan Panic," *Spaces of Identity: Global Media, Electronic Landscapes, and Cultural Boundaries,* eds. David Morley and Kevin Robbins (New York: Routledge, 1995) 147-173, 170.
212 See Elizabeth Grosz, *Volatile Bodies: Toward a Corporeal Feminism* (Bloomington and Indianapolis: Indiana UP, 1994).
213 Ibid., 175.
214 Ibid., 178.

the critique of postmodern mediality and its compliance with the racializing and gendering practices of neoliberal subject formation that it tackles at its level of content. With its edgework of blending the figural and literal – a blending of symbolization and signification that is always on the brink of a 'distasteful' cheesiness – the novel rather enacts and stages a tension between the production of meaning and the desire for an epistemologically unaccomplishable production of presence in literary representations. It thus enacts and makes tangible a tension between what Hans Ulrich Gumbrecht has called "meaning effects" and "presence effects." [215]

For Gumbrecht, contemporary Western culture, and, more specifically, the present situation of the humanities in academia, is marked by the exhaustion of and a growing frustration with both post-Kantian metaphysics and nineteenth-century hermeneutics, and the twentieth-century rejection and deconstruction of these concepts in the spirit of phenomenology and constructivism. Tracing back this "unresolved crisis" [216] of the humanities to the crisis of representation that, according to Foucault, began in the period of Early Modernity, Gumbrecht senses an increasing desire for presence in "a pre-dominantly meaning-based culture."[217] This meaning-based culture ultimately depends on interpretation – the decoding of 'insubstantial' meaning encoded in 'substantial' signs – rather than the experience of "events of self-unconcealment of the world"[218] that, according to Gumbrecht, marks the acquisition of knowledge in a presence culture such as medieval culture. It is because these events cannot be induced by and "never come[s] from the subject," and because "revelation and unconcealment [...] just happen"[219] that Gumbrecht speaks of "presence effects" that are 'produced' in the sense of being 'brought forth' by "the impact that 'present' objects have on human bodies"[220]., rather than produced in the sense of being manufactured. And rather than calling for "a replacement of meaning with presence," Gumbrecht, somewhat pretentiously, argues for "a relation to the things of the world that could oscillate between presence effects and meaning effects."[221]

---

215 Hans Ulrich Gumbrecht, *Production of Presence: What Meaning Cannot Convey* (Stanford: Stanford UP, 2004) 2.
216 Gumbrecht, *Production of Presence*, 3.
217 Ibid., 81.
218 Ibid.
219 Ibid.
220 Ibid., xiii.
221 Ibid., xv.

This is pretentious insofar, as the author delineates in *Production of Presence* a theory of aesthetic experience that clearly privileges a para-religious *Erleben* of auratic substance over the hermeneutic project of decoding culturally and historically contingent significations. In his eagerness to promote the project of a non-hermeneutic field in the humanities that would do away with the prevalence of meaning encoded in signs, Gumbrecht prefers to downplay that even non-semantic qualities (no matter whether those of artifacts or natural objects) are charged with meaning accorded to them by cultural contexts. With reference to artifacts in general, it is questionable if "a pure semantically disinvested experience of presence" can still be defined "as falling into the range of 'communication'."[222] With reference to literary works of art, it seems even more doubtful that something like non-semantic qualities even exists.[223] Most disquieting and most important, in subordinating reflection to a quasi-religious experience of presence effects, the aesthetic theory envisioned by Gumbrecht advocates what seems like a relapse into forms of pre-critical reception. Roberto S. Martinez, after meticulously tracing the philosophical concepts and lines of argument underlying *Production of Presence*, justifiably concludes that its author's privileging of "aesthetic epiphany" ultimately entails the same analytical and historical incapacitation (*Entmündigung*) of art that Martin Heidegger had practiced before him.[224]

Yamashita's aesthetic edgework in *Tropic of Orange* – programmatically announced by the novel's epigraph as "not wild, or crass, or cheesy enough to compete with the collective mindlessness that propels our fascination forward"– does not shy away from concepts such as 'substance' and 'presence,' the recourse to which has "long been a symptom of despicably bad intellectual taste

---

222 Pierpaolo Antonello, "The Materiality of Presence: Notes in Hans Ulrich Gumbrecht's Theoretical Project," *Producing Presences: Branching Out From Gumbrecht's Work* (Dartmouth: U of Massachusetts P, 2007) 15-26, 21.It should be noted that Antonello's essay is, in essence, favorable of Gumbrecht's call for an ontological turn in the humanities.

223 See Roberto Sanchino Martinez, "'Die Produktion von Präsenz'. Einige Überlegungen zur Reichweite des Konzepts der ‚ästhetischen Erfahrung' bei Hans Ulrich Gumbrecht," *Ästhetische Erfahrung: Gegenstände, Konzepte, Geschichtlichkeit*, Sonderforschungsbereich 626 (ed.), (Berlin, 2006). <*www.sfb626.de/veroeffentlichungen/online/aeth.erfahrung/aufsaetze/sanchino.pdf*>n.p.   Martinez points to the significance in literary works of art of non-semantic qualities like sound and rhythm (see paragraph 14).

224 Martinez, "'Die Produktion von Präsenz.' Einige Überlegungen." Paragraph 16.

in the humanities,"[225] as Gumbrecht claims. It neither, however, distances her novel from deconstruction or the hermeneutics of a cultural criticism that reveals political concepts such as race, risk, and security to be representational constructions in the service of global capitalism and free trade. While clearly expressing the "desire for a different epistemology"[226] that Gumbrecht identifies at the core of a crisis in the humanities, Yamashita's aesthetics documents that she does not renounce, as Gumbrecht does, the "hermeneutic maximalism" of "endless interpretation,"[227] to which her novel offers a complex and multiply layered textuality.

Her decidedly fantastic negotiation of time and space shows the epistemological crisis of representation to be enhanced by "some of the 'special effects' produced today by the most advanced communication technologies."[228] It first and foremost exposes them, however, as interwoven with the political-economic rationale of neoliberal subject formation. In representing one of her novel's characters as a 'special effect' of contemporary mediality in an allegory of reading, Yamashita's novel challenges the line between abstraction and allegorical figuration, symbolization and signification, meaning effects and presence effects – without abdicating or betraying her affiliation with the meaning culture, to which Gumbrecht pays mere lip service. Intellectually unintimidated by discursive taboos established by either the ideological crisis in Asian American literature or the call for an ontological turn in the humanities, Yamashita addresses in her novel both the politics of representation and the erotics of presence, and in doing so, challenges the order of literary and academic discourse.

---

225 Ibid., 53. As we have seen, the complex discourse on mediality in *Tropic of Orange* leaves no doubt that substance and presence must remain concepts as long as they are brought forth by the presentification strategies of medial productions, no matter whether those of literary texts or those of electronic media. At the same time, this literary discourse flaunts its own privilege over electronic simulacra, as it prompts in its readers a strong desire for physical presence, and in doing so, allows for an affective experience that might come close to the fleeting moments of presence that Gumbrecht calls "aesthetic epiphany."

226 Ibid., 62.

227 Ibid., 55.

228 Ibid., xv.

4 Monstrous Politics: Epistemological Empowerment, Natural Science, and New Territories of Empire in Larissa Lai's *Salt Fish Girl*

4.1 "THE IDENTITY OF THE BODY HAS NOT YET BEEN CONFIRMED:" EXCESSIVE TEXTUALITY AND DISCURSIVE CONTROL IN LARISSA LAI'S WRITINGS

In a talk given at a workshop dedicated to the re-mapping of Canadian urban activism in 2004,[1] Canada-based, Chinese American author, political activist and prolific academic Larissa Lai strikingly chose as a title "The Identity of the Body Has Not Yet Been Confirmed," a formulaic phrase notoriously applied to unidentifiable dead bodies in the context of official police communiqués. In the talk, Lai retrospectively delineates the history of her own involvement in and identification with Canadian identity politics movements of the 1980s and 90s, and identifies the 2004 political situation of feminist and anti-racist activism in Canada as a stalemate moment of crisis that she traces to political impasses of that earlier period. While acknowledging "the idea of breaking the silence" as "a powerful one" that "allowed the articulation of those experiences which, as good citizens of Trudeau's multicultural Canada, we were taught not to recognize, let alone speak about,"[2] Lai criticizes as "fashionable" and historically contingent

---

1 Larissa Lai, "The Identity of the Body Has Not Yet Been Confirmed: Panel Talk for 'A Walk with Woman Warriors' at Strathcona Community Centre, August 28, 2004."*West Coast Line 58* 42.2 Active Geographies: Women and Struggles on the Left Coast (2008): 137-139.
2 Ibid., 138

the strategy of self-racialization "of the marked body"[3] that characterized the activism of the 1980s and 90s:

> Our current moment is one in which that strategy no longer works. I'd argue, in fact, the radical and productive aspects of this strategy have been largely contained, and what remains effective is its conservativizing function. It assimilates us into liberal democracy through the production of a set of tropes that locates oppression in history, both denies and reproduces it in the present, and further creates target market groups through this re-valorized production of identity. It has come to the point where there are industries, both academic and literary, around these once silenced histories. They have become the expected, and indeed, only recognized discourse of racialized peoples. [...] That liberal democratic state we lobbied so hard to be included in a decade ago is no longer the same. In the meantime our bodies and their representations are circulated in the global economy both as signs of great wealth and extreme poverty. Our status as consumers places us in a relationship to other economies and other racialized bodies in ways that are both more intimate and more exploitative than ever. It is these relationships we need to begin exploring, representing, questioning and fixing in ways we have only just begun to imagine.[4]

Involved in both academic and literary 'industries' concerned with the marked bodies of women of color in Canada, Lai is far from mourning activism as a dead body. Contextualized with the quoted passage, the provocative title of her talk becomes visible as reflecting the "politically correct"[5] absorption of the marked body into an official state multiculturalism that, while acknowledging racial oppression as a historical fact, blinds out its own ongoing racism, and thus renders lifeless and inert this body's efforts at liberation and subversion. While evoking with the pretentiously neutral police jargon the subtle presence of social control and normalizing practices of discipline that are instrumental to this process of absorption (which, as will be shown below, can be read as a process of abjection), the phrase, at the same time, signals the marked body's evasion of these practices, a resistance against a 'confirmed,' and thus arrested identity. Moreover, in the interplay of title and text, the idea of the body, cast by the police phrase as a site of identitarian truth that can and has to be confirmed by state authority, assumes a different – less literal – notion of the body, i.e. the notion of textual bodies and bodies of texts. It is in this sense that the title of her talk suggests a reading of Lai's body of work as part and parcel of a multiply

---

3   Ibid.
4   Ibid., 138-139.
5   Lai, "The Identity of the Body," 138.

coded, interventionist project of political activism, an interminable, liberatory project that "cannot be a freedom machine,"[6] as it has to adapt its strategies to the shifting role of the nation state in the era of neoliberal globalization and its "conservativizing"[7] racist politics of containment.

With its catchy title and perceptive political criticism the talk is representative of Lai's prolific production and circulation of theoretical texts that capture her engagement in politics of race and gender in a language of personal experience and involvement, a language, in which the marked body figures prominently, both in a literal sense and as a metaphor. In the context of her academic traveling as a scholar and theoretical expert on 'minority writing,'[8] and the politics of representation, Lai has repeatedly problematized the circulation of her own racialized and gendered body as an Asian abject that is unwittingly compliant with the branding and marketing of Canada as a multicultural nation.[9] Yet, Larissa Lai is also a fictional writer, the author of two novels and a body of poetic work, and has, in the framework of these theoretical positionings, extensively commented on her own creative writing. While self-consciously circulating her body as an Asian/alien abject defined by the discourse of Canadian state multiculturalism, Lai has thus produced and disseminated an amazing amount of paratextual supplement to her novels, a supplementary body of theoretical texts, navigating the reception, and, as will be argued in the following, curtailing the literary potential of her fictional texts. Although both textual units – text and paratext – remain clearly distinguishable by the conventional markers of their publishing contexts, the 'spillover' of these

---

6 Ibid.

7 Ibid.

8 As Eleanor Ty and Christl Verduyn, editors of a collection of essays on Asian Canadian auto-ethnography, emphasize in their introduction to the volume, the term "minority writing" is increasingly rejected in recent postcolonial literary theory as "a construct and expression of the power and literary politics of a given time and context"(1), since a "racially minoritized writer in North America […] may no longer be associated with the marginal, minor, or Other" (2). *Asian Canadian Writing beyond Autoethnography* (Waterloo, ON: Wilfried Laurier UP, 2008). Without wanting to ignore this legitimate critique, I consider it appropriate to use the term in the context of Larissa Lai's politics of writing which, among other things, aim to reveal an ongoing minoritization of racialized others beneath the political correctness of a deceptively inclusive multiculturalism.

9 See for example: Larissa Lai, "Brand Canada: Global Flows and a People to Come," *Reading(s) from a Distance: European Perspectives on Canadian Women's Writing*, eds. Charlotte Sturgess and Martin Kuester (Augsburg: Wißner, 2008) 23-32.

paratextual remarks and explanations – a prolific paratextuality that by far exceeds the usual amount of authorial auto-commentary – destabilizes their boundaries without, however, achieving the liberating effect widely associated with the metaphor of 'blurred boundaries.' Against the background of this extensive paratextual supplement to her own fiction, the title of Lai's 2004 talk assumes a meta-textual quality, particularly when applied to the composite textuality formed by her novel *Salt Fish Girl* and her commentary on the novel in her theoretical writings: what the paratextual spillover generates is a queer, textual body whose identity has not been, and can indeed not be, confirmed.

Published in 2002, and thus at a point in time between the 1980s and 90s period of the discourse of Canadian multiculturalism, the period, in which Asians and their "breaking the silence"[10] became the "flavor of the month,"[11] and the ensuing stalemate moment of activist crisis that Lai describes in her talk, *Salt Fish Girl* is, significantly, a novel whose diegetic world is set in a mythical, historic China and a hyper-capitalist, near future Pacific Rim. While exempting a politically stagnant present, the Chinese setting offers an alternative myth of origin, whereas the speculative Pacific Rim setting projects a post-apocalyptic, post-national world order governed by six mega-corporations and their relentless economic competition. Both settings are populated by complexly hybrid, queer protagonists and composite bodies; impurity and abjection figure prominently throughout the narrative. Clearly, Lai uses the abject and abjection – defined by George Bataille as "the inability to assume with sufficient strength the imperative act of excluding abject things"[12]– as an important trope in *Salt Fish Girl*.

Abjection, however, does not end there. Commenting on her second novel in numerous articles, talks and interviews, Lai has not only offered background information on the stalemate political moment that conditioned the creative process of *Salt Fish Girl's* production ("I've dealt with these problems at a creative level, if only because it seems my only possible entry point at this moment")[13] but has, in addition, disclosed details on and explanations of the novel's diegetic world that its narrative discourse does not provide. Avid readers of her articles thus learn not merely that the mythical Chinese setting owes its creation to Lai's interest "in the whole question of origins" and has to be read as

---

10 Lai, "The Identity of the Body," 138.
11 Paul Wong qtd. in Lai, "The Identity of the Body," 138.
12 Qtd. in Julia Kristéva, *Powers of Horror: An Essay on Abjection* (New York: Columbia UP, 1982) 56.
13 Larissa Lai, "Future Asians: Migrant Speculations, Repressed History & Cyborg Hope," *West Coast Line 44* 38.2 (2004): 168-175, 170.

a reaction to "the common racist injunction that gets tossed at people of colour in North America to 'go back where you came from'," [14] culminating in a tracing of her own upbringing in California and Newfoundland, and her ancestral origins in Hong Kong and a Chinese village. Lai neither restricts her comment on the "futuristic parts" of her novel to pointing out "some of the major world events" [15] that influenced and inspired her writing of *Salt Fish Girl*:

the cloning of Dolly, the sheep, the arrival of three rusty ships from China on the West Coast of British Columbia carrying 600 Chinese migrant labourers, Monsanto's suing of a farmer whose canola crop, probably through natural pollination, had picked up some of Monsanto's altered DNA, the patenting of slightly modified basmati rice by a large Texas corporation, the construction of Celebration, a fully planned ur-American town, by Disney. [16]

An instance of public authorial "epitext," [17] this provision of "genetic" background information does not, by any means, interfere with Lai's privileging of creative writing "as the only possible entry point" [18] for political activism in an era "heavily controlled by a neo-conservative political and economic agenda," [19] and the "massive corporatization of everything and anything." [20] It certainly navigates, though, the reception of *Salt Fish Girl*, and, even more important, assigns a mere political functionality to the literary text.

While these instances of authorial information on the genesis and the historical and political situated-ness of a fictional text seem to 'merely' imply a subordination or interventionist instrumentality of the literary to the political, the epitextual supplement of details on *Salt Fish Girl*'s diegetic world not provided by the novel's diegesis presents an even more confounding form of discursive control. Minutiae on Evie, *Salt Fish Girl*'s rebellious cyborg protagonist and her

---

14 Ibid., 171.
15 Ibid.
16 Ibid., 172.
17 Gerard Genette defines as 'epitext' "any paratextual element not materially appended to the text within the same volume but circulating, as it were, freely, in a virtually limitless physical and social space" (344), and as 'genetic commentary' all epitextual information – authorial or otherwise – on the conditions and the process of the production of a given literary text. (367) *Paratexts: Thresholds of Interpretation* (Cambridge: Cambridge UP, 1997).
18 Lai, "Future Asians," 170.
19 Ibid., 168.
20 Ibid., 169.

artificial genealogy are, for example, disclosed in the context of the genetic epitext quoted above[21], and a delineation of the exact structure of the novel's corporation governed world order is belatedly given in another one of Lai's nonfictional publications.[22] It is important to note that, while these details might support a comprehensive reading of the novel, they are by no means essential to it. At first glance it rather seems as if political activist and critic Larissa Lai mistrusted literary author Larissa Lai and the workings of her novel's complex aesthetics, although the text works more than effectively without her explanations.

The result is an excessive textuality, a composite textual body with a thick, undulating, and muscled 'tail' of a paratext that is not restricted to the functions of advertisement – the function that Genette has called "temptation"[23] – or generic disambiguation. On the contrary, Lai's interlacing of cultural critique with references to her own biography and supplementary elaborations on *Salt Fish Girl*'s diegetic world in her nonfictional publications generates a generically ambiguous, sprawling textual entity that lingers between the fictional and the factual, and questions conventional textual boundaries. Although discursive authorial control aimed at navigating *Salt Fish Girl*'s reception is mainly exercised in the framework of scholarly talks and publications – a fact that limits its impact as the public thus addressed and reached primarily consists of academics engaged in politics of 'ethnic' writing in general, and/or Lai's work in particular – it, in effect, risks arresting the free play of the fictional text's signifiers, and reducing it to a mere illustration of the agenda of identity politics.

Fictional authorship and risk in Lai are thus contingent upon her double agency as a creative writer and a political activist, who is amenable to political imperatives and taboos originating in an Asian North American discourse on the politics of ethnic representation and articulation. Consequently, the risks inherent to Lai's fictional authorship are, to a certain extent, similar to those taken by

---

21 See Lai, "Future Asians," 175: "Manufactured from the DNA of a Chinese-Canadian woman interned with her Japanese-Canadian husband during the Second World War, combined with the DNA of freshwater carp in order to get around human cloning laws, adopted by the man who patented the process and tossed back into the walled off prison-factories of the future [...]." Interestingly, Lai's epitextual comment provides these details of Evie's genetics – details that the novel withholds – at this point in order to suggest a reading of Evie as "the figure of the cyborg Asian" (175), thus reducing and delimiting the metaphoric potential of a fictional protagonist to an illustration of Lai's own positioning within Asian Canadian identity politics.
22 See Lai, "Brand Canada," 28.
23 Genette, *Paratexts*, 91.

Karen Tei Yamashita. The novels of both authors are speculative fictions concerned with questions of multiculturalism and the nation state; they deal with national and transnational subject formation in the era of, as well as the infiltration of representation by, neoliberal capitalism. Both authors belong to racialized North American minorities, yet can be considered privileged "subjects of speech in the ivory tower,"[24] who obviously apply their academic knowledge to their respective creative writings. Both authors thus have in common the double bind of being racialized, political-economic subjects in multicultural North American nations, and enjoying the privilege of academic education and institutionalization. In both instances this double bind results in the authors' respective vivid interest in and their perceptive critique of neo-colonializing, political-economic practices and discourses, as well as an understanding of literature as a means of political intervention.

However, as the previous chapter endeavored to show, Karen Tei Yamashita embraces the hazards produced by this double bind by way of an intricate aesthetic edgework *within* her novel rather than navigating its reception by epitextual comments. Inscribed in *Tropic of Orange*'s complex aesthetics is a profound – and legitimate – trust in the effectiveness of narrative composition and the free play of literary language. And, although the novel invites political readings, its political subtext is not, and cannot by any means be, channeled into a mere illustration of Asian American identity politics or its claims. Strikingly, as the subsequent analysis of Larissa Lai's novel aims to prove, the same can be said of *Salt Fish Girl*. With its narration conjoining an alternative Chinese myth of origin and a speculation on political subject formation at a near-future, post-national Pacific Rim, the novel parades a generic hybridity that corresponds with its themes of impure origins and composite, transgenic corporeality. Yet Larissa Lai displays little confidence in her novel's aesthetics, and the trope of abjection that her comments foreground as having a key role in *Salt Fish Girl* remains not restricted to the fictional text. Lai's epitextual commentary on the novel further destabilizes conventional generic boundaries and, in the process, produces a queer narration, a composite textual body comprised of the novel's text and the enormous 'tail' of its verbal and performative authorial paratext. One might call this an abject textual body, but the political implications of such a designation are highly ambivalent.

If one follows Lai's epitextual navigation, both textual units – text and paratext – must be read against the background of Julia Kristeva's seminal essay *The Powers of Horror*, a treatise on abjection drawing on the work of Georges

---

24 David Leiwei Li, *Imagining the Nation: Asian American Literature and Cultural Consent* (Stanford: Stanford UP, 1999) 186.

Bataille and Mary Douglas. While focusing on psychoanalytic processes of individuation, Kristeva's concept conjoins Bataille's sociologist definition of abjection as the act of expelling threatening elements that establishes the foundations of collective existence, and Douglas's anthropologist findings on the constitutive function of notions of purity in indigenous communities. In doing so, it provides a theory of abjection that enables a deeper understanding of both individual and collective processes of subject formation. Widely received in the field of postcolonial studies, this theory of abjection has increasingly been used in theorizing the role of the "'strange' (racialized, feminized, alien) body"[25] in the multicultural nation.[26]

Based on the ambivalent, originary moment of the infant's separation from the maternal body, of which it is still a part, Kristeva's idea of abjection is inherently resistant to definition and categorization. Extrapolating from maternal rejection in the subject's individual history and "approaching abjection"[27] instead of defining it, Kristeva circumscribes the abject as a highly ambiguous and excessive being:

---

25 Joanna Mansbridge, "Abject Origins: Uncanny Strangers and Figures of Fetishism in Larissa Lai's *Salt Fish Girl*," *West Coast Line* 38.2 (2004): 121 -133, 122.

26 See also Sara Ahmed, *Strange Encounters: Embodied Others in Post-Coloniality* (London: Routledge, 2000) 39-103; Sara Ahmed, *The Cultural Politics of Emotion* (Edinburgh: Edinburgh UP, 2004) 82-100; Rey Chow, *The Protestant Ethnic and the Spirit of Capitalism* (New York: Columbia UP, 2002)128-152; Donald Pease "National Narratives, Postnational Narration," *Modern Fiction Studies* 43.1(1997):1-23. Notwithstanding the wide range of subject positionalities of, and the implicit differential in perspective represented by these authors their emphasis on the key role of abject, strange bodies in the performative and narrative construction of the nation is strikingly unanimous.

27 Kristeva *Powers of Horror* 1. "Approaching Abjection" is the title of the first chapter of Kristeva's essay. It is quoted at this point, in order to highlight the characteristic elusiveness of Kristeva's text and to caution against insufficiently complex readings that might reduce the abject to connotations of defilement associated with bodily substances such as excrements and menstrual blood. What has to be acknowledged instead, is the metaphoric threat that the abject poses to *any* symbolic order as a constant reminder of the permeability and fragility of its borders, and the high degree of abstraction in Kristeva's essay, whose "difficult and fascinating prose not only describes the idea of the abject," as Megan Becker-Leckrone observes, "but also acts out its strange force." *Julia Kristéva and Literary Theory. (Transitions)* (London: Palgrave, 2005) 151.

[The Abject] lies there, quite close, but it cannot be assimilated.²⁸

[...] It is something rejected from which one does not part, from which one does not protect oneself as from an object. Imaginary uncanniness and real threat, it beckons to us and ends up engulfing us. [...] It is thus not a lack of cleanliness or health that causes abjection but what disturbs identity, system, order. What does not respect borders, positions, rules. The in-between, the ambiguous, the composite.²⁹

A topos of ambiguity, the abject is both a constituent of and a menace to any symbolic order defined by an identitarian logic of sameness. As a non-object, th"has only one quality of the object – that of being opposed to *I*."³⁰ Likewise describing a process – the, however incomplete, incorporation and/or expulsion of the abject – and an affective quality, the term abjection, then, refers to moments of personal and collective crisis: as the abject "threatens the purity of origins and the integrity of boundaries while disrupting the distinctions between self/other, inside/outside, pure/impure", and in so doing induces "fascination and horror, desire and dread."³¹

In the context of state multiculturalism, this unsettling ambiguity of abjection is embodied by the figure of the stranger who, as Sara Ahmed observes, is "temporarily assimilated *as* the unassimilable."³² Caught in the deadlock of a perpetual chiastic movement, "the strange body is constructed through a process of incorporation and expulsion,"³³ and is, in turn, assigned a crucial role in the paradoxical construction of the multicultural nation where it enables a deceptive incorporation of difference. Abjection thus belongs to the workings of what Rey Chow has termed the "ethnicity management apparatus,"³⁴ i.e. the workings of a government policy whose celebratory awareness and inclusion of ethnic difference "serves, in the end, to mask and perpetuate the persistent problems of social inequality."³⁵

While *Salt Fish Girl*'s investment in and aesthetic negotiation of abjection as a critique of the incorporation of otherness by the multicultural nation state have been explicitly pointed out by Lai's paratextual references to the concept, and

---

28 Kristeva, *Powers of Horror*, 1.
29 Ibid.
30 Ibid., italics in the original.
31 Ahmed, *Strange Encounters*, 54.
32 Ibid., italics in the original.
33 Ibid.
34 Chow, *The Protestant Ethnic*, 122.
35 Ibid., 133.

have been widely acknowledged in the critical reception of the novel, the abject textual body comprised of the fictional main text and Lai's authorial epitext keeps producing political contingency. Of course, this contingency can be read as a politically programmatic rejection and disturbance of a dominant generic categorization confining the production and the reception of minority writing. What comes to mind in this context is Jacques Derrida's notion of parergonality, developed in his discussion of Kant's *Critique of Judgment*, a notion that does not define the framing paratext as a mere liminal structure marking the boundary and thus an ontological difference between the inside – "the intrinsic beauty"[36] – of a text and its "extrinsic,"[37] paratextual outside. Instead of defining the framing 'parergon' as a supplement to a preexisting 'ergon,' Derrida emphasizes the paradox double movement of the frame that contributes to the constitution of the very identity which defines its own quality as a secondary other:

Parerga have a thickness, a surface which separates them not only (as Kant would have it) from the integral inside, from the body proper of the ergon, but also from the outside, from the wall on which the painting is hung, from the space in which statue or column is erected, then, step by step, from the whole field of historical, economic, political inscription in which the drive to signature is produced. [...] No "theory", no "practice", no "theoretical practice" can intervene effectively in this field if it does not weigh up and bear on the frame which is the decisive structure of what is at stake, at the invisible limit to (between) the interiority of meaning (put under shelter by the whole hermeneuticist, semioticist, phenomenologicalist, and formalist tradition) and (to) all the empiricisms of the extrinsic which incapable of either seeing or reading, miss the question completely.[38]

Against this background, it could be argued that it is not necessarily a lack of confidence in the expressive power of "the body proper" of her fiction that motivates Lai's paratextual proliferation. The "thickness" of *Salt Fish Girl*'s paratextual 'tail', its excessive blurring of the boundaries between novel and paratext might rather be read as a programmatic, performative confirmation of the principle of abjection that Lai emphasizes to be so prominent in her novel: By dissolving the boundaries of the "interority of meaning" and blending this

---

36 Jacques Derrida, *The Truth in Painting* (Chicago and London: U of Chicago P, 1987) 63.
37 Ibid.
38 Derrida, *The Truth in Painting*, 60-61.

with the "empiricisms of the extrinsic,"[39] the author, once again, affirms the "in-between, the ambiguous, the composite"[40] that is the abject.

The composite, abject discourse thus produced appears to offer – at least temporarily as a "narrative in the gaps of history"[41]– a solution to the problems arising from the complex relationship between ethnicity and representation that Lai discusses in many of her critical texts. Repeatedly, she describes the extent to which many racialized Canadian writers of color – fraught with the tacit obligation to be representative in the sense of identity politics and ethnic belonging, and motivated by a strong desire for recognition and "entry into a national imagination" [42] – used autobiography as a mode of breaking the silence in the 1980s and 90s. While acknowledging the need for recognition, Lai cautions against the pitfalls of ethnic autobiography – the, however involuntary, reproducing of racializing stereotypes in response to what Rey Chow has termed "coercive mimeticism,"[43] and to the "race ritual"[44] that conditions its reception – and makes a strong argument for fiction as preferable over autobiographic writing: "I seem, at this point, to be arguing in favor of metaphoricity, as more liberatory and more productive than texts that presume to artlessly represent experience, if only because the latter cannot, in the end, produce experience for the reader."[45]

Lai's own, decidedly fantastic, speculative fiction clearly avoids the pitfalls of auto-ethnograpy, and definitely succeeds in offering its readers experience by way of an intricate narrative technique and a productive metaphoricity. *Salt Fish Girl* in particular is a case in point as it provides polyvalent metaphors that can represent "an inherited, shared condition of social stigmatization and abjection"[46] that is important to Lai and many other Asian American writers. The

---

39 Ibid.
40 Kristeva, *Powers of Horror*, 4.
41 The quote refers to the subtitle of Larissa Lai's essay "Corrupted Lineage: Narrative in the Gaps of History", *West Coast Line 33* 34.3 (2001): 40-53. In this essay Lai discusses the need of minority writers in Canada for new strategies in view of the infiltration of capital in representational politics.
42 Larissa Lai, "Strategizing the Body of History: Anxious Writing, Absent Subjects, and Marketing the Nation," *Asian Canadian Writing Beyond Autoethnography*, eds. Eleanor Ty and Christl Verduyn (Waterloo, ON: Wilfrid Laurier University Press, 2008) 87 -111, 107.
43 Chow, *The Protestant Ethnic*, 138.
44 Robert Stepto qtd. in Lai, "Strategizing the Body of History," 99.
45 Lai, "Strategizing the Body of History," 105-106.
46 Chow, *The Protestant Ethnic*, 146.

metaphoricity of the novel can, however, not be restricted to this narrowly defined political subtext. What Lai creates, then, by extending the diegesis of the novel into her nonfictional work, and by blending it with political comments and autobiographical empiricisms, is a hybrid, contingent textuality that, strikingly, reintroduces the autobiographical 'I' that she avoids in her fiction. Implicitly, the authorial self-conception inherent to this abject textuality appears to respond to Kristeva's call for an alternative authorship formulated in conclusion of "Powers of Horror:" "Who, I ask you, would agree to call himself [sic] abject, subject of or subject to abjection?"[47] Using the trope of abjection in her fictional text, where it signifies both the unassimilable racialized other and the body politic that excludes it in including it, and in her theoretical texts, where it signifies the same, Lai's construing of an 'abject authorship' reproduces the chiastic structure of abject assimilation. This not only raises the question, if the excessive textuality and the abject, non-identitarian textual body it produces succeed in "disturbing identity, system, order"[48] of a voracious state multiculturalism that immediately incorporates and commodifies that which it interpellates as its abject other. More important, Lai's authorial strategy is self-contradictory as it brings in through the backdoor the "compulsive self-referentiality"[49] of the very genre she criticizes.

What emerges when the trope of abjection that controls Lai's novel collapses with the rhetoric of abjection that controls her nonfictional writings is a textual body that – while intended to be liberated and liberatory – is 'contaminated' by discursive control. Lai's extensive exercise of discursive control appears to testify to a strangely uncritical adherence to the Romanticist concept of authorship whose claim to ultimate authority over the meaning of a fictional text has been sustainably dismantled by both twentieth-century literary production and criticism. This dismantlement famously climaxed in the seminal essays of Roland Barthes and Michel Foucault, who have pronounced defunct the Romanticist figure of the author as the singular locus of textual authority (Barthes "The Death of the Author," 1968), and have identified the author as one powerful discursive function among others (Foucault "What is an Author?," 1969).

Of course, the author is not and never has been dead, as not least the strong authorships of Barthes and Foucault show. Yet obviously, Lai's political strategy of abject textual contamination complicates her authorial position, and her attitude towards postmodernist and poststructuralist definitions of literature as a

---

47 Kristeva, *Powers of Horror*, 209.
48 Ibid., 4.
49 Chow, *The Protestant Ethnic*, 127.

discursive game and the author as a mere 'scriptor' is telling in many ways. Dictated by the political demands of minority writing, her strategy of self-referentiality and abject contamination – a strategy that is in and of itself contradictory – appears to interfere, in addition, with the notion of the obsolescence of an outdated model of authorship. It comes as no surprise that Lai has commented on her authorial self-conception and the challenges posed by late-twentieth-century criticism's renunciation of the author as the singular site of literary meaning-making in her nonfictional publications. In a particularly conclusive interview, conducted by Robyn Morris, she states:

I probably do have alliances with postmodernism as an artistic movement but I don't really think of my work in those terms. Certainly, when I was beginning, I thought about postmodernism as a Euro-centric movement that I didn't particularly want to be allied with it. Whose modernity was it that we were supposedly "post"? *I found the notion of the "death of the author" particularly annoying, as it seemed to be widely in play at precisely the moment when many marginalized people were finally beginning to find their voice.* But regardless of whether I took postmodernism on in an overt way or not, I suppose it was hard to avoid. I [...] am as much a product of western intellectual and political movements as people of so-called "European" descent. It's only that the trajectory of my lineage is a bit more broken and scattered. *I am interested in the notion of truth as a construction.* Is that an idea that belongs to postmodernism? Or could it equally well belong to liberatory movements from the margins?[50]

In its claiming of an eccentric political and cultural position that refuses to be regulated by a "Euro-centric" power/knowledge complex, Lai's statement displays a theoretical eclecticism and a staged theoretical naiveté that further illuminate her authorial self-positioning as an ambiguous, contingent endeavor. As both her critical and fictional publications show, Lai is well aware that "the notion of truth as a construction" cannot be separated from the "liberatory movements from the margins,"[51] for whose anti-essentialist politics it provided a crucial epistemological foundation. Yet formed and constrained by the imperatives and taboos created by politics of representation demanding the constant display of an "awareness of writing from a racialized and gendered position,"[52] she is compelled to reject "the power of the universal (white) man"[53]

---

50 Larissa Lai,"'Sites of Articulation'- An Interview with Larissa Lai: Robyn Morris in Conversation with Larissa Lai," *West Coast Line 44* 38.2 (2004): 21-30, 24-25, italics added.
51 Ibid., 25.
52 Ibid., 26.

and "the editorial power of white privilege"⁵⁴ in prayer- wheel-like repetitions that, ultimately, result in theoretical inconsistency. Again, Lai's struggle for discursive control over her fictional texts is folded back into the political activist's struggle for recognition and empowerment; literary authorship is collapsed with activist authorship and its compulsion for ideological disambiguation.

As a consequence, contradictions abound, even within the limited scope of one interview: Although Lai explicitly wants her fiction "to move beyond the instructive mode" and renounces a "certain kind of didacticism" that she acknowledges to have been "in play" in the discourses that were formative to her "coming of age, coming to politics,"⁵⁵ this very didacticism is slipped in by way of her excessive epitextual self-commentary and threatens to paralyze any fictional move beyond the instructive mode. In spite of her claim "to put [...] aside" her "own and other people's politics of representation" in her creative writing, Lai feels compelled to proclaim that her novel constructs a reader in her "likeness" in a "kind of contingent essentialism of the moment."⁵⁶ And in the same breath with disavowing "storytelling as a civilizing force, as a way of imposing an ethics, a morality" she keeps directing an ethical reception of *Salt Fish Girl* not only by characterizing it as a "much darker book" whose protagonists are "implicated in systems they cannot control,"⁵⁷ but by imposing another disambiguating interpretation of the cloned 'Sonias'⁵⁸ of her novel's diegesis.

---

53 Ibid., 29.
54 Ibid., 28.
55 Ibid., 23.
56 Ibid., 22. In order to avoid distortion in this rendition of Lai's statement on the 'construction' of her reader, her elaboration on this point should not be withheld: "In my fiction I try to centralize the experience of people like myself. *But I mean 'like myself' in the loosest and most fluid way possible.* Sometimes it can be racialized or gendered or of a particular sexual orientation. Sometimes it's reactive. Sometimes it's constructive. Sometimes it is a lot of contradictory things at once. But I am definitely trying to break away from a unitary Western liberal subject." ("sites of articulation" 22, italics added) The passage is characteristic of Lai's oscillating between an understanding of the literary as a 'fluid' discourse whose metaphoricity enables a wide range of receptive experience, and her compulsion to channel and direct this experience according to the demands of the politics of representation.
57 Lai, "Sites of Articulation," 25.
58 A full literal quote of this passage seems to be in order here as a characteristic instance of Lai's exercise of epitextual navigation: "In many ways, *Salt Fish Girl* is a

Contradictions like these vividly illustrate Lai's authorial self-conception as deeply entangled in a tight-knit net of contingent conventions: The self-conscious circulation of her marked body as a site of authorial control and meaning-making, and the construction of a reader in her "likeness"59 implicitly invoke an essentialism that immediately has to be designated as a temporary strategic device as it collides with the 'politically correct' avowal of truth as a construction. In addition to this activating of a strategic essentialism, Lai's explicit embracing of a "politics of contingency,"60 and the repeated expression of her interest in the "figure of the traitor"61 are telltale indicators of a struggle to come to terms with a predicament established by a very specific "field of historical, economic, political inscription in which the drive to signature is produced."62 Besides evoking the risk taken by Karen Tei Yamashita, who has captured her perception of the "predicament of Asian American articulation"63 in the trenchant term of the "mine field,"64 Lai's interest in the transgressive figure of the traitor suggests a parallel to 'Hollywood transgressor' Kathryn Bigelow and her entanglement with the contingent politics of the Hollywood middlebrow-machine. And despite the differences in the heterogeneous fields that condition the creative work of all three authors, these fields appear to have

---

much darker book [than Lai's first novel *Fox*, S.W.]. I'm thinking a lot more in terms of systems and a lot less in terms of individual capability, individual power. Nu Wa and Miranda are both implicated in systems they cannot control. The future is more violent than the past. Hope lies in the random – the idea that even out of the worst situations sometimes mutations occur in a liberatory direction. You get this with the Sonias, the cloned women who somehow escape and manage to reproduce without the intervention of the corporation. It's not about having learned anything, consciously or subconsciously. It's about a bit of will and a bit of luck. Or a lot of luck even – what the Sonias have done is in some ways quite miraculous – to have achieved this sort of superhuman fertility beyond anything technoscience could ever bestow. It's a breaking out beyond the imagination of the technology itself." Lai, "Sites of Articulation," 25.

59 Ibid.
60 Ibid., 22.
61 Ibid., 23, 24.
62 Derrida, *The Truth in Painting*, 60.
63 David Leiwei Li, *Imagining the Nation:Asian American Literature and Cultural Consent* (Stanford: Stanford UP, 1999) 21.
64 Karen Tei Yamashita, "Traveling Voices," *Café Creole: Circle K* (June 2000): Web, 12 Jul. 2011, <http://www.cafecreole.net/travelogue/karen/circleK2.html#june2000 >.

in common the prompting of a "drive to signature"⁶⁵ that they simultaneously constrain and regulate by very particular inscriptions.

Obviously, for the racialized and gendered activist writer in Canada at the beginning of the twenty-first century, these inscriptions require the "drive to signature" to be distinctly pronounced, and authorial signature to be defended against theoretical concepts that might interfere with the politics of representation. Bound by conflicting inscriptions that demand the positivist⁶⁶ embodiment of a strong meaning-making authority *and* the acknowledgement of the "notion of truth as a construction," Larissa Lai has to resurrect the author as the site of meaning-making in the name of an anti-racist and feminist empowerment of the marked body. Suffused with the empiricism and the self-referentiality that she and others have disqualified as an unfit strategy for the 'ethnic' literary text, the body politics informing her sprawling epitextual comment on *Salt Fish Girl* produce a 'contaminating' parergon⁶⁷ that threatens to arrest and 'paralyse' the novel.

The strikingly consistent use of pathologizing metaphors in otherwise heterogeneous definitions of discursive authorial control points beyond the desired effect of abject alienation to fundamental hazards inherent to Lai's prolific paratextual control. Significantly, Jacques Derrida has outlined the dangers of the parergon as "a sort of pathology of the *parergon*"⁶⁸ in his reading of Kant's *Critique of Judgment*. In contemplating the effects of framing parergonality, Derrida cautions against the "seductive adornment" produced by "the gilding of the frame done in order to recommend the painting to our attention by its attraction:"⁶⁹

The deterioration of the *parergon*, the perversion, the adornment, is the attraction of sensory matter. As design, organization of lines, forming of angles, the frame is not at all

---

65 Derrida, *The Truth in Painting*, 60.

66 It testifies to Larissa Lai's acute awareness of the political conundrum that complicates her authorial position, when she addresses the problem of positivism in the same interview: "Productivity is always a positive act. And positivism, as much of the history of the twentieth century has borne out, is a breeding ground for fascism. To stake out a place of belonging, however much comfort one gets from doing so, is also to commit an act of violence."("Sites of Articulation," 23-24)

67 The word is used here, according to Derrida's definition, as "a hybrid of outside and inside." *The Truth in Painting*, 63.

68 *The Truth in Painting*, 64.

69 Ibid.

an adornment and one cannot do without it. But in its purity it ought to remain colorless, deprived of all empirical sensory materiality.[70]

Read with Derrida, the slew of empiricisms in the body politics informing Lai's epitextual navigation of her novel's reception constitutes a seductive "gilded frame" that is definitely not "colorless," a frame that risks impeding the metaphoric productivity of the fictional text. It is important to note, though, that the terms "purity" and "perversion" in Derrida's deconstruction of Kantian aesthetics can be read as telltale signs of the "hidden essentialism"[71] that Diana Fuss has identified at the core of deconstruction against the grain of its perception as the "most rigorous anti-essentialist discourse."[72] Motivated "by an interest in uncovering the ways in which deconstruction deploys essentialism against itself" and "leans heavily on essence in its determination to displace essence,"[73] Fuss traces an essentialist logic in Derrida that even informs "Derrideanisms"[74] such as "undecidability, contradiction, and heterogeneity."[75] In conclusion, she posits:

It is important to note that essence is a sign, and as such historically contingent and constantly subject to change and to redefinition. Historically we have never been very confident of the definition of essence, nor have we been very certain that the definition of essence is to *be* the definitional. Even the essence/accident distinction, the inaugural moment of Western metaphysics, is by no means a stable or secure binarism. The entire history of metaphysics can be read as an interminable pursuit of the essence of essence, motivated by the anxiety that essence may well be accidental, changing, unknowable. Essentialism is not, and has rarely been monolithically coded.[76]

Derrida's demand for a purity of aesthetics has thus to be treated with caution, as it seems to reiterate, if inadvertently, the essentialism that it aims to deconstruct. What can be read with Fuss, as a "reactionary" "lapsing into"[77] essentialism in

---

70 Ibid.
71 *Essentially Speaking: Feminism, Nature, and Difference* (New York and London: Routledge, 1987) 13.
72 Ibid., 12.
73 Ibid., 13.
74 Ibid.
75 Ibid.
76 Fuss, *Essentially Speaking*, 20.
77 Ibid.

Derrida, thus contrasts the "interventionary,"[78] strategic deployment of essentialism, the temporary taking of "the 'risk' of essence"[79] that characterizes Lai's embracing of an activist politics of contingency. Against this background, Derrida's "pathology of the *parergon*"[80] and its insistence on the colorless purity of the frame appears itself to be 'contaminated' by an inadvertent evocation of aesthetic essence. This essentialist contamination complicates a critique of Lai's parergon to *Salt Fish Girl* as contaminated by "empirical sensorial materiality."[81]

It becomes obvious, at this point, that it is not the sensorial materiality of the marked body evoked by the language of experience and justified by a strategic essentialism that is in turn legitimized by the agenda of activist identity politics, but the collapsing of this agenda with the extensive exercise of epitextual discursive control that threatens to 'contaminate' Lai's novel. Even against the background of a post-Kantian view that acknowledges that "the experience of aesthetic form is implicated, through its necessary tie to critical discourse, in the social and political conflicts inherent in the formations of the public sphere,"[82] Lai's authorial commentary on her novel appears to be "both didactic and incantatory, worked by the compulsion of mastery."[83] Its conflation with the ethic commitment to empiricist body politics of representation expressed in a language of personal experience risks arresting the very experience of *Salt Fish Girl*'s aesthetics in the framework of a narrow political agenda.[84]

---

78 Ibid.
79 Ibid., 1."The 'Risk' of Essence" is the title of Fuss's introductory chapter in *Essentially Speaking*.
80 *The Truth in Painting*, 64.
81 Ibid.
82 John Brenkman, "Extreme Criticism," *What's Left of Theory: New Work on the Politics of Literary Theory*, eds. Judith Butler, et al. (New York: Routledge, 2000) 114-136, 120.
83 Derrida, *The Truth in Painting*, 154.
84 The host of references to Lai's authorial epitext in critical readings of *Salt Fish Girl* shows that Lai's epitextual 'drive for signature' has been effective in navigating the novel's reception. Accordingly, most of these readings, including my own articles, have elaborated on Lai's fictional representation of the concept of abjection, its function in the construction of the multicultural nation in the era of free market capitalism, and its potential of disrupting corporate power. See for example Joanna Mansbridge, "Abject Origins: Uncanny Strangers and Figures of Fetishism in Larissa Lai's *Salt Fish Girl*," *West Coast Line 44* 38.2 (2004):121-13; see also Susanne Wegener, "Pacific Trans-Formations: Politische Ökonomie, Körper und Geschlecht in Larissa Lais *Salt Fish Girl*," *GENDER: Zeitschrift für Geschlecht, Kultur und*

However, just like the textual body of Lai's parergon that evades terminal definition, the identity of the textual body of her novel has not yet been confirmed. Beyond the political agenda foregrounded by Lai's epitextual commentary, *Salt Fish Girl*'s speculation on the future of bio-politics in the twenty-first century offers "to the impatient objector, if s/he insists on seeing the thing itself at last,"[85] a complex literary extrapolation from historical and contemporary scientific and political-economic constructions of human essence. Projecting a body politic, whose production of biological citizens rests upon the molecularization, the fragmentation, and the recomposition of the living body, the novel exposes the hazards inherent to biological technologies, by which "life itself has become open to politics."[86]

While, in the futurist setting of its diegetic world, the essentialism/ constructivism divide becomes moot as the very 'essence' of biological identity can be constructed by the transfer of DNA-fragments, the novel suggests an essential residue of the "accidental, changing, unknowable,"[87] a living potential that eludes control by scientists and medical practitioners. This projection of chance as an uncontrollable agent of subject formation and biological development of the human species offers a glimpse of hope at the end of the novel, eventually adding a utopian twist to a dystopian narrative. At the same time, paradoxically, it ties in with the dynamics of hope that propel contemporary bio-medical research to develop ever more refined methods of biological control.

Against the grain of Larissa Lai's epitextual directions the subsequent close reading of *Salt Fish Girl* aims to highlight the literary world-making that privileges the novel's complex speculation on the risks of biological citizenship in a genetically engineered, near future. In other words, the analysis sets out to show that it is by way of this literary world-making in the futurist strand of the

---

Gesellschaft 3.2 (2010): 92-106. Although most of the articles on *Salt Fish Girl* also discuss the topic of genetic engineering and the liberatory possibility that lies in a post-humanistic subjectivity, the narrative strategies of the novel and the philosophical and political implications inherent to its speculation on a bio-economic future have hardly been sufficiently explored. For an insightful reading, focusing on the entanglement between science and capital, see Tara Lee, "Mutant Bodies in Larissa Lai's *Salt Fish Girl*: Challenging the Alliance between Science and Capital," *West Coast Line 44* 38.2 (2004): 94-110.

85 Derrida, *The Truth in Painting*, 63.
86 Nikolas Rose, *The Politics of Life Itself: Biomedicine, Power, and Subjectivity in the Twenty-First Century* (Princeton and Oxford: Princeton UP, 2007) 15.
87 Fuss, *Essentially Speaking*, 20.

novel that biological control and its formation and management of risky bodies can be experienced as an all-encompassing episteme that is neither completely futuristic nor restricted to the construction of the nation-state and its abjection of alien bodies. Conditioned by a growing inseparability of bio-politics and bio-economics, this episteme is continuously gaining pertinence since the time of the novel's publication. Reading the salience and "the normalization of the term 'biocapital' as both an indicator and a precursor of a "new turn,"[88] Nikolas Rose convincingly argues:

The very emergence of the language of bioeconomics brings into existence a new space for thought and action. The bioeconomy has appeared as a space to be mapped, managed, and understood; it needs to be conceptualized as asset of processes and relations that can be known and theorized, that can become the target of programs that seek to increase the power of nations or corporations by acting within and upon that economy.[89]

This emergence of a new space that is to be "mapped, managed, and understood" raises the question, by whom? Can a culture afford to leave this project to the life sciences, or, to put it differently, can the utopian imaginary of the life sciences replace the imaginary of literature and its function of political and cultural synthesis? What happens when the utopian imaginary of the life sciences assumes the role of a guiding culture, while art and literature are in danger of becoming a subculture *sui generis*?[90] Clearly, the stakes are high in Larissa Lai's fictional speculation on the implications of a thoroughly biologized, hyper-capitalist future. At content level, *Salt Fish Girl*'s futurist strand negotiates the hazards arising from an unprecedented alliance of science and capital, the growing prevalence of an economized life science as a form of biopolitical governance. Less conspicuous, and subtly inscribed in the novel's exposition, a meta-representational discourse points to questions of epistemology and power, the epistemological history of the life sciences, the epistemological conditions of their constructions of alterity. The point of departure of the present analysis will therefore be a close reading of three expository passages as intricate epistemological gestures of empowerment, targeted at holding the ground of the literary against an impending loss of cultural significance.

---

88 Nikolas Rose, "The Value of Life: Somatic Ethics and the Spirit of Biocapital," *The Right to Life and the Value of Life: Orientations in Law, Politics, and Ethics*, ed. Jon Yorke (Burlington, UK: Ashgate, 2010) 85-99, 91.
89 Ibid.
90 See Peter Sloterdijk, *Regeln für den Menschenpark: Ein Antwortschreiben zu Heideggers Brief über den Humanismus* (Frankfurt/Main: Suhrkamp, 1999).

4.2 OFFERING ODORS – EPISTEMOLOGICAL EMPOWERMENT AND NATURAL SCIENCE

Salt Fish Girl's narration begins with the exposition of its two first-person narrators and their respective historical settings in its first two chapters. This exposition of the diegetic world of a novel that conjoins an alternative myth of origin and a bio-punk speculation on the near future is preceded by an epigraph, a quotation from Gertrude Stein's collection *Useful Knowledge*. Presented at the threshold of the fictional text, this epigraph effectively foreshadows, disambiguizes, and enhances the function of the expository chapters. It suggests that what happens at *Salt Fish Girl*'s beginning is nothing less than the positing of an epistemologically privileged, non-mimetic disorder that underlies and is being suppressed by a dominant symbolic order. As corresponding gestures of epistemological empowerment these three parts of the novel announce the inauguration of a new 'order of things,' emerging at a new threshold of knowledge.

4.2.1 Useful Poetics

Placed before the table of contents, on a page after Lai's dedication of her novel to her Chinese grandmother Tsui-Pun Wai-Chee, the epigraph reads: *"I don't like rain. I don't mean that thunder scares me. You know very well what I mean I mean that sometimes I wish I was a fish with a settled smelling center."*[91] In using a quotation from one of Stein's modernist texts as an epigraph to her postmodern novel, Larissa Lai certainly applies the conventional gesture of the epigraph to align her own claiming of a strong authorship with the famously strong authorship of one of the most prominent writers of trans-Atlantic modernism. Though equally conventional, the positioning of this alignment after the dedication of the novel to her biological grandmother, at the same time, summons the notion of an ideational, matriarchal genealogy exceeding a biological concept of lineage and its inherent determinist constructions of identity. By quoting Stein at the peritextual threshold to her fictional text, Lai thus not only augments her own authorship with Stein's symbolic capital, but programmatically identifies herself and her novel's poetics with those of an exceptional woman writer, whose texts have been immensely influential to literary modernism's project of sustainably shattering the claim of mimetic representation.

---

91 Larissa Lai, *Salt Fish Girl* (Toronto: Thomas Allen, 2002), italics in the original. Future references will be given parenthetically by page numbers in the text.

At first glance, Lai's choice of the quote seems to be motivated merely by a conspicuous thematic correspondence of its reference to fish to the eponymous salt fish girl who, as the title announces, is at the center of the novel's narration. At the same level, the quote can further be read as a foreshadowing of the tone of the first-person narrative of Nu Wa, the Chinese goddess, whose hybrid body combines features of fish, snake, and human anatomy, and whose narration provides an alternative myth of origins in the first chapter of the novel. And finally, the quote, equally conspicuously, forestalls the centrality of olfaction to *Salt Fish Girl*'s plot and protagonists. Conjoining these arguments, critic Paul Lai's reading of the "enigmatic and querulous epigraph"[92] exemplifies such an interpretation:

The cantankerous quality of the speaker's voice prefigures Nu Wa's later voice, but the epigraph also yokes the fish to "a settled smelling center," suggesting an olfactory sensory organ that is more stable than what humans possess. The desire to be a fish, too, points to Salt Fish Girl as the desirable and desired figure of the novel.[93]

These observations are as correct as they are reductive. They limit the correspondence between epigraph and fictional text to the level of content in both textual units. They neither account for the eccentric status of Gertrude Stein's authorship and poetics nor for the aesthetic and epistemological implications inherent to Larissa Lai's gesture of selecting – and, as will be pointed out below, arbitrarily trimming – a passage from Stein's "Farragut or a Husband's Recompense," a very personal Stein text, published in the volume *Useful Knowledge*.

Intended to address an American audience by a collection of texts that were not meant to form a unified book when they were written (most of the pieces originated between 1915 and 1926), *Useful Knowledge* was first published in 1928, and is mainly comprised of "selected works that reflected the theme of America."[94] According to Stein's own recommendation of the book in *Advertisement*95, a short text added to the collection as a first page, "Useful Knowledge has been put together from every little that helps to be American." Beyond its obvious purpose of marketing the book by flattering the patriotic

---

92 "Stinky Bodies: Mythological Futures and the Olfactory Sense in Larissa Lai's *Salt Fish Girl*," *MELUS* 33.4 (2008):167-187, 169.
93 Paul Lai, "Stinky Bodies," 169-170.
94 Edward Burns, "Foreword: Useful Knowledge about *Useful Knowledge*" (1988), *Useful Knowledge* (Barrytown, NY: Station Hill/Barrytown, LTD., 2001) vii-xvii, vii.
95 *Useful Knowledge* (Barrytown, NY: Station Hill, 2001) n.p.

pride of its intended American readers, *Advertisement* also provides reasons for the inclusion of pieces in *Useful Knowledge* that are not as conspicuously 'American' as "Business in Baltimore," "Patriotic Leading," or the portraits of Sherwood Anderson and Woodrow Wilson. In one of the characteristic twists that have earned her texts labels such as 'enigmatic' or 'hermetic,' Stein describes in *Advertisement* as "a romantic thing that has been so added to the history of living for a whole generation" her belief that "in America the best material is used in the cheapest things because the cheapest things have to be made of the best material to make them worth while making it," and concludes: "This is the American something that makes romance everything. And romance is Useful Knowledge."

It is by way of this affirmation of American exceptionalism and its amalgamation with an unconventional version of American pragmatism that "romance" could be and has been included in *Useful Kowledge*. While Stein's use of the term 'romance' is ambiguous – although she suggests a specifically American meaning, it is not clear if this implies a reference to the American genre of romance as exemplified by the stories of Nathaniel Hawthorne, whose fictional worlds border on the fantastic – it might account for the admission to the collection of an "intimate"[96] text such as "Farragut or A Husband's Recompense."[97]

Organized in six sections on eleven pages, "Farragut"[98] is quite obviously a piece that, like many other Stein pieces, ridicules linguistic conventions and

---

96 Burns, "Foreword," xii.

97 Gertrude Stein, "Farragut or a Husband's Recompense," *Useful Knowledge* (Barrytown: Station Hill, 2001) 5-16. Future references will be given parenthetically by page numbers in the text.

98 The piece hardly gives any clues that allow for more than a speculative interpretation of the inclusion of the name "Farragut" in its title. It can be read, for instance, as a reference to David Glasgow Farragut, who, although a Southerner, had a leading role as an Admiral in the Union Navy during the American Civil War. While this engagement of a Southerner in the war effort of the Union might evoke the connotation 'traitor,' Farragut has been widely memorialized in the U.S. – in the form of monuments and by a number of American cities, which were named after him – mostly for his courageous behavior in the 1864 Battle of Mobile Bay, a courage trenchantly captured in his famous battle cry: "Damn the torpedoes, full speed ahead!" See *"Union Generals: General David Glasgow Farragut, USA,"* HistoryCentral.com. Web. 05 Jan. 2012 *<http://www.historycentral.com/Bio/UGENS/USAFarragut.html>*. Stein's evocation of these connotations adds a belligerent and, at the same time, a decidedly patriotic ring to her struggle for self-assertion in her relationship with

behavioral norms. But it is also a text that reflects Stein's struggle to come to terms with her relationship with Alice B. Toklas at a point in time when the tone in this relationship indicated an impending turn from romance to power play.[99] Like all Stein texts, "Farragut" is by no means unambiguous, and certainly calls for more profound and encompassing research that would go beyond the scope and the purpose of a contextualization of Salt Fish Girl's epigraph. However, in order to give an idea of its thrust and tone, its striking accumulation of polite phrases and apologetic explanations that alternate with statements of resistance and authorial self-assertion should not go unmentioned. Marked by simple grammar and an obscuring use of pronouns that refuses any unequivocal identification of speaker, subject and addressee, the first sections of "Farragut" seem to tackle a process of adaptation to social rule represented by sentences such as "How do you do", "Very well thank you" (6), "Please be neat" (7), or "Every one was pleased" (9). Not unusual in Stein, these phrases seem "like the mere recording of the banalities and niceties of everyday 'polite' chitchat,"[100] as Marjorie Perloff observes with reference to "Marry Nettie" (1916), Stein's poetic reply to Marinetti's misogynist Futurism.

In "Farragut," after apparently referring to childhood memories of oppressive socialization at school and at home in the sections "Early years" and "Earlier years," Stein in the subsequent section "Crossing" begins to interlace the phrases "of social ritual and boredom"[101] with the speaker's confessions of insubordination and resistance.

A few lines after admitting "I was naughty" (8) – a confession at once both childlike and fraught with connotations of sexual transgression – the tone and, obviously, the age and the situation of this speaker have changed remarkably, when she/he announces: "I'm now going to begin telling everything"(9). The 'crossing' announced in the title of the section could thus refer to the transition

---

Toklas. Even when read in a less referential mode, the 'gut' in Farragut equally connotes 'reckless courage.' It thus points in a similar direction, suggesting that what Stein feels compelled to summon and display in the piece is 'guts'.

99 As an earlier piece, "Farragut" thus foreshadows a development that Stein biographers ascribe to a later stage in the Stein/Toklas relationship, in particular to the period of the late 1920s and early 1930s when Stein wrote and published *The Autobiography of Alice B. Toklas*. See Linda Wagner-Martin, *Favored Strangers: Gertrude Stein and Her Family* (New Brunswick, NJ: Rutgers UP, 1995). Especially Chapter 13 "Alice's Book and 'La Gloire'." 195-207.

100 Marjorie Perloff, "Grammar in Use: Wittgenstein/Gertrude Stein/Marinetti," *South Central Review* 13. 2/3 *Futurism and Avantgarde* (1996): 35-62, 53.

101 Perloff, "Grammar in Use," 54.

from childhood to adulthood, implying that the ability of "telling everything" is dependent on the competent use of language and a critical, detached perspective. It could, even more likely, refer to Stein's crossing of the Atlantic as an expatriate who lived in France for a long period of time, implying a more conscious use of a language that was different from the one in use in the chosen country of residence. And it could, finally, refer to the crossing of a gender boundary by a lesbian who lived in a marriage-like relationship with another woman. According to Marjorie Perloff, these latter 'crossings' resulted in a "double bind of sexual and national difference" that "produced a very special relationship to language"[102] and, ultimately, in "Stein's refusal to 'mean,' her dislocation or disruption of patriarchal language."[103]

It is this special relationship to language that adds a double entendre to the striking accumulation of expressions of reluctant non-compliance in "Crossing." In this section of "Farragut," the images of quarrel and controversy evoked by such words as "shoving," "shouting," and "dispute" (9) that the speaker discloses after announcing "to begin telling everything," are interlaced with polite expressions of a still cautious refusal to comply. Only at one level can sentences like "I don't really mean to be a slave" (10), "I say that I offered odours" (10), "I don't mean to be foolish (10), and "I said not so sweet" (11), be read as references to the speaker's attempt to negotiate the conventions regulating proper behavior in, say, a love relationship. The multiply coded references to odors and taste in particular point beyond a negotiation of behavioral norms and beyond erotic connotations to the speaker's more general refusal of conventional linguistic representation[104].

This rather polite refusal to comply with an all-encompassing, dominant symbolic order makes way for a more belligerent attempt at asserting authority in "Principal parts," the final section of "Farragut." Similar to Stein's use of the principle/principal pun in "Marry Nettie,"[105] the title of the section playfully

---

102 Ibid., 38.

103 Ibid., 51.

104 It is worth noting that in these references to sensual qualities Stein does not use the word 'mean,' whereas in the quoted sentences, in which she uses it, it can be read either as an expression of intention or volition (I don't really *want* to be a slave; I don't *intend* to be foolish) or as expressing the will to signify by her poetic work (I don't really *signify in order* to be a slave; I don't *signify* to be foolish) The latter interpretation ties in with the subtle, yet ubiquitous struggle for authority over meaning-making in "Farragut," a meaning of 'mean' that Stein's poetics at the same time rejects.

105 See Perloff, "Grammar in Use," 53.

indicates a will to dismantle the principle of a male-coded authority over language as meaning-making, as well as, paradoxically, a determination to claim the equally male-coded 'principal part' in the lesbian relationship, the quarrels of which seem to be the object of the section. With the plural form 'parts,' the title even evokes the idea of the phallus that would grant the speaker both the authority of the husband in this marriage-like lesbian relationship *and* the more encompassing authority over meaning making.

Fraught with the double purpose of simultaneously tackling a 'phallogocentrism' *avant la lettre* and asserting a powerful, signifying position both in the love quarrel and the dominant symbolic order, Stein's language in "Principal parts," while still polite and marked by a lover's eagerness to please, becomes more explicit in its refusal to comply. The speaker, for instance, announces a willingness to fight by declaring "By this means we conquer" (11) in the fourth line at the beginning of the section, a battle cry that is picked up and reinforced a few lines below: "[…] and by this time I conquer" (12). And, in a later passage towards the end of the piece, the speaker, somewhat obstinately, asserts

> I said go home if you like.
> I said I am an authority.
> I said I could be angry.
> I said nothing. (15)

Intermingled with these expressions of pugnacious resolution, however, are many phrases that point to a struggle for 'settlement' and indicate a defiant insecurity behind the articulation of bold self-assertion, as the following passage exemplifies: "I will not be coerced. But I was. Was I. I was coerced. I see it."(12)

Significantly, Stein uses the word 'settle' six times in this section, exploiting and playing with the broad array of its denotations.[106] And it is amidst this struggle

---

106 The *Oxford English Dictionary* lists 35 meanings of the verb "to settle." *OED Online* (March 2011) Web, 31 Jan 2012 <http://www.oed.com/view/Entry/176867?rskey=Gqhdhe&result=3&isAdvanced=false#eid>. In order to mention but a few denotations that, apart from more customary usages, might be pertinent to Stein's use of the word in "Farragut," I want to emphasize the *OED*'s definitions of 'settle' as an expression of 'calming down' or 'subsiding'(of passion, see *OED* entry 19a), of establishing a domestic state (see *OED* entry 28b), of securing by decree, ordinance, or enactment (see *OED* entry 30 a), of directing the course (of a body of persons) to a common point (see *OED* entry 9a), but also, applied to hounds in the

for 'settlement' in "Principal Parts" that the passage containing the quote that Larissa Lai uses as an epigraph to *Salt Fish Girl* can be found. In "Farragut" the passage reads: "I don't like rain. I don't mean that thunder scares me. You know very well what I mean I mean that sometimes I wish I was a fish with a settled smelling center. I don't like it. I think it's an ugly word." (12) The framing composed of the very short first two sentences and the equally short concluding statements navigates all attention to the enigmatic sentence "You know very well what I mean I mean that sometimes I wish was a fish with a settled smelling center." The enigma of the curious desire to be "a fish with a settled smelling center" is enhanced by the ambiguous pronouns "you" and 'I' and Stein's conflating of two sentences by the omission of a period. This refusal to comply with the rules of punctuation as a structuring principle of a dominant grammar results in the flamboyant doubling of the phrase 'I mean' at the center of the phrase. What is emphasized and ascribed centrality by this conspicuously doubled "I mean I mean" is the claiming and the assertion of an authority that playfully subverts the linguistic authority of and the coercion by grammatic rule. Yet, at the same time, this doubling can be read as a stammer, and thus as a sign of the same elusive insecurity that marks Stein's attempt at asserting authorial dominance in the struggle for 'settlement' throughout the piece.

Unsettled by the quarrel with a counterpart whose refusal to understand can only be perceived as obstinacy – "You know very well what I mean" – ,the speaker 'conquers' with the droll riddle of her wish to be "a fish with a settled smelling center." Upon close scrutiny, however, the riddle and its drollery dissolve in a vapor of smelly connotations. Apart from connotations of slippery elusiveness, the word fish, particularly in conjunction with the idea of "odours" in a text full of sexual innuendo, unmistakably alludes to the purportedly fishy smell of female genitalia, and thus invokes the devaluation of a female coded odor[107] by an epistemologically dominant patriarchal center. Yet, in fore-

---

context of hunting, as an expression of keeping steadily to the scent (see *OED* entry 9b).

107 Jane Gallop, Carol Mavor, and others, have traced the privileging of a masculine coded authority of visual signs prevalent in Western cultures to Sigmund Freud's *Civilization and its Discontents* (1930). Describing and performing civilized culture's "diminution of the olfactory stimuli" (Freud 99) by elaborating on women and smell in a "fetid footnote" (Mavor 281), Freud's text lays down modern Western civilization's depreciation of female coded olfaction. Sigmund Freud, *Civilization and its Discontent*, *The Standard Edition of the Complete Psychological Works of Sigmund Freud* vol. 21 (London: Hogarth Press 1953-74) 59-145. Carol Mavor "Odor di Femina: Though You May Not See Her, You Can Certainly Smell Her,"

grounding with the "smelling center" a particularity of fish anatomy, Stein, at the same time, subverts the misogynist symbolic connotations by pointing to 'the thing itself' rather than its patriarchal coding. The elusiveness of Stein's fish is the elusiveness of the object itself, the object that an 'exhausted' patriarchal language fails to capture.

Stein's image of the fish resonates with the other-worldly monstrosity of sea serpents and many-headed hydras that medieval and early Renaissance mapmaker's drew at the edges of their maps, an appropriating signification that marked the border between known and unknown territories.[108] As Stein's fish is not only 'smelly,' but a monstrous animal, endowed with an organ to discern smells, it not only eludes but counters the phallogocentrism of patriarchal signification. Privileged and empowered by "parts" – the "settled" and thus incorruptible, olfactory organ – Stein's fish can 'settle' a different order. It becomes obvious that what is expressed in the desire to be a fish with a settled smelling center is Stein's desire to overcome the contradictions inherent to her drive for authorial self-assertion: endowed with monstrously different, yet empowering and incorruptible "parts" that enable the positing – the 'settlement'– of a different, sensual, epistemological order, the dilemma of a female claiming of "principal parts" would be solved, and "odours" could be "offered."

At this point, the poetic function of the sentences that frame the one expressing the wish to be a fish becomes more transparent. In order to emphasize that the fish in this passage is no longer just a noun, but an object, a body 'caressed' by poetic composition,[109] the initial statement "I don't like rain" provides the contrasting example of a phrase that is depleted of meaning by the conventionality of an 'exhausted' language. Arrested by the conventional syntax of a phrase resonating with connotations "of social ritual and boredom,"[110] the noun 'rain' does not allow for immediate emotional experience. So fixated is 'rain' by the conventional syntax of this phrase that it cannot trigger in any reader the receptive affect, the emotional excitement that is the objective of Stein's poetics.[111] The juxtaposition of the statement "I don't like rain" thus

---

The Smell Culture Reader, ed. Jim Drobnick (Oxford/ New York: Berg, 2006) 277-288. See also Jane Gallop *The Daughter's Seduction: Feminism and Psychoanalysis* (Ithaka, NY: Cornell UP, 1982) especially 26-27.

108 See Margaret Atwood, *In Other Worlds: Science Fiction and the Human Imagination* (New York: Doubleday, 2011) 67.

109 See Gertrude Stein, *Lectures in America*, 1935 (Boston: Beacon, 1985) 231.

110 Perloff, "Grammar in Use," 54.

111 In *Lectures in America* Stein describes her poetic project as motivated by the semantic deficiency of the 'names' of conventional language. Particularly critical of

serves to heighten and to expose the destabilizing emotional effect of the subversive syntax of the fish-sentence.

It is only by way of the poetic monstrosity, the 'stammer' in the poetic syntax of this sentence that a signifying potential of the noun 'fish' can be retrieved from language.[112] A poetic composition that unsettles and displaces conventional language, the fish-sentence can be read as a programmatic plea for the monstrous stammer of an experimental writing, targeted at renewing a fixated, exhausted language. The affective experience of its elusive, yet different 'odor' hence makes palpable a poetic program whose epistemological criticism motivates the drive for authorial self-assertion and the positing of a female-coded epistemology. While the reference to water in the rain-statement, at first glance, suggests a confounding correspondence with the fish-sentence, its fixated emptiness indicates that it, in fact, corresponds with the concluding sentences of the passage "I don't like it. I think it's an ugly word." This subtle correspondence of the concluding sentences with the initial "I don't like rain" does not simply point to the difference between the prevailing epistemological order and its desired poetic and sensual alternative. By forming a framing verbal bracket that encloses the sentence articulating the desire for alternative epistemological empowerment, these corresponding sentences also expose this desire to be suppressed and contained by the conventions of a dominant language.

Strikingly, Larissa Lai did not include the last two sentences of the passage in her epigraph to *Salt Fish Girl*. Her choice of the quote indicates that, for her, the issues of difference and poetic epistemological empowerment are far from being 'settled.' It implies a programmatic identification of her novel with Stein's modernist objective of dislocating or disrupting a conventional language that "is

---

'exhausted' nouns – "A noun has been the name of something for such a very long time" (214) – because they made it impossible "to feel anything and everything that for me was existing so intensely" (242), she ultimately rejected and increasingly replaced them with pronouns in later stages of her writings. Qtd. in Perloff "Grammar in Use" 38-41. See also Claudia Franken, *Gertrude Stein, Writer and Thinker* (Münster: LIT-Verlag, 2000) 301.

112 Stein's unsettling of conventional language by the stammering "I mean I mean" at the center of the fish-sentence can be read as prefiguring the programmatic "stuttering in language" that Gilles Deleuze declares to be the task of the writer: "[…] it is no longer the character who stutters in speech. It is the writer who becomes *a stutterer in language*. He makes language as such stutter: an affective and intensive language, and no longer an affectation of the one who speaks." "He Stuttered," *Essays Critical and Clinical* (Minneapolis: U of Minnesota P, 1997) 107-114, 107, italics in the original.

patriarchal not because it *is* male, but because it exaggerates, hypostasizes, exclusively valorizes male modes of signification, silencing the female presymbolic, pluridimensional modes articulated by experimental writing."[113] Lai's omission of the last two sentences of the passage is irritating, at first glance, as it obscures this subtext of poetic empowerment and appears to invite interpretations such as the one by Paul Lai that reduces the correspondence between the Stein quote and her novel to the level of content. Yet this omission can also be read as a conscious 'trimming,' targeted at reopening a hermetic epistemological enclosure and containment of the devalued, pre-symbolic odors that the monstrous, composite body of her fictional text endeavors to set free.

4.2.2 The Gaze of Natural Science

Announced as a fundamental epistemological critique, such "not so sweet"[114] odors are prominently and programmatically offered in the expositions of *Salt Fish Girl*'s first-person narrators where they serve as signs that expose and unsettle the epistemological order of natural science. Comprised of two narrative strands, one told by Nu Wa, an ageless Chinese Goddess/shapeshifter/trickster figure, and set in various periods of historic China, the other one told by Miranda Ching, a young woman of Chinese descent and set in a post-national, near-future North American Pacific West, the novel begins with the world- and self-creation of the primal Chinese Goddess. Feeling "lonely in a way even the most shunned of you have never known loneliness" (1), Nu Wa interrupts the space-time continuum of a yet unformed, pre-symbolic world by inserting her narration of a myth of origin.

The materials of life still lay dormant, not yet understanding their profound relationship to one another. There was no order, nothing had a clear relationship to anything else. The land was not the land, the sea not the sea, the air not the air, the sky not the sky. The mountains were not yet mountains, nor the clouds clouds.

But wait. Here comes the sound of a river, water rushing in to fill the gap. Here comes the river. Hussssssssh. Shhhhhh. Finger pressed vertically against lips, didn't I tell you? Of course I have lips, a woman's lips, a woman's mouth, already muttering secrets under my breath. Look. I have a woman's eyes, woman's rope of smooth, black hair, extending past my waist. A woman's torso. Your gaze slides over breasts and belly. The softest skin, warm and quivering. And below? Forget modesty. Here comes the tail, a thick cord of

---

113 Marianne DeKoven, *A Different Language: Gertrude Stein's Experimental Writing* (Madison: U of Wisconsin P, 1983) xix, italics in the original.

114 Stein, "Farragut," 8.

muscle undulating, silver slippery in the early morning light. Lean closer and you see the scales, translucent, glinting pinks and greens and oily cobalt blues. (1-2)

It is a fabulous, hybrid, amphibian blend of woman, fish and snake that is washed up by the waters of the Yellow River and instantly charges the scene with signals of erotic seduction. In the eternal present of the myth it is unclear who is being addressed by this seduction, who is being courted by whispered secrets, glossy hair and the translucent scales of the fishtail. Read as an appeal to the reader, this exposition in any case touts for trust: trust in a colorful, iridescent, sensual, and playful narrator and a narration beyond logic and reason; it touts for confidence in a stinking, slime-born, divine fertility outside any symbolic dichotomy. What is being presented here is the intrusion of *logos* into *mythos* by the positing of a symbolic order, and it is literally significant that the title of this first chapter is "The Bifurcation."[115]

This title only at one level refers to Nu Wa's failing attempt to form replicas of herself from river mud and her enraged splitting of her creations' fishtails after they start making fun of their maker before the act of creation is even finished. While the 'bifurcation' at this naive-mythical level casts humanization as a result of punishment for an originally immanent hubris, it denotes, at a deeper, more subtle level, the introduction of a binary symbolic regime, which always implies hierarchy and dissymmetry. Yet as her fantastic body boldly signals, Nu Wa is the figure of a hybrid third, neither fish nor fowl, neither completely human nor unambiguously animal, and her attempt to form creatures in her likeness does not fail by chance.

Rather, this failure seems programmatic as it indicates a characteristic disinterestedness to exercise the power of signification, and points to the alternative procreative principle that Nu Wa embodies. This libidinal principle becomes unmistakable when she is described as enjoying and envying her creations' sexual pleasures (which the narration links to the human anatomy that emerges after the splitting of the fishtail, and thereby casts as enabled by difference and deviation from the divine model). *Salt Fish Girl's* narration thus suggests that it is the principle of difference and multiplicity, as well as a dionysian desire for desire that propel Nu Wa's incarnation as a lesbian woman who falls in love with the eponymous salt fish girl and the subsequent series of

---

115 Clearly resonating in this expository scene's poetic language is Julia Kristeva's hypothesis of a pre-discursive, semiotic dimension of language associated with the maternal body and its repression by the paternal law of the symbolic that structures all signification, a hypothesis that Kristeva explores in *Revolution in Poetic Language* (New York: Columbia University Press, 1984).

both her and her lover's re-incarnations and lifecycles in eighteenth- and nineteenth-century China throughout the novel.

It is almost impossible to miss the feminist critique and the deconstruction of the phallogocentrism inherent to the Western narrative of the paradise garden in this mythic representation of Nu Wa. There are, however, contradictions in the exposition of Nu Wa that call into question the sole explanatory potential of its interpretation as a feminist cultural critique. By interrupting the solitude of a timeless "abandonment to the vertiginous fascination of the undefined, of chaos, of the anticosmos"[116] the narrator thus introduced paradoxically terminates an order-less, pre-symbolic state that can be described, with George Canguilhem, as marked by the "sleep of reason" that "begets monsters;"[117] and yet, by the very act of telling, this narrator initiates the order that defines her own monstrosity. Moreover, in inviting and exposing herself to an obviously masculine-coded, objectifying gaze that immediately construes this monstrosity as other, the narrator seems to resort to the 'ancient' strategy of a stereotypically feminine-coded, erotic seduction as a means of pacifying the predatory instincts of an equally stereotypical male.

This provocative play with gender stereotypes casts doubt on an interpretation of the alternative myth of origin as a narrative gesture of feminist epistemological empowerment. Its contradictions subtly point to a related, yet more fundamental epistemological challenge. It is the challenge of capturing forms of life and classifying them in representations of nature, a scientific challenge that Michel Foucault has identified as the concern of natural history in the classical age in *The Order of Things*.[118] Upon closer scrutiny, the primal moment that the subtitle of *Salt Fish Girl*'s first chapter locates at the "Bank of the Yellow River, pre-Shang dynasty" (1) significantly reflects the threshold of knowledge that, according to Foucault, marked the emergence of natural history in seventeenth-century Europe. Foucault argues that before signs became modes of representation in the seventeenth century, they were part of things themselves, and an organization of knowledge that could distinguish between observation,

---

116 Georges Canguilhem, *Knowledge of Life*, 1965 (New York: Fordham UP, 2008) 138.

117 Canguilhem follows Goya in repeating that "the sleep of reason begets monsters." *Knowledge of Life* 140. Shortly after this passage, Canguilhem emphasizes the dependency of any concept of monstrosity on normative judgment and the existence of "a strict legality imposed on nature by mechanistic physics and philosophy" (141).

118 Michel Foucault, *The Order of Things: An Archaeology of the Human Sciences,* 1970 (New York: Vintage, 1994).

documentation, and fable did not exist. With the rising awareness of the split between what de Saussure would later term 'signifier' and 'signified,'

natural history finds its locus in the gap that is now opened up between things and words – a silent gap, pure of all verbal sedimentation, and yet articulated according to the elements of representation, those same elements that can now without let or hindrance be named. Things touch against the banks of discourse because they appear in the hollow space of representation.[119]

In the seventeenth century, as Foucault has it, natural history began to fill the gap between things and words with a cataloging project that accounted for "the living being in its anatomy, its form, its habits, its birth and death," yet removed "the whole of animal semantics."[120] The living being was purified, "stripped naked"[121] of "Litteraria"– that is, stripped of "traditions, beliefs, and poetical figures."[122] Guided by objectives of "mathesis"[123] (defined by Foucault as a science of calculable order), an emerging natural history relied on the eye to capture the things that it named and classified in a 'table' without connecting them to discourse.

While Lai's fable of Nu Wa clearly and programmatically draws on ancient Chinese mythology, its wording strikingly resembles that of Foucault in the passage quoted above. What the "sound of a river" and its "water rushing in to fill the gap" announces, is, read with Foucault, the filling of the epistemological gap left by the mere naming of European natural science in the age of the catalogue. A poetical figure charged with multiple cross-references to fables and fairy tales, Nu Wa fills "the hollow space of representation"[124] with 'litteraria' that the seventeenth-century catalogue of natural history had silenced. The text alludes to this silencing by presenting the sound of the river as a "Husssssssh" followed by "Fingers pressed vertically against lips, didn't I tell you"(1). With the reader thus prepared for the disclosure of silenced "secrets" of China – and here Lai, again, plays with a stereotype – the fantastic narration of NuWa re-inserts into the "silent gap, pure of all verbal sedimentation" "elements of

---

119 Ibid., 129-130.
120 Ibid., 129.
121 Ibid.
122 Ibid., 130.
123 Ibid., 73.
124 Ibid., 130.

representation"[125] that the calculable order of natural history and its barren grid of knowledge did not account for.

It is the cataloging eye of natural science to which Lai's rendition of the myth of Nu Wa offers the grotesque spectacle of the goddess's voluptuous, composite body. Rather than evoking some general 'sleep of reason,' this invocation of the fabulous monster addresses the blanks left by an incipient natural science that "is not the effect [...] of a rationality formed elsewhere," but must be considered "a separate formation, one that has its own archaeology."[126] The gaze that Nu Wa's exposition aims to seduce is thus neither merely the objectifying gaze of a stereotypically gendered male nor the analytic, yet unspecific gaze of post-enlightenment rationality. It is the masculine coded, classifying gaze of a science that, throughout its history, construed monstrosity to illustrate and to affirm the norms it had established.

Tracing back the function of monsters in the history of eighteenth- and nineteenth-century life sciences, historian of science George Canguilhem shows how the concept of monstrosity became an epistemological instrument to the scientific study of the normal and the pathological. Perceived by eighteenth-century natural history as "aberrant organisms,"[127] and used as a substitute for experimentation and a comparative means to better understand the rules of regular natural organization, the 'monsters' that had been displayed and enjoyed as a spectacle in the bestiaries of the Middle Ages and the Renaissance – exemplified in Canguilhem by a "child with a rat's tail coming out of his head," a "magpie-woman," or a "pig with a human head"[128] – were, in the nineteenth century, naturalized against the claims of a positivist anthropology:

In his *Histoire des anomalies de l'organisation* (1837), Isidore Geoffrey Saint-Hilaire [...] achieves the domestication of monstrosities, ordering them among anomalies, classifying them according to the rules of the natural method, applying to them a methodical nomenclature still in use today, and, above all, naturalizing the composite monster, that is, the one in which we find the complete or incomplete elements of two or more organisms united.[129]

---

125 Foucault, *The Order of Things*, 130.
126 Ibid.
127 Canguilhem, *Knowledge of Life*, 141.
128 Ibid., 140.
129 Ibid., 142.

According to Canguilhem, Saint Hilaire's formula, "There are no exceptions to the laws of nature, only exceptions to the laws of naturalists,"[130] marks the turning point, at which 'teratology' – the study of physiological abnormalities – not only became part of biology as a natural science, but allowed for an experimental science that, under the label 'teratogeny,' tried to create its own objects.

Significantly, in showing how monstrosity, at this point, "appears to have revealed the secrets of its causes and laws, while anomaly appears called upon to explicate the formation of the normal,"[131] Canguilhem emphasizes a crucial distinction between monstrosity and the monstrous when he concludes "Henceforth, the transparency of monstrosity to scientific thought cuts monstrosity off from any relation to the monstrous."[132] With monstrosity firmly in the grip of a life science that had been cleansed of depreciated myths and their artistic representations, the monstrous is banished to the realm of fantastic art, where, motivated by "a nostalgia for the nondistinction of forms, for panpsychism, for pansexualism," "monsters are called upon to legitimate an intuitive vision of life, in which fecundity effaces order."[133]

Against the backdrop of Canguilhem's remarks on monstrosity and the monstrous, *Salt Fish Girl*'s exposition of Nu Wa becomes visible as doubly programmatic. As both an avowal of the fantastic genre and a critique of the biological categories established by Western life sciences, it displays and celebrates the body of a chimera, a monster, like the spectacle of strange animals in the bestiaries of the Middle Ages and the Renaissance. In doing so, it expresses a desire for a fecundity that might efface an order of knowledge, whose definition of species has been linked to constructions of race and heteronormativity from the moment of its inception.[134] Indulging in this fecundity, Lai's exposition of Nu Wa not only invites and challenges the categorizing gaze of biology but, at the same time, mocks this gaze by endowing Nu Wa with a fetid smell of unknown provenance, immediately after the primal scene quoted above: "In the beginning there was me, the river and a rotten-egg smell. I don't know where the smell came from, dank and sulphurous, but there it was, the stink of beginnings and endings, not for the faint of heart" (2). With this passage, Lai links the trope of composite monstrosity to a stench that is circumscribed as reminiscent of decomposing organic matter.

---

130 Qtd. ibid., 142.
131 Canguilhem, *Knowledge of Life*, 143.
132 Ibid.
133 Ibid., 141.
134 See ibid., 144.

This circumscription is significant in several ways. First, its very quality as a circumscription points to the "semiological ambiguity"[135] of olfaction. This ambiguity is conditioned by the extreme elusiveness of smell as "an object that always escapes, and "distinguished by formlessness, indefinability and lack of clear articulation."[136] And second, its choice of descriptive similes both at once exposes and makes skillful use of "the determination of olfactory meanings by non-olfactory contexts."[137] Described as "the stink of beginnings and endings" (2), the stench of Nu Wa's primal setting alludes to biological processes of birth and death, processes whose smelly 'filthiness' has been suppressed and contained by medical hygiene in Western cultures. Lai's wording retrieves these smelly biological connotations and embeds them into the ideational context of a religious culture that greatly contributed to their suppression: in describing the smell of rot and decomposition as "dank and sulphurous" the passage evokes the cultural coding of smells by pre-enlightenment Christianity, whose belief in a heavenly "odor of sanctity" was complemented by the idea of a sulfurous "stench of hell."[138] Lai's re-interpretation of the Christian paradise garden and its critique of natural science's constructions of biological norm, purity, and order are thereby invested with the stench of hell. Read as a menace to the orderly garden of biology, this stench might even allude to the medical practice of an emerging nosography that Foucault describes in *The Birth of the Clinic*: "Until the end of the eighteenth century *the gaze of the nosographers was a gardener's gaze*; one had to recognize the specific essence in the variety of appearances."[139]

These subtly blended olfactory connotations ideally supplement the exposition of Nu Wa's composite, monstrous body that invites, yet evades the categorizing gaze of natural science. The passage particularly foregrounds that the source of the multiply coded smell cannot be identified. In having Nu Wa claim "I don't know where the smell came from" Lai's exposition asserts the mocking persistence of an element of contingency, despite Nu Wa's unwitting positing of an order that ends the state of undefinable chaos. The sentence emphasizes the volatile aggregate state of smell, a disconnection of airborne

---

135 Alfred Gell qtd. in Jim Drobnick, "Introduction: Olfactocentrism," *The Smell Culture Reader*, ed. Jim Drobnick (Oxford/New York: Berg, 2006) 1-17, 5.

136 Alfred Gell, "Magic, Perfume, Dream...," *The Smell Culture Reader*, ed. Jim Drobnick (Oxford/New York: Berg, 2006) 400-410, 402.

137 Ibid.

138 Constance Classen, "The Breath of God: Sacred Histories of Scent," *The Smell Culture Reader*, ed. Jim Drobnick (Oxford/New York: Berg, 2006) 375-390, 382.

139 Michel Foucault, *The Birth of the Clinic: An Archaeology of Medical Perception*, 1973 (New York: Vintage, 1994) 119, italics added.

molecules from their sources that, according to critic Paul Lai, "endows them with confusion or lack of clarity about categories and origins." While the "intuitive vision of life, in which fecundity effaces order"[140] can only grant a brief, imaginary moment of undefined chaos, the introduction of stink provides a transcendent reminder of the undefinable that evades categories, a sensual revenant apt to haunt and to unsettle any given political and epistemological order that might be posited to replace the chaos.

The disparaging designation of a smell as stink exemplifies a process of cultural coding that takes advantage of the physical contingency of traveling, airborne molecules in order to affirm a dominant symbolic regime. As Sara Ahmed points out, in her trenchant analysis of *The Cultural Politics of Emotion*,[141] it is the performativity of the disgust reaction that attributes offensiveness to an object that it casts as being inherently offensive. The culturally coded, emotional operation of the disgust reaction works to "hierarchise spaces as well as bodies."[142] The disembodied, elusive volatility of a smell that is designated as stink particularly enables a "metonymic slide,"[143] i.e. the contagion /contact /contingency by which the sickening quality ascribed to disgusting objects is transferred to anything in their proximity. In describing the smell that pervades the setting of Nu Wa's exposition as a stink that is "not for the faint of heart"(2), Lai foreshadows a subversive re-coding of the over-determined trope of stink, the recoding of a trope that has always been an integral part of the most pervasive, racializing and gendering Western stereotypes.

Both the physical contingency of traveling, airborne molecules and the historical contingency of the cultural coding of smell privilege the trope of stink as a leitmotif of monstrosity linking the alternative Chinese myth of origin to *Salt Fish Girl*'s second narrative strand and futurist North-American Pacific Rim setting. Announced by the epigraph as a poetic sign of epistemological privilege, and picked up in Nu Wa's exposition that charges it with contingent connotations of fecundity, rot, and subversive power, stink is the marker of an unclassifiable disease that endangers the biologized governance of Saturna, a transnational corporation in the hyper-capitalist, dystopian world of Miranda. As the elusive sign of a monstrous "contagion," stink disturbs the clinical pastorate of a bio-economic corporation and thus threatens a collective body that is a monstrous body politic in the literal and the figurative sense of the word.

---

140 Canguilhem, *Knowledge of Life*, 143.
141 Sara Ahmed, *The Cultural Politics of Emotion* (Edinburgh: Edinburgh UP, 2004).
142 Ibid., 88.
143 Ibid., 87.

4.2.3 Expanding the Gaze

It is the year 2044, and in the city of "Serendipity" everything seems to be under control. Situated at the Pacific coast of today's British Columbia, shielded by walls and governed by "Saturna," one of six mega-corporations that rule the market and thus the world, Serendipity is populated by well-to-do middleclass citizens, who subsist on virtual, computer-game-style labor and flawless, genetically engineered foods. The task of these citizens is the administration of corporate profit and production, a production, notably, that is predominantly delegated to female, genetically engineered clones. While life in Serendipity and other corporation-governed cities all over the world is determined by the potency and the sterile luster of a hypertrophic technology, a class of outlaws and untouchables carves out a miserable, filthy, dangerous, and yet strangely glamorous existence in the "Unregulated Zone," the remnant of the national state that has been deprived of its governmental power and functions.

This futurist setting of *Salt Fish Girl* clearly conjoins a critical speculation on the ends of Pacific Rim utopianism with a bio-political extrapolation from "an emergent form of life,"[144] enabled and procured by the new technologies and the "new style of thought"[145] that mark twenty-first-century life sciences. This new style of thought – a threshold of knowledge summed up by Nikolas Rose as "the molecularization of vitality"[146] – heavily relies on visualization techniques "that opened the gene to knowledge and technique at the molecular level."[147] While Rose is careful to avoid a premature prediction of an ontological change that the new episteme might entail, *Salt Fish Girl*'s fictional speculation is less reserved. Projecting exactly this ontological change of the human species, its bizarre, futurist scenario, on the one hand, celebrates the possibility of a post-human subjectivity, yet on the other, expresses the same ethic concern that already resonates in George Canguilhem's 1965 remarks on monstrosity and the monstrous: "[...] how can we resist to find the monstrous again at the very heart of the scientific universe from which it was believed expelled – to find the biologist himself partaking, *in flagrante delicto*, in surrealism."[148]

Significantly, Lai's exposition of the novel's surreal, futurist setting begins with an intricately coded comment on the centrality of visual and linguistic representation to the ideational history of Western natural science, a comment,

---

144 Rose, *Politics of Life*, 80.
145 Ibid., 12.
146 Ibid., 13.
147 Ibid., 14.
148 *Knowledge of Life*, 144, italics in the original.

more precisely, on the interplay of these forms of representation in scientific constructions of gender, race, and monstrosity. This meta-representational comment is subtly inscribed in the individual myth of origins of Miranda Ching, the novel's second first-person narrator. Lai obviously plays with the generic conventions of autobiographical narration, when she has Miranda reconstruct the story of her own conception by means of a photograph depicting her mother Aimee in a moment shortly before that conception.

In doing so, Lai artfully links Miranda's speculation on her parents' relationship prior to her conscious recollection to an elaborate photographic composition: the photograph shows Aimee Ching who, sitting in front of the mirror of her vanity, is photographed by her husband Stewart, whose camera and body are, reflected by the mirror, in the picture as well, whereas his face is blinded out by the reflection of the camera's flashlight. Miranda's speculative narration thus conjures up a highly charged symbolic image that shows Aimee as a glamorous, yet aging 'dragon lady' and ex-star performer of Serendipity's Chinese nightclub, and Stewart Ching as her unloved, lackluster, and featureless husband. This pictorial exposition of the elderly couple, who, despite their age, are about to become Miranda's parents, is further laden with symbolism by a careful arrangement of "elegantly cut perfume bottles" on "the dark wood vanity"(10). It thereby prepares the stage for the olfactory fall of man that first leads to Miranda's conception and birth, and, ultimately, to the family's expulsion from the corporate 'paradise' of Serendipity.

Both its symbolically charged, elaborate composition and its speculative interpretation by the narrator subtly insinuate an affinity of the photograph with Diego Velazquez's painting *Las Meninas*. Painted in 1656, *Las Meninas* is still considered one of the most mysterious and, as a consequence, one of the most widely discussed paintings in art history. It is largely regarded as a meta-paining, a painting about questions of representation and interpretation, and has preserved its mystery, although the people it seems to represent had already been identified by art historians in the early eighteenth century. Among the most prominent of *Las Meninas*' philosophical interpretations is a reading by Michel Foucault that serves as the opening chapter to *The Order of Things*, since, for Foucault, Velazquez's painting symbolizes the very epistemological threshold of knowledge that, by conjoining image and word, cataloging table and discourse, gave rise to natural science.

The picture composed by Velazquez shows the painter himself in the act of painting King Philip IV and his wife in a vast studio or a room of the Spanish royal court. Brush in hand, the painter stands in front of his canvas, the back of which faces the spectator, while his gaze is directed at a point outside the picture, exactly the point that any spectator of the picture occupies. Placed in the focus of the painter's gaze, the spectator thus shares with the model posing for the artist a position outside the picture. Since the spectator cannot see the front of the painter's canvas, and the model, like the spectator, is not in the picture, it is only by way of a mirror hanging on the far wall of the studio and presumably reflecting the painter's subject, that this subject becomes visible as the royal couple.

At first glance, this simple, yet intricate setting is, as Foucault suggests, "a matter of pure reciprocity: we are looking at a picture in which the painter is in turn looking out at us. A mere confrontation, eyes catching one another's glance, direct looks superimposing themselves upon one another as they cross."[149] This exchange of gazes, enabled by the shared position of spectator and model outside the picture, has, however, unsettling consequences, both for the illusion of mimetic representation and for the spectator. In the "neutral furrow" of the painter's gaze, Foucault writes, "subject and object, the spectator and the model, reverse their roles to infinity."[150] The painter's gaze, suspended in the moment of its movement between the model/spectator position outside the picture and the canvas depicted in the painting, thus sets up a triangle of invisibilities: as the back of the canvas does not reveal the subject of the painting, "it renders forever unstable the play of metamorphoses established in the centre between spectator and model. Because we can only see that reverse side, we do not know who we are, or what we are doing. Seen or seeing?"[151] For Foucault, *Las Meninas* is therefore a painting whose subject is representation per se, a meta-painting that unsettles the idea of the image as a mere object of the gaze of a universal, sovereign subject.

It is this meta-representational quality that resonates in the expository fiction of a medial interplay between the photograph taken by her father and Miranda Ching's ekphrastic verbal interpretation. Miranda's ekphrasis clearly suggests a parallel of the photographic image to Velazquez's painting with regard to both content and composition. In minutely describing Aimee Ching's careful make-up, elegant jewelry, and glamorous dress, as well as her father's tall appearance "in a well-cut suit" (12), her interpretation picks up the ceremonial dress code of the scene at the royal court depicted in *Las Meninas*. While this description subtly insinuates the royalty of the couple who are about to become her parents, and thus endows the narrator herself with an ennobled, royal lineage, the photographic setting in front of the mirror of Aimee's dresser activates the same

---

149 *The Order of Things*, 4.
150 Ibid., 5.
151 Ibid.

4.2 Offering Odors – Epistemological Empowerment and Natural Science | 243

self-reflexivity that renders precarious any demarcation between subject and object, visible and invisible, seeing and seen in *Las Meninas*.

It is important to emphasize that what is reflected by the looking glass in Stewart Ching's photo is not in itself an inverted version of the confounding crisscrossing of gazes and invisibilities of *Las Meninas*. The triangle of invisibilities that allows for the unsettling experience of the contingency of representation in *Las Meninas* is, in the exposition of *Salt Fish Girl's* futurist setting and narration, established by the experience of ekphrasis. It is Miranda's tentative description of the photographic image that sets up a meta-representational triangle of invisibilities and thus the unstable play of metamorphoses described by Foucault. Whereas in *Las Meninas* the position of the artist – the painter – is safely within the picture and in turn the painter's subject and the spectator share a precarious position outside, it is Stewart Ching whose very act of taking the picture of his wife annihilates his own depiction in the photograph by the reflection of the camera's flashlight that renders his face invisible.

Like his daughter, who contemplates the photograph that depicts a moment prior to her existence, Stewart Ching is not in the picture. At first glance, it appears as if this were the standard situation of any representation, since it seems to be the artist – the photographer – and the spectator who are absent from and thus invisible in the picture. One has to keep in mind, though, that both the photographic image and its invisibilities are conjured up by the narrative of a first-person narrator who conspicuously flaunts the speculative nature of her narrative. After a meticulous description of the photograph's setting, Aimee's outfit and her pose within that setting the narrative continues:

From her sad smile and from the faded way her eyes shine you can tell she thinks of herself as old. Certainly she has no premonition of my arrival, at least not in this photograph. About my father, because you can't see his head, you can't tell. Maybe he knows something she doesn't, but I doubt it. But if you look really carefully into the brilliance of the flash reflected in the mirror behind my mother, you can see the outline of the camera's lens, and in the centre of that lens is a teensy black squiggle. It might just be a hair on the negative, but I like to think of it as a twinkle in my father's eye, a wriggly little premonition of my coming. When we look at the photograph together, no one notices the squiggle but me. No one really even notices the reflection of the man in the mirror. Once when my parents weren't around, I pointed the squiggle out to my brother Aaron, but he just laughed and said, "It's not possible, stupid. When you look in a camera you look through the viewfinder. Your eye won't appear in the lens." I never mentioned it again. (12)

The passage clearly foregrounds that it is Miranda's narrative that paints a picture, and the picture thus conjured is, without doubt, intended to illuminate the shortcomings of photography as a "certificate of presence."[152] The passage also conveys that, different from the painter's gaze depicted in *Las Meninas*, Miranda's gaze is anything but a "neutral furrow."[153] And while the painter's gaze in *Las Meninas*, according to Foucault, "renders forever unstable the play of metamorphoses established in the centre between spectator and model,"[154] it is the process of speculative ekphrasis that re-inscribes instability and subjectivity into a visual medium that transforms the living subject into an arrested object.

An instance of the *"studium"*[155] by which the spectator makes meaning of a photographic image, the ekphrastic passage resonates with Roland Barthes's reflections on photography: the theatricality of the photographic setting and Aimee's mask-like make-up unambiguously reflect Barthes's definition of photography as "kind of theater, a *Tableau Vivant*, a figuration of the motionless made-up face beneath which we see the dead."[156] The description of Aimee's "sad smile and the faded way her eyes shine" (12) conspicuously echoes Barthes's comment on the "faint smile" of the person "posing for the lens"[157] as well as his assessment that it is the "return of the dead"[158] that photography enables. And the emphasis on the elimination of the photographer by the reflection of the camera's flashlight mirrors Barthes's perception of the photographer as a mere *"operator,"* and, at the same time, his notion of the *studium* "as a kind of education (knowledge and civility, 'politeness') which allows me to discover the *Operator*, to experience the intentions which establish and animate his practices, but to experience them 'in reverse,' according to my will as *Spectator.*"[159]

Miranda's *studium* of the photograph, her will as a spectator, is motivated by her search for identity and the "truth of lineage," the only "little truth"[160] that photography can provide, according to Barthes. The focus in the narrative on the

---

152 Roland Barthes, *Camera Lucida: Reflections on Photography* (New York: Hill and Wang, 1981) 87.
153 Foucault, *The Order of Things*, 5.
154 Ibid.
155 Barthes, *Camera Lucida*, 27, italics in the original. The italics in all subsequent quotes from Roland Barthes' *Camera Lucida* are the italics used in the original.
156 Barthes, *Camera Lucida*, 32.
157 Ibid., 11.
158 Ibid., 9.
159 Ibid., 28.
160 Ibid., 105.

technical specifics of the camera – the flash, the lens, the viewfinder – shows these technical devices, however, to be incapable of "wakening" the "intractable reality"[161] of "what has been."[162] Foregrounding the invisibilities produced, yet at the same time concealed, by the "tyranny"[163] of photography, the narrative of Miranda's *studium* casts her narration as forced "to enter the picture,"[164] as compelled to find and re-inscribe the annihilated *operator*, and to become a 'painter' whose intuitive, speculative language is privileged to fill the epistemological gaps left by photography's deficiency.

Miranda's speculative reading of the "teensy black squiggle" (12), the tiny flaw in the photographic image, as a foreshadowing, a sign of an "arrival" that lies in the past from the *studium's* point of view, yet is in the future from the point in time captured by the picture, provides an instance of the spectator's interest in the kind of disturbing detail that Barthes has called the "*punctum*."[165] In directing attention to the *punctum* that catches her interest as it allows for speculation, the narrator signals her will to dismiss the knowledge and the cultural coding that regulates the *studium* of photography, since, as Barthes has it, "the *studium* is ultimately always coded, the *punctum* is not."[166] Lacking a proper name and a referent it is the *punctum* of the "teensy black squiggle" (12) that disturbs the photographic claim to realistic representation, and that incites and legitimates a pointedly speculative, fictional narration. Miranda's reading of the *punctum* as the sign of a "premonition" of her "arrival" in a photograph taken at a point in time prior to her existence, spotlights photography's "stasis of an arrest," its "immobilization of time that assumes [...] an excessive, monstrous mode,"[167] and, at the same time, undoes this stasis by introducing a different temporality.

Devalued by her brother Aaron as a lack of cultural knowledge – a 'stupidity' pointedly exposed by his condescending remark "it's not possible, stupid" (12) – Miranda's reading of the *punctum* becomes the speculative focal point privileged to illuminate the invisibilities and the unstable play of metamorphoses that photography's pretension to reveal everything conceals and arrests. Beyond the insufficiency of photography, there resonates in the *punctum's* lack of a proper name and referent, in its speculative reading by

---

161 Ibid., 119.
162 Ibid., 85.
163 Ibid., 118.
164 Foucault, *The Order of Things*, 5.
165 Barthes, *Camera Lucida*, 51.
166 Barthes, *Camera Lucida*, 51.
167 Ibid., 91.

Miranda's ekphrasis, Foucault's contemplation on the incompatibility of language and visual representation, articulated in his reading of *Las Meninas*:

> [...] the relation of language to painting is an infinite relation. It is not that words are imperfect, or that, when confronted with the visible, they prove insuperably inadequate. Neither can be reduced to the other's terms: it is in vain that we say what we see; what we see never resides in what we say.[...] But if one wishes to keep the relation of language to vision open, if one wishes to treat their incompatibility as a starting point for speech instead of as an obstacle to be avoided, so as to stay as close as possible to both, then one must erase the proper names and preserve the infinity of the task. It is perhaps through the medium of this grey, anonymous language, always over-meticulous and repetitive because too broad, that the painting may, little by little release, its illuminations.[168]

In the exposition of *Salt Fish Girl*'s surreal, futurist setting, the first-person narrator's speculative ekphrasis thus not merely reflects, but flaunts the infinite relation of language and visual representation. The excessively uncertain language of speculative fictionality in Miranda's ekphrasis exposes the incompatibility of language and vision and, at the same time, uses it as "a starting point for speech."[169] With its references to Velazquez's *Las Meninas*, Miranda's reading of the photograph points to the contingency of representation, its dependence on thresholds of knowledge that condition its production and reception. While *Las Meninas* marks a threshold of knowledge at which the modern subject emerges, and which thus, for the first time, allows for self-reflection and therefore a reflection on the nature of aesthetic representation, the photographic image stands for an epistemological shift by which the power of visual evidence and authentification begins to repress other forms of representation. The photograph is the icon of an age in which, as Johannes Fabian contends, "the ability to 'visualize' a culture or society almost becomes synonymous for understanding it."[170] The exposition of *Salt Fish* Girl's futurist setting foregrounds, however, the centrality of an always culturally coded ekphrasis to this process of meaning-making, and the contingency inherent to the interplay of language and vision.

Eluding both forms of representation, smell is particularly suited to expose this contingency, and, at the same time, the decidedly political nature of any cultural coding of both language and vision. While the array of glittering

---

168 *The Order of Things*, 9-10.
169 Ibid., 9.
170 Johannes Fabian, *Time and the Other: How Anthropology Makes its Object* (New York: Columbia UP, 1983) 106.

perfume bottles arranged on Aimee's dresser, at first glance, appears as a mere adornment to the theatrical scene set up for the photograph that serves as an exposition of Miranda's parents, and as a point of departure for her auto-fictional myth of origins, a closer look reveals its important contribution to the meta-representational subtext of the exposition. The image of bottled perfume on a woman's vanity evokes the hetero-normative promises of a scent-selling industry to augment the erotic desirability of a gender that it casts as precarious and therefore in constant need of olfactory disambiguation.[171] Sold as bottled essences of desire, women's perfumes are not only supposed to reinforce a culturally coded hetero-normativity, but, more generally, to cover up the purportedly stronger smells of female sexuality that were devalued and suppressed by a white European post-enlightenment culture eager to distance itself from the miasma of a "'primitive' animal past."[172]

What is evoked with the collection of perfume bottles displayed on Aimee's dresser is thus a cultural critique that ties in with the critique of the primacy of visualism, yet at the same time exceeds it. It is obvious how the detail of the perfume bottles supplements the critique of the photographic image as an artifact that not only fails to capture the truth of what has been, but "blocks memory," as it represents "no odor, no music, nothing but the exorbitant thing."[173] Yet there is more to this detail than a critique of photography: the display of the perfume bottles on a Chinese woman's dresser in a photograph seen and mediated through the gaze of a lesbian spectator who is this woman's daughter, and who, as the reader learns shortly after the ekphrastic exposition, is marked by a piercing stench, directs attention to the sense of smell that a male-coded, scientific ocular-centrism has linked to devaluing constructions of race and gender by the means of ekphrasis.

Tracing such devaluing constructions in scientific theories of sexuality of the early twentieth century, Carol Mavor shows how smell was connected to the feminine, the pathological, and the primitive, while a masculine coded

---

171 Mark Graham shows that the perfume industry increasingly addresses a gay market as well, and, while now equally capitalizing on homosexual phantasies of bottled desirability, construes homo-normative notions of scent. "Queer Smells," *The Smell Culture Reader* ed. Jim Drobnick (Oxford, UK/New York: Berg, 2006) 305-319, esp. 308-312.

172 Carol Mavor, "Odor di Femina: Though You May Not see Her, You Can Certainly Smell Her," *The Smell Culture Reader* ed. Jim Drobnick (Oxford, UK/New York: Berg, 2006) 277-288. See also Alain Corbin, *The Foul and the Fragrant: Odor and the French Social Imagination* (Leamington Spa et al.: Berg, 1986).

173 Barthes, *Camera Lucida*, 91.

preoccupation with the visual was cast as a marker of higher development and civilization. Mavor particularly mentions "the Darwinian spin on smell"[174] in Freud's studies on hysteria and in the work of his contemporary Havelock Ellis, a sexologist, who "described the smell of peoples that he regarded as lower on the evolutionary scale as musky," and who specifically related "the smell of animalistic musk to black women, to lactating women, to women in general, to the Chinese, and even to the demented."[175] Using photographs of their objects of study and descriptive comments and captions to establish their theories – two forms of representation, neither of which can capture smell – it is, in fact, Freud's and Havelock's ekphrasis, the "regular alternation of speech and gaze,"[176] analyzed by Foucault in *The Birth of the Clinic,* that allowed for their theories' devaluing classifications. It becomes obvious that "the picture's only role is to divide up the visible within an already given conceptual configuration."[177] It is this conceptual pre-configuration that determines Freud's and Havelock's scientific descriptions, a syntactic organization of pictures resulting in devaluing constructions of alterity.

Juxtaposing this syntactically organized, photographic gaze with "Lacan's conceptualization of the gaze as an expanded constellation of the senses, in which sight loses its pride, its authority, and its maleness,"[178] Carol Mavor, strikingly, uses Jacques Lacan's reading of *Las Meninas* as an example of the Lacanian gaze as *objet petit a,* as pure desire. She argues that, for Lacan, the central invisibility in *Las Meninas* is the *odor di femina* emanating from the genitalia of the infanta, the royal couple's young daughter who is at the geometric center of the painting. While Foucault's reading neglects this figure and focuses on the invisibilities and the exchange of gazes that, for him, renders *Las Meninas* subjectless, for Lacan, as Mavor shows, the subject of the painting is the annihilated subjectivity of the spectator and the gaze, the desire for that which is hidden under the hoopskirts of the infanta's dress.[179] Following Lacan's ekphrasis, and presumably referring to the latency of the purportedly feminine odor in a child, Mavor contends that the infanta's 'odor di femina' is doubly unseen like the canvas depicted in the painting, and thereby becomes the *objet petit a,* the fetish of a pure desire that seeing cannot fulfill. In conclusion, Mavor

---

174 "Odor di Femina," 282.
175 Ibid., 282-283.
176 Michel Foucault, *The Birth of the Clinic:An Archaeology of Medical Perception,* 1963 (New York: Vintage, 1994) 112.
177 Ibid., 113.
178 Mavor, "Odor di Femina," 277.
179 See Mavor, "Odor di Femina," 285.

remarks: "Lacan's one drop of *odor di femina* loosens the gaze into an expanded constellation of the senses. No longer overcome by the look, bodies come into play... 'a wild odor emanates'."[180]

Without resorting to Lacan's (and Mavor's) somewhat mystifying language, Miranda's ekphrasis is driven by a desire that the photograph of her parents does not fulfill. Whether read as a desire for a sign of her own arrival – a sign that would assign her the position of the infanta's un-representable, feminine smell – or as a desire for the 'true' smell of the mother, Miranda's gaze, her *objet petit a*, is expanded and can thus expose the violence of the perfumed photograph, its hetero-normative, sexist, and racializing annihilation of subjectivity, its erasure of the living body and its smelly, animal past. Legitimized by the epistemological contingency of scientific ekphrasis, the fantastic, speculative narrative that is about to follow is cast as privileged to bring to the fore wild odors and bodies that have been repressed and depreciated by male-coded, scientific modes of signification and classification.

Announced as epistemologically privileged, Miranda's ensuing narration conjures up the same scenario as the photograph, yet casts it as a fantastic, highly erotic, primal scene and relates it to the desire for a penetrating stench. The erotic scene that Miranda imagines as the moment of her conception is initiated by Aimee's desire for a durian, the Asian fruit that is known for its pungent, musty stench, and that grows and is popular mostly in Asian countries. Aimee Ching's desire for the fruit is triggered when she discovers a durian tree thriving in the Unregulated Zone outside Serendipity, despite the harsh climate of North American Pacific coast. Against all risks – and these include the illicit trespassing of the Unregulated Zone as well as the illicit consumption of a fruit that is not corporation grown and controlled – Stewart Ching succeeds in bringing Aimee one of the wild durians whose smell unleashes memories of her Chinese childhood – and a wave of passion for her unloved husband:

"Durian," he said. "Come eat." He stood in the doorway and did not move. She rose from the worn seat of her ancient vanity, and on her dainty, small, now lithe feet, practically wafted up to him and pressed her warm lips to his. He dropped the durian in surprise. As they tumbled to the floor, it tumbled between them, its green spikes biting greedily into their flesh, its pepper-pissy juices mixing with their somewhat more subtly scented ones and the blood of the injuries it inflicted with its spiky green teeth. (14-15)

Depicting a spectacular, primal scene of monstrous hybridity, the passage evokes the racializing, misogynist stereotype of a sex-obsessed Asian 'dragon-lady' and

---

180 Ibid., 287.

links its hegemonic ascriptions of an aggressive, and always excessive eroticism to the representation of the durian as a hybrid of animal and fruit that is cast as equally aggressive and excessive. The scene thus implies that Aimee Ching[181] is culpable of multiple transgressions: in keeping with the racializing stereotype, she is unable to control her desire for her 'smelly, oriental' origins, and breaks the corporate law that forbids the consumption of wild, uncontrolled fruit. Driven by her 'lowly instincts' she then, in addition, breaks the law of nature by having sex with another species which, on top of that, is not even unambiguously classifiable.

With this double breach of law Aimee fulfills the criteria that, according to Michel Foucault, define the abnormal individual,[182] a legal category of modernity that reworks biological conceptualizations of monstrosity. In the modern figure of the abnormal individual that emerged in the nineteenth century, Foucault finds the monstrosity that Canguilhem considers to have become tamed and naturalized by natural science in the course of the eighteenth century. Different from Canguilhem, who shows how an emerging natural science relied on the eye to determine "aberrant organisms"[183] as monsters, and who claims that monstrosity was naturalized after having "revealed the secrets of its causes and laws,"[184] Foucault traces the genealogy of the modern abnormal individual to the very monstrousness that Canguilhem considers extinguished and banished to the realm of fantastic art.

Foucault acknowledges that morphological deviations of the body had, in the nineteenth century, ceased to challenge the laws of both natural science and jurisdiction. He argues, however, that, beginning at the end of the eighteenth century, regimes of normalization increasingly construed an invisible, internalized monstrosity, a monstrosity of the soul and the mind. Counter to positivist concepts of nature, this invisible, internal monstrosity of the abnormal individual is, for Foucault, an effect of legal constructions of nature rather than their cause. Accordingly, any breach of the law of nature is, from that point on, inextricably linked to a breach of the law of a given culture and its inherent codification of nature. Summing up the implications of Foucault's genealogy of the abnormal individual as a modern descendant of the monster, Andrew N. Sharpe writes:

---

181 Strikingly, and equally catering to a racializing stereotype, Stewart Ching's role in this scene is, again, merely that of an operator, a partner in a doubly coded crime.
182 See *Abnormal: Lectures at the College de France 1974-1975* (New York: Picador, 2003), esp. 60-67.
183 Canguilhem, *Knowledge of Life*, 140.
184 Ibid., 143.

Today it is only the normal type, Tarde's 'zero of monstrosity' (1897 (1999)), that is distanced from the monster. All those who deviate from the norm bear a relationship by degree to monster status, one that can be endlessly reworked for the purpose of recreating the coherence of human identity.[185]

What Lai's representation of Aimee's transgression in the primal, erotic scene, teases out, is, read with Foucault and Sharpe, the presence of a cultural regime that construes 'the Asian woman' as the locus of invisible monstrosity. The sexist and racializing stereotypes inscribed in Aimee's double breach of law and its connotations of uncontrollable, excessive sexuality are exposed as contemporary instances of the reworking of biological conceptualizations of monstrosity. The fantastic spectacularity of the scene thus serves to visualize the modern construction of a monstrosity the invisibility of which allows for constant re-workings and re-ascriptions of the monster status according to the political-economic needs of a given culture. What at first seems like an irritating affirmation of race and gender stereotypes both in the primal erotic scene and in Nu Wa's exposition becomes visible, at this point, as an effective correspondence that brings to the fore the shift from body to mind, from visible organic aberrance to invisible, internal deviance in successive historical constructions of monstrosity. The idea of a monstrous, matriarchal lineage summoned by this correspondence resonates with Foucault's notion of the modern figure of the abnormal individual as a descendant of the monster of previous historical periods. In linking this matriarchal lineage to the trope of an elusive, yet persistent stench as its monstrous marker, Lai points to the persistence of scientific, legal, and broader cultural constructions of monstrosity, and, simultaneously, to their shift from visibility to invisibility.

At the same time, Miranda's narration rings with a tone of resistance and empowerment that signals the willingness to undermine and reframe a prevalent construction and regulation of monstrosity. This tone, moreover, appears to posit the epistemological privilege of a speculative fiction that, just like the scientific imaginary it projects, experiments with monstrosity. In a passage immediately following the spectacular, primal scene of monstrous hybridity, Lai, for instance, very skillfully has Miranda draw a conclusion that pretends to relativize the scene's fantastic spectacularity by acknowledging the speculative quality of her narration:

---

185 Andrew N. Sharpe, *Foucault's Monsters and the Challenge of Law* (Oxon/ New York: Routledge, 2010) 48.

As for the precise nature of my conception in this incident, what shall I say? That the third gender is more unusual and more potent than most imagine? That my conception was immaculate, given the fact that my mother was a good eight years past menopause? I can tell you none of these things because I know nothing about them. (15)

Almost in passing, and casually 'clad' in the tone and gesture of unreliable narration, this passage casts a fantastic form of parthenogenesis as the origin of the first-person narrator, and, at the same time, relates the primal, erotic scene of her conception to the Christian dogma of Immaculate Conception. Even more provocatively, the passage casually instantiates an "unusual" and "potent" third gender as the product of Immaculate Conception, and fantastic speculation as its privileged mode of tackling "the coding of trans bodies, practices and desires as 'unnatural' within medico-legal, as well as broader cultural, domains" (Sharpe 11). The idea of an immaculate purity is thus subtly linked to that which evades the knowledge and classification of Western natural science; speculative fiction – to know nothing – is posited as its privileged epistemology.

Inscribed with topoi of monstrosity – which include the monstrous durian as well as the racializing and sexist stereotypes – Lai's exposition of the futurist strand of her novel, once again, appropriates the patriarchal Christian myth of the paradise garden, and, at the same time, by locating it at a corporation-governed North American Pacific coast in the year 2044, the utopianism of the Asia Pacific myth. This exposition foreshadows the ongoing centrality of constructions of monstrosity, the reworking of its legal and biological conceptualization, to *Salt Fish Girl*'s futurist diegetic world order. In the new territories of empire of this bio-economic world order we encounter both Foucault's modern figure of the abnormal individual, whose invisible monstrosity poses a threat to the production and governance of biological citizens, and Canguilhem's eighteenth-century figure of the "biologist himself partaking, *in flagrante delicto*, in surrealism."[186]

4.3 NEW TERRITORIES OF EMPIRE

In *Salt Fish Girl*'s futurist setting, Larissa Lai projects the blueprint of a hyper-capitalist, post-apocalyptic, and thoroughly biologized society whose laws and civil code of conduct are determined by the economic interests of six multinational mega-corporations that have divided global dominance among

---

186 *Knowledge of Life*, 144, italics in the original.

themselves. Merged in a coalition treacherously called the "Pacific Economic Union (PEU)," yet far from having settled their distribution battles, the "Big Six" (11) provide the citizens of their walled compounds with a humble salary, the safety of the corporation-owned product range, and protection against uncontrolled, possibly contaminated foods or biological assaults by hostile rival corporations. In exchange, they demand unquestioning law abidance, a clinical visibility and availability, as well as an unconditional identification with and commitment to corporate politics.

At first glance, this form of corporate governance appears to rely on the systematic distribution of political subjects in milieus of inclusion that Foucault has described as characteristic of disciplinary societies. At the same time, it seems to rest upon a code of honor strongly reminiscent of the work ethic generally associated with Asian employees and their notoriously uncompromising devotion to a company . A passage in which Miranda Ching recollects her father's adaptivity to corporate rule conspicuously foregrounds such a work ethic:

In his past life, my father would not have sold Saturna out for any price. He understood what we had. He understood the safety of the compound. *He was not a greedy man.* Our life was comfortable in a middle-class, suburban sort of way. *It was not excessive. My father was content with that.* He was proud of having fathered a child at such late age. At seventy-five, he was proud that he was able to continue working for the company, that they valued his labour and his trust. That he could not afford to retire on the meager pension offered did not bother him. (95, italics added)

The passage describes virtues such as industriousness, a deluded pride, and modesty, a self- and frictionless functioning in the gears of a company, whose interests are unquestioningly internalized as personal goals, a company that, however, remains strikingly featureless and disembodied. While the italicized sentences ostensibly sketch an image of loyal subjectivity, their accumulation of negations subtly slips in the spirit of the elusive mega-corporations, a spirit decidedly contrasting the modesty of their employees. In emphasizing that Stewart Ching was "*not* a greedy man" and that his life "was *not* excessive," these sentences highlight the mega-corporations' excessive global proliferation as propelled by greed and the compulsion for growth, transgression, and excess that Karl Marx identified at the core of the capitalist mode of production.[187] Embedded in the context of Miranda's early childhood impressions, this

---

187 See Karl Marx, *Das Kapital. Band 1: Der Produktionsprozess des Kapitals*, 1867, Marx Engels Werke, Vol. 23 (Berlin: Dietz, 2008) 167.

representation of an excessively capitalist dominion thus casts corporate governance as resting upon both the spatial distribution and surveillance of political subjects, *and* the 'gas' of governmentality, on Foucault's disciplinary power which hides itsself *and* the encrypted elusiveness of the Deleuzian control society.[188]

With the concise brevity of its sentences, the passage, at the same time, suggests a fragmentation of the political subjects thus produced. In her article on the alliance between science and capital in *Salt Fish Girl*, Tara Lee describes this fragmentation as a strategy that is characteristic of the "scattered hegemonies" and the "multinational power network" of global capitalism:

This network is premised on a breaking apart of bodies and a blurring of boundaries that were previously considered stable. Late capitalism imposes itself on the globe by fragmenting the body until it is nothing more than pieces for power dispersal. [...] Just as power moves in a state of disjuncture, the objects and people affected by this power are subject to fragmentation and dispersal themselves.[189]

In the framework of Miranda's childhood recollections, Lai stages global capitalism's fragmentation of bodies and charges it with an ambivalent gender coding that draws on and simultaneously deconstructs gender stereotypes of the American Pacific Rim discourse and official North American discourses of multiculturalism. Miranda's remark that her father was proud of "having fathered a child at such late age" (95) not only serves to underline his general contentment or complacency but supplements the image of a man who, represented as living in an unhappy marriage and as deeply insecure of his gender role, is characterized, at another point, as "soft, gentle and bookish" (27). Miranda's remark reveals that Stewart Ching's contentment rests upon illusions in two different ways: it exposes as illusionary Stewart's assumption that Saturna truly appreciates his labor and loyalty (only a fair salary and pension would be an appropriate appreciation of his labor's value; this appreciation would, however, curtail corporate capitalization on the unpaid surplus value of this labor); and it spotlights his illusion to have sired Miranda. In characterizing Stewart Ching as soft, placid, economically naïve, and unmanly, Lai evokes the

---

188 See Michel Foucault, *Discipline and Punish: The Birth of the Prison* (New York: Vintage, 1995); and Gilles Deleuze, "Postskriptum über die Kontrollgesellschaften," *Le Autre Journal* 1(Mai 1990) Web, 20 Jul. 2011. <www.nadir.org/nadir/archiv/ netzkritik/postskriptum.html>.

189 Tara Lee, "Mutant Bodies in Larissa Lai's *Salt Fish Girl*: Challenging the Alliance between Science and Capital," *West Coast Line 44* 38.2 (2004): 94-110, 95.

template of the effeminate Asian 'coolie,' the clichéd symbol of a class of male, Asian immigrant laborers, whose construction as un-free, servile, and easily exploitable served as a foil to highlight the stylizing of the white American laborer as the "American freeman," at the end of the nineteenth century, a subtext resonating in an over-determined, racializing stereotype to this day.[190]

Sharply contrasting this ideologically charged stereotype of 'the Asian' as a sign of deficient masculinity, Lai shows Stewart Ching, at another point in Miranda's narrative of her early childhood, as a terminator-like superhero. The complex scene in which Stewart Ching demonstrates to his young daughter his work as a tax-collector for Saturna and the function of his "Business Suit" to that task is one of the novel's most impressive. The shiny black Business Suit is a kind of whole-body interface that enables its wearer to move virtually, as in a computer game, in "Real World," a simulacrum of the illicit Unregulated Zone outside the walls of the corporate compound. Assembled from separate parts for arms, legs, torso, and head, this dystopian version of a business suit boldly symbolizes the destabilization, de-composition, and re-composition of the body according to the logic and the needs of a de-territorialized capitalism.[191] The fragmentation and functionalization of the body is carried on in Stewart Ching's virtual metamorphosis in the "Real World" game, a stunning transformation, watched breathlessly by his pre-adolescent daughter on the video screen that comes with the suit:

It was my father, but a much stronger, younger, more heroic version of him, both like the man I knew and entirely without the soft, gentle, bookish demeanour with which he carried himself through family life. A woman and child appeared at his feet. Their clothes were ragged. The woman's cheek was bleeding. The child was screaming and scrabbling with its sharp desperate little claws for her breast *which jutted through her clothing just a little too sexily for one so abject.* My father helped the woman to her feet. He unhooked a canteen from his belt and gave it to her to drink. Suddenly a flock of something like birds swooped towards them – round discs with razor-sharp edges that screamed like crows. My father's eyes turned red and shot lightning bolts at them. He raised his arm. It was a gun, shooting rapid machine-gun fire. He continued to walk and as he put each knee forward a spray of bullets shot out. The birds were subdued. The swooping became slow tumbling. *They flickered, lost their solidity, became a thin stream of digits.* My father opened his mouth wide and swallowed them. (27, italics added)

---

190 See Christine So, *Economic Citizens: A Narrative of Asian American Visibility* (Philadelphia: Temple UP, 2008) 10.
191 See Lee, "Mutant Bodies," 96.

The scene summons the image of a heroic, super-masculine body, oscillating between charitable redeemer figure and egoshooter, a body that is both at once religiously and erotically charged. While the subtext of religious charity subtly inscribes this body with connotations of the good shepherd who cares for the helpless in his flock, the erotic subtext, evoked by the boldly aggressive transformation of limbs into firearms, is further enhanced by the seemingly casual reference to the "too sexily" jutting breast of the woman in the dystopian setting of the computer game that is Stewart Ching's place of work. Beyond erotic connotations, this reference underlines that Ching's work as a tax-collector is a virtual adventure; it exposes its embeddedness in a sentimental narrative, and thus the double fictionality of the situation, and in doing so, insinuates that the boundary between virtual mise-en-scène and an experience of reality as mediated by the body has become precarious. This precarious boundary is marked by the Business Suit. The Business Suit as interface enables the paradox of the Real-World- Game; it dissolves and renders the body redundant by transforming it into a current of digital signs that have lost their referentiality.

It appears consistent that this representation remains vague about the identity of the taxpayers whose taxes are being collected, and says nothing about how the digits thus collected are transferred to Serendipity and Saturna's financial world, or which value they represent. Instead of offering referential disambiguation, the scene establishes within *Salt Fish Girl*'s futurist diegetic world a hyper-fictional level that corresponds with and points to the hyper-fictionality of electronic monetary transactions and "its dizzying linkages between finance and computer technology."[192] Read against the background of the isomorphism linking the representational symbolism of money and language, Lai's introduction of a second-order fictional narrative exposes the postmodern decoupling of both systems of representation from a universal equivalent.[193] Global capital's borderless space of possibility becomes perceptible as a space of pure representation, with its agents and operations dissolving almost without a trace in an interminable chain of reciprocal references and deferrals.

In keeping with this logic, the programmers and beneficiaries of the Real World-Game remain hidden and bodyless. Lai's narration, however, counters and contrasts the virtuality of their money flows with the reality of the suffering, racialized, and gendered, subaltern body on which they capitalize. Her use of Miranda's young self as the medium of both levels of fictionality allows for their

---

192 Jean-Joseph Goux, "Cash, Check, or Charge," *The New Economic Criticism: Studies at the Intersection of Literature and Economics*, eds. Martha Woodmansee and Mark Osteen (New York: Routledge, 1999) 114-127, 122.

193 See ibid., 120-126.

dramatic collision: while watching virtual policemen beating Stewart Ching and his tax collector colleagues with truncheons in order to 'extract' the digital flows that the men have swallowed on the video screen, Miranda simultaneously witnesses her father's body squirming next to her in the Business Suit with the real pain inflicted by these virtual beatings. Miranda's spontaneous impulse to end her father's virtually induced, yet sensually felt pain by flipping the switch of the business suit is thwarted by a surprisingly determined motion by which Stewart Ching, despite his agony, pushes her hand away, and by his sharp rebuke: "Don't you ever do that. You must never interfere with the business suit." (28).

Tara Lee reads Stewart Ching's incomprehensible behavior as expressing a self-denying complicity with the elusive, disembodied hegemony of capital. For her, Ching's command "don't interfere" is "the motto for the individual's role in the global market. Be active participants, but above all, don't interfere."[194] While this would be a perceptive political interpretation, if it referred to a factual text, it fails to account for the decidedly literary quality of the passage, its specific narrative situation. It is, however, with a comment by Miranda that Lai ends her first-person narrator's recollection of this scene from her early childhood: "I felt I'd betrayed him deeply by witnessing what I had witnessed" (29). With this conspicuously periphrastic wording, Lai takes recourse to a topos of ineffability and concludes the scene by pointedly emphasizing her first-person narrator's young age, her sensitivity to the deceptive fictionality of the virtual game in which her father is involved, and her inability to articulate what she senses.

This ending of the Business-Suit scene corresponds with self-reflective comments that, at different points in Miranda's recollection of her early childhood, flaunt her narration as being contingent upon the narrator's young age and thus the psychological and intellectual limitations of her perception. When Miranda recollects a conversation between her five-year- old self and her mother, Lai has her wonder, for instance, "Have I pieced these things together from memory or did I really think about them as I do know?" (22) At another point, Lai puts an even more conclusive comment in her first-person narrator's mouth: "I was a sheltered child living out my parents' utopian dream as though it were reality. They did not show me the cracks. And out of loyalty and love for them, when I sensed the cracks, I refused to see them. But of course this unspoken pact could not last." (71)

It is this unspoken pact of loyalty that conditions Miranda's perception of the Business-Suit scene. Evoked by the simultaneous experience of a fictional scene, presenting a sugary, sentimental narrative with blatant erotic connotations and

---

194 Lee, "Mutant Bodies," 97.

distinctly religious undertones, and Stewart Ching's actual suffering, Miranda's feelings of shame and betrayal pertain to her father's naïve susceptibility to a deluding fiction that is designed to occlude his sheer instrumentality to the ends of the corporation. Despite her inability to articulate her feelings, this conclusion of the scene picks up the idea of an epistemologically empowered difference, the notion of a potent third gender that, while knowing nothing, is privileged to uncover a deluding fictionality that is instrumental to the mode of government effective in Saturna's territories of empire. While the periphrastic wording of Miranda's sentiment shows this potential to be still clouded and pre-conscious, at this point, it foreshadows a narrative development that conforms to the patterns of the *bildungsroman*. It indicates that *Salt Fish Girl*'s futurist strand is a narrative of formation evolving with the protagonist's coming of age that is also a coming to politics;[195] it announces and foreshadows the achievement of a political consciousness that ultimately allows for a perceptive representation of the corporations' political structure and objectives.

Significantly, the narrative of Miranda's *bildung* is a clinical narrative, a narrative of medical pedagogy, and a narrative of disease and disease control in the age of biogenetic capitalism, and it is in the context of this clinical narrative that the most conclusive details on the corporate political order effective in Serendipity are revealed. Since the moment of her birth, Miranda's body has been surrounded by the same ambiguous durian stench that her speculative myth of origins relates to her conception as an instance of transgressive monstrosity. At first experienced by her parents as an aphrodisiac triggering a blissful resurgence of passion between the elderly couple, Miranda's stench successively turns into a social, medical, and political problem jeopardizing her family's citizenship in the walled compound of a community whose collective imaginary

---

195 See Franco Moretti, *The Way of the World: The* Bildungsroman *in European Culture* (London: Verso, 1987). According to Moretti, "the Bildungsroman [...] had always held fast to the notion that *the biography of a young individual was the most meaningful viewpoint for the understanding and the evolution of history*. (227, original italics).The narrative of Miranda's coming of age, her *bildung*, corresponds to many of the conventions of the European Bildungsroman, as delineated by Moretti: it entails the experience of individuality as a risk and a burden, the experience of societal injustice as a reaction to this individuality, the gradual recognition that her stigmatization as a carrier of disease is an unjust accusation deriving from the aberrant logic of the medical regime governing the society into which she was born. It further entails the realization of the pathologized condition as an epistemologically privileging, individual trait, that she eventually accepts and values as her nature and part of her inheritance.

is obsessed with phantasms of purity and scientific control. And it is, again, Stewart Ching whose uncritical compliance with the prevalent order gives decisive clues to its organizing principles. Contrary to his wife, who is reluctant to pathologize a smell that she finds peculiar but not unpleasant, Stewart Ching soon conceives of Miranda's abnormality as a disease that has to be cured as it threatens the family's safe position within the compound.

Using the Business Suit and his privileged access to the Real World simulacrum of the illicit Unregulated Zone, Stewart increasingly spends his working hours secretly roaming Real World in order to find medical treatment for his daughter's stench, without giving her away to Serendipity's watchful authorities. In having Miranda describe the "deathly pallor" of his skin and the "sheen of the waking dead" (60) in Stewart's eyes after his medical exploration of the Unregulated Zone, Lai effectively enhances Saturna's representation of this zone as a necropolis, a decaying counter-city, marked by a crumbling cityscape and populated by a destitute multitude of living dead. Dirty, dilapidating, and anarchic, the Unregulated Zone is cast as the inverted image of Serendipity; pointedly promulgated by Saturna's media as dangerous to the life and health of its citizens, its disorder is supposed to highlight Saturna's political regime as a pastorate, whose first and main concern is the health of its population.

It is in the course of the clinical narrative of what is soon designated as her disease that Miranda gradually becomes aware of the deceptive fictionality in this representation of the Unregulated Zone; progressively she discovers the true character of Saturna's regime as a monstrous body politic whose medico-scientific ontology "entails the creation of aberrant logics."[196] After her father's failed attempts at finding a cure for the stench that surrounds Miranda, the Ching family is forced to leave the corporate city and make a living in the Unregulated Zone. Once established there, the dreaded zone, while crumbling and disorderly compared to Serendipity's sterile luster, turns out to be a fertile ground for livelihood in several ways. It is here that the Ching family opens a produce store that specializes on the sale of wild durians. It is here that Aimee Ching sets out a lush and exuberantly growing garden in the back-yard of the store. And it is here, in the remnant of the crumbling national state, that rumors about Saturna and their rival corporations' true objectives are spread, take root, and trigger the growth of resistance and subversion.

---

196 Eugene Thacker, "Necrologies or, The Death of the Body Politic," *Beyond Biopolitics: Essays on the Governance of Life and Death*, eds. Patricia Ticineto Cough and Craig Willse (Durham and London: Duke UP, 2011) 140-162, 146.

Mirandas's first unmediated encounter with the Unregulated Zone takes place at the age of six when her father takes her there after several failed attempts at having her peculiar smell treated by Saturna's medical practitioners. Having subjected his daughter to these treatments in the form of pills that come in various colors and entail nothing but undesirable side effects, Stewart Ching, significantly, resorts to a strangely old-fashioned, traditionally Chinese mode of transportation to bring Miranda to practitioners of traditional Chinese medicine whose shops are located in the illicit zone. Stowed in a plastic milk-crate on the back of her father's bicycle, Miranda first watches Stewart bribe the guard at the city-gates, and, on the ensuing ride through the "vast city mushrooming up into a pinkish purple sky" outside Serendipity's walls, takes in the view of dilapidating, windowless buildings that had "clearly been bombed" (37), and the foul smell that pervades the crumbling city. Miranda soon recognizes this city as the one that serves as the setting of the Real-World-Game, yet is represented there in a romanticized fashion, and, above all, without the stench. She also realizes that a similarly romanticized and odorless representation of this city is used as the setting for a televised advertisement for shoes produced and marketed by a corporation-owned factory. Presented as the marker of a denied reality, the stench of the forbidden city is the first clue affirming Miranda's tentative perception of the deceptive fictionality that not only enables the corporation's misleading information politics, but also its amalgamation of biopolitical governance and economic profit seeking.

Further clues in the episode point to the persistence of a historical paradigm of socio-medical regulation in *Salt Fish Girl*'s futurist diegetic world. In having Miranda describe the inhabitants of the bombed out city as "too poor to afford socks" and as wearing plastic shopping bags instead, and in linking this poverty to the overwhelming stench "of old petrol, sulphur, urine and rotten food" (37), Lai projects to her novel's futurist setting the idea of an industrial *lumpenproletariat* and its "secretions of poverty." It is, strikingly, the same concept of reeking poverty the regulation of which by public health policy in nineteenth-century France is at the center of Alain Corbin's seminal study *The Foul and the Fragrant*.[197] Corbin points to the pertinence of sociological and medical studies that linked what they construed as the "heavy scent" and "the fetidity of the laboring classes"[198] to the risk of epidemic diseases: "Doctors and Sociologists had just detected that a type of population existed which contributed

---

197 *The Foul and the Fragrant: Odor and the French Social Imagination* (Leamington Spa et al.: Berg, 1986).
198 Corbin, *The Foul and the Fragrant*, 143.

to epidemic: the type that wallowed in its fetid mire."[199] Underlying this construction of the poor in terms of filth was the assumption

that some individuals exhaled an animal stench. The human who had always wallowed in the depths of poverty smelled strong because his humors did not have the necessary digestion and "the degree of animalization proper to man." Therefore, if he did not have a human odor, it was not because he had regressed but because he had not crossed the threshold of vitality that defined the species.[200]

What Lai's depiction of the Unregulated Zone evokes is thus the historical notion of a dehumanized type of population, whose poverty was construed as posing the 'fetid' risk of epidemic disease. This depiction suggests that the corporate regime in *Salt Fish Girl*'s futurist diegetic world resorts to historical strategies of socio-medical regulation, to strategies that are neither purely fictional nor completely futuristic: In erecting walls around its cities, the corporation uses the historical, bio-political instrument of a topographical partition that marked, in fact, a threshold of vitality, a threshold, separating and protecting a population defined as human from a population that was construed as a different species altogether. Mediated through the perspective of a child and foregrounding this child's sensitivity for aestheticizing fictionalization, this representation of the foul-smelling zone uses the potential of speculative fiction to conjure up in, skillful detail, the image of a historically coded, futurist riskscape. Contrasting the idealizing fictions of the diegetic Real-World-Game and TV-ad, this literary fiction flaunts as an epistemological privilege its capacity of amalgamating the projection of a dystopian future world with the denied and repressed memories of various historical instances of biopower and biopolitics.

Thus marked as epistemologically superior, Miranda's narration blends historically coded connotations of a fetid *lumpenproletariat* with nationally coded connotations of racialization and warfare from different historical periods. The great number of shop signs in Asian letters that Miranda cannot decipher summons images of a smelly Chinatown and conjoins them with those of the smelly sweatshop. Throughout this description, Lai's wording links the stereotype of the ethnic other as a stinking primitive with animalistic food habits to connotations of the camp (i.e. connotations of both the American detention camp for Japanese Americans during WW II, and, conjured by the mention of groups of loitering and drinking youths, of the Indian reservation). And while

---

199 Ibid., 144.
200 Ibid.

summoning with these connotations of the camp, "the fundamental bio political paradigm of the West"[201] Lai evokes, with her description of the "vast city mushrooming into a pinkish purple sky" (37), images of Hiroshima after the U.S.-American atomic bombing, images, in other words, of the most extreme warfare and the most toxic pollution. Ultimately, the text amalgamates heterogeneous historical forms and instances of biopower and biopolitical governance exercised by European and North American nations in one impressive metaphor.

While pointing with this dense historical subtext to the persistence of "the enormous fetidity of social catastrophes"[202] in the futurist corporate regime, Lai, again, links the trope of foul smell to a discourse on nature and its scientific and legal codification. With meticulous consistency, she uses in her representation of the corporate empire an imagery of surface aesthetics that juxtaposes metaphors of surface sealing prevalent in the depiction of the corporate city with metaphors of eroding structures and fertile, open soil, prevalent in the depiction of the Unregulated Zone. The smelly fecundity of the illicit zone's unregulated nature and dilapidating polity is linked to the trope of unsealed, eroding soil, while the corporate cities gleam with the shiny surfaces of the sleek medical and scientific technology in the age of genomics. Miranda's narration gradually reveals that this technology not only allows for an unprecedentedly penetrating, scientific gaze, but for molecular scientific interventions that recode as nature the products of genomic artifice.

Legally sanctioned by corporate laws that prioritize the protection of intellectual property over the protection of civil rights, corporate science is engaged in seed design and the 'optimization' of natural bodies. Miranda's discovery of so-called "janitors" who work in the basement of Serendipity's elementary school vividly illustrates the co-presence of medical regimes from different historical periods. Made from the racialized bodies of illegal, female immigrants, the janitors are primitive service workers, produced by a blend of bio-political regulation and surgery. The aberrant corporate logic first pathologizes these illegal immigrants by stigmatizing them as carriers of the so-called "drowning disease," and then surgically alters and rebuilds their bodies under the pretext of medical treatment. Significantly, clear film windows in the janitors' backs grant a permanent and total surveillance that transcends the boundaries of the body.

The immaculate surface and hypertrophic size of the Saturna apples of Miranda's childhood, on the other hand, betrays their origin in the genomic

---

201 Agamben, *Homo Sacer*, 181.
202 Corbin, *The Foul and the Fragrant*, 143.

laboratories of the corporate seed designers. The designing and patenting of seeds for the sake of corporate profit is, as Rosi Braidotti argues, "the ultimate colonization of the interior of living organisms. [...] As a privatized icon for commercialized biodiversity the seed connects the old 'universalist' idea of nature to the financial reality of global culture."[203] What the co-presence of biopolitical and scientific practices from different historical periods in *Salt Fish Girl*'s speculation on a futurist corporate world showcases, then, is the shifting of "capitalist looting" [...] from the former colonies to the 'new frontiers', or the 'natural resources' represented by [...] genetics."[204] It is in the sleek laboratories of the mega-corporations' medical practitioners and scientists that nature is re-defined, re-organized, produced and owned – no matter whether in the form of racially marked and surgically altered bodies or patented seeds.

The meticulously consistent use of an imagery of surface aesthetics in this speculative projection of biogenetic capitalism subtly conveys contradictory historical codifications of sterility and fertility, risk and risk control. Re-organized in sterile operation theaters, the surgically altered bodies of the janitors are reminiscent of a twentieth-century eugenic practice of nation states: In the name of "a kind of pastoral eugenics unproblematically operating within the context of a developing paternalistic welfare state,"[205] people who were deemed unfit for reproduction were forced into being sterilized. Contrasting this connotation, while equally connected to the sterile luster of clinical laboratories, the corporate practice of seed design, its production of a commercialized biodiversity, evokes the notion of a controlled, optimized fertility. Sealed, impermeable surfaces are thus linked to a codification of nature that rests upon the ultimate control over and the colonization of the interior of living organisms. They signify a taming of chance, the repression of unpredictable agents that might interfere with the ends of biogenetic capital, agents whose very unpredictability qualifies as pathology in the corporate book of nature.

The crumbling, eroding surfaces of the Unregulated Zone, on the other hand, stand for an unpredictable nature that cannot be owned and controlled. Reverberating with Canguilhem's "fecundity that effaces order," and truly fertile in the sense of biodiversity, the fetid zone generates life without classification, selection, and control. Its permeable soil and structures let through the stench

---

203 Rosi Braidotti, "Locating Deleuze's Eco-Philosophy between *Bio/Zoe*- Power and Necro-Politics," *Deleuze and Law: Forensic Futures*, eds. Rosi Braidotti, Claire Colebrook, and Patrick Hanafin (Basingstoke: Palgrave Macmillan, 2009) 96-116, 102.
204 Ibid.
205 Rose, *Politics of Life*, 61.

that comes with unsanitized, organic life; they exude the miasma of chance, the stench of a living multiplicity that is the resource of and, at the same time, as it cannot be controlled, a danger to corporate cash flows. The contradictory connotations of sterility and fertility thus evoked and ascribed pointedly contrast the official self-marketing of Saturna as a pastoral custodian of health and life, and the corporate representation of the illicit zone that surrounds its cities as a hotbed of risks against which their citizens have to be safeguarded. Ultimately, the over-determined symbolism of the surface aesthetics in Lai's depiction of the corporate garden of life epitomizes the corporations' codification of nature. It draws attention to the paradoxes of biogenetic capitalism, its colonizing of life itself and its dependence on forms of propaganda that, quite literally, bank on strategically triggered anxieties.

It is by way of these contrasting and multiply coded images embedded in the clinical narrative of Miranda's disease that the political structure of the corporate empire is gradually revealed: cast as a protective shield against the biological risk of a disease that might endanger its citizens' health, Serendipity's walls figuratively and literally represent the immunological border of a body politic whose living, vital order is dependent upon "the notion that the *bios* itself can be defended."[206] Enclosing forms of life that are produced, exploited, and defined as worthy of protection, and excluding forms of life that are devalued and construed as a biological risk, these walls are the constitutive symbol of a thoroughly biologized body politic in the age of genomics and its immunological management of multiplicity. Collapsing the figurative and the literal, Serendipity's walls protect the health of a political body that is vitally threatened by a biological multiplicity that can no longer be monitored and controlled. While its media construe unclassified forms of life as "not safe" and a menace to the life of individual bodies, it is, in fact, the body politic itself, the health of the political-economic body that is 'plagued' by the epidemic disease of (the) multitude.[207]

As a threshold of vitality in the age of genomics, Serendipity's walls define not the species, as did the hygienic measures in Corbin's nineteenth-century France, but mark the threshold between a *bios* that is included in a legal order resting upon a re-coding of nature and a *zoe*, existing outside legal and scientific codification; the walls serve to distinguish the type of population that is

---

[206] Eugene Thacker, "Necrologies or, The Death of the Body Politic," *Beyond Biopolitics: Essays on the Governance of Life and Death*, eds. Patricia Ticineto Cough and Craig Willse (Durham and London: Duke UP, 2011) 140-162, 158, italics in the original.

[207] See ibid., 154.

construed as biological citizens from a type of life that does not live up to the standards of the *bios*. The very notion of biodefense that the walls embody entails, however, that this *zoe* is not once and for all defined by a clear-cut opposition between biological life (in the sense of Agamben's bare life) and political life; rather, it denotes what Eugene Thacker calls

> a *whatever*-life in which biology and sovereignty, or medicine and politics, continually inflect and fold onto each other. Whatever-life is the pervasive potential for life to be specified as that which must be protected, that which must be protected against, and as those forms of nonhuman life that are the agents of the attack.[208]

Serendipity's walls have to be porous and permeable in order to enable these flexible, circulating re-definitions of life upon which the functioning of any bio-economic regime in the age of genomic rests. Blending the goal of unbridled economic growth with the objectives of a scientific gaze that penetrates bodies until they disappear and are reconfigured in terms of genetic programs,[209] Saturna is a genomic body politic, a body politic whose creation and marketing of patented life forms depends upon the controlled circulation of information. While the Real-World-Game promulgates the fiction of a disciplinary power over bodies, Miranda's narration gradually uncovers the corporation's use of genomics as a security apparatus whose function and purpose differs significantly from the disciplinary apparatus of the nation state that relied on eugenics.

Delineating the distinction between eugenics as a scientific discourse and a disciplinary apparatus designed to maximize the fitness of nation states, and genomics as the regulation and control of global populations, Marina Levina explains that

> genomics, as a security apparatus, emphasizes a shift from power/knowledge to control/ information. The former establishes parameters, disciplines bodies, and fixes categories. The latter gathers information, directs flows, and controls movement. Freed from establishing norms and disciplining racialized bodies, genomics' *raison d'être* is to gather, qualify, and manage information. Information, however, can never be stabilized as knowledge, otherwise

---

208 Thacker, "Necrologies," 159, italics in the original.
209 See Marina Levina, "Regulation and Discipline in the Genomic Age: A Consideration Of Differences Between Genomics and Eugenics," *A Foucault for the 21st Century: Governmentality, Biopolitics, and Discipline in the New Millennium*, eds. Sam Binkley and Jorge Capetillo (Newcastle upon Tyne, UK: Cambridge Scholars, 2009) 308-319, 315.

processes of gathering will stop and apparatuses will cease to function. As such, it is never done; its very existence depends on constantly being in-flux. [210]

Whereas Serendipity's permeable walls thus aptly symbolize the dependence of genomics on the neoliberal restructuring that allows the global free movement of information encoded in genetic programs and electronic signs, the use of the concept of the body politic as a metaphor for corporate governance appears to contradict the decidedly disembodied quality of the new episteme of biogenetic capitalism and its use of genomics as a security apparatus. In other words, it appears inconsistent to represent a global bio-economic system that capitalizes on the "collection, distribution, and circulation of information about life itself"[211] by taking recourse to the ancient metaphor of the body politic, a historical metaphor that has been widely used in self-conceptions of political bodies, where it has illustrated and legitimated principles of unity, hierarchy and centralization.[212]. However, as Eugene Thacker emphasizes, beyond unity, hierarchy, and centralization, the body politic is characterized by inconsistencies and permutations that constitute a fourth, significant principle:

The concept of the body politic entails the creation of a logically coherent monstrosity [...] raised as it is to address a problem of political ontology, [it] often entails the creation of aberrant logics, that is, modes of thinking that make sense logically but that result in an image of the body politic that can only be described as teratological.[213]

Read with Thacker, Lai's recourse to the old metaphor of the body politic in the futurist strand of her novel makes sense at several levels. First, the medical

---

210 Ibid., 316, italics in the original.
211 Ibid., 317.
212 According to Eugene Thacker, the concept of the body politic has been a surprisingly persistent response to the challenge of thinking political collectivity and is characterized by equally persistent principles, albeit with variations responding to specific historical conditions. Based on an analogy between the anatomy of the natural, individual human body and the anatomical organization of the political, collective body, the body politic metaphor, throughout its history, symbolizes principles of unity, hierarchy, and centralization. Its persistent central concern is the relation between the individual, natural body and the political body of the collectivity. While "the former is said to preexist the latter, and often serves as its model, it is essential that the latter governs, manages, and regulates the former." Thacker, "Necrologies," 143.
213 Ibid., 146, italics in the original.

ontology that is inscribed in the body politic concept per se gains a conclusive and particular significance in *Salt Fish Girl* as it collapses with the diegetic corporations' distinctly bio-medical rule and their self-stylization as pastoral guardians of life. Second, the creation of a logically coherent monstrosity that Thacker identifies as a marker of any body politic collapses with the corporations' engagement in teratogenic experiments. In collapsing the literal and the figural, Lai extends the organicist symbolism of the body politic concept to a political allegory that exposes the hidden persistence of elements of sovereignty and totalitarianism in the ultimately abstracted political economy of a globalized biogenetic capitalism. Above all, her depiction of the monstrous corporate empire as a body politic in *crisis* vividly affirms Eugene Thacker's judgment of the "rather gothic longevity"[214] and the unabated relevance of the concept:

> If today we no longer speak of a body politic, this is not because the concept has ceased to exist. Perhaps it is because the issues that are raised by the body politic concept have never been so relevant as they are in contemporary discussions of 'the state of exception,' 'biopolitics,' and the 'multitude.' The body politic concept is never so *vital* as when it ceases to be an explicit part of the debate, and its ontological categories invisibly serve to make possible political discourse.[215]

In keeping with the medical logic of the body politic, the state of exception in *Salt Fish Girl*'s corporate empire is prompted when the so-called drowning disease reaches epidemic scale. Miranda, meanwhile living in the Unregulated Zone after enduring an impressive range of bizarre, yet futile medical treatments against her durian stench, first learns about the nature of the epidemic when she applies for a job as a laboratory assistant in a private clinic. After finding the clinic, a surprisingly polished establishment hidden on "the top floor of a crumbling office tower on a street of ancient crumbling office towers" (98), and after signing a confidentiality clause, Miranda is given information about the disease by Dr. Seto, "a roundish Asian woman […] in a neat white lab coat"(99): "It hasn't got an official name. It hasn't got an official anything. None of the corporations want to acknowledge it, but some call it the dreaming disease or the drowning disease" (100). When Miranda inquires about the number of cases discovered, Dr. Seto replies:

---

214 Ibid., 159.
215 Ibid., 159-160, italics in the original.

We're not sure how many. The symptoms are so peculiar, and so unlike any other known disease – foul odours of various sorts that follow the person without actually emanating from the body, psoriasis, sleep apnea, terrible dreams usually with historical content, and a compulsive drive to commit suicide by drowning. (100)

With great attention to detail this description evokes and conjoins connotations of civilization diseases whose symptoms belong to a spectrum disorder rather than a particular morbus. The peculiarity of the symptoms listed here lies in their disembodied elusiveness, their lack of a classifiable agent, their evasion from a diagnostic medical apparatus that since its emergence struggled to get hold of and to classify deviances from its established standards of the normal. Significantly, this list of elusive symptoms culminates in "the compulsive drive to commit suicide by drowning," thereby insinuating that it is, above all, a behavioral deviance from the normal that alerts the corporate authorities and motivates their official denial of the epidemic. With this detail, Lai subtly charges *Salt Fish Girl*'s medical discourse with the historical connotations of suicide statistics that became all the rage in nineteenth-century science and a disciplinary bone of contention between sociology and medicine. According to Ian Hacking, nineteenth-century medical science struggled to claim suicide as a medical topic by trying to prove that madness, its alleged cause, was an organic disease. Late-nineteenth-century sociology, on the other hand, defined suicide, "the most morbid of behaviors,"[216] as an *"anomie"*[217] that indicated social and moral decline, alienation and disintegration, thwarted the growth of the population, and was, ultimately, considered a sign of communal pathology.

Amalgamating these connotations, Dr. Seto's description of the disease that is soon called "the contagion" alludes to regimes of normalization and the notion of abnormal individuals whose invisible pathology and increasing number call for statistical registration and medical measures as they threaten to infest and weaken the body politic. Significantly, the private clinic that offers Miranda a job belongs to Dr. Rudy Flowers, a famous former medical scientist for Painted Horse, one of Saturna's rival corporations; its polished luster betrays its status as a heterotopia of scientific regimes of regulation amidst the crumbling Unregulated Zone.[218] With subtle clues, the text insinuates a causal relation

---

216 Ian Hacking, *The Taming of Chance* (Cambridge et al.: Cambridge UP, 1990) 64.
217 Emile Durkheim qtd. in Hacking *The Taming of Chance* 64, italics in the original.
218 Given the medical ontology of the body politic that entails an analogy between the physician and the ruler (see Thacker 150) Flowers's establishment amid the Unregulated Zone can be read as representing a heterotopia in the medical sense of displaced tissue at a non-physiological site. A sovereign infiltration of the zone that

between Flowers's desertion from Painted Horse and the spreading of the syndrome that soon affects the populations of all corporations. It remains unclear, whether Flowers was dismissed, because he failed to find the cause of and a treatment for the disease, or had to leave, because he insisted on information politics that interfered with the economic interests of Aries Williams, the corporate CEO and owner of a seed-design enterprise. Whatever the circumstances, Flowers's defection can be read as the beginning of a crisis, a state of exception, inaugurated by the intermediate suspension of legal rule in the corporate body politic whose bio-economic objectives require the double sovereignty of the physician and the CEO, the doctor and the corporate manager. Despite its ambiguity, this backstory seems to suggest an incompatibility deeply engrained in the alliance between life sciences and capital, an irreconcilability that troubles the bio-economic regime and entails a permanent state of exception.

It is in the course of her training as a laboratory assistant for the dubious Dr. Flowers and his secret experimental project that Miranda meets many carriers of "the contagion." While scraping skin cells and drawing blood samples, she encounters the patients' various peculiar smells and is told about their memories and dreams of historic instances of political oppression, economic exploitation, and colonization; she listens to tales and legends that the patients remember without ever having read or heard about them. With these instances of a biological resurgence of the repressed history and the 'litteraria' that have no place in the biologized culture of the novel's diegetic corporate empire, Lai brings Miranda's narrative discourse and its rich blend of historical connotations in line with the narratives of the pathologized carriers of "the contagion." It becomes obvious that what is designated by corporate politics as a disease afflicting monstrously abnormal individuals must, in fact, be read as an embodied cultural archive of repressed historical knowledge and memory.[219]

---

represents a space of exception from corporate law during the crisis of corporate rule, it might be read as a metaphor for the perpetual nature of sovereignty that persists even during the time of an *interregnum*, in the sense of Ernst Kantorowicz's *The King's Two Bodies: A Study in Mediaeval Political Theology* (1957) as read by Giorgio Agamben, *Homo Sacer: Sovereign Power and Bare Life* (Stanford: Stanford UP, 1995) 91-94.

219 Strikingly, Lai's representation of the carriers of the contagion as a cultural archive is reminiscent of evolutionary biologist Niles Eldredge's definition of the species as "information repository." See John Brockman, *The Third Culture: Beyond the Scientific Revolution* (New York: Touchstone, 1995) esp. Chapter 6, 119-128. Lai seems to make a point, though, that the information 'reposited' in the bodies of the

This revelation, however, dawns on the reader before it dawns on Miranda. While Miranda is somewhat disenchanted with the corporations' rule and politics at this point, she is still far from realizing the scope of their monstrosity.

This changes when Evie enters the picture. Consistent with the expositions' subtext of an alternative epistemological empowerment, Lai links the point at which the narrative of Miranda's clinical education turns into a narrative of political education to the trope of a smell that triggers the sexual desire of a potent third gender. During her working hours in the laboratory, Miranda meets the rebellious clone Evie, whose pungent salt fish smell at first prompts a strange feeling of familiarity, and, eventually, Miranda's love and erotic desire. Ironically, it is Evie, the clone, who informs Miranda that disease is a state of suffering, and suffering the only indicator by which the individual can judge the transition from the normal to the pathological.[220] It is Evie, who in the course of the evolving romance, discloses the truth about the corporate seed designers and their transgenic blending of human and animal genes, a secret teratogenic experiment resulting in the mass production of the clone series 'Sonia' and 'Miyako' and providing the corporations with an army of unpaid, female workers. And it is Evie, who reveals that the conspicuously 'ethnic' names of the clone series as well as the clones' uniformly dark hair and eyes betray their origins in the Diverse Genome Project and its collection of gene material of "peoples of the so-called Third World, Aboriginal peoples, and peoples in danger of extinction" (160).

Disclosed in the novel's diegesis by "Sonia 113,"[221] this nightmare scenario of ultimate corporate control and exploitation of subaltern female and animal bodies obviously comments on the biotechnological "creation of biovalue"[222] and the excesses of neoliberalism and global free trade in the age of genomics. It boldly showcases the unethical implications of an alliance between the life sciences and capitalism and the new, de-territoralized imperialism in its wake. At first glance, this scenario appears to affirm Patricia MacCormack's trenchant

---

carriers of the contagion is of a literary kind and does not consist of biological adaptations and biological survival mechanisms.

220 See Canguilhem, *Knowledge of Life*, 106; and Rose, *Politics of Life*, 85.
221 "Sonia 113" is Evie's corporate production number, the cynical designation of a tool that is not considered a citizen in the novel's corporate empire. Her self-chosen name "Evie" signals the claiming of civil rights and, at the same time, the positing of the founding myth of an embodied political resistance.
222 Rose *Politics of Life* 133.

remark that "women and animals are territories of new empire."[223] Drawing on Deleuze's philosophy of becoming, MacCormack calls for "Vitalistic FeminEthics"[224] and a new activism vis-à-vis the deadening disappropriation of female and animal bodies that she attributes to "the rise of capitalism, technology and other tropes of modernity to postmodernity."[225] However, in its imprecision, her catchy phrasing fails to capture the spirit of the new politics of visualization and circulation, the new episteme that rests upon a "molecularization of vitality"[226] and "produces ever-shifting waves of genderisation and sexualisation, racialization and naturalisation of multiple 'others'."[227] MacCormack's phrasing fails to acknowledge that the politics of a new "schizoid"[228] capitalism depend upon the circulation of disembodied information and have "effectively disrupted the traditional dialectic relationship between empirical referents of Otherness (women, natives, and animal others) and the processes of discursive formation of genderisation/racialization /naturalization."[229]

Larissa Lai's speculative fiction of a corporation-governed, near-future North-American Pacific West leaves no doubt that the new politics combining visualization and the circulation of information constitute a regime under which difference is produced as a commodity, and ambiguity multiplies as the figure of the strange, monstrous, abnormal body can no longer be easily identified by obvious markers. Intricately inscribing this figure in the gestures of literary epistemological empowerment in its expositions, the novel traces the cultural and scientific re-codifications of its monstrosity to the beginnings of natural science. And in taking recourse to the poetics of the body politic in her literary speculation on a futurist corporate empire, Lai impressively visualizes the persistence of sovereignty and totalitarianism within the new episteme that conditions the elusive reign of biocapital.

Less convincing is, however, Lai's speculation on the possibilities of agency and resistance in an age when the "body itself has become the battleground."[230]

---

223 Patricia MacCormack, "Vitalistic FeminEthics," *Deleuze and Law: Forensic Futures*, eds. Rosi Bradotti, et al. (New York: Palgrave Macmillan, 2009) 73-95, 78.
224 Ibid., 73.
225 MacCormack, "Vitalistic FeminEthics," 79.
226 Rose, *Politics of Life*, 13.
227 Braidotti, "Locating Deleuze's Eco-Philosophy," 104.
228 Ibid., 103.
229 Ibid., 104.
230 This is, for once, a quotation from one of Larissa Lai's many epitextual remarks: "The question is how to fight back when your body itself has become the

As the figure of Evie exemplifies, the hybrid genetic texts embodied by the protagonists of the novel are not merely cast as objects of the "informatics of domination," [231] as Donna Haraway has called the new forms of biogenetic power, but are presented as codes of transgressive and emancipatory possibility. Unmistakably an homage to Haraway's concept of the cyborg,[232] Lai's depiction of Evie is committed to the ethics and the imaginary of a non-anthropocentric, post-humanistic philosophy that considers the cyborg and her political agency a solution to the challenge of thinking a non-essentialized, embodied subjectivity. A mutated clone with implanted techno-control devices, Evie manages to transcend her genetic script and to rally organized resistance against corporate power. Her rebellious potential and vital subversive energy (an energetic agency that Rosi Braidotti would likely describe as "*zoe*-driven"[233]) trigger Miranda's

---

battleground." "Brand Canada: Global Flows and a People to Come," *Reading(s) from a Distance: European Perspectives on Canadian Women's Writing*, ed. by. Charlotte Sturgess and Martin Kuester (Augsburg: Wißner, 2008), 23-32 , 29.

231 Donna Haraway, *Modest_Witness@Second_Millennium. Female Man Meets Oncomouse* (London /New York: Routledge, 1997) 174.

232 In an article on Georges Canguilhem and his conceptualization of the human/ machine relationship, Ian Hacking traces the idea of the cyborg back to its origins in space research, where it was developed by Manfred Clynes and Nathan Kline in 1960 as a computerized bio-feedback machine, an extension to the body that freed astronauts from taking care of bodily needs in a "human-hostile environment." Hacking criticizes Haraway's embrace of the cyborg metaphor for blurring fact and fiction: "Haraway is with the monsters, who need have no history, no fall from grace, no paradise lost, no mother, no Oedipal relationships, and, of cardinal importance for her, no gender. Casting about for a model for socialist-feminists to strive for, she proposes the cyborg itself. Whereas many feminists have resisted technology as an aspect of patriarchal dominance, Haraway, always intensely aware of her own paradoxes, says, in part, embrace technology, embrace a technology that reaches far past any existing reality. Let us become cyborgs, not bodies enhanced with computerized bio-feedback, but bodies without a prehistory. In such a community gender will, to say the least, be transformed." "Canguilhem amid the Cyborgs," *Economy and Society* 27.2-3 (1998): 202-216. 212. Notwithstanding its polemic tone, Hacking's criticism seems to identify at least some of the reasons for the vagueness marking the celebratory usage of the cyborg metaphor in Haraway's wake.

233 See Rosi Braidotti, *Transpositions: On Nomadic Ethics* (Cambridge, UK: Polity Press, 2006) 41. According to Braidotti's definition, *zoe* "refers to the endless vitality of life as continuous becoming" and "supports a notion of subjectivity in the

love and desire, initiate her political awakening, and enable the utopian twist at the end of a bleak, dystopian narrative: after Evie and Miranda have become a couple – and by then it has become obvious that both are re-incarnations of the mythical Nu Wa and her salt fish girl lover – Miranda, too, conceives a child by eating a wild durian, thus closing a cycle of alternative procreation that produces ever new, unclassifiable, and transgressive life forms.

4.4 Until the Next Time

This decidedly fantastic ending of *Salt Fish Girl* with yet another miraculous parthenogenesis leading to the birth of yet another monstrously hybrid, fertile, female body certainly caters to Patricia MacCormack's ideal of "vitalistic feminethics."[234] It also seems to promote what Rosi Braidotti has called "biocentred egalitarianism," a "philosophy of radical immanence and affirmative becoming, which activates a nomadic subject into sustainable processes of transformation."[235] Obviously, *Salt Fish Girl*'s final scene, in which Miranda and Evie, acting as her midwife, give birth to a baby girl, indulges in the gender trouble of a transsexual imaginary. The scene symbolically re-appropriates a female power of procreation that, as the novel has shown, has been colonized by male modes of scientific signification under the protection of intellectual property rights. The scene seems to revel in the female monstrosity that Braidotti and others greet as the emblem of a new teratological, post-humanistic philosophy that captures "difference in nonpejorative terms."[236] Braidotti's celebration of the cyberteratology that she sees proliferating in new feminist science fiction culminates in her call for "a culture of affirmation and joy" that

---

sense of qualitative, transversal and group-oriented agency". In "Locating Deleuze's Ecophilosophy," Braidotti describes the *zoe*-driven body as "marked by the interdependence with its environment through a structure of mutual flows and data transfer" with "the relentless generative force of *bios/zoe* and the specific brand of trans-species egalitarianism" as its starting point.113 -114.

234 MacCormack, "Vitalistic FeminEthics," 73.
235 Rosi Braidotti, "Cyberteratologies: Female Monsters Negotiate the Other's Participation in the Far Future," *Envisioning the Future: Science Fiction and the Next Millennium,* ed. Marlene S. Barr (Middletown: Wesleyan UP, 2003) 146-171, 147.
236 "Cyberteratologies," 154.

"cultivates the art of complexity" and her conclusion that "the presence of monsters can provide both solace and a model."[237]

But different from Lai's speculative fiction, Braidotti, notwithstanding her otherwise perceptive criticism, fails to consider that legal, scientific, and cultural re-workings and re-codifications of monstrosity merely re-configure the devaluing constructions of race, class, and gender, and thus, ultimately, serve to keep the old triad in place. While Lai ends Miranda's narration, the final scene, and her novel with the sentence "Everything will be all right, I thought, until next time"(269), thus displaying her narrator's (and her own) awareness that these displacements are preliminary at best, Braidotti celebrates embodied monstrosity as a resistant mode of 'becoming.' Her praise of embodied monstrosity might even partake, if involuntarily, in the somatic ethics and the economy of hope that are "intrinsically linked to the 'spirit of biocapital'."[238] In other words, the vitalistic ethics of embodied monstrosity, promoted by Braidotti and others, might tie in with an increasingly biological understanding of personhood in the age of genomics. Even more important, they hardly affect the new practices for the government of persons, practices that have changed significantly with the emergence of the molecularization of vitality. This new episteme entails, as Nikolas Rose observes, a shift from unclassifiable abnormalities to symptomless susceptibilities; it requires an active biological citizenship and a scientific, biological literacy that extend the neoliberal imperative of a prudent, managerial self-care to include a promissory self-management of genetic predispositions:[239]

The active responsible biological citizen must engage in a constant work of self-evaluation and the modulation of conduct, diet, lifestyle, and drug regime, in response to the changing requirements of the susceptible body. In tracing out, experimenting with, and contesting the new relations between truth, power, and commerce that traverse our living, suffering, mortal bodies, and challenging their vital limits, such active biological citizens are redefining what it means to be human today.[240]

The skepticism expressed in the last sentence of *Salt Fish Girl*'s final scene reflects Lai's awareness of the ideological hazard implicit to her decision to have the novel end with a celebration of monstrous maternity and female powers of

---

237 Ibid., 166.
238 Nikolas Rose,"The Value of Life: Somatic Ethics and the Spirit of Biocapital," 98.
239 On the emergence of a promissory culture and the growing significance of susceptibility see Nikolas Rose, *The Politics of Life Itsself*, esp.84-94.
240 Nikolas Rose, *The Politics of Life Itsself*, 154

procreation. The phrase "until the next time" suggests that Lai was careful to relativize the biologism inherent to this feast of alternative, female fertility. Nevertheless, the scene provides a somewhat disappointing ending to the narrative of Miranda's coming of age that is also a coming to politics. This is all the more so, as, throughout the novel, a discourse on "Traditional Culture"[241] (the appreciation of which Miranda 'inherits' from her mother) highlights the lack and the trivialization of this very culture in the biologized corporate empire. In particular, the novel's discourse on lesbian romance and a potent third gender is linked to a discourse on political education that is subtly inscribed with topoi of literacy and literature as a repository of cultural knowledge. Lai depicts Evie not merely as one of the "iron-pumping giant Ninja mutant Barbies" (149) that Braidotti euphorically welcomes in her article "Cyberteratologies;" she makes a point of showing that Evie is willful and witty, but also well-read. It is no coincidence that Evie escapes corporate control by resorting to a tactics she derives from Mary Shelley's novel *Frankenstein* (159); neither is it an accident that the cloned factory workers, whose resistance Evie rallies, sabotage the shoes they manufacture by equipping them with soles inscribed with poems, polemics, and drawings (249). With this latter detail, the symbolism of *Salt Fish Girl*'s surface aesthetics comes full circle: it suggests that it is art and literature that provide insulation and protection against the cultural erosion that comes with the new regime of biocapital and its reductive formation and regulation of political subjects as biological citizens.

The strong argument for the epistemological empowerment of speculative fiction to counter the dominance of scientific modes of signification that Larissa Lai makes in *Salt Fish Girl*'s expositions is thus, in the futurist part of her novel, only faintly inscribed in a subordinate discourse on art and literature. Although the narrative of Miranda's education is linked to the romance with Evie, who gives this education a turn from clinical to political (a narrative development picking up Stein's idea of romance as useful knowledge) the novel's ending does not quite keep the promise inscribed in its beginning. While the text's consistent and productive metaphoricity bleakly captures the risks construed by the molecularization of vitality and biological risk as a new mode of governance in the age of biocapital, its ending insinuates that hope lies in the chance mutations that evade scientific control (an idea ironically encoded in 'Serendipity, the

---

241 In his article "The Third Culture," Paul Rabinow points to an arrogant ignorance of natural scientists and their lack of "Traditional Culture with capital T, capital C." *History of the Human Sciences* 7.2 (1994): 53-64, 53.

name of the corporate city')[242] and resistance remains limited to the celebration of an officially defined monstrosity.

It seems, however, that hope lies not so much in the monstrosity of a third gender as in a literature that challenges the impending dominance of a scientific imaginary promulgated by what Paul Rabinow has called the "third culture." What is eroding in the new territories of empire, no matter whether read as actual territories like the Pacific Rim or as human beings encoded in digital data streams, are the ethics and the cultural synthesis that art and literature can provide, a crumbling, fertile soil emanating both the repressed miasma of national history and the stench of a transnational, bio-economic future at the North American Pacific Rim. Encoded in the phrase "until the next time" is, apart from the insight that new thresholds of knowledge will introduce ever new symbolic regimes and their re-workings of identitarian categories, the anticipatory epistemology of risk and speculation; this epistemology rests on a contingency that is filtered by observation, selection, extrapolation and serial description[243]. *Salt Fish Girl* leaves no doubt that these operations should better not be left to capital and science alone.

---

242 The *OED* defines "serendipity, n." as "the faculty of making happy and unexpected disvoveries by accident." *OED Online* (March 2012) Web, 8 Apr. 2012 http://www.oed.com/view/Entry/176387?redirectedFrom=%3ESerendipity#eid.

243 Joseph Vogl refers to risk as an anticipated chance event, the contingencies of which are filtered, formalized and rationalized by observation and serial descriptions that establish relations between causes and consequences. *Kalkül und Leidenschaft: Poetik des ökonomischen Menschen* (Zürich and Berlin: Diaphanes, 2008) 166-167. The interrelation between the two strands comprising *Salt Fish Girl*'s narrative discourse, or rather, the dissolution of the opposition between their temporal trajectories through the concept of reincarnation, can indeed be read as an instance of serial description. In this respect, Lai once again extracts a different meaning from the epistemology of risk and speculation by applying the principle of serial description to successive historical varieties of capitalist production and to corresponding forms of labor resistance against capitalist exploitation.

5 Towards a Poetics of Risk and Speculation

Risk and speculation, so the study set out to show, are pivotal concepts around which Kathryn Bigelow's *Strange Days*, Karen T. Yamashita's *Tropic of Orange*, and Larissa Lai's *Salt Fish Girl* are organized. Published within a decade around 2000, these artifacts, while otherwise heterogeneous, unanimously display thoroughly economized, dystopian diegetic worlds, in which individuals are pervasively addressed and formed as economic subjects. Thus far, Kathryn Bigelow's Hollywood movie *Strange Days* had mainly been addressed by film scholars who had read it along the paradigm of the vexed relation between gender and the action film; Karen Yamashita's novel *Tropic of Orange* had primarily been praised for establishing trans-Pacific and hemispheric perspectives on multiculturalism and immigrant struggles around recognition and assimilation; in a similar vein, Larissa Lai's novel *Salt Fish Girl* had been received in the framework of critical studies of Canadian multiculturalism and ethnic minority writing.

Yet the texts' striking unanimity on the subtle workings of a new political-economic rationality, formed by an alliance of neoliberalism and neo-conservatism that re-configures race, class and gender, seemed to challenge familiar categories of critical political thinking and call for different readings. The specific time and place of the texts' publication, the setting of their narratives in near-future cities of the North American Pacific coast, and not least their recourse to boldly fictional, speculative devices in their unison projection of a dystopian climate of fear all suggested that the texts react to and reflect the growing salience in North America of an unprecedented framework of governance at the historical moment of their production. Most important, the artifacts' aesthetics of risk and speculation appeared to correspond with both the speculative strategies of an economic Pacific Rim discourse emerging in the closing decades of the twentieth century and the increasing pertinence of risk as a rationality to govern social problems in North American 'rim cities.'

The study's point of departure was thus the hypothesis that aesthetics of risk and speculative fiction became a salient representational strategy in both fictional discourses of cultural artifacts and factual political-economic discourses emerging at the North American Pacific coast at the threshold of the new millennium. In order to make these aesthetic correspondences visible and to highlight the three fictional texts' perceptive and clairvoyant political critique, the introductory chapter offers a survey of the utopianist Pacific Rim discourse and recent theorizations of risk and risk management. These overviews are preceded by an exemplary discussion of three theories of science fiction. Persistent throughout the brief history of science fiction as a genre worthy of academic attention are attempts at establishing a poetics that would both prove the value of science fictional aesthetics against the grain of an enduring disparagement of the genre in 'serious' literary studies, and allow the definition of distinctive generic markers for its numerous subgenres.

The term speculative fiction, introduced as an umbrella term in the 1950s, turned out to be specifically resistant to precise definition. While the studies by Darko Suvin (1979) and Fredric Jameson (2005) focus on and foreground the political potential of science fictional texts in general (Suvin) and of the utopian form in particular (Jameson), Seo-Young Chu endeavors to develop a "Representational Theory of Science Fiction" (2010) that allows the consideration of all fictional texts as to some degree science fictional. Apart from methodological and terminological imprecisions, it is, above all, the presupposition of degrees of fictionality underlying Chu's theory that is neither convincing nor provides points of reference or an inventory of generic conventions for a classification of Bigelow, Yamashita and Lai's texts as speculative fiction.

Turning this shortcoming to advantage, "Restless Subjects" resorts to the double coding of the term 'speculation' as a political-economic and an aesthetic mode of extrapolating representation, and to pragmatic theories of fictionality. According to these pragmatic approaches, the definition of fictionality is based upon speech act conventions that regulate fiction, its production and reception, as a complex cultural practice in Western societies. While, according to these conventions, the signifiers of fictional discourses are freed from extra-textual referentiality, the factual discourses, whose power of meaning-making assigns a marginal cultural status to fiction, are expected to renounce fictionalizing strategies. However, as the delineation of both the utopianist Pacific Rim discourse and the theorization of risk and dominant discourses on risk and risk management set out to show, economic and political-economic practices of extrapolating assessment (speculation) rely on fictionalizing operations that render precarious any conventional distinction between discourses of works of fiction and factual discourses of truth.

While the futurologist rhetoric of North American fashioners of a Pacific Rim imaginary creates a simulacrum of the Pacific region as a homogeneous, transnational marketplace and its prospering community of rational economic actors (and thus takes recourse to aesthetic strategies characteristic of the utopian form to perpetuate older versions of Euro-American symbolic appropriation) the rationalities of risk and practices of risk management in multicultural North American nations resort to dystopian speculations on dangers and their supposed consequences. The chapter on risk theory gives a brief sketch of the controversy between theorizations of risk that are based upon an ontological perception of risks as 'real' (Douglas and Wildavsky, Beck) and theorizations of risk as a dispositif to govern social problems.

Promulgated across disciplines by scholars drawing on Foucault's notion of biopolitics and governmentality, this non-ontological understanding of risk highlights the relevance of fictionalizing narrative to risk scenarios construed by experts and advisors of policy makers. Such highly fictional, dystopian speculations on the probable outcome of dangers not only inform political decision makers, who are in the powerful position to declare dangers as risks. They also serve as fantasies fostering market-compliant behavior of neoliberal subjects and public consent to legal and extralegal extensions of governance. Ultimately, fantasies of risk are at work whenever a political state of exception needs to be established and justified. There is thus an amazing literariness to political discourse in general, and to risk as a dispositif of governance in particular, an entanglement of aesthetic and political practices reminding us that the so-called discourses of truth keep calling for our close attention to rhetoric and representation.

Considering the power assigned to experts and their fictionalizing strategies, the idea of a democratizing effect of discourses on risk in a deliberative public sphere becomes at least doubtful. "The public sphere is," as Judith Butler observes, "constituted in part by what cannot be said and what cannot be shown. The limits of the sayable, the limits of what can appear, circumscribe the domain in which political speech operates and certain kinds of subjects appear as viable actors."[1]. Despite the widely acknowledged efficacy of fictionalizing aesthetic practices in politics and economics, the power differential that marginalizes art and culture remains in place. Against this devaluation of cultural artifacts vis-à-vis the realm of the factual, the close analyses forming the main part of the study

---

1 *Precarious Life: The Powers of Mourning and Violence* (London and New York: Verso, 2004) XVII.

show that the fictional texts of its corpus address and give voice to that which does not appear in dominant political, economic and scientific discourses on risk and security. In other words, the exemplary readings offered in "Restless Subjects" prove that artifacts like Kathryn Bigelow's Hollywood film *Strange Days*, Karen Yamashita's novel *Tropic of Orange*, and Larissa Lai's novel *Salt Fish Girl* are viable, if marginalized actors. These texts make visible the manipulative fantasies of risk in the service of the political-economic interests and the *oikodizee* of neoliberal capitalism. Most important, in performing the narrative selection, ordering and anticipatory establishing of relations between causes and their supposed consequences, their speculative aesthetics spell out the modeling operations of filtered contingency underlying all representations of dangers as risks. In doing so, they outline fundamental principles of a poetics of risk and speculation that would provide a timely analytical tool for contemporary cultural criticism.

5.1 UNITED IN A STATE OF FANTASY

In supplying a theory for the speculative narration that is constitutive of risk scenarios, this poetics need neither be limited to works of fiction in general nor to cultural artifacts conforming to however fuzzy patterns of science fiction in particular. On the contrary, in spelling out the logic of filtered contingency underlying aesthetic and political practices, a poetics of risk and speculation can provide a frame of reference and comparison for fictional and non-fictional discourses against the grain of their institutionalized cultural division. The exemplary readings of the study show that practices and aesthetics of risk and speculation became particularly effective in "the ongoing global-capitalist 'New World Order' emerging after 1990."[2] In the following, a final exemplary reading may at once both shed light on the significance of the year 1991 to the political restructuring that ushered in the rise of risk and speculation, and serve as evidence that a poetics of risk and speculation need not be restricted to science fictional texts or the genre of fantasy.

Compared to the artifacts of the study's corpus, *Divisadero*,[3] a novel written by Sri-Lankan-born, Canadian author Michael Ondaatje and first published in

---

2 Slavoj Zizek, "Is it Still Possible to be a Hegelian Today?" *The Speculative Turn: Continental Materialism and Realism*, eds. Levi Bryant, Nick Srnicek and Graham Harman (Melbourne: re.press, 2011) 202-223, 214.

3 Michael Ondaatje, *Divisadero* (New York: Vintage International 2008).

2007, seems like an unlikely choice. But while displaying no science fictional or fantastic elements, the poetic images in *Divisadero* activate and enable an experience of the enduring historical relationship between fantasy and political culture in the U.S. Such a relationship has been denied by political theory not only in the American context, although it can be traced back to the emergence of the modern nation state, as Donald E. Pease argues. Drawing on Jacqueline Rose's book *States of Fantasy*, and in particular on her insight "that fantasy – far from being the antagonist of public, social, being – plays a central, constitutive role in the modern world of states and nations,"[4] Pease writes in *The New American Exceptionalism*:

The decisive shift in the political fortunes of the modern state took place at the historical moment when the ruler, instead of embodying the state, served a separate constitutional and legal state that it was his duty to maintain. Once real authority was no longer vested in the person of the ruler, it disembodied itself. It was this disembodiment, Rose concluded, that rendered the state itself a fantasy. The state thereafter relied on a ghostly, fantasmatical power no reason could fully account for to enact its authority.[5]

And after emphasizing the state's dependence "upon its subjects' affective investments in fantasy for its legitimation,"[6], Pease describes American exceptionalism as a particularly enduring state of fantasy:

American exceptionalism is a transgenerational state of fantasy and like a family secret it bears the traces of transgenerational trauma. [...]The content of this transgenerational trauma haunted the historical record that could neither be claimed nor completely foreclosed in the state of fantasy. The traumatizing images that insist within American exceptionalism's transgenerational fantasy reach back to events that accompanied the nation's founding [...] and project themselves into the present as images that confront historical narratives with what violates their conditions of representation.[7]

Read with Pease, *Divisadero* is politically perceptive in pinpointing the exact date at which and the representational strategy by which the U.S. as a state whose self-definition had rested on the fantasy of American exceptionalism during the 46-year-period of the cold war, instigated its transformation to a

---

4   Quoted in Donald E. Pease, *The New American Exceptionalism* (Minneapolis and London: U of Minnesota P, 2009) 1-2.
5   Ibid., 3.
6   Ibid., 2.
7   Ibid., 38.

fantasy state of exception in the new post-cold-war world order. At the same time, it addresses both the transgenerational trauma inscribed in and silenced by successive fantasies of American exceptionalism and their conditions of representation. The story of its protagonists Anna, Claire, and Cooper, begins with the following exposition:

By our grandfather's cabin, on the high ridge, opposite a slope of buckeye trees, Claire sits on her horse, wrapped in a thick blanket. She has camped all night and lit a fire in the hearth of that small structure our ancestor built more than a generation ago, and which he lived in like a hermit or some creature, when he first came to this country. He was a self-sufficient bachelor who eventually owned all the land he looked down onto. He married lackadaisically, when he was forty, had one son, and left him this farm along the Petaluma road.Claire moves slowly on the ridge above the two valleys full of morning mist. The coast is to her left. On her right is the journey to Sacramento and the delta towns such as Rio Vista with its populations left over from the Gold Rush. She persuades the horse down through the whiteness alongside crowded trees. She has been smelling smoke for the last twenty minutes, and, on the outskirts of Glen Ellen, she sees the town bar on fire- the local arsonist has struck early when certain it would be empty. She watches from a distance without dismounting. The horse, Territorial, seldom allows a remount; in this he can be fooled only once a day. The two of them, rider and animal, don't fully trust each other, although the horse is my sister Claire's closest ally. She will use every trick not in the book to stop his rearing and bucking. She carries plastic bags of water with her and leans forward and smashes them onto his neck so the animal believes it is his own blood and will calm for a minute. When Claire is on a horse she loses her limp and is in charge of the universe, a centaur. Someday she will meet and marry a centaur. (*Divisadero* 7-8)

At the very beginning of the first chapter, which is entitled "The Orphan," this exposition conjures what Walter Benjamin has called a dialectical image. "Like the opening shot in a montage"[8] this dialectical image amalgamates a whole series of related historical images that are so well-known and so deeply engrained in the fabric of the national imaginary that they can be considered national archetypes. With the "grandfather's cabin" the novel's first sentence evokes the primitive log cabin whose tradition as a national icon for the safe home of civilization amidst the American wilderness can be traced back to authors like Philip Freneau or James Fenimore Cooper. The lone rider on the mountain ridge, wrapped in a blanket and gazing into a distant horizon cites the

---

8 This is Donald Pease's comparison. I use it here for its allusion to the modernist literary techniques of montage and collage, on which Ondaatje's text obviously draws. *The New American Exceptionalism*, 38.

stereotype of the vanishing Indian (whose most popular artistic representation is probably James Fraser's sculpture *The End of the Trail*). In positioning this lone rider on a mountain ridge, dividing the Pacific coast from "the journey to Sacramento and the delta towns" founded during the mid-nineteenth century Gold Rush, Ondaatje's narration unmistakably evokes the idea of the American frontier as a moving concept, and with it the ideology of Manifest Destiny that cast the Anglo-American settlement of the continent from sea to shining sea as a divinely ordained mission. And inscribed in this citation of the historical icons and myths of American progress and exceptionalism is a tradition of aestheticizing artistic compliance with its expansionist trajectory, a symbolic compliance of artists who were instrumental to the silencing of moral doubts in face of the violent Anglo-American appropriation of what would become the territory of the U.S.-American nation.

It is all present in this dense, dialectical image, and yet, the image would not be dialectical, if it were not subtly distorted. To begin with, the most obvious deviation from the iconic stereotypes is the fact that the lone rider is a woman, and this woman is no Native American. She is cast as the sister of a first-person narrator, whose identity is, at this point, indeterminate, and both are presented as descendants of an archetypal male immigrant, who had severed all ties to his genealogical and national origins, and whose speculative vista had propelled his appropriation of what was cast as uninhabited Virgin Land. This mythical concept of Virgin Land is subtly inscribed in the second paragraph of the passage where the dialectical image turns into a full-blown allegory. The myth of Virgin Land resonates in the figure of the female rider of an unruly horse that is named Territorial. Her use of "every trick not in the book" to tame Territorial's wild nature encodes both the patriarchal positing of a symbolic order and this order's exemption of its own law as a cunning strategy of domestication and submission.

Significantly, Claire's trick to tame Territorial, her measure of domestication by deterrence, is a citational, symbolic performance of the physical violence and bloodshed that had been erased from the mythical narrative of Virgin Land. At the same time, the metaphor of representational trickery applies to the fantasy of exceptionalism, by which the cold-war National Security State solicited public consent. And, as Ondaatje's allegory goes on to show us, so adaptable is this fantasy and the symbolic regime that continues to reproduce it, that it can literally incorporate the excessively transgressive and hybrid figure of a female centaur. Given the name of the horse, the figure of the female centaur epitomizes a fantasma that in conjoining woman and animal body feminizes the territory. This incorporation of excessive hybridity into a national fantasy ties in with the unproblematic integration of the figure of the local arsonist into the mythical picture. Neither immigrant hybridity nor ritualized and therefore predictable acts of local protest pose a danger to a nation that has in the second half of the twentieth century reconfigured its mythical founding fantasy of exceptionalism by defining itself at once both as a liberal multicultural nation and a National Security State, a state that formed its political subjects through the cold-war imaginary of permanent threat to its liberal values.

Told in first-person narration, a mythic-historical present and with a striking emphasis on physical presence, this dialectical image is the overture to an ensuing third-person narrative presenting the childhood recollections of Anna, who grew up with Claire and Cooper on a farm in Northern California during the 1970s. Bodies and territory remain central to Anna's fictitious memoir that summons fragmented images of the simple life on an American farm, marked by frugality and hardship, but also by a sense of security derived from land ownership and clearly demarcated boundaries. In fact, the physical presence of land and bodies, the fantasy of their exceptional American amalgamation, is depicted as both origin and ending of the community of Anna's small family.

We soon learn from Anna's narrative that this family is constituted by the same founding acts of violence and extralegal appropriation as the territory they live on. We learn that after Anna's mother had died in childbirth her father, feeling that the small California hospital "owed him a wife" (11), unceremoniously took home with him not only his daughter, but also Claire, a baby girl born in the same week, whose mother, too, had died in childbirth. We also learn that Cooper, who is a little older than the girls and who works as a farmhand for Anna's father, had been taken into the fold of this community after his family had been murdered on the neighboring farm. "The Orphan," the title of the expository chapter, thus applies to all three protagonists. And inscribed in what it depicts as founding acts of violence and appropriation is a libidinal economy resting on that exchange of female bodies that Marcel Mauss and Georges Bataille have described as constitutive of tribal Pacific island communities.

In keeping with these connotations of tribal symbolic economy (and its subtext of eroticism) the family community ends with an eruption of physical violence when the father catches the adolescent Anna and Cooper having sex in the above mentioned grandfather's log cabin. With an impressive scene depicting the annihilating fury of a godlike father figure coming down on his fosterlings who are caught in the act of breaking his law, Ondaatje ends his expository chapter, quite literally, in a storm of violence and bloodshed. And this storm of violence not only invests the novel's allegory on the symbolic economy of the national security state with connotations of archaic drama. This storm of physical violence provides a poetic image for the expulsion of the American Adam from the paradise of territorial fantasy.

Significantly, *Divisadero*'s narration picks up this image of the storm and resolves all doubt as to its political subtext in the second chapter telling the story of Cooper's life after his expulsion from the farm. Depicted as a compulsive risk taker, Cooper becomes a cardsharp, a professional gambler and a member of a group of other gamblers working the casinos of Nevada. This group is shown to be traveling to Vegas where they intend to outperform a rival association of professional gamblers in a kind of gambling showdown. And the novel sets the stage for this gambling showdown in the middle of the second chapter with the following, remarkable passage:

The Gulf War begins at 2:35 a.m. during the early hours of January 17, 1991. But it is just another late afternoon in the casinos of Nevada. The television sets hanging in mid-air that normally replay horse races and football games are running animated illustrations of the American attack. For the three thousand gamblers inhaling piped-in oxygen at the Horseshoe, the war is already a video game, taking place on a fictional planet. The TV screens are locked on mute. There are floor shows, cell-phone hookers, masseurs at work, the click-clacking of chips and nothing interrupts the reality of the casino where the 'eye in the sky' looks down on every hand played on the surfaces of green baize. Simultaneously, in the other desert's night, orange-white explosions and fireballs light up the horizon. By 2:38 U.S. helicopters and stealth bombers are firing missiles and dropping penetration bombs into the city. During the next four days, one of the greatest high-tech massacres of the modern era takes place. The Cobra helicopter, the Warthog, the Spectre, and its twin, the Spooky, loiter over the desert highway and the retreating Iraqi troops, pouring down thermobaric fuel, volatile gasses, and finely powdered explosives, to consume all oxygen so that the bodies below them implode, crushing into themselves. (*Divisadero*, 53)

Ondaatje thus begins his staging of the gambling showdown with a juxtaposition of the casino in the desert of Nevada and Operation Desert Storm, the U.S. military intervention that started the most highly mediated war in American history[9]. According to Donald Pease, the Persian Gulf War was "a transitional object to wean the nation of its cold war mentality"[10] and its unprecedented coverage by U.S. news media "a ruse through which the New World Order had

---

9   See Pease, *The New American Exceptionalism*, 41.
10 Ibid., 45.

taken control of the visual field."[11] And it was not only the extent of the media coverage that was unprecedented, but its technology of electronic animation that transmuted the events covered into a virtual reality. Commenting on the fantasmatic spectacle of the war produced and televised in order to attune the American public to Bush's New World Order, Donald Pease writes:

Positioned within the 'smart bomb's' pinpoint view of their trajectory right up to the point of impact, U.S. televisual publics were deprived of the critical distance necessary to adopt a standpoint on the war. Having been deprived of access to any facts other than this media simulation, these spectators were instead embedded in the unfolding of this spectacle, as part of its production.[12]

The above cited passage from Ondaatje's novel shows exactly this embeddedness, and yet, the spectators in the casino are not spectators at all. As gamblers in a Vegas casino they are absorbed in their own virtual reality, to which the broadcasting of the Gulf War media simulation adds nothing but background noise. The passage not only juxtaposes the virtual reality of the casino in the Nevada desert with the aestheticized spectacle of operation Desert Storm, but ingeniously interweaves these topoi in a chiastic montage that allows the dizzying experience of what Slavoj Zizek has called "the desert of the real."[13] A poetic sleight of hand, the chiasmus in this passage mimics the fictionalization of reality by the aesthetic trickery of a political discourse that erased bodies and their mutilation from its representation of a war staged to replace one state fantasy by another. The chiastic entanglement of bodies that need to be kept alive by piped-in oxygen with bodies, crushed and suffocated by high-tech warfare consuming all oxygen, exposes at once both this artificial erasure of bodies from political speech and its speculative formation of political subjects at the historical moment when American leaders officially inaugurated a New World Order. A highly aestheticized comment on the state's aestheticization of the Gulf War, the passage artfully plays with presence and absence, simultaneously highlighting the absence of the body of the sovereign ruler from modern political speech and the disembodiment of electronic signs as the unprecedented epistemological condition of its postmodern variety.

At the same time, it taps, with its casino setting, the historical American discourse on gambling and speculation already mentioned in this study in the chapter on *Strange Days*. Responding to the growing popularity of stock market

---

11 Ibid., 43.
12 *The New American Exceptionalism*, 42-43.
13 *Welcome to the Desert of the Real* (London/New York: Verso, 2002).

speculation in late-nineteenth/early-twentieth-century America, this discourse reconceptualized the figure of the pioneer and frontiersman as a gambling risk taker, a speculator who, in the hope of getting something for nothing, perceived of economic contingencies as chances of democratic inclusion. In the dialectical image summoned by Ondaatje's chiastic passage, this idea of democratic inclusion translates into a large room crammed with masses of gamblers kept under control by electronic surveillance and brainwash. The text suggests that the experience of presence that had been associated with the decidedly physical thrill of gambling and speculation has been replaced by the ghostly elusiveness marking the semiotics of electronic data transfer. And what is left of democratic inclusion and participation in the desert of the real engendered by this semiotics is an uncritical mass indulging in presence effects rather than making sense of their surroundings, an uncritical mass, united in a new state of fantasy.

With these corresponding dialectical images, the first section of *Divisadero* not only astutely identifies the official staging of the Persian Gulf War in 1991 as the historical turning point marking the American inauguration of a globalized political order. These images showcase the official introduction of a political aesthetics of risk and speculation while subtly relating its unprecedented use of disembodied signs to the historical disembodiment of modern sovereign authority that, according to Jacqueline Rose and Donald Pease, "rendered the state itself a fantasy."[14] 'United in a state of fantasy' hence applies to the long-standing tradition of the entanglement of political and aesthetic practices and the national collectivity of political subjects thus produced, but the phrase also points to the paradox persistence of national sovereign authority in the era of global economic liberalization.

At a different level, 'united in a state of fantasy' fittingly describes the compliance with the doctrine of American exceptionalism of cultural institutions, historians and literary scholars working in the academic field of American Studies. According to Donald Pease, these scholars' "principles of selection of the historical events that would be allowed representation within the historical record"[15] have over a long period contributed to the fantasy of American exceptionalism. It is worth noting, against this background, that *Divisadero's* narrative discourse consists of the speculative conjectures of Anna, the novel's focal protagonist, who is depicted as having become a writer and literary scholar. Situated in France, where she investigates the life and work of a fictitious French poet, Anna, at the same time, fantasizes about and imagines the lives of her foster siblings Claire and Cooper. And time and again, throughout

---

14 *The New American Exceptionalism*, 3.
15 *The New American Exceptionalism*, 11.

her speculative narration, she emphasizes the importance of her ability as a writer to adopt different voices and the privilege of a viewpoint that is detached from the American context. Referring to her home address in San Francisco, Anna, at one point, roughly in the middle of the novel, explains: "I come from Divisadero Street. Divisadero from the Spanish word for division [...]. Or it might derive from the word *divisar*, meaning 'to gaze at something from a distance.' (142)The title of Michael Ondaatje's novel might thus not only reflect the many doublings and lines of division in its plot, but encode and advocate practices of reading and writing that are uncompromised by ideological fantasies.

5.2 Paratexts

That the notion of ideologically uncontaminated practices of cultural signification is a utopian fantasy at best becomes particularly visible in the paratextual analyses of the study. Given at the beginning of each analytical chapter, these readings suggest that the regulation and the politics of authorship effective in the authors' respective fields of artistic production generate contingent scripts that are informed by economic constraints as well as struggles over recognition along the lines of gender and race. These scripts seem to produce a drive for authorial signature that is, at the same time, undermined and constrained by discursive and/or institutional taboos and a demand for identification with the respective field's political and/or economic interests. The hazards arising from such contingent scripts are, as the examples of Bigelow and Lai show, of an aesthetic *and* a political nature.

While the analysis of *Strange Days*' subtexts proves the political message of the film to be consistent with its brilliant aesthetics of risk, and while its aesthetics of risk are shown to tie in with a perceptive, self-referential discourse on the significance of medial representation to risk as a framework of governance, it also shows that the end of the film compromises its complex message with disappointingly conventional imagery. In interpreting this compromised ending as an aesthetic risk not taken that translated into a political risk not taken, the chapter concludes that it was, ultimately, the efficacy of the Hollywood middlebrow-machine and the inconsistencies of its auteur politics that conditioned the failure of Bigelow's film in terms of both economic success and aesthetic recognition.

The chapter on *Salt Fish Girl* comes to a similar conclusion. Concerned with Larissa Lai's complex position as a creative writer, political activist and prolific academic in the era of institutionalized Canadian multiculturalism, the reading of her theoretical writings suggests that this position entails ideological double binds resulting in a rigid understanding of authorship and a demand for authorial control that complicates and curtails the aesthetic potential of her fictional text. Reading *Salt Fish Girl* against the grain of the author's epitextual navigation, the subsequent analysis traces in the novel's speculation on the risks of a biologized subjectivity at a near-future North American Pacific Rim, a discourse on natural science, its history and its recodifications of alterity. But the subtle and perceptive critique of male-coded scientific modes of signification articulated in the epigraph and the expository chapters, and the astute extrapolation of the risks construed by an alliance of molecular biopolitics and biocapital in the futurist strand are shown to be somewhat inconsistent with the celebration of a post-human, transgender monstrosity at the end of the novel. The meta-fictional claim to an empowerment of alternative speculations on risk and risk politics thus turns out to be similarly compromised by ideological scripts as the critique conveyed by *Strange Days*' intricate aesthetics of risk.

A brief sketch of the contingencies that mark the field of Asian American literature, placed at the beginning of the second analytical chapter, shows Karen T. Yamashita's position in that field to be similarly precarious. Different from Larissa Lai, however, the Japanese American author foregoes all epitextual navigation and relies on the efficacy of her novel's aesthetics. In order to capture Yamashita's aesthetic embracing of the political risks construed by the ideological controversies between Asian American critics over French Theory, the chapter takes recourse to the sociological concept of edgework. It argues that edgework – the deliberate encounter with a hazardous boundary condition that requires skillful control – applies to the protagonists' handling of risks construed by political-economic restructuring in *Tropic of Orange*'s plot, and is, at the same time, an apt description of the novel's bold aesthetics. At plot level, edgework signifies the protagonists' skillful tackling of the boundary conditions established by internal colonization, border control, the bankerization of life and deceptive representations enabled by the disembodied semiotics of electronic media.

This medial discourse, at the same time, proves to be a self-reflexive meditation on literary representation. Its highly allegoric quality could be shown to be taken to extremes in the novel's 'cheesy' staging of a medial spectacle, and to come full circle in an allegory of reading that ultimately teases out a desire for presence. In these allegories, the text not only criticizes the epistemological conditions that enable the confidence game of de-territorialized capitalism; its performative oscillation between a shrill and 'distasteful' representation of presence and the production of meaning by a multiply layered textuality stages and negotiates questions of epistemology and ontology that have recently become pertinent to the call for an ontological turn in the humanities. The close reading of Yamashita's literary edgework, however, finds evidence that the author remains in control of her novel by way of a consistent aesthetics of risk, and, unintimidated by discursive and institutional taboos, does not renounce the "hermeneutic maximalism"[16] of "endless interpretation."[17]. The balancing act of Yamashita's precarious aesthetics in *Tropic of Orange* demonstrates that a literary negotiation of risk, unfazed by the contradictory regulation of authorship in a particular field, results in a consistent, complex text that can, at the same time, tackle this very regulation. The acknowledgement of Yamashita's work by a scholar such as Jinqui Ling (as expressed in Ling's recent publication[18] entirely focusing on her novels), allows to conclude that consistent politics and aesthetics even effectuate changes in the contingent prescriptions of a particular field of production.

From within and against these rigid systems of regulation, the speculative fictions analyzed in this study are convincing in their representation of risk and speculation as new aesthetic and epistemological categories that define both discourses of works of fiction and discourses of politics and science emerging at the frontier of capitalist development at the dawn of the 'Pacific Century.' In historicizing risk as a dispositif and a political rationality, delineating the calculating operations of its underlying logic of speculation, and exposing the disembodied semiotics of electronic information transfer as its unprecedented medial condition, these speculative fictions propose a poetics of risk and speculation and outline its distinctive paradigms. Among these paradigms allegory appears particularly significant, because its challenges the order of discourse and enacts a self-reflective meditation on the relation between sign and referent, representation and presence. As a mode of 'other speaking,' oscillating between practices of cultural signification and the world of objects, it both reflects and responds to the increasingly complicated relation between epistemology and ontology.

---

16 Gumbrecht, *Production of Presence*, 55.
17 Ibid., xv.
18 *Across Meridians: History and Figuration in Karen T. Yamashita's Transnational Novels* (Stanford: Stanford UP, 2012). Although the book seems to focus on the hemispheric trajectory of Yamashita's novels, it is worth noting that Jinqui Ling, one of the scholars most skeptical of the recourse to poststructuralist aesthetics in Asian American literature, acknowledges the aesthetic and political significance of her work.

5.3 Contexts

This significance of allegory to a poetics of risk and speculation points to a critical potential exceeding a critique of neoliberal politics at the Pacific Rim and its reconfigurations of race, class, and gender. Besides allowing to adress the claims of a non-hermeneutic field eager to establish a non-critical philology that would revel in a speculative, para-religious *Erleben* of auratic substance, a poetics that theorizes the operations of speculation can provide the theoretical framework to assess from a philologist vantage point the advent of a speculative turn in continental philosophy. In fact, Hans Ulrich Gumbrecht's call for an ontological turn has much in common with the new currents in recent philosophy that "depart from the text-centered hermeneutic models of the past and engage in daring speculations about the nature of reality itself."[19] While not representing a unified philosophical movement, speculative realists and materialists of all stripes are inspired by Quentin Meillassoux's book *After Finitude* [20] and share his critique of "correlationalism," defined by the author as "the idea according to which we only ever have access to the correlation between thinking and being, and never to either term considered apart from the other."[21]

Accordingly, the core thinkers of speculative realism/materialism reject as the origin of correlationalism both Kant's post-critical philosophy and what they call the philosophies of access that developed in its wake for renouncing "any knowledge beyond how things appear to us."[22] Aiming to "grasp an object 'in itself', in isolation from its relation to the subject,"[23] and turning against "the reduction of philosophy to an analysis of texts," speculative materialists find themselves in the demanding position of having to *think* about "the nature of reality independent of thought or language."[24] It is at this point, i.e. the point at which speculative materialists seem to be trapped in "the sticky network"[25] of

---

19 Levi Bryant, Nick Srnicek, and Graham Harman, eds., *The Speculative Turn: Continental Materialism and Realism* (Melbourne: re.press, 2011) cover text.
20 *After Finitude: An Essay on the Necessity of Contingency* (London: Continuum, 2008).
21 Ibid., 5.
22 Levi Bryant, Nick Srnicek, and Graham Harman, "Towards a Speculative Philosophy," *The Speculative Turn: Continental Materialism and Realism* (Melbourne: re.press, 2011) 1-18,4.
23 Meillassoux, *After Finitude*, 5.
24 Bryant, Srnicek, and Harman, "Towards a Speculative Philosophy, 4.
25 This is Levi Bryant's term. See "Sticky Networks," *Larvalsubjects* (4 May 2010): Web. 4 Oct 2012. <http://larvalsubjects.wordpress.com/2010/05/04/sticky-networks/>. Its polemical subtext becomes much clearer when read with Aaron F.

'correlationalism,' that the editors of *The Speculative Turn* introduce their understanding of speculation, and in the process try to downplay the polemical nature and the eliminative implications of their project:

> This activity of 'speculation' may be cause for concern amongst some readers, for it might suggest a return to pre-critical philosophy, with its dogmatic belief in the powers of pure reason. The speculative turn, however, is not an outright rejection of these critical advances; instead, it comes from a recognition of their inherent limitations. Speculation in this sense aims at something 'beyond' the critical and linguistic turns. As such it recuperates the pre-critical sense of speculation as a concern with the Absolute, while also taking into account the undeniable progress that is due to the labour of critique.[26]

Similar to Gumbrecht who, anticipating critical reactions to his project of doing away with the prevalence of meaning in the humanities, speaks of practices of reception that would oscillate between meaning effects and presence effects, the editors of *The Speculative Turn* want to take the edge off their scathing critique of the work of philosophers "from Hegel to Heidegger to Derrida" with a polite nod in the direction of those who still believe in the critical potential of hermeneutics and Kantian epistemology. The similarity between these rhetorical moves is indicative of other parallels, although there clearly are differences between various schools of speculative realism with their shared desire for a philosophical re-turn to "properly ontological questions,"[27] and Gumbrecht's call for an ontological turn in the humanities (e.g. with its emphasis on a Heideggerian being-in-the-world, his metaphysical version of ontology[28] would

---

    Hodges's succinct definition of materialism as a "doctrine that accords some form of priority to matter or material processes," yet is confronted with the "problem that bare indeterminate matter is unthinkable in the strict sense: matter can only *be* insofar as it is formed. Form must therefore be presupposed as both logically and ontologically prior to matter. The matter in an individual being cannot serve as ground for that being's essential determination because matter, when stripped of all predicates, is wholly indeterminate, anything predicable therefore is what it is because of its form." "Martin Hägglund's Speculative Materialism," *CR: The Centennial Review* 9.1 (Spring 2009): 87-106. Web. 30 Jun 2012. < http://muse.jhu.edu/journals/ncr/v0009/9.1.hodges.html> 92.

26 Bryant, Srnicek, and Harman, "Towards a Speculative Philosophy," 4.
27 Ibid.
28 In delineating Meillassoux's distinction between metaphysical and non-metaphysical speculation, Adrian Johnston writes that, for Meillassoux, "Metaphysics is defined as a philosophical position combining an epistemology of access to the asubjective

be considered too anthropocentric by speculative realists.). Besides religious undertones, the most problematic position that both turns to a non-critical ontology seem to share is the rejection of the relevance of any notion of subjectivity as contingent upon cultural, political, and historical conditions (while Gumbrecht's alignment with Heidegger posits the absolute being and thus an absolute, universal subject, speculative realists, in "speculating once more about the nature of reality independently of thought and of humanity more generally," posit an absolute reality).

It becomes obvious, at this point, that speculation acquires in the discourse of speculative realism/materialism a meaning far from the one underlying the present study. It also differs decisively from the one inherent to the call for an ontological turn in the humanities. While, in speculative realist terms, Gumbrecht's subjective *Erleben* of being ultimately amounts to a form of metaphysical speculation, Meillassoux proposes for speculative realism/ materialism a non-metaphysical variety of speculation. Summing up this concept of non-metaphysical speculation, Adrian Johnston criticizes: "For Meillassouxian speculation, with its denial of the principle of sufficient reason, absolute being in and of itself involves no necessity, resting on the baseless base of the ultimate fact of a brute contingency."[29] The "daring speculations about the nature of reality itself," announced by the cover text of *The Speculative Turn*, hence rely on the presupposition of a radical contingency that allows for a non-critical musing about the existence of an asubjective absolute, including "the possibility of a 'God still yet to come.'"[30]

Clearly, this is an understanding of contingency and speculation starkly contrasting the concept of a contingency that is filtered by the calculating operations of a political rationality. It is, above all, an understanding of speculation and contingency in which subjectivity, culture, politics, and history have no place. Speculation on radical contingency certainly serves the ends of a

---

absolute with an ontology in which some being thereby accessed is necessary in the sense of necessarily existent (early modern Continental rationalism with its substance-metaphysics exemplifies this position)." "Hume's Revenge: A Dieu, Meillassoux," *The Speculative Turn: Continental Materialism and Realism* (Melbourne: re.press, 2011) 84-113, 94.

29 Johnston, "Hume's Revenge," 94.

30 Meillassoux qtd. in Johnston "Hume's Revenge," 94. Johnston justifiably problematizes how Meillassoux's "divinology" (Meillassoux's term) goes together with his "polemics against the new fideism of 'post-secular" thought sheltering under the cover of post-Kantian epistemological skepticism regarding claims about the objective nature of being an sich."

self-appointed philosophical avant-garde struggling to overcome various forms of modern idealism and their purported

> preoccupation with such issues as death and finitude, an aversion to science, a focus on language, culture, and subjectivity to the detriment of material factors, an anthropocentric stance towards nature, a relinquishing of the search for absolutes, and an acquiescence to the specific conditions of our historical thrownness.[31]

This list of the alleged shortcomings of the 'philosophies of access' already corroborates a characterization of materialism as an essentially interventionist endeavor that is "just this negative relation to some prevailing tradition, now construed as idealism."[32] But the quality of materialism as an always negatively evoked "polemic stance" becomes fully obvious when the editors of *The Speculative Turn* argue that the "lack of genuine and effective political action in continental philosophy "is a result of "the 'cultural turn' taken by Marxism, and the increased focus on textual and ideological critique at the expense of the economic realm."[33] How speculation on the existence of objects, unmediated by and independent of human thought, could prepare the ground for political action remains as obscure in this discourse as the question of what this philosophical turn to speculation, radical contingency and absolute reality entails for the status of cultural artifacts and humanist critique. While an epistemology that would allow to conceptualize how the materiality of signs and artifacts affects the bodies of readers and audiences is certainly needed to supplement and enrich practices of close reading and their ethics of humanist critique, a philosophy that posits the irrelevance of epistemology altogether puts at stake the cultural significance of art and the academic disciplines that are dedicated to its analysis.

---

31 Bryant, Srnicek, and Harman, "Towards a Speculative Philosophy," 4.
32 Aaron F. Hodges, "Martin Hägglund's Speculative Materialism," 92.
33 Bryant, Srnicek, and Harman, "Towards a Speculative Philosophy," 4.

6 Works Cited

Agamben, Giorgio. *Homo Sacer: Sovereign Power and Bare Life*. Stanford: Stanford UP, 1998.
Agamben, Giorgio. *Bartleby oder die Kontingenz*. Berlin: Merve, 1998. 69-72.
Agamben, Giorgio. "No to Bio-Political Tattooing." *Le Monde* (10 January 2004): Web. 04 May 2011 <*http://www.ratical.org/ratville/CAH/total Control.html*>.
Agamben, Giorgio. *State of Exception*. Chicago/London: U of Chicago P, 2005.
Ahmed, Sara. *Strange Encounters: Embodied Others in Post-Coloniality*. London: Routledge, 2000.
Ahmed, Sara. *The Cultural Politics of Emotion*. Edinburgh: Edinburgh UP, 2004.
Altman, Rick. *Film/Genre*. London: BFI, 1999.
Amoore, Louise, and Marieke de Goede. "Introduction: Governing by Risk in the War on Terror." *Risk and the War on Terror*. Ed. Louise Amoore and Marieke de Goede. London and New York: Routledge, 2008. 5-19.
Antonello, Pierpaolo. "The Materiality of Presence: Notes on Hans Ulrich Gumbrecht's Theoretical Project." *Producing Presences: Branching Out From Gumbrecht's Work*. Ed. Victor Mendes. Dartmouth: U of Massachusetts P, 2007.15-26.
Appadurai, Arjun. *Fear of Small Numbers: An Essay on the Geography of Anger*. Durham: Duke UP, 2006.
Arnoldi, Jakob. *Risk: An Introduction*. Cambridge, UK: Polity, 2009.
Aradau, Claudia, and Rens van Munster."Taming the Future: The Dispositif of Risk in the War on Terror." *Risk and the War on Terror*. Eds. Louise Amoore and Marieke de Goede. London and New York: Routledge, 2008. 23-40.
Atwood, Margaret. "Interview with Margaret Atwood on her Novel *The Handmaid's Tale*." *Reader's Companion to the Handmaid's Tale by Margaret*

Atwood. (20 May 1998): Web. 5 Mar. 2012. <http://www.random house.com/resources/bookgroup/handmaidstale_bgc. html#interview>.
Atwood, Margaret. "The Queen of Quinkdom." *The New York Review of Books.* 49.14 (26 Sept. 2002): Web. 5 Mar. 2012. <http://www.nybooks.com/articles /archives/2002/sep/26/the-queen-of-quinkdom/?>.
Baker, Tom, and Jonathan Simon. "Embracing Risk." *Embracing Risk: The Changing Culture of Insurance and Responsibility.* Eds. Tom Baker and Jonathan Simon. Chicago: U of Chicago P, 2002. 1-25.
Baecker, Dirk. "Volkszählung." *Kapitalismus als Religion.* Ed. Dirk Baecker. Berlin: Kadmos, 2002.
Barthes, Roland. *Camera Lucida: Reflections on Photography.* New York: Hill and Wang, 1981.
Baudrillard, Jean. *Simulations.* New York: Semiotexte, 1983.
Baudrillard, Jean. "The Ecstacy of Communication." *The Ecstacy of Communication.* Ed. Sylvere Lotringer. New York: Semiotexte, 1988. 11-27.
Baudrillard, Jean. "Seduction, or the Superficial Abyss." *The Ecstacy of Communication.* Ed. Sylvere Lotringer. New York, Semiotexte: 1988. 57-75.
Barnouw, Eric. *Tube of Plenty: The Evolution of American Television.* New York: Oxford UP, 1975.
Beck, Ulrich. *World Risk Society.* Cambridge, UK: Polity, 1999.
Becker-Leckrone, Megan. *Julia Kristéva and Literary Theory: (Transitions).* London: Palgrave, 2005.
Benjamin, Walter. "Capitalism as Religion." *The Frankfurt School on Religion: Key Writings by the Major Thinkers.* Ed. Eduardo Mendieta. New York: Routledge, 2005. 259-262.
Berrettini, Mark. "Can 'We All' Get Along? Social Difference, the Future, and *Strange Days*." *Camera Obscura 50* 17.2 (2002):155 -189.
Bourdieu, Pierre. "The Market of Symbolic Goods." *The Field of Cultural Production: Essays on Art and Literature.* Columbia: Columbia UP, 1984. 1-34.
Bourdieu, Pierre. *The Rules of Art: Genesis and Structure of the Literary Field.* Cambridge, UK and Malden, MA: Polity, 2010.
Brandt, Stefan L. "The City as Liminal Space: Urban Visuality and Aesthetic Experience in Postmodern U.S. Literature and Cinema." *Amerikastudien / American Studies* 54.4 (2009): 553-581.
Braidotti, Rosi. "Cyberteratologies: Female Monsters Negotiate the Other's Participation in the Far Future." *Envisioning the Future: Science Fiction and the Next Millennium.* Ed. Marlene S. Barr. Middletown: Wesleyan UP, 2003. 146-171.

Braidotti, Rosi. *Transpositions: On Nomadic Ethics*. Cambridge, UK: Polity Press, 2006.

Braidotti, Rosi. "Locating Deleuze's Eco-Philosophy between *Bio/Zoe*-Power and Necro-Politics." *Deleuze and Law: Forensic Futures*. Eds. Rosi Braidotti, et al. Basingstoke: Palgrave Macmillan, 2009. 96-116.

Brenkman, John. "Extreme Criticism." *What's Left of Theory: New Work on the Politics of Literary Theory*. Eds. Judith Butler, et al. New York: Routledge, 2000.114-136.

Brockman, John. *The Third Culture: Beyond the Scientific Revolution*. New York: Touchstone, 1995.

Brown, Wendy. "American Nightmare: Neoliberalism, Neoconservatism, and De-Democratization." *Political Theory* 34.6 (2006): 690 -714.

Bryant, Levi, Nick Srnicek, and Graham Harman, eds. *The Speculative Turn: Continental Materialism and Realism*. Melbourne: re.press, 2011.

Bryant, Levi, Nick Srnicek, and Graham Harman, "Towards a Speculative Philosophy," *The Speculative Turn: Continental Materialism and Realism*. Melbourne: re.press, 2011. 1-18.

Bryant, Levi. "Sticky Networks." *Larvalsubjects* (4 May 2010): Web. 4 Oct 2012. <http://larvalsubjects.wordpress.com/2010/05/04/sticky-networks/>.

Burns, Edward. "Foreword: Useful Knowledge about *Useful Knowledge*." (1988). *Useful Knowledge*. Barrytown, NY: Station Hill, 2001. vii-xvii.

Burnham, Michelle. "Trade, Time, and Risk in Pacific Travel Writing." *Early American Literature* 46.3 (2011): 425-447.

Buscombe, Edward. "Ideas of Authorship." *Auteurs and Authorship: A Film Reader*. Ed. Barry Keith Grant. Malden, et al.: Blackwell, 2008. 76-92.

Butler, Judith. "Merely Cultural," *Social Text* 52/53 Queer Transexions of Race, Nation, and Gender (1997): 265-277.

Butler, Judith. *Precarious Life: The Powers of Mourning and Violence*. London and New York: Verso, 2004.

Canguilhem, Georges. *Knowledge of Life*. 1965. New York: Fordham UP, 2008.

Carr, Brian. "*Strange Days* and the Subject of Mobility." *Camera Obscura 50* 17.2 (2002): 191 -217.

Castel, Robert. "From Dangerousness to Risk." *The Foucault Effect: Studies in Governmentality*. Eds. Graham Burchell, et al. Chicago: U of Chicago P, 1991.

Chomsky, Noam. "Notes on NAFTA: The Masters of Mankind." *Juarez: the Laboratory of Our Future*. Ed. Charles Bowden. Hong Kong: Everbest, 1998. 13-20.

Chow, Rey. *The Protestant Ethnic and the Spirit of Capitalism*. New York: Columbia UP, 2002.
Chu, Seo-Young. *Do Metaphors Dream of Literal Sleep: A Science Fictional Theory of Representation*. Cambridge, MA, and London: Harvard UP, 2010.
Chuh, Kandice. "Of Hemispheres and Other Spheres: Navigating Karen Tei Yamashita's Literary World." *American Literary History* (2006): 618 – 637.
Classen, Constanze. "The Breath of God: Sacred Histories of Scent." *The Smell Culture Reader*. Ed. Jim Drobnick. Oxford/New York: Berg, 2006. 375-390.
Clay, Karen. "Mexican California: Trade, Institutions and Law." *Studies in the Economic History of the Pacific Rim*. Eds. Sally M. Miller, et al. London: Routledge, 1997. 197-209.
Cohn, Dorrit. "Signposts of Fictionality: A Narratological Perspective." *The Distinction of Fiction*. Baltimore and London: Johns Hopkins UP, 1999. 109-131.
Coleman, Mathew. "U.S. Statecraft and the U.S.-Mexico Border as Security/Economy Nexus." *Geopolitics*. Vol. II. Ed. Klaus Dodds. London, et al.: Sage, 2009. 209-235.
Cook, David A. "Auteur Cinema and the 'Film Generation' in 1970s Hollywood." *The New American Cinema*. Ed. Jon Lewis. Durham, N.C.: Duke UP, 1998.
Corbin, Alain. *The Foul and the Fragrant: Odor and the French Social Imagination*. Leamington Spa, et al.: Berg, 1986.
Corrigan, Timothy. "Auteurs and the New Hollywood." *The New American Cinema*. Ed. Jon Lewis. Durham, N.C.: Duke UP, 1998.
Cronon, William, George Miles, and Jay Gitlin. *Under the Open Sky: Rethinking America's Western Past*. New York: Norton, 1992.
Cumings, Bruce. "Rimspeak: Or, The Discourse of the Pacific Rim," *What Is In A Rim: Critical Perspectives on the Pacific Region Idea*. Ed. Arif Dirlik. Lanham: Rowman and Littlefield, 1998. 53-72.
Cunningham, Hilary. "Transnational Politics at the Edges of Sovereignty: Social Movements, Crossings and the State at the U.S.-Mexico Border." *Global Networks* 1 (4): 369-387.
Davis, Mike. *Ecology of Fear: Los Angeles and the Imagination of Disaster*. New York: Vintage, 1999.
Davis, Mike. *City of Quartz: Excavating the Future in Los Angeles*. London: Verso, 2006.
Dean, Mitchell. *Governmentality: Power and Rule in Modern Society*. 2nd ed. London, et al.: Sage, 2010.

Deleuze, Gilles. "Postskriptum über die Kontrollgesellschaften." *Le Autre Journal* 1 (Mai 1990):Web. 20 Jul.2011 <www.nadir.org/nadir/archiv/netzkritik/postskriptum.html>.

Deleuze, Gilles. "He Stuttered." *Essays Critical and Clinical*. Minneapolis: U of Minnesota P, 1997. 107-114.

Deleuze, Gilles and Felix Guattari. *A Thousand Plateaus: Capitalism and Schizophrenia*. Minneapolis: U of Minnesota P, 1991.

DeLillo, Don."In the Ruins of the Future." *The Guardian*. (22 Dec. 2001): Web. 5 Jan. 2012. <www.guardian.co.uk/books/2001/dec/22/fiction.dondelillo/>1-7.

De Certeau, Michel. "Montaigne's 'Of Cannibals: The Savage 'I'." *Heterologies: Discourse on the Other*. London: U of Minnesota P, 1997. 67-79.

De Man, Paul. "Allegory." *Allegories of Reading: Figural Language in Rousseau, Nietzsche, Rilke, and Proust*. New Haven and London: Yale UP, 1979. 188-220.

De Man, Paul. "The Rhetoric of Temporality." *Blindness and Insight: Essays in the Rhetoric of Contemporary Criticism*. Abingdon: Routledge, 2005. 187-228.

Derrida, Jacques. "The Law of Genre." *Critical Inquiry* 7.1 (1980): 55-81.

Derrida, Jacques. *The Truth in Painting*. Chicago and London: U of Chicago P, 1987.

De Toro, Alfonso. "Jenseits von Postmoderne und Postkolonialität: Materialien zu einem Modell der Hybridität und des Körpers als transrelationalem, transversalem und transmedialem Wissenschaftskonzept." *Räume der Hybridität. Postkoloniale Konzepte in Theorie und Literatur*. Eds. Christof Hamann and Cornelia Sieber. Hildesheim: Olms, 2002. 15-52.

Dirlik, Arif. "The Asia-Pacific Idea." *What Is In A Rim?: Critical Perspectives on the Pacific Region Idea*. Ed. Arif Dirlik. Lanham: Rowman and Littlefield, 1998. 15-36.

Dirlik, Arif. "There's More in the Rim than Meets the Eye." *What Is in a Rim?: Critical Perspectives on the Pacific Region Idea.?* Ed. Arif Dirlik. Lanham, Rowman and Littlefield, 1998. 352 -369.

Doane, Mary Ann. *Femmes Fatale: Feminism, Film Theory, Psychoanalysis*. London / New York: Routledge, 1991.

Drobnick, Jim. "Introduction: Olfactocentrism." *The Smell Culture Reader*. Ed. Jim Drobnick. Oxford/New York: Berg, 2006. 1-17.

Donzelot. Jacques. "The Mobilization of Society." *The Foucault Effect: Studies in Governmentality*. Eds. Graham Burchell, et al.. Chicago: U of Chicago P, 1991. 169-180.

Douglas, Mary, and Aaron Wildavsky. *Risk and Culture: An Essay on the Selection of Technical and Environmental Dangers*. Berkeley and Los Angeles: U of California P, 1982.

English, James F. *The Economy of Prestige: Prizes, Awards, and the Circulation of Cultural Value*. Cambridge, MA, and London, UK: Harvard UP, 2005.

Esteve, Mary. *The Aesthetics and Politics of the Crowd in American Literature*. Cambridge, UK: Cambridge UP, 2003.

Ewald, Francois. "Two Infinities of Risk." *The Politics of Everyday Fear*. Ed. Brian Massumi. Minneapolis/London: University of Minnesota Press, 1993.221-228.

Ewald, Francois. "Insurance and Risk." *The Foucault Effect: Studies in Governmentality*. Eds. Graham Burchell, et al.. Chicago: U of Chicago P, 1991. 197-210.

Fabian, Johannes. *Time and the Other: How Anthropology Makes its Object*. New York: Columbia UP, 1983.

Fiske, John. "British Cultural Studies and Television." *Channels of Discourse: Television and Contemporary Criticism*. Ed. Robert C. Allen. Chapel Hill and London: U of North Carolina P, 1987. 254-289.

Flynn, Dennis O., and Arturo Giraldez. "The Pacific Rim's Past Deserves a Future." *Studies in the Economic History of the Pacific Rim*. Eds. Sally Miller, et al. London: Routledge, 1998. 1-18.

Foucault, Michel. *The Birth of the Clinic: An Archaeology of Medical Perception*. 1963. New York:Vintage, 1994.

Foucault, Michel. *The Order of Things: An Archaeology of the Human Sciences.*1970. New York: Vintage, 1994.

Foucault, Michel. *Discipline and Punish: The Birth of the Prison*. 1975. New York: Vintage, 1995.

Foucault, Michel. *Abnormal: Lectures at the College de France 1974-1975*. New York: Picador, 2003.

Foucault, Michel. "Politics and Reason." *Politics, Philosophy, Culture: Interviews and Other Writings, 1977 -1984*. Ed. Lawrence D. Kritzman. New York: Routledge, 1988. 57 -85.

Foucault, Michel. *Security, Territory, Population*: *Lectures at the College de France 1977-1978*. London: Palgrave, 2007.

Foucault, Michel. *The Birth of Biopolitics: Lectures at the College de France 1978-1979*. New York: Picador, 2010.

Frank, Joseph. "Spatial Form in Modern Literature." 1945. *The Idea of Spatial Form*. New Brunswick and London: Rutgers UP, 1991. 4-66.

Frank, Joseph. "Spatial Form: An Answer to Critics." *The Idea of Spatial Form*. New Brunswick and London: Rutgers UP, 1991. 67-106.

Franken, Claudia. *Gertrude Stein, Writer and Thinker*. Münster: LIT-Verlag, 2000.

Fraser, Nancy. "Heterosexism, Misrecognition, and Capitalism: A Response to Judith Butler." *New Left Review* a. 228 (1998): 140-150.

Freud, Sigmund. *Civilization and its Discontent. The Standard Edition of the Complete Psychological Works of Sigmund Freud*. Vol. 21. London: Hogarth Press 1953-74.

Fuss, Diana. *Essentially Speaking: Feminism, Nature, and Difference*. New York, and London: Routledge, 1987.

Gallop, Jane. *The Daughter's Seduction: Feminism and Psychoanalysis*. Ithaka, NY: Cornell UP, 1982.

Gell, Alfred. "Magic, Perfume, Dream... ." *The Smell Culture Reader*. Ed. Jim Drobnick. Oxford/New York: Berg, 2006. 400-410.

Genette, Gerard. *Paratexts: Thresholds of Interpretation*. Cambridge: Cambridge UP, 1997.

Giddens, Anthony. *The Consequences of Modernity*. Stanford: Stanford UP, 1990.

Giles, Paul. "The Deterritorialization of American Literature." *Shades of the Planet: American Literature as World Literature*. Eds. Wai Chee Dimmock and Lawrence Buell. Princeton: Princeton UP, 2007. 39-61.

Goodman, Nelson. *Ways of Worldmaking*. Indianapolis: Hackett, 1978.

Gordon, Colin. "Governmental Rationality: An Introduction." *The Foucault Effect: Studies in Governmentality*. Eds. Graham Burchell, Colin Gordon, and Peter Miller. Chicago: U of Chicago P, 1991.1 -51.

Gormley, Paul. "Trashing Whiteness: *Pulp Fiction, Se7en, Strange Days* and Articulating Affect." *Angelaki: Journal of the Theoretical Humanities* 6.1 (2011): 155-171.

Goux, Jean Joseph. *Symbolic Economies*. Ithaka, NY: Cornell UP, 1990.

Goux, Jean Joseph. "Cash, Check, or Charge?" *The New Economic Criticism: Studies at the Intersection of Literature and Economics*. Eds. Martha Woodmansee and Mark Osteen London and New York: Routledge, 1999.114-128.

Graham, Mark. "Queer Smells." *The Smell Culture Reader*. Ed. Jim Drobnick. Oxford, UK/New York: Berg, 2006. 305-319.

Grant, Gary Keith. "Man's Favorite Sport?: The Action Films of Kathryn Bigelow." *Auteurs and Authorship: A Film Reader*. Ed. Barry Keith Grant. Malden, et al.: Blackwell, 2008. 280-291.

Grosz, Elizabeth. *Volatile Bodies: Toward a Corporeal Feminism*. Bloomington and Indianapolis: Indiana UP, 1994.

Gumbrecht, Hans Ulrich. "Epilogue: Untenable Positions." *Streams of Cultural Capital*. Eds. David Palumbo-Liu and Hans Ulrich Gumbrecht.Stanford: Stanford UP, 1993. 249-262.

Gumbrecht, Hans Ulrich. *Production of Presence: What Meaning Cannot Convey*. Stanford: Stanford UP, 2004.

Habermas, Jürgen. *The Structural Transformation of the Public Sphere: An Inquiry into a Category of Bourgeois Society*. Cambridge, UK: Polity, 2011.

Hacking, Ian. *The Taming of Chance*. Cambridge, et al.: Cambridge UP, 1990.

Hacking, Ian. "Canguilhem amid the Cyborgs." *Economy and Society* 27.2-3 (1998): 202-216.

Haraway, Donna. *Simians, Cyborgs, and Women: The Reinvention of Nature*. New York: Routledge, 1991.

Hartwell, David. "The Golden Age of Science Fiction is Twelve." *Speculations on Speculation: Theories of Science Fiction*. Eds. James Gunn and Matthew Candelaria. Lanham, et al.: Scarecrow, 2005. 269-288.

Harvey, David. *A Brief History of Neoliberalism*. Oxford: Oxford UP, 2005.

Heath, Stephen. *Questions of Cinema*. London: Macmillan, 1987.

Heise, Ursula. "Die Zeitlichkeit des Risikos im amerikanischen Roman der Postmoderne." *Zeit und Roman: Zeiterfahrung im historischen Wandel und ästhetischer Paradigmenwechsel vom sechzehnten Jahrhundert bis zur Postmoderne*. Ed. Martin Middecke. Würzburg: Königshausen und Neumann, 2002. 373-394.

Hodges, Aaron F. "Martin Hägglund's Speculative Materialism." *CR: The Centennial Review* 9.1 (Spring 2009): Web. 30 Jun 2012. <http://muse.jhu.edu/journals/ncr/v0009/9.1.hodges.html> 87-106.

Hunt, Alex. "Mapping the Terrain, Marking the Earth: William Emory and the Writing of the U.S./Mexico Border." *American Literary Geographies: Spatial Practice and Cultural Production 1500-1900*. Eds. Martin Brückner and Hsuan L. Hsu. Newark: Rosemont, 2007. 127-146.

Ian, Marcia. *Remembering the Phallic Mother: Psychoanalysis, Modernism, and the Fetish*. Ithaka, NY: Cornell UP, 1996.

Jameson, Fredric. *Archaeologies of the Future: The Desire Called Utopia and Other Science Fictions*. London and New York: Verso, 2005.

Jeffords, Susan. *Hard Bodies: Hollywood Masculinity in the Reagan Era.* New Brunswick: Rutgers UP, 1994.

Jermyn, Deborah, and Sean Redmond. "Introduction: Hollywood Transgressor: The Cinema of Kathryn Bigelow." *The Cinema of Kathryn Bigelow: Hollywood Transgressor.* Eds. Deborah Jermyn and Sean Redmond. London/New York: Wallflower, 2003.1-20.

Johnston, Adrian. "Hume's Revenge: A Dieu, Meillassoux," *The Speculative Turn: Continental Materialism and Realism.* Melbourne: re.press, 2011. 84-113.

Kelleter, Frank. "A Tale of Two Natures: Worried Reflections on the Study of Literature and Culture in an Age of Neuroscience and Neo-Darwinism." *Journal of Literary Theory* 1.1. New Developments in Literary Theory and Related Disciplines (2007): Web. 5 Mar. 2011. <http://www.jltonline.de/index.php/articles/article/view/65/258> 153-189>.

Kellner, Doug. "Critical Perspectives on Television from the Frankfurt School to Postmodernism." *A Companion to Television.*Ed. Janet Wasko. Malden et al.: Blackwell, 2008. 29-47.

Kennedy, Liam. *Race and Urban Space in Contemporary American Culture.* Edinburgh: Edinburgh UP, 2000.

Kim, Elaine H. *Asian American Literature: An Introduction to the Writings and their Social Context.* Philadelphia: Temple UP, 1982.

Kristeva, Julia. *Powers of Horror: An Essay on Abjection.* New York: Columbia UP, 1982.

Kristeva, Julia. *Revolution in Poetic Language.* New York: Columbia UP, 1984.

Lai, Larissa. *Salt Fish Girl.* Toronto: Thomas Allen, 2002.

Lai, Larissa. "The Identity of the Body Has Not Yet Been Confirmed: Panel Talk for 'A Walk with Woman Warriors' at Strathcona Community Centre, August 28, 2004."*West Coast Line 58.* 42.2 Active Geographies: Women and Struggles on the Left Coast (2008): 137-139.

Lai, Larissa. "Future Asians: Migrant Speculations, Repressed History & Cyborg Hope." *West Coast Line 44* 38.2 (2004): 168-175.

Lai, Larissa. "'Sites of Articulation'- An Interview with Larissa Lai: Robyn Morris in Conversation with Larissa Lai." *West Coast Line 44* 38.2 (2004): 21-30.

Lai, Larissa. "Strategizing the Body of History: Anxious Writing, Absent Subjects, and Marketing the Nation." *Asian Canadian Writing Beyond Autoethnography.* Eds. Eleanor Ty and Christl Verduyn. Waterloo, Ontario: Wilfrid Laurier UP, 2008. 87 -111.

Lai, Larissa. "Brand Canada: Global Flows and a People to Come." *Reading(s) from a Distance: European Perspectives on Canadian Women's Writing.* Eds. Charlotte Sturgess and Martin Kuester. Augsburg: Wißner, 2008. 23-32.

Lai, Paul. "Stinky Bodies: Mythological Futures and the Olfactory Sense in Larissa Lai's *Salt Fish Girl*." *MELUS* 33.4 (2008):167-187, 169.

Lane, Christina. "From *The Loveless* to *Point Break*; Kathryn Bigelow's Trajectory in Action." *Cinema Journal* 37.4 (1998): 59-81.

Lane, Christina. "The Strange Days of Kathryn Bigelow and David Cameron." *The Cinema of Kathryn Bigelow: Hollywood Transgressor.* Eds. Deborah Jermyn and Sean Redmond. London and New York: Wallflower, 2003. 178 - 197.

Larner, Wendy. "Spatial Imaginaries: Economic Globalization and the War on Terror." *Risk and the War on Terror.* Eds. Louise Amoore and Marieke de Goede. London and New York: Routledge, 2008. 41-56.

Lee, Tara. "Mutant Bodies in Larissa Lai's *Salt Fish Girl*: Challenging the Alliance between Science and Capital." *West Coast Line 44* 38.2 (2004): 94-110.

Leon, Consuelo. "Foundations of the American Image of the Pacific." *boundary 2* 21.1 (1994): 17-29.

Ley, David. *Millionnaire Migrants: Trans-Pacific Life Lines.* Malden, et al.: Wiley-Blackwell, 2010.

Li, David Leiwei. *Imagining the Nation: Asian American Literature and Cultural Consent.* Stanford: Stanford UP, 1999.

Ling, Jinqui. *Narrating Nationalisms: Ideology and Form in Asian American Literature.* New York, et.al.: Oxford UP, 1998.

Love, Heather K. "Close but not Deep: Literary Ethics and the Descriptive Turn." *New Literary History* 41.2 (2010): 371-391.

Lowe, Lisa. "Heterogeneity, Hybridity, Multiplicity: Marking Asian American Differences." *Diaspora* 1.1 (1991): 22-44.

Luhmann, Niklas. *The Concept of Risk: A Sociological Theory.* New Brunswick/ London: Aldine Transaction, 2002.

Luhmann, Niklas. "Die Evolution des Kunstsystems." *Schriften zur Kunst und Literatur.* Frankfurt/ Main: Suhrkamp, 2008. 258-275.

Lyng, Stephen. "Edgework: A Social Psychological Analysis of Voluntary Risk Taking." *American Journal of Sociology* 95.4 (1990): 851-886.

Lyng, Stephen. "Edgework, Risk, and Uncertainty." *Social Theories of Risk and Uncertainty: An Introduction.* Ed. Jens O. Zinn. Malden: Blackwell, 2008. 106-137.

Mailloux, Steven. "Hermeneutics, Deconstruction, Allegory." *The Cambridge Companion to Allegory*. Eds. Rita Copeland and Peter T. Struck. Cambridge, et al.: Cambridge UP, 2010. 254-265.

Mansbridge, Joanna. "Abject Origins: Uncanny Strangers and Figures of Fetishism in Larissa Lai's *Salt Fish Girl*." *West Coast Line* 38.2 (2004): 121-133.

Martinez, Roberto Sanchino. "'Die Produktion von Präsenz'. Einige Überlegungen zur Reichweite des Konzepts der ‚ästhetischen Erfahrung' bei Hans Ulrich Gumbrecht." *Ästhetische Erfahrung: Gegenstände, Konzepte, Geschichtlichkeit*. Ed. Sonderforschungsbereich 626. Berlin, 2006. Web. 3 Sept 2012. <www.sfb626.de/veroeffentlichungen/online/aeth.erfahrung/aufsaetze/sanchino.pdf>.

Marx, Karl. *Das Kapital. Band 1: Der Produktionsprozess des Kapitals*. 1867. Marx Engels Werke. Vol. 23. Berlin: Dietz, 2008.

Massumi, Brian. "Everywhere You Want to Be: Introduction to Fear." *The Politics of Everyday Fear*. Minneapolis/ London: U of Minnesota P, 1993. 3-37.

Mavor, Carol. "Odor di Femina: Though You May Not See Her, You Can Certainly Smell Her." *The Smell Culture Reader*. Ed. Jim Drobnick. Oxford/ New York: Berg, 2006. 277-288.

Meehan, Eileen R. "Watching Television: A Political Economic Approach." *A Companion to Television*. Ed. Janet Wasko. Malden, et.al.: Blackwell, 2008. 238-255.

Melville, Herman. *The Confidence Man: His Masquerade*. New York, et.al.: Norton, 2006.

Michaels, Walter Benn. *The Gold Standard and the Logic of Naturalism*. Berkeley and Los Angeles: U of California P, 1987.

Mihm, Stephen. *A Nation of Counterfeiters: Capitalists, Con Men, and the Making of the United States*. Cambridge, MA: Harvard UP, 2007.

Mitchell, Dean. *Governmentality: Power and Rule in Modern Society*. 2nd ed. London, et al.: Sage, 2010.

Mitchell, Katharyne. *Crossing the Neoliberal Line: Pacific Rim Migration and the Metropolis*. Philadelphia: Temple UP, 2004.

Miyoshi, Masao. "Turn to the Planet: Literature, Diversity, and Totality." *Comparative Literature* 53.4 (2001): 283-287.

Miyoshi, Masao. "A Borderless World: From Colonialism to Transnationalism, and the Decline of the Nationstate." *Critical Inquiry* 19.4 (1993): 726-751.

Miyoshi, Masao. "Sites of Resistance in the Global Economy." *boundary 2* 22.1 (1995): 61-84.

Moretti, Franco. *The Way of the World: The* Bildungsroman *in European Culture*. London: Verso, 1987.
Moretti, Franco."Conjectures on World Literature." *New Left Review* 1 (2000): 54-68.
Morley, David, and Kevin Robbins. "Techno-Orientalism: Japan Panic." *Spaces of Identity: Global Media, Electronic Landscapes, and Cultural Boundaries*. Eds. David Morley and Kevin Robbins. New York: Routledge, 1995.147-173.
Nystrom, Derek. "Hard Hats and Movie Brats: Auteurism and the Class Politics of the New Hollywood." *Cinema Journal* 43.3 (Spring 2004): 18 – 41.
Olkowski, Dorothea. *Gilles Deleuze and the Ruin of Representation*. Berkeley and Los Angeles: U of California P, 1999.
Ondaatje, Michael. *Divisadero*. New York: Vintage International 2008.
Oshinski, Matthew. "The Hurt Locker Movie Review – Kathryn Bigelow Has a Blast in Iraq." *NJ.com* (25 June 2009): Web. 05 Febr. 2011. <http://www.nj.com/entertainment/tv/index.ssf/2009/06/the_hurt_locker_movie_review_k.html>.
Palumbo-Liu, David. *Asian/American: Historical Crossings of a Racial Frontier*. Stanford: Stanford UP, 1999.
Pease, Donald E.. "National Narratives, Postnational Narration." *Modern Fiction Studies*. 43.1(1997): 1-23.
Pease, Donald E. *The New American Exceptionalism*. Minneapolis/London: U of Minnesota P, 2009.
Pelletier, Yvonne Elizabeth. "False Promises and Real Estate: Land Speculation and Millennial Maps in Herman Melville's *Confidence Man*." *American Literary Geographies: Spatial Practice and Cultural Production 1500-1900*. Eds Martin Brückner and Hsuan L. Hsu. Newark: U of Delaware P, 2007. 191 -205.
Perloff, Marjorie. "Grammar in Use: Wittgenstein/Gertrude Stein/Marinetti." *South Central Review* 13. 2/3 Futurism and Avantgarde (1996): 35-62.
Rabinow, Paul. "The Third Culture." *History of the Human Sciences* 7.2 (1994): 53-64.
Rody, Caroline. "The Transnational Imagination: Karen Tei Yamashita's *Tropic of Orange*." *Asian American Identities Beyond the Hyphen*. Eds. Eleanor Ty and Donald C. Goellnicht. Bloomington: Indiana UP, 2004. 130-148.
Rose, Nikolas. *Powers of Freedom: Reframing Political Thought*. Cambridge, UK: Cambridge UP, 1999.
Rose, Nikolas. *The Politics of Life Itself: Biomedicine, Power, and Subjectivity in the Twenty-First Century*. Princeton and Oxford: Princeton UP, 2007.

Rose, Nikolas. "The Value of Life: Somatic Ethics and the Spirit of Biocapital." *The Right to Life and the Value of Life: Orientations in Law, Politics, and Ethics*. Ed. Jon Yorke. Burlington, UK: Ashgate 2010. 85-99.

"Reagan, Ronald Wilson." Thomas L. Purvis, *A Dictionary of American History*. Malden, et al.: Blackwell, 2002.

"Risk." *Stanford Encyclopedia of Philosophy*. (Fall 2011). Web. 20 Dec. 2011. <http//:plato.stanford.edu/entries/risk>.

"Risk, n." *OED Online* (March 2012) Oxford University Press. Web. 20 Mar. 2012. <http://www.oed.com/view/Entry/166306?rskey=5AFGY7&result =1>.

Sadowski-Smith, Claudia. *Border Fictions: Globalization, Empire, and Writing at the Boundaries of the United States*. Charlottesville and London: U of Virginia P, 2008.

Saloy, Mona Lisa. "African American Oral Traditions in Louisiana." *Louisiana's Living Traditions*. (May 1998): Web. 22 Nov. 2011. <http://www.louisianafolklife.org/LT/Articles_Essays/creole_art_african_am_oral.html>.

Salter, Mark B. "Risk and Imagination in the War on Terror." *Risk and the War on Terror*. Eds. Louise Amoore and Marieke de Goede. London and New York: Routledge, 2008. 233-246.

Scannell, Paddy."Television and History." *A Companion to Television*. Ed. Janet Wasko. Malden, et.al.: Blackwell, 2008. 51-66.

Schrader, Paul. "Notes on the Film Noir." *The Film Genre Reader II*. Ed. Barry Keith Grant. Austin: U of Texas P, 1995. 213-226.

Searle, John R. *The Construction of Social Reality*. New York: Simon and Schuster, 1995.

Searle, John R. "The Logical Status of Fictional Discourse." *New Literary History* 6 (1974-75): 319-332.

"Serendipity,n." *OED Online* (March 2012) Web. 8 Apr. 2012. <http://www.oed.com/view/Entry/176387?redirectedFrom=%3ESerendipity#eid>.

"settle,v." *OED Online* (March 2011) Web. 31 Jan 2012. <http://www.oed.com/view/Entry/176867?rskey=Gqhdhe&result=3&isAdvanced=false#eid>.

Sharpe, Andrew N. *Foucault's Monsters and the Challenge of Law*. Oxon/ New York: Routledge, 2010.

Shavers, Rone. "Review of *I Hotel* by Karen Tei Yamashita." *The Quarterly Conversation* 23 (7 Mar. 2011): Web. 5 Nov. 2011. <http://quarterlyconversation.com/i-hotel-by-karen-tei-yamashita >.

Shaviro, Steven. "'Straight from the Cerebral Cortex:' Vision and Affect in Strange Days." *The Cinema of Kathryn Bigelow: Hollywood Transgressor*.

Eds. Deborah Jermyn and Sean Redmond. London/New York: Wallflower, 2003. 159-177.
Shell, Marc. "The Issue of Representation." *The New Economic Criticism: Studies at the Intersection of Literature and Economics*. Eds. Martha Woodmansee and Mark Osteen. London and New York: Routledge, 1999. 53-74.
Simon, Jonathan. "Choosing Our Wars, Transforming Governance: Cancer, Crime, Terror." *Risk and the War on Terror*. Eds. Louise Amoore and Marieke de Goede. London and New York: Routledge, 2008. 79-96.
Simonsen, Kirsten. "Spatiality, Temporality, and the Construction of the City." *Space Odysseys: Spatiality and Social Relations in the 21st Century*. Eds. Jorgen Ole Baerenholdt and Kirsten Simonsen. Burlington: Ashgate, 2004. 43-62.
Sloterdijk, Peter. *Regeln für den Menschenpark: Ein Antwortschreiben zu Heideggers Brief über den Humanismus*. Frankurt/Main: Suhrkamp, 1999.
Smith, Gavin. "'Momentum and Design:' Interview with Kathryn Bigelow." *Hollywood Transgressor: The Cinema of Kathryn Bigelow*. Eds. Deborah Jermyn and Sean Redmond. London/New York: Wallflower, 2003. 20-31.
Smorkaloff, Pamela Maria. "Shifting Borders, Free Trade, and Frontier Narratives: US, Canada, and Mexico." *American Literary History* 6.1 (1994): 88-102.
"Speculation, n." *OED Online* (March 2012) Web. 20 Mar. 2012. <http://www.oed.com/view/Entry/186113?redirectedFrom=speculation>.
"Speculative Fiction." *OED Online* (March 2012) Web. 5 Mar. 2012. <http://www.oed.com/view/Entry/186115?redirectedFrom=speculative%20fiction>.
So, Christine. *Economic Citizens: A Narrative of Asian American Visibility*. Philadelphia: Temple UP, 2008.
Soja, Edward W. *Postmodern Geographies: The Reassertion of Space in Critical Social Theory*. London: Verso, 1989.
Stäheli, Urs. *Spektakuläre Spekulation: Das Populäre in der Ökonomie*. Frankfurt/Main: Suhrkamp, 2007.
Stein, Gertrude. *Lectures in America*. (1935). Boston: Beacon, 1985.
Stein, Gertrude. "Farragut or a Husband's Recompense." *Useful Knowledge*. Barrytown, NY: Station Hill, 2001.
Stepovich, Romy. "Strange Days: A Case History of Production and Distribution Practices in Hollywood." *The Cinema of Kathryn Bigelow: Hollywood Transgressor*. Eds. Deborah Jermyn and Sean Redmond. London/New York: Wallflower, 2003.144-158.

Strange Days. Dir. Kathryn Bigelow. Prod. James Cameron. With Ralph Fiennes, Angela Bessett, and Juliette Lewis. Twentieth Century Fox. USA 1995.

"*Strange Days* Teaser." 20th Century Fox. (22 Apr. 2008): Web. 15 Febr. 2011. <http://www.youtube.com/watch?v=s0zaqWQiXG8&feature=related>.

Streisand, Barbra. "Kathryn Bigelow Winning the Oscar® for Directing." *82nd Edition of the Academy Awards ceremony.* (10 Mar. 2010) Web. 20 Mar. 2011. <http://www.youtube.com/watch?v=e-DPBOTlSWk >.

Suvin, Darko. *Metamorphoses of Science Fiction: On the Poetics and History of a Literary Genre.* New Haven and London: Yale UP, 1979.

"System, n." *OED Online* (March 2012) Web. 20 Mar. 2012. <http://www.oed.com/view/Entry/196665?redirectedFrom=system#eid>.

Tarnoff, Ben. *Moneymakers: The Wicked Lives and Surprising Adventures of Three Notorious Counterfeiters.* London: Pengouin, 2011.

Tasker, Yvonne. *Spectacular Bodies: Gender, Genre, and the Action Cinema.* New York: Routledge, 1993.

Taylor, Mark C. "Discrediting God." *Journal of the American Academy of Religion.* 62.2 (1994): 603-623.

Thacker, Eugene. "Necrologies or, The Death of the Body Politic." *Beyond Biopolitics: Essays on the Governance of Life and Death.* Eds. Patricia Ticineto Cough and Craig Willse. Durham and London: Duke UP, 2011. 140-162,

Ty, Eleanor, and Christl Verduyn. *Asian Canadian Writing beyond Autoethnography.* Waterloo, ON: Wilfrid Laurier UP, 2008.

Ueno, Toshiya. "Japanimation: Techno-Orientalism, Media Tribes, and Rave Culture." *Aliens R Us: The Other in Science Fiction Cinema.* Eds. Ziauddin Sardar and Sean Cubitt. Sterling: Pluto, 2002. 94-110.

"Union Generals: General David Glasgow Farragut, USA." HistoryCentral.com. Web. 05 Jan. 2012. <http://www.historycentral.com/Bio/UGENS/USA Farragut.htm>.

Vogl, Joseph. *Kalkül und Leidenschaft: Poetik des ökonomischen Menschen.* Zürich and Berlin: Diaphanes, 2008.

Vogl, Joseph. *Das Gespenst des Kapitals.* Berlin: Diaphanes, 2011.

Wagner-Martin, Linda. *Favored Strangers: Gertrude Stein and Her Family.* New Brunswick, NJ: Rutgers UP, 1995.

Wallace, Molly. "Tropics of Globalization: Reading the New North America." *symploké* 9. 1-2 (2001): 145-160.

Wacquant, Loic. *Punishing the Poor: The Neoliberal Government of Social Insecurity.* Durham: Duke UP, 2009.

Wegener, Susanne. "Lines and Layers, Grids and Maps: Das Konzept des Rhizoms als Ausdruck postkolonialer Hybtridität in Karen Tei Yamashitas *Tropic of Orange*." *LiLi: Zeitschrift für Literaturwissenschaft und Linguistik 37*.147 (2007): 164-177.

Wegener, Susanne. "Pacific Trans-Formations: Politische Ökonomie, Körper und Geschlecht in Larissa Lais *Salt Fish Girl*." *GENDER: Zeitschrift für Geschlecht, Kultur und Gesellschaft* 3.2 (2010): 92-106.

White, Mimi. "Ideological Analysis and Television." *Channels of Discourse: Television and Contemporary Criticism*. Ed. Robert C. Allen. Chapel Hill and London: U of North Carolina P, 1987. 134-171.

Wise, Raul Delgado, and Mariana Ortega Breña. "Migration and Imperialism: The Mexican Workforce in the Context of NAFTA." *Latin American Perspectives* 33.2 (2006): 33-35.

Walter, William. "Putting the Migration-Security Complex in its Place." *Risk and the War on Terror*. Eds. Louise Amoore and Marieke de Goede. London and New York: Routledge, 2008. 158-177.

Woodside, Alexander. "The Asia-Pacific Idea as a Mobilization Myth." *What Is In A Rim: Critical Perspectives on the Pacific Region Idea*. Ed. Arif Dirlik. Lanham: Rowman and Littlefield, 1998. 37-53.

Wolfe, Gary K. "Coming to Terms." *Speculations on Speculation: Theories of Science Fiction*. Eds. James Gunn and Matthew Candelaria. Lanham, et al.: Scarecrow, 2005. 13-22.

Xiaojing, Zhou. "Introduction: Critical Theories and Methodologies in Asian American Studies." *Form and Transformation in Asian American Literature*. Eds. Zhou Xiaojing and Samina Najmi. Seattle and London: U of Washington P, 2005.

Yamashita, Karen Tei. *Tropic of Orange*. Minneapolis: Coffee House Press, 1997.

Yamashita, Karen Tei. "Traveling Voices." *Café Creole: Circle K2* (June 2000): Web. 12 Jul. 2011. <http://www.cafecreole.net/travelogue/karen/circleK2.html#june2000>.

Zimmermann, David A. *Panic! Markets, Crises, Crowds in American Fiction*. Chapel Hill, U of North Carolina P, 2006.

Zipfel, Frank. *Fiktion, Fiktivität, Fiktionalität: Analysen zur Fiktion in der Literatur und zum Fiktionsbegriff in der Literaturwissenschaft*. Berlin: Erich Schmidt, 2001.

Zizek, Slavoj. *Welcome to the Desert of the Real*. London and New York: Verso, 2002.

Zizek, Slavoj. "Is it Still Possible to be a Hegelian Today?" *The Speculative Turn: Continental Materialism and Realism*. Eds. Levi Bryant, Nick Srnicek and Graham Harman. Melbourne: re.press, 2011. 202-223.